THINKING PRAYER

THINKING PRAYER

THEOLOGY AND SPIRITUALITY

AMID THE CRISES OF MODERNITY

ANDREW PREVOT

University of Notre Dame Press
Notre Dame, Indiana

Manufactured in the United States of America

Library of Congress Cataloging-in-Publication Data

Prevot, Andrew L.
  Thinking prayer : theology and spirituality amid the crises
of modernity / Andrew Prevot.
      pages cm
  Includes bibliographical references and index.
  ISBN 978-0-268-03845-8 (pbk. : alk. paper) — ISBN 0-268-
03845-7 (pbk. : alk. paper)
  1. Prayer—Christianity. 2. Philosophical theology. I. Title.
  BV210.3.P738 2015
  248.3'2—dc23
                    2015031819

∞ *The paper in this book meets the guidelines for permanence and
durability of the Committee on Production Guidelines for Book
Longevity of the Council on Library Resources.*

To the millions who have died in slavery

If you are a theologian, you will pray truly.
And if you pray truly, you will be a theologian.

—Evagrius Ponticus

I've been in the storm so long,
O give me little time to pray.

—slave spiritual

CONTENTS

ACKNOWLEDGMENTS

The labor that generated this text would not have been possible without the gracious financial assistance of the University of Notre Dame, the Lilly Endowment, and the Fund for Theological Education. A special note of thanks is due to my *Doktorvater*, Cyril O'Regan. His responses to earlier drafts of these chapters have immensely improved the final product, and his insights concerning the original idea made the completion of this work conceivable to me. Any errors are undoubtedly my own. To my other committee members, Lawrence Cunningham and J. Matthew Ashley, I am likewise greatly indebted, not only for their constant support over the many years that I have been their student, but also for their distinctive efforts to bridge the modern gap between theology and spirituality which have significantly influenced my own.

Among the many other faculty at Notre Dame that have shaped my self-understanding as a theologian, I would especially like to thank Mary Catherine Hilkert, for enriching my sense of the dynamics of nature and grace; Kevin Hart, for allowing me to understand what it means to adopt a phenomenological attitude; Michael Signer, for teaching me about the horrific history and the unforeseen promise of Christian-Jewish encounter; Nathan Mitchell, for increasing my appreciation for the church's liturgical imagination; Gerald McKenny, for helping me perceive the political significance of authentic Christian witness; and Jamie Phelps, for introducing me to the rich traditions of black and womanist theology. I would like to mention, as well, my teachers and mentors at The Colorado College, without whom I would not have been prepared to do work in theology. In particular, I would like to thank my undergraduate advisor in philosophy, Jonathan Lee; my other extraordinarily formative professors Susan Ashley, Carol Neal, John Riker, and David Weddle; and my sources of spiritual support Melissa Nussbaum, Valerie Vela (of blessed memory), Fr. Bart Geger, and Bishop Richard Hanifen.

I would also like to express gratitude for my mentor at Boston College, M. Shawn Copeland, who has been an incomparable source of counsel and encouragement and for my research assistant Robert Brodrick, who painstakingly proofread the entire text. The final version has been enhanced greatly by the suggestions of reviewers and the careful editorial guidance of Bob Banning. Moreover, many of my friends have listened to me over the past few years as I began to articulate various inchoate features of my argument, and their perceptive responses consistently challenged me to think more clearly and to overcome potential difficulties. In this regard, I am especially indebted to Steven Battin, Brian Hamilton, Noel Terranova, Daniel Castillo, Kevin McCabe, Bridget O'Brien, Todd Walatka, Peter Fritz, Julia Feder, John Thiede, Andrew Downing, Jennifer Martin, David Lantigua, Michael Mawson, Adam Clark, Paul Scherz, Deonna Neal, Katie Grimes, Megan McCabe, Erin Kidd, James DeFrancis, Jordan Wales, John Sehorn, Jay Martin, Matthew Eggemeier, Brandon Peterson, Emeka Ngwoke, Patrick Gardner, Emily Stetler, Awet Andemichael, and Eduardo Gonzalez—but the list could certainly continue. To all of my friends: your words to me have been invaluable, and please let us continue the conversation!

To my parents, my sisters, and my ancestors: I can only say that I owe you much more than can be repaid and that you are now, and will forever be, very dear to me. To Elizabeth: you have been my most cherished companion and partner, and certainly words cannot say all of the things you mean to me. For all of my loved ones, who have formed my thoughts with their kindness, I give thanks. And to God who knows my many debts and faults, who is the eternal source of all good things, and to whom I try to pray, though often failingly: to you I owe everything, perhaps least of all this text, but certainly not excluding it. May it serve only to give you glory.

INTRODUCTION

The Untold Promise of Prayer

The purpose of this book is to encourage theologians and other intellectuals to rediscover prayer as a highly significant source of Christian thought and life amid certain pressing crises of the modern age. It recommends prayer, not as a panacea, but nevertheless as a blessing that needs to be retrieved and reintegrated into Christian theory and practice in order to help Christians and others better meet the demands of this challenging epoch. This is not only a work of scholarship about prayer. Nor is it only a prayer articulated through scholarship. It is both at the same time. Before developing the argument of this text in more detail, a few preliminary remarks are in order.

First, in order to appreciate the specific dynamisms of prayer as the best of the Christian tradition presents it, one must acknowledge the extraordinary gift of freedom that is included within this mystery. Prayer presupposes a creature with the freedom to pray, and it promises unheard-of levels of freedom to all those who dedicate themselves to this practice. At the same time, one must also contemplate a reality that is infinitely greater than even the loftiest creaturely freedom: the absolutely simple, primordially creative, paschally redemptive, historically liberative, and eschatologically transformative freedom of the triune God, which is revealed in the life, death, and resurrection of Jesus Christ and poured out as the grace of the Holy Spirit. God is not merely the addressee of prayer but its primary agent. From a Christian perspective, prayer happens whenever there is interaction between these two freedoms, that is, whenever the triune God and any given creature choose (and we hope and believe that God always makes this choice) to relate in a manner that also necessarily involves other qualitative, experiential, and social (thus not just abstractly self-determining) aspects of their respective freedoms.

The prayerful interplay of Trinitarian and creaturely freedoms cannot be understood apart from love. But the relation between this interplay and love is rather complex. The self-giving, other-welcoming, and extremely costly acts of love through which God initiates and sustains this relationship and through which we are likewise called to participate in it give prayer its definitive orientation. With God as its author, prayer has an inescapably amorous inclination. But to what extent prayer already enjoys and manifests such love is an open question. Prayer seeks the mutual love of God and creation in situations where this love has often been found wanting —or, more gravely still, where it has been rendered inconceivable by its many near-complete experiential refutations (idolatry, murder, oppression, agony of all kinds). Prayer, then, is not in every case a serene experience of love but often a more volatile interaction of freedoms that, however ordered by love it may be, must also yearn for it with no small degree of desperation. Prayer asks for love (perhaps only for love). But it does so in the midst of innumerable loveless and hateful circumstances.

This understanding of Trinitarian and creaturely freedoms interacting for the sake of love is not just an interpretation of explicitly Christian prayer. It is an explicitly Christian interpretation of prayer itself, which is a mystery that takes on various historical expressions more or less congruent with such a Christian interpretation. Many of these expressions do not present themselves as Christian, and those that do are not necessarily more adequate for this reason. A prayer with Christian trappings that is not deeply animated by freedom and love will pale in comparison with a free and loving prayer offered by someone who has little or no concern for Christianity as a distinct faith tradition. But it does not follow that Christianity is irrelevant to the meaning of prayer or that it is just one among many interchangeable vehicles for it. On the contrary, the following argument presupposes that Christian prayer, when experienced and practiced in authentic ways, reveals constitutive features of prayer as such—including above all the supreme mysteries of Trinitarian freedom and love which enable and receive prayer even when not recognized as doing so. A guiding premise of this work is thus that Christian prayer provides an unparalleled glimpse into certain hidden-and-disclosed realities that make prayer, in any given case, the very particular sort of interaction that it is.

These initial reflections have already begun to clarify why one should not think of prayer as just one among many elements of Christianity or of human activity in general and especially why one should not discount it as a mere trivial pastime. To be sure, both Christians and non-Christians must concern themselves with other important ideas and practices that may be meaningfully distinguished from prayer. Indeed, even when one thinks prayerfully, prayer is not the only phenomenon that should occupy one's attention; even when one prays ceaselessly, prayer is not all that one must do. Nonetheless, when prayer clearly unveils itself as the love-oriented interaction of Trinitarian and creaturely freedoms in the context of our severely damaged world, its rightful centrality becomes unmistakable. This all-important interaction reverberates in every aspect of genuinely Christian existence and echoes in the many wounded and lovelorn hearts of the human race. If the skeptics are mistaken and God is not merely an illusory projection of finite consciousness but rather the almighty savior of the world who seeks our loving companionship, then prayer is in a very real sense "the one thing necessary" (cf. Luke 10:42). It is a vital struggle for divine-and-human communion without which any ultimate healing and sanctification for the world will remain inaccessible.

Prayer has shaped the intellectual endeavors of Christian thinkers for centuries, though far from perfectly and often without sufficient awareness of the fact. Moreover, it will continue to do so as long as there continues to be any Christian thought that is worthy of the name. To think as a Christian is to think prayerfully. If this dual vocation of thinking and praying is really conceivable (and one should not be too quick to discount it as a "square circle"), it follows that the fruits of prayer are destined not only for the heart but also for the mind. Prayer is not only an opportunity for holy affections and ritual performances but also an occasion for rigorous reflection. Conversely, it also follows that thought is not sufficient unto itself, at least not when it seeks clarity regarding those realities that are somehow implicated in prayer (but which realities are not?). Therefore, in order to approach the fullness of thinking that is appropriate to an intellectual life, the sort of life that was once called "philosophical," one needs more than a transcendental analytic (thinking on thinking . . .) and more than an ontological framework (in which mind and being become one). One needs the hope of a thorough, albeit perhaps never historically perfectible, synthesis of prayer and thought. Theology is, at its best, nothing other than an approximation of such a synthesis.

Some readers might worry that such an interpretation of theology as the unity of prayer and thought will unhelpfully emphasize contemplation at the expense of action. But this is not the case. The claim here is that thinking, which is itself a practice and which emerges from and shapes other sorts of practices, must be developed in accord with the full Trinitarian and creaturely mystery of prayer, including the embodied acts of love that it both inspires and requires. In other words, the various practical conditions for a free, difference-respecting, and life-affirming love between God and humanity and between all of God's creatures, which are sought and found in the light of prayer, must be incorporated into what we call thinking. Conversely, thinking must be practiced in such a way that it seeks a greater realization of this comprehensive love. The unification of prayer and thought is therefore significant not only for its own sake (that is, for the good of contemplation), but also for the sake of certain practices of freedom and love that this unity alone seems sufficiently prepared to support (including practices in the areas of ethics, politics, etc.). The stakes of this project are thus inseparably theoretical and practical. Moreover, if either of these terms figures more prominently as the goal of this work, it would be the practical, insofar as this is able to integrate contemplation and action.

The cultivation of prayerful thought and life is especially significant in the modern age and for multiple reasons. In the first place, many modern intellectual traditions tend to distort, conceal, or marginalize the mystery of prayer through the exclusive promotion of various forms of secularity, that is, forms of worldliness that can be theorized and practiced without any interaction with the living God (though "God" may still be used in such cases as a trope). Hence, there is a need to understand and reaffirm the viability of prayer in this at least potentially atheistic or prayer-negating situation. However, the rise of secularity is not the only crisis to consider here (a crisis, certainly, for the prayerful, but arguably not only for them). The modern age is also entangled in at least two other crises (or sets of crises), shared among the prayerful and the nonprayerful alike, which can be identified with the troubled fate of Western metaphysics and with various local and global structures of socioeconomic and identity-based violence. The fate of metaphysics affects the intelligibility of prayer in complicated ways, and the structural violence of the world tests the integrity of prayer in the gravest possible terms.

In each of these three crises, there is a negation—the disregard for God, the descent of thought into nihilism, and the wanton destruction of life—that calls for a new decision regarding how to proceed. This is why it is appropriate to call them "crises." Each of these crises directly concerns prayer and may, in fact, be best interpreted as an effect of its nonrealization. In other words, if there is but one crisis here, it is this: that all of the integrated goods that prayer represents have not yet come to pass, not prior to modernity and, most crucially for us, not within it. This central problem has distinct manifestations. The differences between these crises are important, but so too are their multiple interconnections.

Although prayer is jeopardized by these crises, it is not merely their passive victim. On the contrary, prayer offers a promising, though still largely unexamined, response to them. What is the nature of this response? In brief, prayer resituates and thereby significantly

qualifies the meaning of secularity by affirming humanity's critical freedom and locating it in interactive relation with God; prayer
opens a doxological path beyond the potentially nihilistic trajectory
of metaphysics without losing the holistic sense of wonder and keen
theoretical insight that have been generative of this tradition; and
prayer inspires liberative movements of personal and social transformation in resistance against the violent structures of the world, while
awaiting God's definitive victory over them. At its best, therefore,
prayer intervenes decisively in each of the crises of secularity, metaphysics, and violence and thereby prepares for a new postmodern
and transmodern advent of freedom and love.

The ostensible division of theology and spirituality is another
problematic feature of the modern age, which is very relevant to
the present discussion and not exactly reducible to the other crises
mentioned above. In response to this specific issue, the best strategy
seems to be this: to reconceive of theology and spirituality as two
inseparable aspects of the one mystery of prayer. Once one adopts
this intrinsically unified perspective, additional questions about
how to relate the two in practice will certainly remain, but the basic
principle of their integration (i.e., prayer) will at least be established.
Nevertheless, the core question of the present argument will not be
how to bridge any apparent gap between theology and spirituality
but rather what sorts of theoretical and practical benefits the mystery of prayer, which already bridges this gap in principle, holds in
store for a crisis-ridden humanity.

In the six chapters that follow, we shall trace this question
through a series of relevant thinkers and conversations in order to
develop a cumulative response to it. The next section of the Introduction will highlight the main contributions of each chapter and
thereby give an overview of the argument as a whole. The other tasks
that remain to be accomplished in the Introduction are these: to define more clearly certain key terms, including especially prayer, doxology, theology, spirituality, secularity, metaphysics, and violence; to
foreshadow the debates concerning these terms (since the act of definition already brings us into controversial territory); to distinguish
the present work from analogous projects associated with radical

orthodoxy, liturgical theology, and the interdisciplinary study of spirituality; and to confess some important limitations of scope.

THE STRUCTURE OF THE ARGUMENT

The argument of this text is divided into two parts, "From Metaphysics to Doxology" and "Spirituality in a World of Violence," each with three chapters. Although the crisis of secularity does not appear in the title of either part, one should not conclude that it has, therefore, dropped out of consideration. On the contrary, it remains an ever-present concern, as does the question of the modern separation of theology and spirituality. The reason to prioritize prayer's response to the other two areas of crisis is that these seem to require a greater level of clarification. The mere appropriation of prayer as a basis for thought and life already challenges the absolute claims of secularity and presages a possible reintegration of theology and spirituality. How exactly such an appropriation might helpfully intervene in debates about metaphysics and violence is somewhat less obvious. Hence, we shall treat these two crises directly, while recognizing their intersections with one another and with the other crises of modernity.

The first part, "From Metaphysics to Doxology," begins with a chapter-length examination of the conceptually and politically distorted mode of doxological thinking that Martin Heidegger develops in response to certain problems that he associates with metaphysics. These problems include the technological, nihilistic, and ontotheological concealments of being and its difference, as well as the loss of a proper relation between humanity and divinity. The first half of this chapter critically analyzes Heidegger's diagnosis of these problems, especially insofar as he connects them with Christian theology. The second half of the chapter then interrogates his recommended alternative. This alternative emerges largely from his reading of the poet Friedrich Hölderlin and other figures of a very selective Greco-German cultural tradition. These sources give rise to a dangerous type of highly autochthonous doxology, which domesticates and disintegrates the mystery of God and, moreover, implicates Heidegger's work in various anti-Jewish and destructively colonial forms of inhospitality. Thus there is much to resist in Heidegger's (admittedly non-Christian) approximation of a prayer-like thought. At the same time, he allows one to glimpse the possibility and the possible appeal of postmetaphysical doxology, and it is for this reason above all that he remains an important reference point for Christian thinkers of prayer, as we shall see throughout.

The next chapter details Hans Urs von Balthasar's critical encounter with Heidegger. It highlights not only what Balthasar appropriates from Heidegger, both in terms of his own critique of metaphysics and his strategy of doxological aesthetics, but also how he seeks to correct Heidegger on both counts. Moreover, it raises critical questions regarding, on the one hand, whether Balthasar does enough to overcome the dangers of metaphysics that Heidegger somewhat perceptively identifies and, on the other hand, whether Balthasar sufficiently avoids the perils that are evident in Heidegger's proposal. We shall see that, with some qualifications, it is possible to respond mainly in the affirmative to both of these questions.

The key here is that Balthasar proposes Trinitarian freedom and love, not the finite event of being, as the most appropriate context in which to think the mystery of prayer. More specifically, Balthasar's analogical account of being preserves difference, not only within the world, but also between the Creator and creation; his Christian doxological aesthetics concretizes this difference in the revelation of God's mysterious glory and word, which appear within humanity's bodily experiences of nature and history and particularly in the radically self-giving presence of Christ; and, finally, his dramatic interpretation of salvation situates this difference in the realm of prayerful and prayerfully informed interactions between divine and human freedom, that is, spirituality. In all of these ways, he endeavors to think prayer from itself while resisting both what is problematic about various types of difference-concealing metaphysics and about Heidegger's particular sort of doxological impurity.

The remaining chapters attend to a variety of Christian perspectives that not only exhibit many of the most salient features of

Balthasar's doxological thought but also enhance the postmetaphysi- cal and counterviolent potential of this sort of thought. Although Balthasar's elucidation of Christian prayer sets us on an auspicious course, in many ways his basic approach needs to be refined, ad- justed, and supplemented to address the crises of modernity more ef- fectively. Each of the Christian thinkers and theologians that follow offers important critical emendations of Balthasar's prayerful vision.

The third chapter concludes the first part of the book by dis- cussing the many subtle ways that Jean-Luc Marion, Jean-Yves Lacoste, and Jean-Louis Chrétien distinguish their postmetaphysi- cal treatments of Christian doxology from metaphysics in general; from Heidegger's problematic alternative to it; from Balthasar's still somewhat metaphysical theory, on which they nevertheless greatly depend; and from a rival school of radically apophatic, deconstruc- tive discourse, represented by John Caputo and others, which seeks to retrieve prayer after metaphysics only while largely severing its ties with doxology. Marion, Lacoste, and Chrétien are aided by their adaptations of certain phenomenological methods of inquiry. Never- theless, these methods also pose some difficulties, which this chapter will allow us to consider. Among the three theologically oriented phenomenologists studied here, Chrétien does the most to address these difficulties in a manner that opens the way toward a full and uncompromising style of postmetaphysical doxology. In fact, his work stands at the apex of presently conceivable arguments regard- ing prayer's significance in relation to the end of metaphysics. He introduces a new approach that is thus far without equal.

The second part of this project, called "Spirituality in a World of Violence," presupposes certain insights regarding this theme that already appear in the preceding chapters. In particular, it presup- poses the prayerful confrontations with Heidegger's inhospitality that are discernible in Balthasar's doctrine of Trinitarian love, in Em- manuel Levinas's ethical turn to the other, and in Caputo's, Marion's, Lacoste's, and Chrétien's distinct ways of blending these two possi- bilities. It also presupposes the sense of prayerful responsibility that runs throughout these sources. And yet, here it will be necessary to become more concrete regarding both the conditions of modern violence and the ways that specific forms of Christian spirituality powerfully counteract them. That is, without forgetting the question of metaphysics—and, indeed, while remaining cognizant of its ambiguous effects—the remaining chapters shift the focus toward certain structures of socioeconomic domination and anti-Jewish and antiblack oppression. In short, the central question becomes how the postmetaphysical doxology developed in the previous chapters already supports, and may also be deepened and sharpened in order to more effectively support, the kinds of liberative theory and practice that are necessary to resist these violent structures.

To this end, the fourth chapter discusses the development of Johann Baptist Metz's political theology in connection with his understanding of prayer and the virtue of spiritual poverty. First, this chapter argues that Metz's early Rahnerian affirmation of the human subject does not involve an uncritical endorsement of modernity's secularizing, metaphysical anthropocentrism (as certain post-Balthasarian thinkers might worry) but rather stems from a profound awareness of the human being's doxological poverty of spirit. The chapter then shows how Metz transforms this subject-affirming account of the poverty of spirit into a theory of solidaristic political agency, which is both inspired and importantly delimited by an apocalyptic expectation of the glorious action of God at the end of time. The prayerfulness of Metz's political theology distinguishes it in crucial ways from the immanentized critical theories of the Frankfurt School, as well as from the no less secular "political theology" of Carl Schmitt. Finally, this chapter considers how Metz addresses the question of prayer after Auschwitz. It is at this phase of his thought that his interpretation of the poverty of spirit becomes most provocative. He connects it with a cry of lament that, like the tradition of deconstructive apophasis, verges on the nondoxological. At the same time, he argues that this cry depends on a somewhat determinate experience of memory and hope rooted in biblical revelation. In these ways he continues, like the Jewish poet Nelly Sachs, to allow for some kind of deeply troubled doxology. In each of these three stages, Metz's prayerful understanding of the poverty of spirit highlights the Christian theological and spiritual tradition's still insufficiently realized potential to work against various structures of modern violence.

The fifth chapter then studies the doxological proposals of several figures of Latin American liberation theology. In part, the goal is to rebut Balthasar's much-too-negative assessment of this tradition, while taking the prayerful motivations of his concerns seriously. More importantly, however, the purpose of this chapter is to clarify in what ways doxology and liberation prove to be inseparable. It recommends a particular practice of spiritual discernment that is able to uncover concrete cases where doxology and liberation fulfill and express one another nonreductively. The chapter begins by considering two liberation theologians, Enrique Dussel and Juan Luis Segundo, whose works leave something to be desired in this regard. Specifically, whereas Dussel appropriates Levinas's quasi-doxological ethics and the early Segundo affirms a doxologically Ignatian alternative to Pelagianism, both ultimately concede too much to a modern, and particularly Marxian, humanism that does not encourage one to embrace prayer or doxology on their own terms. By contrast, Gustavo Gutiérrez, Leonardo Boff, and Ignacio Ellacuría argue that liberation theology can best be understood in the context of a rigorously doxological spirituality, which seeks to glorify God not only through politics but also through prayer, and indeed through a dynamic and nonreductive integration of the two.

While drawing attention to the distinctive contributions of Gutiérrez and Boff, this chapter culminates with a more extended discussion of Ellacuría. His phenomenological, poetic, and Ignatian reflections on liberative spirituality enable us to bring his work into close contact with Balthasar and the other representatives of postmetaphysical doxology considered above. Moreover, through his life and death, he gives a compelling martyrial witness to the real-world significance of his prayerful practice of spiritual discernment. All in all, this chapter highlights the deep connections between doxological contemplation and socially transformative action on behalf of the poor. It thereby illuminates some of the ways that prayer promises to counteract the violent structures of worldwide socioeconomic injustice.

Finally, the sixth chapter draws attention to the spiritual songs of the slaves that form the core of James Cone's black liberation theology. The purpose of this chapter is not only to understand Cone's writings but also to consider how his profoundly prayerful thought both incorporates and augments the many elements of the mystery of prayer that have appeared in the previous chapters. That is, the goal is to let the doxological wisdom of the slaves, as transmitted by Cone, become a principle of integration with respect to the entire project. This approach contravenes a problematic tendency, which remains fairly widespread, of segregating black spirituality from other theological traditions and dismissing it as a mere contextual concern. Here this spirituality provides the interpretive framework that knits everything together and, moreover, raises our understanding of the significance of prayer to a higher level of adequacy.

The synthetic potential of Cone's thought for this discussion is established in two ways. On the one hand, the tradition of slave spirituals enables Cone to preserve the essential aspects of the post-metaphysical and counterviolent interpretation of prayer that we have been pursuing throughout. Cone continues the foregoing arguments, not only through his Christian theological affirmation of difference, doxological aesthetics, and liberative soteriological drama, but also through his prayerful support of responsible, hospitable action in relation to impoverished and excluded others—and even in relation to oppressors. On the other hand, the same tradition of black spirituality allows Cone to resist the damaging effects that modernity's metaphysically implicated conceptions of race and racist structures of violence have had on black human beings, on those who have victimized them, and on the practice of prayer itself (insofar as this practice begins contradictorily and disastrously to glorify an idolatrous "white" god).

In short, by retaining many of the key ideas about prayer that we discovered in other thinkers and addressing grave challenges that they overlook, Cone safeguards the catholicity of prayerful thought and in certain respects does so more effectively than the other theologians in this study. The fact that his black doxological spirituality confronts those complicit in antiblack racism and affirms the beauty of blackness makes it more, not less, adequate and inclusive than other projects which ignore the life-crushing and prayer-falsifying realities of modern racism. To disregard his critical interventions and the black traditions of prayer on which they depend is to leave prayer vulnerable to certain destructive forces in modernity which it actually has the inner potential to overcome (that is, if the full implications of its freedom and love, as sung in the spirituals, were authentically embodied). In the end, therefore, Cone's theology supplies a trustworthy and vital point of access to the holistic significance of prayer in the modern age.

Nevertheless, although it is reasonable for this book to culminate with an interpretation of Cone, the integrative task that this interpretation illustrates is not thereby exhausted. Beyond the particular argument that develops throughout these six chapters, there is immeasurably more to be contemplated, experienced, and enacted in the many uncharted spaces that continue to arise between Trinitarian and creaturely freedom. Moreover, the provisional synthesis that Cone's retrieval of the spirituals allows does not render the other perspectives on prayer that appear in this study obsolete; rather, this synthesis depends on the possibility of a reciprocally enriching dialogue with them. The whole sweep of the following argument must therefore be read together and, even then, recognized as only one not strictly necessary but also not merely arbitrary entryway into a broader, still-emerging, and perpetually incomplete conversation regarding the theoretical and practical significance of prayer.

DEFINITIONS OF PRAYER AND RELATED TERMS

The preliminary remarks above have already presented prayer as a love-oriented interaction of Trinitarian and creaturely freedoms. However, one might object that this definition deviates from the simpler and more exact meaning of prayer as the making of a request. Although this petitionary meaning is somewhat etymologically precise, at least if one considers the English word and several of its cognates and synonyms in other languages (e.g., *precaria, prière, plegaria, Gebet*), it is nevertheless both too general and too restrictive to match current popular and theological usage. It is too general because it omits any explicit reference to God as the ultimate addressee of prayer, a reference that is usually presupposed today, even in those cases in which one asks for intercession from others (whether from saints or from immediate contemporaries). The sense of request is also too restrictive, insofar as it seems to pinpoint only one aspect of the vast range of interactive experiences that have been associated with prayer throughout the Christian tradition, including its biblical origins.[1] In a wider sense, therefore, prayer is not limited to acts of supplication but also includes countless other forms of concourse between God and humanity—and, in fact, not merely humanity but the whole of heavenly and earthly creation, insofar as everything from angels to elements likewise joins in the hymn.[2] And yet, the sense of request remains essential to the meaning of prayer throughout all of its permutations precisely to the extent that desire, the very heart of a request, remains a constitutive feature of any conceivably free relation between Creator and creature. As Thomas Aquinas suggests, prayer can be understood as an "interpreter" of desire: an act by which the intellective power of practical reason articulates and makes sense of something desired by the appetitive power, and there is nothing that the soul desires more than God.[3] Moreover, as Teresa of Ávila and many other contemplative interpreters of the Song of Songs have shown, God is the one who desires first, and with an infinitely greater intensity, to draw close to the beloved.[4] God pines for us and makes this yearning known through revelation; in this sense, God also prays to us.

In contrast with prayer, *doxology* is typically defined not as an act of request but as an act of praise. It may accompany supplication as a prelude or more often as a concluding flourish, in which one proclaims or sings the grandeur of God. Nevertheless, here too there is a wider sense, in which virtually the entire field of relations between divine and creaturely freedom might be counted as doxological, insofar as the "content" of these relations is determined by the participated and intrinsic glory (*doxa*) and word (*logos*) of God.[5]

To be sure, desire remains an inescapable factor in doxology, since there is always more of God to be enjoyed. But this desire is itself a gift that we receive as part of the self-donation of God through the media of our perception and language—that is, through *doxa* and *logos* in the primordial meaning of these terms.[6] While receiving this gift, moreover, it is necessary to offer it, not only as a gift of praise returned to God, but also as a blessing to be shared with others. Doxology, therefore, has the potential to refer to any act of receiving, offering, and desiring the glory and word of God.

We find ourselves, then, on a somewhat slippery discursive terrain. On the one hand, doxology could be classified as one kind of prayer among many (alongside lament, petition, thanksgiving, meditation, etc.). On the other hand, prayer could be treated as a mere aspect of doxology (namely, the aspect of interpreted desire). In each instance, the meaning would depend on the breadth that one wishes to grant either term. However, the most promising approach seems to involve an unbounded exploration of the implications and co-implications of both. If within the semantic range of prayer there is a certain emphasis on the unfulfilled longings of the heart (the cry *de profundis*), the field of interpretive possibilities opened up by doxology provides a counterbalancing emphasis on the gracious advent of God in glory and word (i.e., revelation), which is the reason for our praise. Both emphases are undoubtedly necessary. Moreover, both find an incomparable witness in the human and divine person of Christ, who can be approached precisely as the incarnate fullness of both prayer and doxology.[7] He is the ground of their unity and the reason to avoid any excessive one-sidedness in the matter.

Whereas prayer seems to mean a free and mutually desirous discourse with God, *theology* seems to mean an intellectually sophisticated discourse about God. If we make too little of this distinction, it becomes difficult to explain why theology could not be done simply by praying or prayer simply by "theologizing" (in the generic sense of speaking or thinking about God). These sorts of undesirable conflations compel us to retain some sense of the difference between prayer and theology. And yet, if we make too much of this distinction, the obvious danger is that we will begin to construe them as entirely separate realms of conversation, in such a way that we will find ourselves simultaneously unable to say anything meaningful about the God whom we address in prayer and unable to pray to the God about whom we might nevertheless have much to say. Whether the latter, the "God" that has been isolated from prayer, has any relation to the living God or is perhaps nothing more than a conceptual idol becomes a serious question. Conversely, whether the former, the "God" of an unreflective or uncritical affect, is actually worthy of the worship that it receives is likewise a matter that calls for close scrutiny.

In order to address these concerns, it is perhaps enough to interpret theology as a practice of thought that seeks to make sense of the mystery of prayer and simultaneously as a practice of prayer that strives to meet the rigorous demands of thought, hence as *thinking prayer* in both senses of the term. According to this conceptual arrangement, theology would be defined by the double criterion of thoughtfulness and prayerfulness and in two different but complementary ways: "thinking" can be read as a gerund with the direct object of "prayer," and "prayer" can be read as a subject modified by the active participle of "thinking." In view of the latter emphasis, it clearly does not suffice for theologians to think about prayer as a mere phenomenon. Rather, in addition to this, they need to allow prayer to supply a decisive hermeneutic for their reflections on God and other things in relation to God. That is, they need to ask whether what they have to say regarding these topics appropriately expresses the distinctive ways of understanding and engaging reality that prayer brings to light.[8] In this sense, prayer exercises a significant degree of subjectivity. At the same time, the former emphasis reveals that the many labors of thinking—intervening in scholarly debates, posing critical questions, striving for conceptual coherence, respecting the manner in which things present themselves, and so on—remain crucial. In other words, prayer does not replace the rigor required by the academy; it adds an extra set of obligations to it. Without sacrificing its constitutive relation with prayer, theology needs to be committed to thought. It exists only as both. Compromises on either side (however inevitable these may be in practice) generally result in its diminishment or even distortion.

If theology, then, can be defined as thinking prayer, *spirituality* can be defined analogously as *living prayer*: that is, as that way of life which prays and as that practice of prayer which lives. In this instance, the double criterion has to do with the simultaneous affirmation of prayer and life. The root word "spirit," in its wide range of meanings, generally evokes a sense of life that is more than mere life. Spirit is an animating force, an inner mystery, or a vital principle that makes life deeply and truly alive. In the Christian tradition, this principle finds a particular luminosity in the corporeal and breath-filled spaces of prayer, perhaps especially in those spaces that have been set aside exclusively for this purpose: the small pockets of life in which one aims to do nothing but pray. And yet, the dynamic co-respiration between the Spirit of God and the fleshly spirits of the world that appears in discrete acts of prayer is not limited to them. It continues throughout the whole course of humanity's prayerfully informed activity. It can be discovered in working, preaching, fasting, and almsgiving, as well as in other less frequently emphasized practices such as eating, walking, conversing, gardening, dancing, protesting, mourning, and even thinking. These activities, insofar as they flow from prayer and preserve its dynamisms, are the ingredients of a sanctified and thus profoundly "enlivened" manner of existence. They are spirituality. And spirituality is, therefore, nothing other than prayer without ceasing. It is prayer spread across the many works and habits of each day.[9]

Any genuinely Christian sense of ethics and politics belongs to this more fundamental category of a constitutively prayerful way of life. The whole spectrum of humanistic and ecological efforts through which Christian communities rightly seek to promote the liveliness of the world should be understood, neither in opposition to, nor as a suitable replacement for, but rather as an integral aspect of the life of prayer. At the same time, one must not lose sight of those moments of life that may be reserved for prayer alone. Spirituality finds its footing here. In the quiet intensity of "pure" prayer, it comes into contact with the movements of a divine spirit that is not reducible to the dialectics of world history but transcends them absolutely and calls us into the unimaginable heights of an unknown freedom and love.

There are many historical traditions that organize the shared vocation of ceaseless prayer in different ways, and it is not unreasonable to speak of them as distinct "spiritualities," so long as one remembers their common origin in the abundant generosity of the one Spirit of God. Moreover, if spirituality introduces a pneumatological accent that appropriately complements the more nearly christological accent of doxology, it does not thereby authorize any sort of separation between the salvific missions of the Son and the Spirit but rather provides a context in which the two can powerfully intermingle in an unending economic perichoresis.[10] In this sense, spirituality becomes virtually synonymous with *imitatio Christi* and, thus, the following of Jesus.

Finally, as noted above, the understanding of prayer as a constitutive source of both theology and spirituality does not settle every possible question regarding the relationship between these two, but it does provide a principle that strongly suggests the need for some kind of integration, especially given the modern tendency toward separation.[11] The desired integration might be conceived as entailing not only a reciprocal influence of the one upon the other but also a significant degree of indistinguishability: if thought is not (impossibly) isolated from the concrete existence in which it arises, and if life is imbued with some level of reflective intentionality, and if both of these are formed according to the specific dynamisms of prayer, then we may be dealing not so much with the reciprocity of two (or three) realities but rather with one complex reality glimpsed from different angles. Whether we speak of this reality as the mystery of prayer together with all of its implications, as the embodied expression of genuine theology, or as an intellectually sharpened spirituality matters little, so long as we understand that it is in fact all of these while remaining one.

THE CRISES OF MODERNITY

In the context of modernity (which, for the purposes of this argument, emerges roughly over the course of the last five centuries), the possibility of thinking and living in a prayerful manner cannot be taken for granted. As Charles Taylor suggests, the fragility of this sort of "religious" theory and practice is a defining characteristic of contemporary *secularity*. With this term, he means to indicate not so much the absence of theological commitment as its destabilization by the modern development of exclusive humanism as a widely available option.[12] In short, Taylor shows us—and he is by no means the only one to do so[13]—that the same modern culture in which the church presently finds itself has partly resulted from a high degree of collective resistance against prayer or at least against some of its major presuppositions. The widespread decision in favor of this humanistic resistance among the intellectual elite has not been arbitrary. Rather, many modern thinkers have sought to support it by formulating various arguments against the supposed immaturity, irrationality, and irresponsibility of traditional forms of religious devotion. Immanuel Kant is just one example of this trend, but he is a crucial example.[14] Furthermore, although G. W. F. Hegel and Friedrich Nietzsche distance themselves significantly from Kant, they do not deviate from this tendency.[15]

The potential for such a decision against prayer is perhaps already discernible in the ancient human capacity for critical reflection and free self-determination, which is exhibited as much by Socrates as by any other ancient figure.[16] Nevertheless, the critical and self-assertive posture of humanity has undeniably acquired greater mobilizing force and argumentative power since the Enlightenment. It has also morphed in many ways in the subsequent centuries of reaction and counterreaction, up to and including the latest phases of postmodern suspicion. In short, it has taken on many forms, which warrant distinct evaluations. But whatever the variety may be, the fact remains that those who continue to pray in the modern epoch are confronted with the crisis of determining how to make sense of this practice in the midst of such a potentially prayer-negating intellectual culture.

The crisis of secularity becomes more complicated for Christian thinkers to the extent that they begin to recognize, as Taylor does, that our present culture has also made many significant advancements over its clearly imperfect premodern forebears, advancements that stem precisely from the same exercise of critical freedom that seems to challenge the viability of prayer as a mature, reasonable, and responsible vocation.[17] In order to respond most effectively to this complex situation, it seems that theologians should not simplistically protest the aspirationally free spirit of modernity but rather draw it into some kind of preservative and yet deeply transformative contact with the infinite freedom of God—that is, into a renewed experience of prayer, which would be capable of validating some of this modern spirit's legitimate concerns, while pointing the way toward a deeper realization of freedom and a more thoroughly life-affirming style of critique. The conditions under which such prayerful contact might occur today remain greatly in need of further elaboration.

Although the challenge of modern secularity is extraordinarily significant, it is not the only crisis to consider. As noted above, there are two other crises or sets of crises, both related to it and related to each other, which can be concisely designated as the purported end of metaphysics and as the structural manifestation of violence. The relations between these three areas of crisis are complex. Another study would be needed to give a thorough account of their interconnected emergence in modernity and to distinguish them adequately from certain premodern analogues—which, to be sure, were in their own ways no less grave. The threats of metaphysical idolatry and structurally entrenched hostility have deep roots in our collective past (including Christendom and before). But the most pressing question here does not concern the historical developments that concretized these problems in different eras but rather the future possibilities that are starting to open up in the present. We need to ask how the theoretical and practical retrieval of prayer might help the church, and contemporary society more broadly, better diagnose and address these diverse crises precisely as they appear in the current era.

The meaning of "metaphysics" and the meaning of its so-called end are matters of some dispute. Since Nietzsche, the debate between defenders and despisers of metaphysical philosophy has been largely characterized by dueling accusations of nihilism. It seems, in fact, that both parties have a point. That is, there is a need to seek an alternative path beyond, on the one hand, a tradition of apodictic metaphysics that ultimately shows itself to be nihilistic insofar as it reduces reality to a system of ontic knowledge under reason's supervision and control and, on the other hand, a mere deconstruction of metaphysics that in its abstract indeterminacy risks becoming a nihilistic parody of it.[18] The hope of overcoming this aporia lies in doxology. At its best, a doxological style of contemplation differs significantly from the sort of allegedly certain and comprehensive theorization that strictly qualifies as metaphysical and from any merely contrarian or disintegrative responses to it.

To take metaphysics seriously is to recognize that, since Aristotle's foundational treatise (and arguably before, under other names), it has generally been intended as a "science," that is, a determinate field of demonstrable knowledge, distinguished from mere myth or opinion—and, thus, from any mere narrative, however "meta"—by the fact that its claims are supposedly known with some high degree of objective certainty to be true and not false. The area of knowledge proper to metaphysics is being qua being, that is, the set of principles, causes, or traits that is definitive of being in its essence and its totality. For Aristotle, this would include theories of substance, of the categories, of the four causes, of the unmoved mover, and so on.[19] The reference to God as Creator (which has at times been counted as a metaphysical doctrine, even though Aristotle himself does not endorse any kind of creation ex nihilo) and the sense of wonder at being (which Aristotle cites as the experiential source of metaphysics)[20] are neither strictly dependent on metaphysics in the exact sense of a science, nor thoroughly definitive of its specific manner of proceeding. What is definitive is the supposedly demonstrable knowledge of the formal features of being as such and as a whole.

It does not suffice, therefore, despite various recent attempts, to construct an apology for metaphysics by appealing to the need for a

Creator-creature distinction or the promise of a natural experience of wonder.[21] These are indispensable goods, but they are not the exclusive property of metaphysics and may even be imperiled by it. Moreover, they do not settle the other issues associated with this intellectual practice, particularly its tendency to reduce experience to a set of objective certitudes; to elevate the status of the knowing subject beyond what can be sustained or believed; to conceal the wondrous, phenomenal arrivals of difference and alterity; to instrumentalize, reify, or otherwise distort the mysteries of God, humanity, and nature; to offer a supposedly rational explanation for suffering, potentially in the mode of a theodicy; and perhaps to serve, usually without critical awareness of the fact, the specific interests of a dominating will-to-power, whether this is located in oneself, in a particular class (elite or bourgeois), or in a politico-cultural region (Europe or the West). In order to make all of these charges against metaphysics, one arguably needs a wider sense of the term, which would be symbolized but not exhausted by the "science": that is, metaphysics as a highly dispersed and hubristic tendency of human consciousness. And yet, even in this wider sense, the idea of an overreaching attempt at conceptual mastery remains paradigmatic.

Granted, these dangers of metaphysics can be greatly mitigated by this or that specific formulation of it, especially by formulations that include enough epistemic humility to uncouple the meaning of metaphysics from the traditional criterion of strict scientificity. Moreover, these dangers or very similar ones can reappear in projects that show no intention of being metaphysical and, perhaps, are explicitly intended not to be. Finally, the refusal of metaphysics is by itself no proof that other serious problems have been successfully avoided or resolved. As a rule, those thinkers who have attempted to enter into a postmetaphysical mode of thought without the guidance of some kind of doxology have tended to fall into certain excessively immanentized and uncompromisingly apophatic patterns of discourse that are rightly critiqued for their deflation of transcendence and their general paucity of consolation.[22] In the most extreme cases, there is very little that seems to occasion the experience of awe any longer except for oneself and one's own mastery of suspicion.

For these reasons, it has become necessary to move beyond not only the uncritical affirmation of metaphysics but also its hypercritical (deconstructive) denial, precisely in order to seek a genuine path of doxological eminence. Phenomenology may be helpful in this regard, especially in its more experientially disclosive, and thus less methodologically apodictic, occurrences. Indeed, there is only a short step from *phenomenon* to *doxa*. Nevertheless, Christian forms of doxology, especially those that have been deepened by phenomenological insight without losing themselves in it, tend to fare better than the efforts of "mere" phenomenology, insofar as they allow one to pursue a richly mediated contemplation of the simultaneously hidden and revealed glory and word of the triune God. The place of poetry, and more broadly of aesthetics (sensation, art, and beauty), is significant here as well. The phenomena that concretize doxology do not arise as perfectly comprehensible objects but rather as finely textured mysteries, which admit of description and creative presentation but not complete eidetic reduction. These are the finite occasions for a loving encounter with the infinite.

Any ostensibly postmetaphysical discourse, whether more nearly phenomenological or aesthetic, that fixes a horizon of immanence and allows no divinely initiated doxology to transpierce it remains, whatever its merits, very close to the dangers of metaphysics, much closer perhaps than it would like to admit. In the end, more is needed than reverence for experience (approached implicitly as a sphere of certain knowledge); we need reverence for that divine excess which, in experience, also surpasses it. Thus we need meditations and songs that dare to become hymns to an absolute, indomitable love.

To be clear, the advertence to a postmetaphysical doxology does not require one to side with Karl Barth against all manner of "natural theology," nor to dispute the doctrine of the First Vatican Council regarding the accessibility of God to the "natural light of reason."[23] Natural theology remains conceivable precisely to the extent that prayer can in some cases continue to take place "naturally," that is, without the explicit acceptance of Christian revelation.[24] Moreover, one might reasonably expect that some knowledge of the mystery of

God is available in the light provided by this kind of prayerful practice. In fact, much of the Western philosophical and theological tradition needs to be reread with precisely this orientation in mind, in order to discover in what ways certain figures that we tend to think of as purveyors of metaphysics have actually been more fundamentally interested in doxology, even if perhaps of a more nearly "natural" variety. Nevertheless, in the end, the purest and most christologically focused thinkers of doxology will tend to be the most reliable, and Barth's warnings are, therefore, well taken.[25]

Nor are the mere buzzwords of metaphysics—"being," "cause," "substance," and so on—necessarily inimical to a doxological manner of thinking that seeks to guard itself against the dangers of metaphysics. To be sure, such words have some problematic histories that one needs to acknowledge and perhaps resist. But no particular words are actually illicit in the context of prayer. The question is how they are used and, more specifically, how this usage expresses and affects the interactions between God and God's creatures. Metaphysics has been troublesome for theology only insofar as it has employed its standard vocabulary in ways that limit reception of the glory and word of God, overly aggrandize the finite intellect of the creature, or in some other way compromise the freedom and love that are supposed to characterize their relationship. Like the best sorts of metaphysics, doxology asks one to believe in something rather than nothing and encourages awe at the fact that there is something rather than nothing. However, its discursive responses to the vibrant shocks and contingencies of being are oriented not toward a mere triumph of human reason but toward a somewhat conceptually clarified act of divine praise.

Although the crises of modern *violence* appear to be in certain respects closely related to the modern culmination of metaphysics, it is nevertheless important to avoid collapsing these two clusters of issues into one massive, undifferentiated problem. To some extent, these sets of crises need to be treated on their own terms. Moreover, a responsible discussion of violence cannot be developed without attending to the concrete histories and contexts in which it has exerted its destructive force. The same requirement of concreteness undoubtedly applies to the discussion of metaphysics as well, especially insofar as it intersects with violence, but there is still a difference in the sorts of realities that are most immediately at stake: a difference between the wonder of being and actual flesh-and-blood human beings living in an environment with other living things. Furthermore, there is a difference in the kinds of responses that are necessary to affirm and protect these realities: mere contemplation must become a historically engaged practice of contemplation-in-action. And yet, although we therefore need a somewhat differentiated approach, one of the contentions driving this project is that a doxological and prayerful spirituality holds out the greatest promise of addressing both sets of crises and, moreover, of doing so in an integrated fashion. A unified response is possible because, and to the extent that, both of these areas of crisis stem from a refusal to think and embody prayer together with all of its implications.

To speak about the structures of violence is to refer not merely to isolated incidents but rather to established patterns of harm and destruction, which are no less constitutive of modernity than are the dreams of the Enlightenment.[26] Within the general category of structural violence, it is possible to distinguish between a grossly imbalanced socioeconomic order that has shown no serious intention of supplying the legitimate and urgent demands of much of the world's population and an aggressive politics of dominant identities that rejects and marginalizes whatever it regards as other, but there are in fact no strict boundaries between these kinds of consistently deleterious power. The impoverished can be othered and the othered can be impoverished, and this seems to be the case more often than not. Nevertheless, the distinction has some value insofar as it acknowledges various kinds of subaltern status in addition to those that are exclusively characterized by a maldistribution of (the control of) resources. In the present argument, we shall consider the particular examples of Jewishness and blackness, without pretending thereby to exhaust the field of relevant cases of identity-based oppression.[27]

The counterviolent potential of prayer stems, in part, from its ability to cultivate subjects who are prepared to resist unjust structures of power and who are likewise capable of understanding why this resistance is necessary regardless of the costs, that is, even when there is only the slightest hope of actual victory and a serious risk of real personal sacrifice. However, no less significantly, prayer shows its counterviolent potential insofar as it gives glory to God as the savior of the world and thereby at least potentially subverts the idolatrous self-glorification of particular parties, nations, or leaders, who may be tempted to misunderstand themselves as the masters of history.[28] In other words, prayer both empowers humanity and importantly reveals the limits of human power. Some theorists have employed the idea of a weak messianism in order to avoid concentrating power in any fallible human projects or institutions while still retaining some hope for a better future.[29] It seems, however, that what we need is not exactly a "weak" but rather a rigorously doxological messianism, whose worldly aspirations would be chastened by the requisite humility of prayer but simultaneously emboldened by a somewhat determinate Christian hope. This would be a messianism that praises the liberating work of the triune God, while asking humanity to play its own finite but indispensable part. This is precisely the sort of powerful but nondominating spirituality that emerges from the prayerful struggles of many Christian communities of the poor and oppressed.[30]

In another respect, prayer promises to work against violence insofar as it provides unparalleled training in the ways of hospitality and responsibility. By requiring one to receive the wholly other God, prayer constitutes a paradigm for the radical form of welcoming that must be extended toward every other other. It accesses the mysteries of *kenosis* and *Gelassenheit* at their source, and lets the self be for the other in a maximal sense. Similarly, by calling one to respond before the judgment seat of God, prayer grounds and strengthens all manner of inner-worldly responsibility—and, indeed, does so much more reliably than the autonomous modern subject, which passes all too quickly from Kant's moral rigorism (still supposedly informed by the "spirit of prayer") to Nietzsche's attempted transcendence of good and evil. By regularly situating ourselves *coram Deo*, we learn to see who we are, what we have done, and what we are meant to do, all in the quite possibly disconcerting light of the transcendent counterintentionality of God.[31] There is likewise a particularly valuable practice of spiritual and ethical discernment that can take place only through an intimate dialogical meditation on the relationship between Christ's existence and our own. In short, therefore, prayer offers us a lesson regarding loving receptivity to the other, while simultaneously granting us a disambiguating perspective on our obligations, and perhaps serious shortcomings, in the midst of this violent world.

Furthermore, it is necessary to recognize that there are horizons of human liberation that only doxology can reach and yearnings of the human spirit that only God can finally satisfy. These aspects of the blessed life are such that no merely secular theory or practice could ever hope to approximate them. Prayer discloses them as nothing else can. One might consider, for example, the hope in resurrection and justice for the dead, the confidence that one is definitively loved despite the hatred of the world, the promise that sins will be forgiven and that even the most horrifically damaged relationships will be mended, and the unshakable joy that comes from an ever-deepening friendship with God. In the absence of prayer, these goods begin to seem illusory, and, as a result, the full scope of historical and eschatological goodness is left unacknowledged. Whatever conceptions of the good may arise in nonprayerful forms of ethical discourse (which may very well be compelling in their own right), the fact remains that still more will be required in order to overcome the world's radical propensity for evil and to experience the fullness of goodness as such. To pray rightly is to understand that, in the final analysis, divine peace alone will suffice.[32]

No doubt, there have been many distortions of prayer that betray this counterviolent potential and pervert the mystery of divine-and-human encounter into an instrument of unspeakable violence. Baptized and believing Christians who prayed to a nominally Christian God have murdered Jews, brutalized indigenous communities, let the poor starve and die, and sold shackled black bodies to the highest bidder. Obviously, such distortions need to be identified and combated with great urgency, wherever and however they occur. But it does not follow that prayer itself is the problem. On the contrary, as the Hebrew prophets have never ceased to remind us, it is precisely the idolatrous and violent *falsification* of prayer that continually produces the sorrow of the world and provokes the righteous anger of God.[33] The appropriate recourse, therefore, is toward a rigorous and active *verification* of prayer as an indispensable sign of obedience to the covenant and, hence, as a thoroughly unified expression of the love of God and love of neighbor (including human, animal, and every other kind of creature). A prayer that would not cease and that would be true would open up unanticipated and liberating possibilities of theory and practice, which it seems we can no longer afford to ignore.

ADJACENT DISCOURSES

The perspective developed here is somewhat similar to, but also in several ways significantly different from, the theological style of *radical orthodoxy*. The present work shares this movement's commitment to "right" doctrine grounded in traditional Christian *doxa*. Moreover, it likewise treats this commitment as the "root" of any promising theoretical and practical engagement with the crises of modernity.[34] However, the argument of this text diverges from the general strategy of radical orthodoxy insofar as it urges theologians to be, by comparison, more appreciative of various aspects of modernity's developments of critical freedom, more attentive to the richly textured phenomenalities of prayer beyond the patristic and medieval periods, more troubled by the prayerful forms of lament that disrupt excessively positive expressions of doxology, more cognizant of the profound doxological possibilities that are constitutive of many traditions of liberation theology, and generally more mindful of the prayerful ways of thinking and living that have emerged among oppressed communities throughout the world.

Many of these recommendations are summed up in the last one. In order to access the deepest and most credible doxological vision, it is necessary to give a clear priority to the prayers of the victims of history. These are the sources for an understanding of prayer that has been tested and sharpened by the body-and-soul-crushing realities of worldly existence—an understanding which is not sufficiently conveyed, for example, by the rather abstract theory of Platonic "participation," however useful this theory may be in many respects. To praise God with integrity, one must be inhabited by the voices of those who perhaps have nothing left except to cry out to God or even against God. Adoration is possible only if it is possible in this context. Moreover, the decision to take these perspectives seriously is that which most clearly prohibits any one-sided denunciations of modernity's characteristic approbation of critical freedom. Many of the "correlations" that have arisen between secular and theological hopes are best interpreted, not as impositions of an extrinsic ideology, but rather as entailments of a practice of Christian prayer that has been forged within the hellacious conditions of this violent world order. For this sort of prayer, modernity is not simply negative but rather ambiguous. The signs of the Spirit's movements within this epoch, therefore, need to be discerned carefully and not decided a priori.

The present argument is likewise related to the field of *liturgical theology*, albeit perhaps only tangentially. It can certainly be counted as part of the effective history of Prosper of Aquitaine's famous dictum, *lex orandi, lex credendi*.[35] However, whereas this principle has inspired many studies of the sacraments and sacred rites of the church, here its effect is more general, namely to draw attention to prayer itself, with liturgy serving only as an occasional (and admittedly underdeveloped) example. As a general rule, it seems appropriate to treat liturgy as the first and last theology and as theology's most definitive source, as many liturgical theologians recommend,[36] only insofar as the specific liturgies under consideration continue to form and be formed by the many prayerful ways of thinking and living that are constitutive of Christian spirituality as a whole. For this reason, there is a need for broader examinations of the mystery of prayer, such as this one, which are not limited to a liturgical context. At the same time, the specific field of liturgical theology remains crucial insofar as it highlights liturgy as a paradigmatic manifestation of the church's prayerful and doxological existence.[37]

The recently emergent and increasingly complex field known as the *interdisciplinary study of spirituality* resists being identified as a mere ascetical or mystical subfield of Christian dogmatics, as it would appear to have been *avant la lettre* in the once standard formulation of Giovanni Battista Scaramelli. This formulation established the parameters for discussion among Catholic theologians from the eighteenth through the early twentieth centuries, when the term "spirituality" suddenly began its meteoric rise.[38] With time the field of spirituality-studies has come to include not only various aspects of Christian life that may not be entirely explicable in terms of traditional doctrinal considerations but also a massive range of interreligious, secular, and other kinds of phenomena reaching far beyond the limits of canonical Christianity. Certainly there is some value in studying this material in order, as Sandra Schneiders suggests, to "understand" it—by which she means to describe, critically analyze, and constructively appropriate it.[39] Moreover, the present work might be read as making a small contribution to this collective effort.

Nevertheless, it seems that any strong methodological distinction between theology and the study of spirituality has the potential to hinder thinkers from constructively appropriating the Trinitarian-and-creaturely fullness of Christian spirituality and perhaps even from describing and analyzing it most thoroughly as it gives itself from itself. Explaining why she believes they should become and remain distinct disciplines, Schneiders suggests that theology is mainly concerned with general doctrines (possibly illustrated by experience) and that the study of spirituality is primarily focused on particular experiences (possibly informed by doctrine).[40] She likewise suggests that the distinctiveness of the study of spirituality could be at least partly determined by its more nearly anthropological, as opposed to theological, horizon; that is, it concentrates on the human being's openness to transcendence instead of the transcendence itself.[41] These distinctions institute a threefold dialectic of generality-doctrine-divinity and particularity-experience-humanity that will call for various kinds of relation and resolution but may be left without any disciplines that are prepared to seek them, since the two likely candidates (theology and spirituality-studies) have already been assigned to one pole or another.

We noted above that it is possible to distinguish spirituality (as a prayerful way of life) from theology (as a prayerful mode of thought). At the same time, we also recognized that a close identification of the two (an identification that is so close as to approach indistinguishability) is demanded by the mystery of prayer that radically unites them. These are not two separable entities that we may or may not choose to combine but rather intrinsically unified aspects of the interactive relations between Trinitarian and creaturely freedoms. Here it is necessary to clarify further that, at least for Christians (but perhaps not only for them), the *study* of spirituality should be oriented toward contemplating this same wondrous reality. In other words, both theology and the study of spirituality should be (and there may actually be only one type of thought here) thoroughly defined by an intellectual responsibility to the phenomenal features and hermeneutical principles that are disclosed by the same prayerful interactivity—which, according to the consensus of the Christian tradition, is constituted at least as much by the self-disclosive actions of the triune God as by the passionate strivings of creation.

In this light, Schneiders's methodological distinction between theology and spirituality-studies begins to seem somewhat too strong. It may legitimately remind us that both ideas and lives need to be researched. But if pressed regarding what the ideas and the lives mean, both in themselves and for us now, we will be returned again and again from one to the other, since they will inevitably be mutually interpreting. Thought finds its only verification in existence, and existence finds its only clarity in thought. We, therefore, need an interpretive space that is open to the reciprocal dynamisms of a prayerfully thoughtful existence and is not divided against them. Schneiders recommends the limited reciprocity that can happen in a dialogue between two clearly demarcated scholarly disciplines; by contrast, the present work seeks to inhabit a more holistic space that is located before or beyond any such division.

To be sure, Schneiders's desire for an interdisciplinary approach, in which the resources of history, psychology, sociology, and other areas of scholarship might be employed freely, in whatever ways they prove useful or necessary, can be entirely incorporated into this unified theological and spiritual space, so long as these other disciplines are not used in a way that contradicts the basically prayerful orientation of this space. Moreover, although academic labor almost certainly needs to be differentiated in some way, it does not follow that the divisions should occur primarily along the lines of universal theological theory and particular anthropological experience.[42] Instead, one might envision other patterns of academic concentration corresponding to different periods, regions, traditions, or debates, all undergirded by a much more explicit sense of a shared vocation. The vocation would be to shed light on the Trinitarian-and-creaturely reality of prayer in all its dimensions.[43]

The scope of the present work is limited by several intentional, but not strictly necessary, choices regarding such points of concentration. The period is primarily contemporary; the regions are somewhat various, though still very few, and mostly confined to certain "Western" locales within Europe and the Americas; the traditions are largely Roman Catholic, with some ecumenically catholic extensions (i.e., traditions that are recognizably Christian according to certain universally normative features of Christian doctrine and practice); and the debates mainly concern the significance of Christian prayer as a response to the crises of modernity. Hence, this text represents only a small thread of the thought that has been, and might yet be, pursued within the vast tapestry of Christianity's prayerful existence—not to mention the nearly limitless field of possibilities for comparative and dialogical study that remain open for further exploration.[44] Indeed, there is nothing in the present work that is meant to dissuade Christian thinkers from seeking deeper levels of respectful engagement with the immense spectrum of non-Christian "spiritualities" (if, in fact, this remains the best general category). There is only the conviction that this engagement should not occur at the expense of in-depth reflections on the meaning and significance of prayer within the Christian tradition. This sort of reflection is indispensable for Christians and highly recommended for everyone else, who would of course remain free to doubt the veracity of this tradition's claims, even while learning to see what it might mean for someone not to doubt them.

It is worth stating clearly that, although Jewish traditions of prayer implicitly contribute a great deal to this study, and although we shall have occasion to consider briefly the obligations that Christians have to pray in solidarity with the Jews, especially in remembrance of the horror of the Shoah, for which the Christian tradition is significantly (though not exclusively) culpable, it remains the case that no thorough treatment of the topic of Jewish prayer, precisely as understood and practiced by Jewish people, will be found in these pages. Moreover, it is also important to acknowledge that the voices of women—and, indeed, the entire field of questions concerning the relationship between prayer, gender, and sexuality, which are certainly bound up with the crises of modernity, even as elaborated here—are not sufficiently represented by the following discussion.[45] These serious limitations, together with the many others that might be mentioned, are products of my own and the present work's finitude. They should not be taken as endorsing a posture of indifference with respect to such concerns but rather merely as clear evidence that this text does not, and cannot, offer a final word on the subject of prayer.

Having completed the clarificatory tasks of the introduction, let us now turn to the first chapter. This chapter will develop the central argument of this book in critical dialogue with Heidegger. His post-Christian work has had an extraordinary influence on many Christian thinkers, as well as their secular interlocutors, and he merits attention here largely because he puts an approximately prayerful or prayer-like way of thinking at the center of a contemporary intellectual culture that includes both of these demographics. His work suggests a connection not only between prayer and Christian theology but also between prayer and *thought as such*. Nevertheless, many theological and nontheological interpreters have recognized a number of reasons to move beyond Heidegger. Although he begins to elucidate what might be gained in a paradigm shift from metaphysics to doxology, the very particular and questionable form that his doxology takes reveals some of the ways that this endeavor

can go badly astray. An initial effort to untangle these Heideggerian knots will prepare for a decisive return, in subsequent chapters,
to an explicitly Christian tradition of prayerful thought (a tradition
which, nonetheless, remains rather preoccupied with Heidegger's
challenging meditations).

PART 1

FROM METAPHYSICS
TO DOXOLOGY

CHAPTER 1

DOXOLOGICAL IMPURITY
Martin Heidegger

Prayer is not the only issue at stake in a Christian confrontation with Heidegger, but the centrality of prayer to Christian thought and life makes this a crucial line of inquiry—one that, moreover, warrants greater attention. In relation to the topic of prayer, Heidegger is a perplexing and troubling figure. His philosophy seems more prayerful than most of its modern predecessors and contemporaries and can even be read as a defense of (something like) prayerful thinking and living amidst the destructive forces of our technocratic age. Nevertheless, it remains, at least by Christian standards, not prayerful enough and even in some significant respects deleterious to the practice and understanding of prayer. Heidegger moves away from metaphysics and toward a recovery of doxology (this is the primary form through which prayer starts to enter his thought) only while maintaining problematic ties to metaphysics and refusing the most serious demands of doxology. This ambivalence allows him to resist certain crises of the modern age (though not as effectively as he might) and to neglect and even become substantially implicated in other crises. On the whole, therefore, his philosophy provides an instructive example of *doxological impurity*—that is, a case in which the promise of doxological contemplation is compromised by various rival commitments.

There is an apparent irony here: Heidegger's promotion of a certain kind of "purity," involving various intellectual, cultural, and political aspects, is the very feature of his thought which proves most detrimental to the purity of his doxology precisely as a doxology. However, there is in fact very little irony in this case. There is really only an equivocation between two senses of purity that have almost nothing to do with one another: on the one hand, a doxological purity of heart and mind that starts from a divine gift of self-bestowing, other-welcoming love and then seeks to express this uncompromisingly hospitable love in the world; on the other hand, an earthly ideal of "purity" that guards a very regional and structurally violent experience of being and appropriates divinity to this limited horizon. Insofar as Heidegger's thought primarily follows the latter route, it jeopardizes its status as a doxology. It becomes imperiled by principles and restrictions that are not consistent with doxological thinking. This is the sort of impurity (disguised as "purity") which we shall investigate in this chapter—while, nevertheless, seeking to recover a sense of the genuine doxological possibilities that it both imitates and obscures.[1]

The positive significance that Heidegger has for the present study consists to some extent simply in the fact *that* he thinks doxologically in response to the crises of modern metaphysics. This fact alone is remarkable, and we shall see in subsequent chapters that many Christian thinkers have followed his lead in this respect. They have done so for good reasons: his account of the dilemmas facing contemporary humanity and his initial steps in the direction of a re-unification of prayer and thought have some merits to them. Nevertheless, his *specific* formulation of this strategy needs to be corrected on several counts in relation to both his critique of metaphysics and his positive doxological proposal.

THE ARGUMENT IN BRIEF

Our critical analysis of Heidegger's itinerary from metaphysics to doxology will proceed in two stages. First, we shall examine his critique of metaphysics in relation to the crises of technology, nihilism, and the forgetting of being and its difference. Although some aspects of this critique are helpful, problems arise insofar as it implicates the Christian theological tradition without seriously considering this tradition's doxological orientation. Second, we shall consider what doxological avenues remain open to Heidegger through the *doxa* and the *logos* that he discovers in Hölderlin's poetry, as well as in other analogous Greco-German cultural figures. In his readings of these sources, Heidegger receives, announces, and seeks the mystery of divinity and the mystery of being,[2] and it is in these two senses that he thinks doxologically and thus somewhat prayerfully. The focus of his doxology is divided between an idiosyncratically theological consideration of the "gods," which, appearing within the event of being (*Ereignis*), hint at the ever-distant "last God," and a postmetaphysically ontological meditation on *Ereignis* itself.[3] Our concern here will not only be to describe these two apparent routes into (something like) doxology but also to note the ways in which they ultimately compromise it.

Because this chapter involves complex analyses of a challenging and (as far as prayer is concerned) rather ambiguous thinker, it will be helpful to begin with a preliminary articulation of the main theses of each of the two stages mentioned above and then advance to a textually mediated elaboration of them. The central point to be made against Heidegger's critique of metaphysics is that it does not pay sufficient attention to the doxological modes of thought that are constitutive of the best forms of Christian theology. The first stage of our analysis will develop three arguments in support of this point.

First, Heidegger does not interpret the history of Christian thought in the precise doxological manners in which it most promisingly gives itself but rather as it is polemically construed by a post-Nietzschean narrative regarding the nihilistic teleology of the West. Although this narrative may legitimately implicate *some* aspects of the Christian tradition, it also reduces a great deal of it to oblivion and makes many questionable judgments about what it does accurately describe. In short, what holds true for the fate of metaphysics may not hold true for the fate of the best sorts of Christian prayerful thought. More distinctions are needed in this area.

Second, Heidegger suggests that there is a direct correspondence between the affirmations of God as the highest being or cause (which he argues are integral to the ontotheological constitution of metaphysics) and the impossibility of prayer. To the extent that these theological names facilitate the technological and nihilistic tendencies of metaphysics and prevent the disclosure of difference, they can understandably prove detrimental to prayer. However, Heidegger does not consider whether the very same names are simultaneously indispensable for prayer. By leaving this question unasked and unanswered, he fails to clarify that the decisive issue is not whether one thinks these names at all but rather whether one ultimately thinks them metaphysically or doxologically.

Third, Heidegger admittedly interprets Christian theology not only as implicated in metaphysics but also as a relatively autonomous discipline grounded in faith. The fact that Heidegger grants philosophy the right to correct this sort of theology is certainly questionable, though perhaps not entirely unreasonable in every case. The much greater problem has to do with his classification of theology as an ontic science. This classification keeps Heidegger from recognizing the ways that Christian doxology has been deeply informed by the eventful manifestation of being among beings and has, therefore, addressed—and not merely ontically—many of the questions that animate his own phenomenological ontology. In short, Heidegger respects the relative independence of faith only on the condition that he is able to decide in advance, without thorough exploration, and quite negatively, the question of its significance.

These three problems in Heidegger's critique of metaphysics, which the question of prayer brings to light—namely, the myopic post-Nietzschean narrative, the one-sided account of theological names, and the positioning of faith as irrelevant to serious thought—stem from a general failure to think Christian doxology as it gives itself from itself. A characteristically modern decision against the thinking of prayer lies at the root of all three. Thus, for all his efforts to transcend modernity, in this respect Heidegger remains thoroughly within its sway. A more decisive break with the prayer-negating tendencies of modern thought would have enabled him to specify the points of convergence and divergence between his critique of metaphysics and Christian doxology. Unfortunately, however, he makes no such break and accordingly leaves the nuances of this relationship in obscurity.

Heidegger's Hölderlinian alternative to Christian doxology, which frames the second stage of our analysis, also comes with major difficulties. The central problem has to do with an ambiguity, subtly but consistently exploited, in the notion of *Ereignis*—and, particularly, in Heidegger's sense of what it means to be appropriated to that which is native, essential, original, and proper (*eigen*: "own"). Heidegger's use of this term demands respect not only for things as they give themselves in their *own* way but also for that Greco-German intellectual, cultural, and political region or homeland (his *own* land) in which he believes that being and thought have and will come into their own. But these are two commitments, not one, and to some extent they work against each other. One might call them, respectively, the principles of *hospitality* and *autochthony*. Heidegger thinks *Ereignis* by reducing the one to the other: openness is restricted by rootedness; distance is sought within *Dasein*'s ontological horizon; the foreign is made to comply with the logic of the home or else is simply forgotten. This autochthonous restriction occurs in at least three different ways.

First, Heidegger's reading of Hölderlin exalts a particular region of theory, culture, and politics that is not only significantly estranged from the primary wellsprings of doxology in the Jewish and Christian traditions but also proves to be (arguably for related reasons) gravely inhospitable to anyone who is insufficiently German. To be clear, Heidegger's Hölderlinian doxology is not problematic simply because it is *somehow* regionally located, as any intellectual work must be, including the present one. Within Christian doxology, as within Heidegger's thought, some degree of regional and traditional rootedness is inevitable. The transparency of any such autochthonous positioning to the desired fullness of doxology will always be questionable, and explicitly Christian works are no exception to this rule: they must, like all others, receive the highest possible scrutiny on the basis of prayer's most deeply held criteria of freedom and love. Conversely, some sort of autochthony is a very good and urgently needed feature of doxological contemplation and action, especially in a globalized technological age which is so prone to uproot us from our local cultures and ecologies.

Nevertheless, Heidegger's sort of autochthony does become particularly problematic insofar as it glorifies its own specific region in a way that dismisses the deepest sources of biblical prayer and, correlatively, prayer's most serious ethical implications. One cannot avoid mentioning, in this regard, the politically disastrous consequences of Heidegger's ostensibly doxological proposal. His poetic thinking manifests a nationalist and racially supremacist spirit, which not only supports his now widely lamented affiliation with National Socialism and the concomitant rejection of Jewish thought and life, but also implicates his project in a less widely recognized colonial logic and politics that has had adverse effects on the (for Heidegger, forgettable) masses of the non-European world. These political outcomes are consistent with his autochthonous version of doxology but inimical to the divine freedom and love that constitute doxology as such.

Second, Heidegger's commitment to autochthony leads him to speak of the mystery of God only as thoroughly appropriated by, and therefore subordinated to, the event of being. Hence, he does not speak of this divine mystery strictly as it gives itself in prayer but rather as another intellectual preoccupation (existential ontology or ontological poetics) requires him to think it. Whether *Ereignis* is understood merely as a symbol of Heidegger's Greco-German culture or more sympathetically as a term that reveals something significant about the manner in which being is always and everywhere disclosed, the problem is similar: to assign divinity a place exclusively within the logic of *Ereignis* is to endorse a kind of intellectual domestication of divinity that can only be threatening to prayer. Under the control of *Ereignis*, the mystery of God comes to be disintegrated into the domains of immanence (the gods) and transcendence (the last God) in such a way that the import of both is decreased. The gods are at most finite messengers (angels, in the strict sense) and are, therefore, not especially deserving of praise or adoration. The last God, which Heidegger suggests is truly divine, remains absent to the point of seeming powerless, indifferent, or wholly abstract, but this is not a God before whom one can meaningfully pray.

Finally, where there is a simple, awe-inspiring, and powerful interplay of immanence and transcendence, this mystery is dissolved into the *logos* and *doxa* of *Ereignis* itself—which is to say, ultimately, into the history and destiny of being. Here the principles of hospitality and autochthony converge, revealing their real point of resolution for Heidegger. Welcoming *Ereignis* as it gives itself and dwelling poetically on the earth are two ways of saying the same thing. However, although there is something admirable in this essentially mortal vocation, it can in the end be little more than an unequal imitation of prayer. Interpreted rigorously, it replaces and has no further use for prayer in the strict sense. The event of being is not God but comes to function analogously: that is, as the ultimate point of reference for an onto-doxology that is not exactly doxology. The inhospitality of *Ereignis* toward the divine and human other is amplified in this instance by an inhospitality toward any change that is not a homecoming to the native conditions of one's being, whether this change is envisioned as a historically liberative transformation of society or an eschatological resurrection of the dead. Thus Heidegger refuses prayer, in the final analysis, precisely by refusing its hope.

Heidegger's threefold autochthonous restriction—which defines doxology in terms of a particular region that is not receptive to doxology's biblical sources, domesticates and disintegrates the mystery of God, and finally allows the event of being to take the place of the hopeful reality of prayer—comes to seem more problematic to the extent that it indicates an affiliation with the very metaphysical tradition from which he seeks to distance himself. There are, no doubt, many ways in which his Hölderlinian thought is importantly distinct from metaphysics, especially in its modern manifestations, as well as from his own earlier phenomenological work. And yet, these distinctions are not entirely decisive as far as the question of prayer is concerned. Heidegger's persistent prioritization of the

Greco-German event of being exacts a high price from prayer, not unlike that which is exacted by the metaphysical tradition. He does not seem to recognize the extent to which his particular version of autochthony proves inhospitable to prayer and its ethical embodiment. Nor does he perceive that his work thereby exemplifies a crisis that is no less (and arguably more) central to the problematic condition of modernity than are technology, nihilism, and ontotheology, a crisis that gives rise to these others and reveals their true form, namely the denial of prayer and the particular patterns of thought and life that it implies. In what follows, then, we shall consider in more detail what Heidegger has to offer in terms of a *general* itinerary from metaphysics to doxology and, moreover, the various ways in which his *specific* approach succumbs to a troubling form of doxological impurity.

CRITIQUE OF METAPHYSICS

Let us now consider more closely the reasoning behind Heidegger's critique of metaphysics and the ways that it does not do justice to Christian doxology. Heidegger argues that we need a very different way of thinking that which metaphysics attempts to think, and it is in this limited sense that he distinguishes his own thought from metaphysics throughout his diverse body of works. Heidegger's "critique," then, if one can use this term without implying any overly specific ties to Kant's philosophical method, is no mere negation of metaphysics but rather a contrastive moment within a larger effort to outperform metaphysics by pursuing a more original, essential, and truthful understanding of the question of being that is proper to it.[4] Although his arguments differ from one text to another, they can be treated collectively (especially after his post–*Being and Time* "turn") as a series of variations on one unifying theme: metaphysics arises in the history of being and discloses it only while, at the same time, greatly preventing its disclosure. Metaphysics is thus a largely self-contradictory manifestation of being which for the most part does not let being manifest itself, even though this is exactly what it purports to do. Metaphysics says "being" but forgets its wondrous coming-to-presence. In the effort to attain certain knowledge of being as such and as a whole, metaphysics fails to correspond with the overwhelming mystery that it desires to think. Instead, it produces various allegedly comprehensive systems of ontic concepts (i.e., objectified representations or abstractions of finite beings organized into a totality), which seem to say more about the intellectual ambitions of the philosopher than they do about the unveiling of the world and its eventful time-space (*Ereignis*). As a consequence of its concealment of being, metaphysics also endangers an appropriate sense of humanity, divinity, and their proper forms of relation. In short, metaphysics does not treat being, the human being, or God with the proper kinds of reverence and contemplation.

Throughout his arguments, Heidegger targets virtually the entire tradition of Western philosophy, from the Greeks through Nietzsche, showing how each philosopher significantly obscures but also partly reveals something about the original and essential phenomenality of being, as well as the roles of the human being and the god(s) that are implicated in it. Nevertheless, his critique acquires its greatest intensity in confrontation with the crises of the modern age. In this era, he contends, metaphysics becomes particularly dangerous. On the one hand, there are new notions of certainty and subjectivity associated with Descartes's *ego cogito*, which shift metaphysics in a self-grounding, epistemological direction that greatly compromises philosophy's openness to the arrival of being.[5] On the other hand, there are related manifestations of technology and nihilism, which pass beyond the limits of metaphysics as a supposedly strict "science," but nevertheless find their sources in a very similar kind of modern subject. We shall focus on Heidegger's interpretations of technology and nihilism, in order to clarify what is concretely at stake for the culture as a whole and not merely for the history of philosophy (though these remain deeply interconnected in his account).

In "The Question concerning Technology," Heidegger maintains that the danger of modern technology coincides with a hyper-extension of the problematically reductive distinction between object and subject (a distinction which arises in modernity and is still operative in Edmund Husserl's phenomenology). Heidegger argues that, through the pull of technology, we now tend to think of ourselves, together with the things around us, as mere units of potential energy, that is, as "raw material" or "standing-reserve" (*Bestand*). In this way, we give ourselves and other people and things a status that is even less dignified than that of an intentional object. Everything becomes disposable. At the same time, we paradoxically tend to grant ourselves an illusory dominion over the whole of being. This is what enables us to think of everything as a mere representation of our own powerful consciousness and to view ourselves, not merely as intending subjects, but as the "lord[s] of the earth" and as the masters of the whole "enframing" structure (*Ge-stell*) of reality.[6]

According to Heidegger, the metaphysics that shows itself in the form of modern technology threatens not only our dignity as human beings but also the very dignity of God. He warns that "where everything that presences exhibits itself in the light of a cause-effect coherence, even God can, for representational thinking, lose all that is exalted and holy, the mysteriousness of his distance."[7] Thus, in Heidegger's judgment, to think of God within the framework of a causal explanation of reality is to risk practicing theology as a kind of philosophical technology, in which God, like everything else, is made to function as part of a system of ordering or enframing through which nothing, not even divinity, is allowed to come from itself into its proper mode of presence. His concern is that even a deity that we describe as causing us, and thus implicitly prior to us, can be employed as a kind of instrumental cause of our own unsustainable greatness: a conceptual device giving us an illusory sense of cognitive mastery over the whole.[8] Whether every invocation of God as cause automatically entails this negative outcome is certainly questionable, but that there may be something perilously technological about the attempt to understand God as part of a science of causes is an aspect of Heidegger's critique of metaphysics that deserves serious consideration. At stake here is the divine freedom that is constitutive of prayer.

Heidegger's account of modern technology intersects at several points with his discussion of the essence of nihilism. In his essay

"The Word of Nietzsche: 'God Is Dead,'" he contends that nihilism is "the fundamental movement of the history of the West" and that "its unfolding can have nothing but world catastrophes as its consequence." In other words, nihilism names both the whole of occidental history and the demise of global history. This Eurocentric, eventually all-consuming negation can be summed up in the statement that "God is dead." Heidegger believes that one must interpret this saying in a particular and rigorous manner. "God" indicates precisely, because historically, the "Christian God," but also "the suprasensory world in general": that is, any ideal realm that one understands as transcendently grounding the value of all physical, sensorial, or natural life. "Dead" means, precisely, murdered: in the words of Nietzsche's madman, "*We have killed him*—you and I." Nihilism is, therefore, not so much the belief that God is nonexistent (which one might call an atheistic opinion) as it is the condition of human thought and existence in or through which "we" (that is, the people of the West) have rendered meaningless or ineffective the idea of a divine foundation of value.[9]

Heidegger argues that this condition is nothing other than metaphysics itself: "In its essence metaphysics is nihilism."[10] He holds that this rule applies no less to the metaphysical theology of the Christian tradition than it does to Nietzsche's allegedly nihilistic philosophy of the *Übermensch*.[11] On the one hand, Heidegger agrees with Nietzsche that the first perpetrators of the death of God were not modern atheistic philosophers but rather Christian "believers and their theologians," adding that "the heaviest blow against God . . . is not that God's existence is demonstrated to be unprovable, but rather that the god held to be real is elevated to the highest value."[12] In other words, Heidegger suggests that Christians are culpable for the death of God insofar as they attempt to situate God within their metaphysical systems of evaluation. On the other hand, Heidegger controversially contends that Nietzsche only manages to reformulate metaphysics and, therefore, never opens up a genuine path beyond it. According to Heidegger, the *Übermensch*'s positing of a new system of values, grounded in the certainty that being is essentially the will to power, belongs, in all relevant respects, to the same fateful concealment of being that is manifest in other metaphysical doctrines and in modern technology.[13]

Heidegger, therefore, rejects what he considers to be Nietzsche's *prescriptive* nihilism only while, at the same time, endorsing Nietzsche's *description* of the entire Western intellectual tradition, including Christianity, as a constitutively nihilistic tradition. As a result, Heidegger is not particularly attentive to those respects in which the doxological features of Christian theology resist being strictly identified with metaphysics. His post-Nietzschean narrative seems to imply that whatever distinctions might be made in this regard are less significant than the mere fact that Christian thinkers have, like metaphysicians, sought to establish an evaluative connection between what they call God and the natural realm of worldly life. Heidegger does not consider whether a specifically prayerful way of approaching this relation, which might be possible and necessary for Christian thinkers, subverts its potentially nihilistic implications. He does not even raise this as a question. Instead, he allows the monolithic perspective of Nietzsche's anti-Christian and antimetaphysical polemic to foreclose serious inquiry into the particular manner in which Christian doxology shows itself from itself. In short, Heidegger proclaims the first words of Nietzsche's madman, "I seek God! I seek God!"[14] having already prematurely concurred with Nietzsche that, in the history of Christianity, which is supposedly embedded in the history of metaphysics qua nihilism, the truly divine God is not to be found.[15] But this is not the only way to read the history of Christianity. Prayer provides a more adequate hermeneutic.

The locus classicus for Heidegger's critique of theology as metaphysical is his seminar "The Onto-Theo-Logical Constitution of Metaphysics." This text, however, is not directly an interpretation of Christianity but rather part of "a conversation with Hegel," a point that should alert us to its specifically philosophical and nondoxological orientation.[16] According to Heidegger, metaphysics is defined by the fact that, within it, "being shows itself in the nature of the ground [*Wesenart des Grundes*]." He clarifies that the nature of the ground is manifold. The ground is the logos of being, hence the manifestation of being as thought, as *ratio*, as knowledge, as truth. But the ground as logos also admits of a further distinction: namely, between the *logos* which grounds being *as such* (onto-logic) and that which grounds being *as a whole* (theo-logic). It is by gathering together these three senses of the ground of being that metaphysics comes to be constituted precisely as "onto-theo-logic."[17] Metaphysics is thus the thinking of being that locates its intelligibility simultaneously in the generality of being (i.e., its universal essence) and in the highest being, which Heidegger calls variously the "first cause," the "*causa prima,*" the "*ultima ratio,*" the "*causa sui,*" the "metaphysical concept of God," and the "god of the philosophers."[18]

In a now widely cited remark,[19] Heidegger laments that "man can neither pray nor sacrifice to this god. Before the *causa sui,* man can neither fall to his knees in awe nor can he play music and dance before this god. The god-less thinking which must abandon the god of philosophy, the *causa sui,* is thus perhaps closer to the divine God."[20] According to Heidegger, therefore, to the extent that theology exhibits the ontotheological structure of metaphysics, by virtue of this fact alone it negates the very possibility of prayer, whether experienced as sacrifice, adoration, or celebration. Why does Heidegger think that metaphysical theology and prayer are incompatible? One answer relates directly to the preceding analyses: Heidegger presents ontotheology as the constitution of thought through which modern technology and nihilism attempt to take charge of God and thereby (as it were) effectively commit deicide. In other words, he treats ontotheology as a template for the kind of deleterious thinking that is prone to distort the divine mystery into a mere instrument of our own power and values.

However, his central argument in this text does not concern technology or nihilism but rather the forgetting of difference. He maintains that the ontotheological constitution of metaphysics is problematic precisely insofar as it represents conceptually the difference between being and beings without thinking this difference as such, that is, as "the circling of Being and beings around each other," through which "one overcomes the other, one arrives in the other," in a dynamically and perpetually reciprocal relation.[21] Heidegger calls this mutual grounding and encircling of being and beings *der*

Austrag. This is the more or less untranslatable name for his under-standing of the original essence of the difference as it shows itself from itself. The problem with metaphysics is that it conceals this manifestation of difference by construing the being of beings as a general concept, on the one hand, and as a highest being, on the other, instead of receiving it as a reciprocal event "of unconcealing overcoming [as being] and of self-keeping arrival [in beings]."[22]

Heidegger's understanding of difference is not irrelevant to the question of prayer. At least one must say that prayer seems to entail some never-fully graspable encounter with the presence of things and that which exceeds this presence, hence with the irreducible but mutually implicating difference of the two. But Heidegger does not greatly develop this connection here, even though he hints at it. He does not clarify how his own understanding of the difference between being and beings should prove more conducive to prayer than a Christian doxological interpretation of God as the Creator (first cause), as the great "I AM" (highest being), or as the supremely diffusive good (highest value).[23] He makes the case that in order to think difference from itself it is necessary to step back out of the grounding, totalizing, and reifying structure of onto-theo-logic, which is particularly evident in Hegel's dialectical philosophy, but he provides very little clarity here regarding what prayer is, how his own understanding of difference supports it, what sort of doctrine of God it implies, and how this doctrine differs from or resembles (if at all) the metaphysical conception of "God."

After reading Heidegger's now famous few lines, one can be left with the impression that certain divine names are in themselves anti-thetical to prayer, and one can begin to think that they must therefore be avoided, whereas all that Heidegger has shown is that, to the ex-tent that the ontotheological constitution of metaphysics functions technologically and nihilistically and, moreover, fails to think differ-ence from itself, the particular manner in which it leads one to speak of God cannot be compatible with prayer. But Heidegger does not give anything like a rigorous description of a Christian doxological manner of divine speech, nor does he elucidate the particular ways of preserving difference and receiving God that it brings into play.

Heidegger's somewhat oracular passage regarding the incompatibility of prayer and metaphysics does not raise, therefore appears to close, but in fact leaves wide open the question of the logos of prayer and the ways in which it depends on, transforms, or transcends the logos of ontotheology. The very same names may acquire an extraordinarily different significance when said in the context of a hymn of praise or a moment of reverent contemplation.

Of course, it might be objected that Heidegger does not entirely reduce theology to the form that it takes within the ontotheological constitution of metaphysics. This objection is fair. To the extent that theology seeks to interpret faith, Heidegger allows it some degree of formal autonomy, which shields it (though only thinly) from his critique of metaphysics.[24] However, this complexity does not alter his general tendency to neglect the significance of Christian prayer but rather reproduces it in a different way. In "Phenomenology and Theology" (1927), Heidegger characterizes theology as an ontic science of historical Christian faith, which, although it by no means falls within the domain of philosophy (understood as phenomenological ontology), nevertheless makes use of certain supposedly "pre-Christian" concepts concerning constitutive features of *Sein* and *Dasein* which he argues are open to some degree of philosophical oversight.[25] Theology, then, has its own proper domain with respect to which philosophy has a limited advisory role to play. One could insist here, against Heidegger, that the sorts of concepts that he treats as pre-Christian are more accurately understood as post-Christian secularizations of themes that first emerged within the faith tradition of the church.[26] However, this clarification would not necessarily prevent theologians from finding some value in Heidegger's phenomenological descriptions of the essential features of human existence.

For this reason, Heidegger's idea that phenomenology can function (in some respects) as a helpful advisor for theology is, in the end, somewhat less problematic than his classification of theology as an ontic science. This classification greatly limits beforehand any possible significance that theology might have for rigorous thought regarding the original and essential truth of all things (whether this is properly called being or not). It thereby encourages one to under-estimate the stakes of various Christian practices of doxological contemplation, whether one considers, for example, Dionysius's hymn to the unknown Source, Aquinas's teachings on divine *esse*, Francis of Assisi's canticle of creation, or Teresa of Ávila's interior friendship and spiritual marriage with God—none of which are strictly reducible to a consideration of entities.[27] Heidegger's position would have been more plausible if he had claimed, less apodictically, that theology, no less than philosophy, can lose touch with the question of being and, consequently, pay insufficient attention to the manners in which being comes to light. But Heidegger does more than warn against the possibility, or even a de facto state, of theological decline; he implies that the decline is definitive of theology itself. At this stage of his thought, he leaves no room to envision a Christian way of thinking of God which would not be thoroughly ontic and, hence, situated in principle outside of the realm of serious intellectual inquiry into the truths of reality. Therefore, Christian doxology will be henceforward strictly unintelligible to him.

In a letter written many years later (1964), after his pivotal encounter with Hölderlin, Heidegger offers what one might call a phenomenological intervention, aimed at the basic understanding of thought-as-science that faithful theology has typically employed, at least in its scholastic mode. What is needed, he says, is a nonscientific, "non-technological . . . thinking and speaking in today's theology," which may be sought precisely in the direction of a "poetic thinking." He explains that "poetic thinking is being in the presence of . . . and for the god . . . purely letting the god's presence be said."[28] Expressed in these broad terms, Heidegger's proposed corrective has much to recommend it, especially insofar as the practice of theology as a metaphysical "science" has to some extent participated in the separation of prayer from thought, as well as the technological, nihilistic, and difference-concealing crises of modernity. We shall see that several Christian thinkers have taken Heidegger's poetic letting of God be God to heart. And yet, the best have done so while, on the one hand, prioritizing explicitly Christian forms of poetic doxology and, on the other hand, clarifying that *many* theologians in the

Christian tradition who have understood their task as "scientific" have not thereby intended to promote anything other than an intellectually rigorous practice of doxological contemplation.

In light of the foregoing discussion, including the still barely glimpsed possibility of a Christianization of Heidegger's poetic thinking, it seems necessary to replace his early distinction between an ontic theology and an ontological phenomenology with a much more complex distinction between five divergent modes of thought: (1) a theology that is faithful, therefore relatively independent, and yet merely ontic; (2) a metaphysical philosophy or philosophical theology that is ontological only as ontotheological, and accordingly technological, nihilistic, and forgetful of difference; (3) an existential philosophy that is ontological as phenomenological but not yet in explicit dialogue with poetry (as in *Being and Time*); (4) a thinking that is poetically phenomenological, thus reverently open to the disclosure of being as event, but also to the mysteries of divinity and humanity that are intimated therein; and (5) an explicitly Christian form of doxology that refuses to subordinate God to any metaphysical system or to the event of being. What is decisive for Heidegger's post-Hölderlin period is the fourth mode of thought—that is, poetry as the doxology of *Ereignis*. Heidegger's categorization of Christian theology as merely ontotheological, ontic, or both (numbers 1 and 2) keeps him from thinking of the Christian tradition as a viable source for a postmetaphysically doxological mode of thought (number 5). Hence, he looks elsewhere, to an aesthetic experience that lies beyond Christianity. His arrangement of terms leaves him without the space to consider the fifth option as a coherent possibility, but this is precisely what must be questioned and studied.

Although the limitations of Heidegger's critique of metaphysics are multiple and serious, especially in relation to Christian doxology, he is to be credited with proposing some sort of doxology as a promising response to the crises of metaphysics in modernity, which he analyzes with some (though not enough) critical insight. Even in its more prayerful forms, theology cannot afford to declare itself immune to these dangers. Its own purity is by no means guaranteed by the name "Christian." It is, therefore, no accident that many Christian thinkers have taken to heart Heidegger's suspicions concerning the technological and nihilistic fate of Western thought and appropriated certain general features of his response to this situation. From Heidegger it seems possible to learn, if somewhat indirectly, that the retrieval of Christian doxology demands some degree of caution, particularly concerning those respects in which Christianity has been implicated in a metaphysical manner of thinking that may seek to control too much about, and thereby threaten to negate or distort, the mysteries of God, being, and humanity. At the same time, however, Heidegger's refusal to think Christian doxology as such keeps him from providing anything like an adequate interpretive framework by means of which one would be able to discern clearly what is promising and problematic in the Christian intellectual tradition. In the end, it seems what we need is a critical hermeneutic that is informed by Heidegger's critique but is not overdetermined by it—a hermeneutic that especially resists those areas of his thought where, in thoroughly modern fashion, he appears more likely to impede than to enable a rigorous thinking of prayer.

HÖLDERLINIAN DOXOLOGY

We shall now consider the particular form of doxology that Heidegger brings to light, especially through his readings of Hölderlin.[29] Heidegger's engagement with Hölderlin begins publicly in 1934 and continues throughout the period of Heidegger's later writings.[30] We have noted already that this engagement enables Heidegger to think doxologically in two distinct ways: that is, with respect to the gods and to the last God, which belong to *Ereignis*, and with respect to *Ereignis* itself. These two can be distinguished as his idiosyncratically theological doxology and his onto-doxology, respectively. In order to understand both of these options, it is necessary to begin with a discussion of *Ereignis* and then consider how this pivotal idea relates to Heidegger's conception of "the fourfold" (*das Geviert*) and his argument concerning the poetic vocation of humanity in the modern age.

After *Being and Time*, *Ereignis* becomes one of Heidegger's most preferred ways of speaking about the essence of phenomenality or manifestation. It refers to the mutually appropriating event of being and beings, through which being is disclosed precisely in its difference from beings, and through which beings are likewise disclosed in their difference from being but also in their various relations with other beings. These disclosures always involve some degree of concealment. Hence, *Ereignis* preserves a sense of the mystery of distance and nearness that constitutes the never-fully graspable truth of being. In *Ereignis*, each being and being as such is appropriated to itself (*er-eignet*)—that is, comes into its own and enters into its proper measure. This appropriation takes place historically and temporally and constitutes history and time as such. *Ereignis* is not merely an event but *the* event. It is that which happens in every happening, the dynamic yet lasting structure of the time-space in which being holds sway as being and beings emerge as beings. As much as *Ereignis* demands respect for the original, essential, and proper manner in which everything appears (i.e., hospitality), it also assigns things a place and roots the thinking of being within a poetically and philosophically Greco-German experience of the world and of history (i.e., autochthony).

In several texts, Heidegger approaches *Ereignis* through an understanding of the fourfold, which is composed of earth, sky, mortals, and gods. These four poetically spoken phenomenological-ontological features are given together in the gathering that constitutes the appearance of anything as a "thing" (*Ding*).[31] For Heidegger, no worldly manifestation thoughtfully received as it gives itself will lack any of these four features. He describes the gods of the fourfold as "the beckoning messengers of the godhead."[32] Through their arrival and their flight, they hint at the last God that is to come, the truly divine divinity that abides in withdrawal.[33] By contrast, he characterizes the mortals as those who are called to dwell upon the earth and beneath the sky.[34] He specifies that the proper manner of mortal dwelling is *poetic*. By this he means that our way of living among things should involve a "distinctive kind of measuring" that preserves the mystery of the fourfold and, correlatively, resists the excessively calculative sort of measuring that is encouraged by modern science and technology.[35] Poetry belongs to the original, not the modern, sense of *techne*: instead of concealing the event of being, it discloses its truth.[36]

Heidegger contends that the experience of divinity that is proper to the fourfold is particularly threatened by the technological and nihilistic fate of modernity. In such an apparently godforsaken age, there is a great need for the poet. The poet's task is "to attend, singing, to the trace of the fugitive gods."[37] The poet is called to speak of the gods, to receive them as they appear, to seek them as they flee, all in preparation for a final coming of the truly divine God that has not yet been granted. Poetic speech names the thing-constituting features of the fourfold, which are the definitive conditions of the event of being, and as part of this naming draws particular attention to the traces or intimations of the divine that appear therein. In short, poetry offers doxology as a response to modernity. Poetic dwelling implies a kind of prayerful dwelling, a dwelling that seeks and praises both being and the godly figures that it hides and manifests—and Heidegger argues that this is precisely what the modern world needs.

There is much to admire in Heidegger's description of *Ereignis* according to the fourfold appearance of the thing and in his understanding of the poet as called to give voice to the hints of divinity that remain amid the crises of modernity. These reflections indicate some degree of openness to prayer. A problem arises, however, insofar as the gods have their place—indeed, arrive in their own proper measure—as a structural element within the fourfold. The realm of the gods is not revered as the transcendent *source* of the thing's appearance but rather as a native or autochthonous *aspect* of it. Heidegger sets up a hierarchy in which *Ereignis* is of higher standing than the gods. But the same must also be said even of the last God. In his *Contributions to Philosophy* (1936–38), he insists on "the admission by [the last] god that it needs be-ing [*Seyn*]."[38] In *Mindfulness* (1938–39), he explains that the "*last* God" is that which "is most remote in the hardly revealed 'time-space' of the truth of be-ing."[39] Divine distance is, accordingly, conceived as the absence of a divinity that nevertheless needs and belongs to ontology. The poet sings of the gods and of the last God only as *proper to*—that is, always already appropriated by or possibly (in some indefinite future) to be appropriated again by—the event of being.

Heidegger's idiosyncratically theological doxology thus seems to welcome the mystery of God but in fact domesticates it by subordinating it to *Ereignis*. This domestication has a disintegrative effect on his understanding of this all-important mystery and, moreover, exposes the inhospitality that his thought shows toward prayer (insofar as prayer and its intelligibility depend very directly on the mystery of God). As messengers, the gods in Heidegger's theory point beyond themselves to something that they are not.[40] Thus even should they, despite the desperate state of the modern era, manage to return from their flight and grace us with their presence, they would still have no power to disclose the divinity of God but merely to signify it. Moreover, the unique sort of nearness-in-distance that Heidegger associates with the last God is almost completely devoid of content. However paradoxically close it may be, this "deity" remains very abstract, indeterminate, barely even legible or recognizable *as* God. One of the clearest indications of this is that it does not invite prayer in any traditional sense of interpersonal dialogue or request.[41] Indeed, it seems almost as though "the last" would suffice as a name for it,[42] and that one could, therefore, prepare oneself for this final end of the event of being without any expectation of divinity in any meaningful sense. The fact that Heidegger holds on to the word "God" and its analogues (*Gott*, *Götterung*, *göttern*, etc.) says something important about his thought: in the end, or as his doctrine of the end, he does not want to advocate any sort of straightforward atheism. Nevertheless, what he offers in its place is not a rigorously doxological contemplation of the mystery of God but rather an ontologically subordinated divine discourse that is stretched between a somewhat opaque angelology and a rather empty eschatology.

And yet, Hölderlin's poetry gives Heidegger a concrete way to think doxologically even in this bifurcated and impoverished theological framework. Hölderlin brings into view the essential elements of the structure of doxology: the reception, offering, and desiring of divine *logos* and *doxa*. In "Hölderlin and the Essence of Poetry"

(1936), Heidegger argues that Hölderlin—whom he calls "the poet"—speaks and sings of the gods by receiving this language or *logos* from the gods, who address him first and place him "under their claim."[43] Moreover, Heidegger indicates that the light, the radiance, the *doxa* of the divine is something that the poet experiences from above: "The poet is exposed to the god's lightning flashes." Quoting Hölderlin, Heidegger clarifies that the poet is called not only to receive the word and glory of the divinity, but also to "offer to the people / The heavenly gift wrapped in song."[44] Thus the doxological element of offering is by no means excluded. Finally, Heidegger's understanding of the distance that separates the "hints of the gods" received by the poet and "the god who is coming" incorporates an unmistakable element of *eros* into his poetic thinking.[45] The gods arrive and flee in an almost alluring manner, in a kind of erotic play, while the true God, whom one deeply desires, remains strictly beyond reach and, thus, infinitely desirable.

The doxological features of the essence of poetry that Heidegger associates with Hölderlin's poetic verses are therefore clear already in this early lecture. However, so too are the extraordinarily problematic aspects of this particular expression of doxology. It is important to recognize that Heidegger's decisive turn to Hölderlin occurs near the time of his political involvement with National Socialism (shortly following his Rectorship in 1933) and that this temporal proximity is no mere coincidence.[46] Hölderlin had become a great cultural icon of the German spirit and played what Robert Savage characterizes as a "massive role" in Nazi propaganda. Savage demonstrates that the myth of Hölderlin as "the purest of all German poets" and as the one who most clearly prefigures the divine redemption or full realization of the German people can be traced back to the exegetical work of Norbert von Hellingrath, a fallen German soldier of the First World War, whose mythico-nationalist reading of Hölderlin was recovered vigorously by German intellectuals and propagandists during the 1930s and 1940s.[47]

Heidegger clearly understands himself as contributing to this poetically *political* movement. He offers his "Hölderlin and the Essence of Poetry" explicitly "in memory of Norbert von Hellingrath

/ Who was killed in action / On December 14, 1916." Moreover, in this text, as in many others, he quotes a line from Hölderlin's hymn "Remembrance" ("Andenken"): "But what remains is founded by the poets."[48] This line has an ominous ring to it. To proclaim it in the specific context and manner in which Heidegger does is effectively to stipulate that *nothing* should remain *except* that which is opened up by the divine speech and radiance that Hölderlin, as the purest of the poets, communicates to and for the German people. The plurality—"poets"—is restricted in advance by the identification of the essence of poetry with Hölderlin. For Heidegger, this unique poet is the ultimate standard by which anyone or anything else can be called poetic. Hölderlin—not Christ—is the criterion that determines the adequacy of any future doxology.

Heidegger's 1943 lecture on Hölderlin's "Remembrance" corroborates and expands upon these points. Here Heidegger presents the poet as a "demigod," who arises out of the "wedding festival of men and gods," that is, the "primal event" (*Ereignis*) of greeting between divinity and humanity—a greeting that might be likened to prayer. Heidegger contends that the poet's vocation is precisely to recollect (*andenken*) this eventful source of all destiny (*Geschick*) and history (*Geschichte*), which he insists means precisely "German history."[49] Heidegger explains, moreover, that the poet is supposed to think back to this originating encounter of the gods with humanity in order to foretell "what is coming." The poetic calling or recalling is thus not only anamnestic but also *"prophetic,"* though decidedly not "according to the Judeo-Christian sense of the term."[50] Heidegger stresses that the holy (*das Heilige*) which the poet anticipates is not equivalent to the salvation (*das Heil*) in which Jews and Christians place their hope.[51] The holy is far more indeterminate; it is merely the opening for a possible arrival of the gods or, finally, the unknown last God. But one should not forget, here, that everything that is distinguished from that which Hölderlin discloses, however accurate the distinction may be descriptively, is also thereby prescriptively negated, precisely because Hölderlin functions as the *norma normans non normata* for all future thought. Heidegger thus permanently exiles from serious consideration the covenantal greeting between God and the Hebrew people, which finds expression in biblical prayer, poetry, and prophecy. He lets the supposed authority of Hölderlin's particular style of remembrance render insignificant this most promising wellspring of doxological thinking.

In the same lecture, Heidegger also introduces an *exitus-reditus* structure according to which the poet's "communal spirit" (*Volkgeist*) travels into the foreign land in order thereby to make an authentic return to the homeland.[52] The echoes of German idealism (which must be understood as both a theoretical and political movement) are hardly faint in these words. Heidegger acknowledges this resonance, although he maintains that something essentially different from the metaphysical subjectivity of Schelling and Hegel is at work in Hölderlin's poetry.[53] For in Hölderlin's case, the spirit moves not by means of speculative reason but rather through poetic thought, therefore doxologically, and for Heidegger this makes all the difference. Indeed, the recourse to poetry preserves a sense of *difference as such*—something which, as we have seen elsewhere, is compromised by the ontotheological constitution of metaphysics that Hegel exemplifies. Hölderlin is, therefore, to be distinguished sharply from his philosophical contemporaries.

And yet, as Jacques Derrida reminds us, the affinity between the communal and self-actualizing *Geist* of Hölderlin and that of the German idealists remains considerable, however distinct they may be in certain respects.[54] Thus it seems necessary to question whether Heidegger's effort to distance Hölderlin from those who forget difference wholly succeeds, even though his distinction between two kinds of spirit (speculative and poetic) is significant. It would be a gross overstatement to suggest that Hölderlin, instead of providing resistance to the metaphysical tradition, merely encloses Heidegger's thought within it. Nevertheless, the idea that Hölderlin definitively liberates Heidegger from the dangers of this tradition and, thereby, preserves difference as such from all oblivion is also misleading. There are subtle lines of co-implication which, without erasing these differences, do significantly qualify them.

It is important to study carefully Heidegger's various characterizations of that which is foreign and that which is of the home. He thinks the foreign initially as "the *fire of heaven*" that is proper to the Greeks, for whom the gods have always already arrived in their nearness.[55] On the one hand, then, there is a sense in which the foreign names the presence of the divine that the poet calls us to remember prayerfully, that is, by recalling the primordial greeting of the gods and humanity in their wedding festival. The foreign is the otherness of the gods or of God to which we are originally exposed in a nuptial embrace.[56] On the other hand, however, the foreign is associated explicitly with the divine fire of *the Greeks*, that is, of a particular historical people with their own "national character." But the poetic spirit has also gone "far beyond Greece to the East," to the "Indies," for the "*spirit . . . loves the colony.*"[57] The movement of the poetic spirit into distance is, therefore, not merely prayerful but also colonially geopolitical. As such, too, it is destined for a return "home," a return precisely to "the historical place in which German humanity must first learn to become at home."[58]

The spiritual remembrance (*Andenken*) of the poet forgets everything that it encounters in distance except "that foreignness that is to be transformed through what is proper to one." Only that which is suitable for the self-realization of the German people through the founding-saying of the poet "is preserved."[59] The Greeks have a privileged place here: the Hölderlinian-Heideggerian conception of the German essence and destiny is constitutively Greek. And the others? They are largely forgotten. To remember poetically, for Heidegger, is to leave in oblivion the colonized peoples themselves and to think doxologically in a manner that fundamentally excludes them, except as exotic resources for the *Volkgeist*. Precisely *resources* in two senses: for it is through this foreignness that the poetic spirit seeks its primal source *and* that European modernity acquires its material resources (its *Bestand*).

At the very least, it must be admitted that Heidegger is not sufficiently critical of the extent to which his promotion of poetically founded Germanness remains implicated in the worldwide "technological dominion" which it, in another sense, nevertheless enables him to critique.[60] But it also seems necessary to make a stronger claim here: namely, that Heidegger in certain respects misdiagnoses what is problematic about modernity or only partially diagnoses it. If the crises only have to do with technology, nihilism, and ontotheology, then Hölderlin's poetry seems to offer an attractive starting point for a different manner of thinking that promises to restore the original sense of wonder at the difference and eventful mystery of being that had been swept away by metaphysics. And perhaps, too, Hölderlin could help us to recover something of the divine, at least insofar as the divine mystery can be approached adequately within the logic generated by the poetic saying of *Ereignis*. However, if one recognizes—and Heidegger does not—that the modern world has been brought to a state of crisis in large part because of the devastating legacy of European nationalistic and colonial culture (which is inseparable from Europe's poetic building and dwelling), then Hölderlin, at least as an idealized figure, comes to seem much more implicated in the problem and much less convincing as a possible solution.

Heidegger's subordination of divine distance to the event of being directly mirrors, and is indeed articulated in the same terms as, his expropriation of the foreign other for the sake of the German spirit's own arrival, cultivation, and homecoming. In both cases, the other, whether divine or human, is under too much control, not by modern metaphysics (although it would appear to do the same), but by a very particular sort of poetic thinking, which imitates prayer but does not adequately accommodate it. The political and theological problems are, therefore, deeply connected and flow from the same source: namely, an excessive concern for a particular sort of autochthony. Heidegger's unquestioned prioritization of his own cultural location and of the event of being that it prescribes as a paradigm for all future thought does not let the phenomenon of doxology—together with its own particular manner of letting things be appropriated and transformed within the glory and word of God—come fully to light. Moreover, his nontotal, but nevertheless significant, inhospitality toward doxology correlates, quite directly in the case of Jewish and Christian traditions, but also in other cases, with a refusal of those human persons, societies, and intellectual endeavors that do not belong to a Greco-German experience of being.

An argument still needs to be made for the claim that Christian doxology, thought on its own terms, at least potentially fares better on the question of hospitality than does Heidegger's Hölderlinian doxology and, moreover, provides what is necessary in this area. This argument will be pursued in subsequent chapters. For the moment, it suffices to indicate the problem as it arises in Heidegger's thought. The prayerful openness to the divine, to others, to difference in its varied appearances—indeed, to prayer itself—is secured by *Ereignis* only as simultaneously compromised by it.

Before leaving Heidegger behind, we should consider the second way that he thinks doxologically, which for the most part surpasses and subsumes the first: namely, his mindfulness regarding *Ereignis* as such. This line of thought differs in some significant respects from his prayerful remembrance and foretelling of the gods and of the last God, but it nevertheless gives rise to similar difficulties. Although, for Heidegger, being is not divine—at least not in the way the gods and the last God are—there is nevertheless a doxology of being, an *onto-doxology.* He thinks being explicitly in relation to *doxa.* In his *Introduction to Metaphysics* (1936), he observes: "*Doxa* means aspect, namely the respect in which one stands. If the aspect, corresponding to what emerges in it, is an eminent one, then *doxa* means brilliance and glory. . . . Glory, for the Greeks, . . . is the highest manner of Being."[61] If being, then, shows itself as *doxa*, it also comes to us in *logos*, in language. Heidegger famously says in his *Letter on Humanism* (1947) that "language is the house of Being."[62] Being thus makes its appearance in language, which shelters it and clears a space for it to arrive in its glory. Language is not merely a human instrument but rather that source of all speech and truth (*aletheia*) that always already precedes us and calls to us. Heidegger discovers this calling in the words of Hölderlin's poetry: he argues that the poet receives the beauty of being and wraps it in song.[63]

Heidegger clarifies, however, that being is not fully transparent in its appearance or in language. To some extent, being, like the last God, abides in withdrawal, distance, silence, and mystery. And yet, in contrast to the last God, who is "not granted,"[64] being *is given.* Heidegger makes this clear in his 1962 lecture "Time and Being," in which he argues that *Ereignis* gives both being and time and appropriates them to themselves and to each other. This is the meaning of the German expression *es gibt* ("there is" or, literally, "it gives"). The givenness of time and being together in *Ereignis* presupposes a withdrawal or expropriation, which Heidegger describes as "the denial of the present and the withholding of the present." But this denial of presence is given precisely together with and through "a manifold presencing."[65] It is because being, even though abidingly transcendent, nevertheless shows itself in presence and as gift that Heidegger elsewhere understands the thinking (*Denken*) of being as a kind of thanking (*Danken*).[66] His meditative approach toward being is, therefore—in a non-Christian but nevertheless significant sense—*eucharistic*. To think is to receive the nearness and distance of being with gratitude.

This joining of thinking and thanking occurs in Heidegger's "Conversation on a Country Path," a dialogue contained in his short book entitled *Gelassenheit* (1959). In the "Memorial Address," which is included in the same volume, he explains that "that which shows itself and at the same time withdraws is the essential trait of what we call the mystery (*das Geheimnis*)." We are called to be open to this mystery, to let it be, and therefore to pursue a mode of thinking characterized not by calculative reasoning but rather by what the translator renders as "releasement toward things [*Gelassenheit zu den Dingen*]."[67] With this recommendation, Heidegger recovers a theme that has been developed throughout the Christian tradition of prayerful spirituality—from patristic reflections on *apatheia* to the Ignatian understanding of *indiferencia*, and beyond—though, for reasons which are perhaps already clear, he chooses to highlight one of its greatest *German* representatives: Meister Eckhart.[68] In his "Conversation on a Country Path," he invokes Eckhart as an authority but immediately disavows Eckhart's theological commitments. In contrast to Eckhart, Heidegger does not understand *Gelassenheit* as an exercise of "letting self-will go in favor of the divine will," but rather as a mode of waiting in which we relinquish transcendental representation and allow ourselves to be "*appropriated (ge-eignet)* to that . . . from whence we are called." That which

Heidegger awaits and desires to let-be, in this precise context, is not God but rather *Ereignis*, the event of being in its simultaneous nearness and distance.[69] And yet, Heidegger approaches this ontological mystery precisely by recalibrating a reverent attitude central to the history of prayer.

One of the crucial arguments of the *Gelassenheit* volume is that "the *autochthony* of man [*die* Bodenständigkeit *des Menschen*] is threatened today at its core."[70] The word *Bodenständigkeit*, rendered by the translator as "autochthony," names, literally, the condition of standing on the ground. It calls to mind the theme of dwelling upon the earth which we encountered above. The meditative approach toward being that Heidegger proposes in response to the technological fate of the modern world can therefore be understood not only in terms of a thankful thinking, a releasement toward things, and an openness to mystery, but also in terms of a poetic dwelling, which receives its measure at least as much from the event of being as it does from the unknown godhead.[71] The poet is meant to sing not only of the divine but also of worldly being. As Heidegger puts the point: "To sing the song means to be present in what is present itself. It means: *Dasein*, existence."[72]

Heidegger's onto-doxology is appealing in some respects. To the extent that being emerges as a question for doxology—that is, to the extent that the glory and word of God are received, offered, and desired through the sway of being (and presumably there is *some* extent to which this is the case)—Heidegger's reverential openness is much more conducive to prayer than are the sorts of metaphysical and calculative thinking that he resists. The problem with his approach does not have to do with the fact that he develops a doxological contemplation of being but rather with the unquestioned primacy and finality that he accords to it. The positive significance of his onto-doxology is clarified, and becomes much less misleading, when it is interpreted in the context of a traditional form of doxological thinking that unambiguously situates the mystery of being within the mystery of God, and not the other way around. However, because Heidegger refuses this arrangement, and instead adopts autochthony as an overarching framework for thought, the promise of his onto-doxology is largely compromised. The valuable role that it could play *in* prayer comes to seem less evident than the threat that it poses *to* prayer.

Coming very close to conceptual idolatry (if not in fact succumbing to it), Heidegger employs the event of being in many respects as a substitute for God. The substitution is, admittedly, unequal and inexact. Heidegger does not simplistically identify the two. The "properties" of the one and the other are not interchangeable. Nor does he forget his meditations concerning the gods and the last God, which, as we have seen, he understands in a distinct way as features belonging to, though by no means exhausting, *Ereignis*. Nevertheless, the fact remains that in Heidegger's prayer-*like* ontology, *Ereignis* usurps the place that is occupied in the prayerful thought of the Christian tradition by the divine will, the divine vocation, and the divine end. It is for the sake of the manifestation of being, not the sovereign will of God, that we are meant to let our own wills go.[73] It is in response to the call of being, not the vocation of God, that we are meant to live and to die.[74] It is upon (or, finally, *within*) the earth, not in the heart of God, that we are meant to find peace and rest.[75] Divine *doxa* and *logos* are not decisive in any of these cases. On the contrary, the presence and the language of being constitute, virtually without remainder, that which is most definitive for thought and existence, that around which everything is to be oriented, that which demands the highest forms of commitment and sacrifice. The prayerful interaction of divine and human freedoms has no serious role to play here.

Heidegger's substitution of ontological resignation for prayer proves to be especially problematic insofar as it gives mortality the final word. Instead of acknowledging our exposure before the God of salvation and venturing more freely and more deeply into this exposure (i.e., instead of praying in this most general sense), Heidegger encourages us, with reference to Rainer Marie Rilke's poetry, to "affirm our unshieldedness" in the orbit of being and thereby say "yes" to its law of death.[76] He emphasizes one sort of exposure (fatal and worldly) over another (liberating and divine). He affirms death as a maximal limit, which he claims is constitutive of our nature,[77] and thereby leaves virtually no room to contemplate an immortal other who might yet have something else in store. In the final analysis, his onto-doxology is about accepting the ways things are and, therefore, not about hoping in the grace of God. It is determined more by fate than by promise.[78]

In a similar way, Heidegger's onto-doxology works against the sense, vital to prayer and to the various sorts of committed social action that it empowers (which we shall consider in subsequent chapters), that many things of this world need to be transformed. Of course, it is necessary to acknowledge a distinction between the original and essential conditions of being, on the one hand, and the endangered state of being in our modern technological and nihilistic age, on the other. Heidegger's onto-doxological "letting-be" does not promote tolerance of the latter but rather a possibly revolutionary return to the former. There is thus a sense in which his prayer-like thought regarding being, even—or precisely—as autochthonous powerfully resists the status quo, at least insofar as this is conceived as a loss of autochthony.

And yet, the fact remains that whatever Heidegger classifies as native or proper to the eventful manifestation of being—including, especially, Greco-German political culture—he likewise treats as sacred and, therefore, as essentially irreformable. The only change that his onto-doxology permits and demands is homecoming. He wants to return to a specific condition of worldly existence that is largely purified of otherness: of the people who are foreign to the land; of the biblical mystery of God that is foreign to the local experience of being and divinity; finally of the prayer which is supposedly foreign to rigorous thought and which, moreover, demands hospitality to many other sorts of foreignness. In the end, far from envisioning a new way of being, oriented toward a new heaven and a new earth, in which relations of greater justice and love among beings and between humanity and God might prevail, and for which one would be presently called to work and to pray, Heidegger's ontological and autochthonous analogue of prayer builds a shrine around the already given time-space of being, whose future is a recurrence of the same, a repetition made secure by an ever-deepening mindfulness regarding a poetic saying that already knows where everything and everyone belongs.

Heidegger, therefore, passes from metaphysics to doxology in a highly problematic manner. His critique of metaphysics disregards the distinctive characteristics of Christian doxology, and his own doxological proposal is overdetermined by a theologically and politically damaging exaltation of the event of being. In particular, his attempt to implicate Christianity in his critique of metaphysics is compromised by his selective prioritization of post-Nietzschean polemic over phenomenological rigor, by his sustained inattention to the manner of theological speech that is proper to Christian prayer, and by his refusal to recognize that faithful forms of contemplation can have more than ontic significance. Moreover, his specific way of formulating a poetic doxology, particularly in dialogue with Hölderlin, suffers from a threefold subordination of hospitality to autochthony. Heidegger treats his own cultural and political region as definitive of being; he lets the resulting account of being disintegrate divinity into two ineffectual spheres (the gods and the last God); and he reveres being in a manner that is structurally similar to, but less prayerful and hopeful than, the way in which the Christian doxological tradition glorifies God. These many problems are signs of a considerable degree of doxological impurity.

Nevertheless, these grave shortcomings do not warrant anything like a complete dismissal of Heidegger's perspective. On the contrary, certain aspects of both his critique of metaphysics and his poetic doxology are worthy of positive attention—including, not least, the mere fact that he turns to doxology precisely in order to address the crises of modern metaphysics. His diagnosis of these crises in terms of a technological enframing of being, humanity, and God that endangers all three; a nihilistic will-to-power, which Nietzsche both names and possibly exemplifies; and an ontotheological concealment of difference and mystery that fixes all things within a comprehensive "scientific" system is, to some extent, a very apt diagnosis. To be sure, a more adequate assessment of the contemporary situation would have to clarify, on the one hand, how these crises are connected with certain modern decisions that have been made against prayer and against the radical practice of hospitality that authentic prayer demands and, on the other hand, to what degree various traditions of Christian doxological spirituality perhaps already powerfully counteract these crises. These are clarifications that we shall pursue in subsequent chapters. But the point here is that Heidegger's critical account of modernity, despite its many limitations, needs to be taken seriously, even by Christian theologians who have valid reasons to be suspicious of it.

Likewise, it is noteworthy that, in turning to doxology, Heidegger finds considerable support in both poetry and phenomenology and, moreover, seeks to develop a new manner of thinking that is capable of integrating the two. From poetry he gains a sense of intimacy with what is given; from phenomenology, he acquires the commitment to analyze this given reality rigorously and deeply and to think through its many implications. We shall see that this intellectual style is particularly well suited for a thick retrieval of Christian doxology and need not be limited to the problematic sources and horizons that Heidegger considers normative. All in all, although Heidegger's itinerary from metaphysics to doxology is very troubled, it nevertheless manages to open up certain possibilities for the future of Christian thought and life that he does not seem to anticipate.

CHAPTER 2

DOXOLOGICAL THEORY
Hans Urs von Balthasar

Hans Urs von Balthasar's retrieval of Christian doxology —which he develops most thoroughly in his multivolume trilogy of (ana)logical, aesthetic, and dramatic theological theory—maintains a rather complex relationship with Heidegger's postmetaphysical thought.[1] In many respects, Balthasar's divergence from Heidegger is as great as can be: Balthasar retains metaphysics (of a particular sort); he immerses himself in the Christian traditions of theology and spirituality; and he replaces Heidegger's horizon of finite being with the all-encompassing reality of Trinitarian freedom and love, which he argues finds its clearest expression in the paschal mystery. And yet, there are other respects in which Balthasar's project manifests an intriguingly Heideggerian character: he strongly resists the metaphysics of the modern period; he turns to the poets (including some of Heidegger's favorites) as wellsprings of doxological thinking; and he seeks to receive the eventful mystery of being as it shows itself from itself. In short, Balthasar affirms several features of Heidegger's path from metaphysics to doxology, while simultaneously avoiding many Heideggerian pitfalls and offering a rigorously Christian counterproposal. All in all, whereas even the partial emergence of prayer in Heidegger's thought is compromised by his particular autochthonous commitments, Balthasar's theology allows the mystery of prayer to shine forth in much of its fullness.

Nevertheless, Balthasar's approach remains questionable on two distinct fronts. On the one hand, to the extent that Balthasar's systematic treatment of ontology and partly speculative understanding of the Trinity continue to be implicated in metaphysics, his work may not sufficiently dispel all of Heidegger's potentially legitimate concerns regarding the technological, nihilistic, and difference-concealing tendencies of the Western metaphysical tradition. Put concisely, the danger is that Balthasar would, as a knowing subject, attempt to decide and control too much. However, the claim of this chapter is not that Balthasar obviously succumbs to this charge. The point is merely that particular aspects of his thought clearly retain *some* kind of positive relationship with metaphysics and are perhaps, therefore, *somewhat* problematically affected by it. On the other hand, Balthasar's critical appropriation of Heidegger does not seem to overcome, without remainder, all of the difficulties that are discernible in Heidegger's postmetaphysical doxology. In particular, one might consider the perhaps overly sanguine nature of Balthasar's doxological contemplation, which may encourage releasement to rather than resistance against suffering; the primarily Eurocentric character of his engagement with culture, which disregards non-European others; and the insufficiently nuanced assessment that he makes of liberation theology partly on the basis of Heidegger's concerns about modern metaphysical subjectivity. In these ways, Balthasar's work (somewhat like Heidegger's, though less drastically) leaves the promise of prayer partly undisclosed. We shall examine Balthasar's doxological theory in light of these two broad areas of potential questioning: that is, his possible points of vulnerability *to* and *with* Heidegger.

However, while considering these critical questions and vulnerabilities, we shall also attend to the many ways that Balthasar's doxological theory does powerfully resist what is most problematic, not only about metaphysics, but also about Heidegger's still rather prayer-denying alternative to it. In general, Balthasar's reflections regarding the mystery of creaturely being and the mystery of the triune God demonstrate his great reverence for the *doxa* and *logos* that are given in prayer, together with the interactive experiences of freedom and love that they imply. His thought is thus constituted much more deeply by a prayerful, doxological practice of *theoria* than it is by any technological, nihilistic, or difference-concealing theory (whether metaphysical or otherwise). For Balthasar, "theory" means *theoria*. It means a contemplative, meditative, intellectually rigorous act of, and reflection on, prayer in its various Trinitarian and creaturely dimensions. Moreover, in sharp contrast to Heidegger, Balthasar emphasizes the close connection that must exist between any genuinely Christian *theoria* and an actively embodied practice of Christic holiness, which includes centrally the kenotic gift of oneself to others. In these ways, he sheds light on the great promise of Christian doxology as a source for an integrated—that is, contemplative and active—response to both the metaphysical and violent crises of modernity.

This chapter will interpret and assess Balthasar's doxological theory in three sections, through which the prayerful interplay of divine and creaturely freedoms will take on an increasingly concrete appearance—passing from analogy, to aesthetics, to dramatics. In the first section, we shall consider how the somewhat metaphysical, but also somewhat postmetaphysically phenomenological, account of analogy that Balthasar formulates in accord with Erich Przywara's *Analogia Entis* and Heidegger's elucidations of the mystery of being neither contradicts doxology nor adds something wholly extraneous to it, but rather discloses a formal intellectual and existential structure that seems to be entailed by it. Whether this analogical structure has to be articulated in a recognizably and, moreover, problematically metaphysical manner are questions that we shall examine more deeply in the next chapter (though we shall begin to address them here). However, the primary goals of this section will be somewhat different: first, to examine in what ways Balthasar's (in some sense and somewhat) metaphysical construal of analogy enables him to resist the technological, nihilistic, and difference-concealing crises that both he and Heidegger associate with modern metaphysics; and second, to show that and how the doctrine of analogy provides a more suitable framework for thinking through the implications of prayer than does Heidegger's more monistic theory of *Ereignis*.

The second section of this chapter demonstrates that, although Balthasar treats analogy as a necessary condition for the possibility of doxological contemplation, he does not regard it as a *sufficient* condition. In a somewhat postmetaphysical gesture, he argues that one must move beyond—without, however, denying the value of—the abstract theorization of the *analogia entis* in order to pursue a richly aesthetic encounter with the glory and word of God that constitute divine revelation. In this respect, he seeks to combine Heidegger's poetic turn with the christological concreteness of Karl Barth's *Church Dogmatics* and an extensive retrieval of the aesthetic sources of Christian scripture and tradition. This more-than-analogical, revelation-saturated thinking of prayer appears in Balthasar's book on contemplative prayer, as well as throughout *The Glory of the Lord* and, indeed, the whole trilogy.

Granted, the epistemological confidence displayed by Balthasar's highly kataphatic doxological aesthetics may leave room to desire a greater degree of apophasis (as one finds in some of the post-Balthasarian figures considered in the next chapter). But his approach still conveys in its own way the sense of ontological and theological mystery that is demanded by prayer. Furthermore, although Balthasar favors a European cultural canon, his symphonic style enables him to welcome a much wider plurality of voices than Heidegger does, and this style could be adapted to include many other prayerful perspectives and traditions that Balthasar neglects. Similarly, his universal soteriological hope makes his doxological project significantly less exclusive than Heidegger's Greco-German homeland. Finally, the type of *Gelassenheit* that figures prominently in Balthasar's doxological aesthetics does not support the fatalistic passivity that characterizes Heidegger's onto-doxology but rather offers a way for the creature to participate actively in the freedom and love of the Trinity, a point which is attested most clearly by Balthasar's Ignatian account of *indiferencia*.

The third section of this chapter draws attention to Balthasar's *Theo-Drama*, along with some related essays, in order to highlight his understanding of the close bond between contemplation and action. We shall see that, for Balthasar, human freedom has a significant role to play in the drama of salvation. This role takes shape through various prayerfully inspired forms of loving action in the world, as well as through the potentially effective practice of petitionary prayer that occurs in Christ and, therefore, in the Trinity. Although Balthasar's somewhat Hegelian discussion of the Trinitarian distance as the "ground" of inner-worldly negation may rightfully provoke some Heideggerian suspicion—as well as other kinds of postmetaphysical suspicion related to the question of theodicy—Balthasar's doxological corrective of Hegel's philosophically distorted theodrama seems to do more to resist the dangers of modern metaphysics than to repeat them. Moreover, although Balthasar's partly Heideggerian and partly de Lubacian assessment of the crises of modernity in relation to the atheistic tendencies of modern subjectivity leads him to develop a rather unconvincing (because largely undifferentiated) critique of liberation theology, there are many ways in which his dramatic theory and even his particular concerns about the perils of modern subjectivity have the potential to facilitate a deeper appreciation for the rigorous doxological vision that is central to many expressions of liberation theology (as we shall see in subsequent chapters).

Finally, in a concluding "coda" to this chapter, we shall encounter Balthasar's interpretation of Charles Péguy: a poet who, like Hölderlin, responds doxologically to the crises of modernity but, unlike Hölderlin, crystallizes the most promising features of Balthasar's distinctive approach to Christian contemplation and action, including all of those features mentioned above. Arguably better than any other figure, Péguy shows what both unites Balthasar with, and divides Balthasar from, Heidegger's much more doxologically ambiguous thought. At the same time, Péguy builds a bridge to the counterviolently political formulations of Christian spirituality that we shall investigate in the second part of this project.

ANALOGICAL METAPHYSICS

The first task, then, will be to consider how Balthasar's adoption of the *analogia entis* shapes his treatments of metaphysics and doxology. In *Wahrheit* (*Truth*, 1947), an early work that would eventually become the first volume of *Theo-Logic*, Balthasar proposes a rather Heideggerian understanding of truth as the "unconcealment (*aletheia*) of being" and as "*poeisis*." He adds a scriptural term to this Heideggerian pair: truth is "*emeth*: fidelity, constancy, reliability." More decisive than this addition, however, is Balthasar's assertion, against Heidegger, that the ultimate measure of truth must be understood as "the identity of thinking and being in God."[2] Thus Balthasar posits divine *esse* as the absolute source of the poetically and ontologically disclosive truth that Heidegger would prefer to restrict to the finite horizons of *Sein* and *Dasein*.[3]

A further similarity and difference between their respective theories of truth and being is relevant here. Like Heidegger, Balthasar highlights a dynamic interplay between that which is given and not given from the overwhelming fullness of being. Both thinkers argue that this interplay characterizes the whole gamut of worldly beings and renders them mysterious even in their phenomenal coming-to-presence. However, whereas Heidegger makes this point through his discussion of the ontological difference or *Austrag*, Balthasar makes it by drawing on a traditional Catholic doctrine of the analogy of being. In keeping with his teacher Przywara, Balthasar distinguishes two levels of this doctrine. The creaturely level includes dynamic inner-worldly tensions between the givenness of being (the essence of things present within their existence) and the hiddenness of being (the essence of things transcending their existence).[4] By contrast, the theological level of the doctrine (which Heidegger largely excludes) refers to dynamic tensions between the immanence of God within creation (as attested by similarities between finite beings and divine being) and the supreme transcendence of God beyond creation (which implies a dissimilarity that is always greater than any given similarity).

Balthasar clarifies that the doctrine of analogy, as it appears on both of these levels, is not merely a teaching about truth and being. Rather, it is ultimately a teaching about the conditions of love—and, therefore, of prayer. As he puts the point: "If love (which is always just) possesses the measure of the revelation of truth, then it necessarily possesses the measure of truth's nonrevelation."[5] Love, or one might just as easily say hospitality, entails a respect for that which both shows itself and hides itself in the concrete existence of another. Love, therefore, necessarily, if at times only implicitly, affirms the analogy—that is, the nearness-in-distance—of that which it loves, whether it be a mere phenomenal appearance, a fellow human subject, or the God of all things. Love recognizes and reveres the manifest and reserved freedom of the other, the freedom that is largely constitutive of the other's mysterious truth and being. This is the deepest meaning, or at least the most important consequence, of analogy.[6]

In a final section of *Wahrheit*, entitled "Confession," Balthasar turns his attention to the prayerful practice of analogy-conditioned love that takes place between humanity and God. He describes it as an act in which the creature acknowledges and actively receives itself as a participant in the analogical structure of truth and being that is given to it by the Creator. According to Balthasar, this participation involves a humble recognition not only of the fact that we do not fully understand ourselves (since our definitive essence lies partly hidden in the mysterious Godhead, as the German mystics emphasize) but also of the fact that God's knowledge and love of our creaturely existence is infinitely more precise and intimate than our own (as Augustine recognizes when he says *interior intimo meo*).[7] Moreover, Balthasar avers that we need to do more than recognize our inescapable finite participation in the absolute mystery of truth and being that comes forth from God. We must also freely offer ourselves to it, welcoming our "ontological unveiledness by a voluntary unveiling."[8] This loving gift of ourselves is, for Balthasar, our confession. It is a prayerful affirmation of the analogical form of our existence in an attitude of total exposure and surrender before God. It is an act of freedom through which we not only express the wondrous reality of our creaturely being but also praise the ineffable glory of the Creator.

Therefore, despite what Heidegger's critical discussion of onto-theology might lead one to suspect, Balthasar's account of the traditional philosophical and theological doctrine of analogy leads quite directly to a prayerful conclusion. The last sentence of the text is hardly consistent with any doxology-negating kind of metaphysics: "But because love is ultimate, the seraphim cover their faces with their wings, for the mystery of eternal love is one whose superluminous night may be glorified only through adoration."[9] Balthasar's final recommendation is not to gain mastery over being as an objective system of entities and causes but rather to adore the unknown depths of everlasting love. If this is where the analogy of being leads, it seems necessary to ask whether it actually belongs to metaphysics and, if so, in what sense. A brief discussion of this question will help to clarify in what respects Balthasar's appropriation of the *analogia entis* as an integral feature of his doxology is and is not susceptible to Heideggerian critique. In the end, we shall have to be content with a somewhat complex response.

First, it should be noted that both Przywara and Balthasar employ the term "metaphysics" in a rather broad sense that applies to any formal reflections regarding the ultimate ground, purpose, and meaning of being as such, even when these occur in the faithful theology of the church.[10] Przywara, in particular, understands the *analogia entis* as a specifically theological form of metaphysics that "carries within itself the positive-ecclesial theology as its living ground [*Lebensgrund*]."[11] To some extent, then, Christian faith gives rise to the understanding of being that Przywara articulates in terms of a formal analogical principle. Moreover, his account draws not only on the kataphatic but also, and perhaps even primarily, on the apophatic dimensions of this faith. He stresses that his analogical metaphysics is oriented toward the absolute mystery of God, a mystery that we do not grasp but that rather "grasps us," a mystery that we know finally only in "unknowing" (*Nicht-Erkennen*).[12] At the same time, however, Przywara argues that the analogy of being begins in, and is grounded (*begründet*) in, the most basic logical axiom of Western philosophy: that is, the "principle of contradiction."[13] He also sees this analogy reflected, albeit imperfectly, in the ontological doctrines of Plato and Aristotle. Thus, although Przywara's analogical metaphysics ultimately emerges from and finds its clearest expression in the *via positiva* and *via negativa* of Christian theology, it is by no means alien to the classical tradition of occidental philosophy that Heidegger identifies with metaphysics.

If one asks whether Balthasar's *Wahrheit* is metaphysical in Przywara's sense, the answer has to be put mostly in the affirmative, though Balthasar's addition of certain aspects of Heideggerian phenomenology may call for some degree of qualification. However, if one poses the same question using Heidegger's definition of metaphysics as technological, nihilistic, and ontotheological, the response has to be expressed considerably more in the negative, though even here there are ways in which the judgment becomes complicated. For example, one must admit that, although Balthasar by no means exhibits the worst form of a modern technological will-to-power, he does offer something like what Heidegger calls an "onto-logic." In short, Balthasar gives an account of being as such in terms of a fundamental distinction between subject and object—without, however, pushing these terms to the extreme positions of the orderer of the enframing (*Gestell*) and the ever-disposable standing-reserve (*Bestand*) that Heidegger warns against.[14] Similarly, Balthasar understands being as a whole as grounded in the absolute subjectivity of God, which he certainly thinks as *causa prima*, if not also in some sense as *causa sui*. To be sure, he does not impose any simplistically univocal notion of causality onto the mystery of God's inner self-relation. Nevertheless, his explicit discussion of God as "self-grounding" cannot be far from what Heidegger has in mind in his account of the particular "theo-logic" that is proper to ontotheology.[15]

For his part, Heidegger explicitly critiques the Christian doctrine of the *analogia entis* in his 1931 lecture course on Aristotle's *Metaphysics*. The clear implication of this text is that Heidegger would not be prepared to receive Przywara's and Balthasar's retrievals of the analogy of being as anything other than additional examples of the largely being- and difference-forgetting history of

Western metaphysics. Heidegger argues that the *analogia entis* illegitimately seeks to reduce all things, including God, to an ontic horizon. He suggests that, instead of seeking a phenomenologically rich meditation on the mystery of being as it gives itself from itself, this tradition rests content with a formal account of the relation between *ens infinitum* and *ens finitum*.[16]

Nevertheless, Balthasar has considerable grounds for rebuttal in this debate. In the first place, Heidegger's objection in the Aristotle lecture course depends upon a sense that it is predominantly the finite notion of *ens* that determines the significance of the *ens infinitum* of the theological level of analogy, whereas a more sympathetic interpretation might locate the significance precisely in the *infinitum*. Moreover, there is perhaps something to be said for Balthasar's eventual preference for the Thomistic understanding of divine being not as *ens infinitum* but rather as *esse subsistens*: a term that seems to warrant a more complicated assessment than Heidegger suggests, even though its meaning differs considerably from Heideggerian *Sein*.[17] But whatever term is used for God's absolute being, the fact remains that Heidegger underestimates the apophatic dimensions of the doctrine of analogy, as well as the support that the analogy gives to doxology. Therefore, although Heidegger helpfully identifies what may be dangerous about the *analogia entis*—insofar as any effort to theorize the mysteries of God and being on the basis of *ens*, or any finite concept, can become implicated in the destructive self-elevation of human subjectivity—he does not grasp what is deeply promising about the very same analogical doctrine, insofar as it opens up an intellectual space for prayer and, thus, for a prayerful overcoming of the crises of metaphysics.

Furthermore, Heidegger does not foresee the possibility that Balthasar enacts (and Balthasar does this more explicitly than Przywara): namely, that of interpreting the analogy of being in concert with several of the postmetaphysical modes of thought which Heidegger himself pursues. Balthasar, as we have seen, offers a Heideggerian account of truth as *aletheia*. Like Heidegger, moreover, Balthasar contends that any restriction of truth to a finite sphere conquerable by the knowing subject would be "nihilistic, self-destructive, and

self-contradictory." For Balthasar, the poetic "spontaneity of knowledge is wholly at the service of receptivity" to that which shows itself from itself. The subject and the object that make up Balthasar's
construal of the generality of being are steeped in mystery, that is, in
"unveiled veiling."[18] In all of these respects, Balthasar mirrors central
features of Heidegger's postmetaphysical phenomenology, while simultaneously and in the same terms specifying what it means to say
that being is analogical. For Balthasar, the two are not divided: the
analogy of being unfolds itself precisely in the wondrous disclosure
and withdrawal of being that occurs among beings.

By situating this inner-worldly dynamic in the context of the
mystery of God, Balthasar is able to open the way toward adoration, sacrifice, and love (practices supposedly incompatible with ontotheology). Moreover, he is able to do so with a level of consistency
that Heidegger's theory of *Ereignis* simply cannot attain. Indeed, it
is precisely on the basis of the *analogia entis* that Balthasar objects
to Heidegger's ontology as too monistic and, therefore, as ultimately
bound up with the prayer-negating crises of modernity. In the fifth
volume of *The Glory of the Lord* (1965), Balthasar argues that the
modern tendency toward a philosophy of identity—that is, toward a
totalizing conception of being that undermines the reverent sense of
divine transcendence that is safeguarded by the *analogia entis*—lies
at the root of the very dangers (technology, nihilism, the concealment of difference) which Heidegger seeks to counteract. Balthasar
contends that these crises are perpetuated most directly and "cata-
strophically" in the modern traditions of "transcendental philosophy" and "philosophy of Spirit," insofar as these traditions promote
a "prayer-less glorification of the Spirit, which takes not only itself
but also all that remains to it under its control."[19] Balthasar has in
mind here thinkers such as Descartes, Leibniz, Kant, Fichte, Hegel,
and Marx—that is, many of the philosophers whom Heidegger
critiques on similar grounds. Heidegger, together with the Greco-
German tradition of poetic thinking upon which he draws, fares
better in Balthasar's judgment. Something akin to both analogy and
prayer survives in his effort to respect difference as such. But these
features of Christian doxology have nevertheless been compromised

by Heidegger's neglect of the absolute freedom and glory (*Herrlichkeit*) of God, which is much more successfully protected by the *analogia entis* than it is by Heidegger's autochthonous thought.

Before Balthasar takes on Heidegger directly, he discusses Hölderlin and thereby effectively identifies and critiques the principal source of Heidegger's doxology.[20] Balthasar positions Hölderlin's work in relation to three traditions: German idealism, ancient Greek cosmology, and the Christian experience of prayer. He argues that "there is not one among Hölderlin's poems that could be described as prayer-less, that is, in which his faith does not say in advance an all-embracing 'yes' to reality." Balthasar likewise discovers a certain pervasive, though never fully crystallized, christological and kenotic subtext in Hölderlin's hymns.[21] However, despite these promising doxological features, Hölderlin remains a tragic figure in Balthasar's account. The tragedy is precisely that the other two elements of the threefold constellation—namely, the Greek cosmos and the German *Geist*—ultimately exert a decisively negative influence on his poetry by undermining the theological level of the *analogia entis* and by distancing his sense of the divine mystery from biblical and ecclesial sources of doxology.[22]

Balthasar continues this line of argument in his direct engagement with Heidegger. He acknowledges that Heidegger's "powerful warnings against technocracy and the ever more terrible philosophical nihilism which is emergent within it are justified." Moreover, he contends that "Heidegger's project is the most fertile one from the point of view of a potential philosophy of glory." Nevertheless, he holds that Heidegger's project proves problematic precisely because "no *analogia entis* prevails in the distinction between Being and existent, but rather an *identitas* which both generates the distinction and embraces it at the same time." According to Balthasar, Heidegger's is thus an ultimately monistic philosophy. He grants that Heidegger's understanding of the ontological difference includes an inner-worldly analogy between "limitless non-subsisting" being and finite beings, but he also clarifies that it lacks a "transcendental analogy of Being between God and the world," of the sort which Aquinas formulates in his affirmation of God as "subsisting and absolute Being."

Without something like this Thomistic and thus properly *theological* analogy, all difference, all glory, every play of revelation and concealment, occurs within the scope of an indeterminate abundance of being without any reference to the "sovereign and majestic freedom of the God of gracious covenant and absolute love."[23] What is lost, then, in Heidegger's ontological difference (or ontological reduction of difference) is an openness to love itself. For Balthasar, this means that there is a loss of prayer and all that it implies. In the midst of the present technological and nihilistic age, Heidegger's Hölderlinian ontology fails to safeguard prayer; whereas the analogy of being, conceived in an innovative phenomenological way, and because of its respect for absolute difference, is able to do just that.

Ultimately, therefore, we must wrestle with the fact that Balthasar largely accepts Heidegger's analysis of the abysmal fate of modern metaphysics only while at the same time elucidating certain ostensibly metaphysical entailments of Christian doxology (namely, the concepts proper to the *analogia entis*) as constituting the only viable response to this predicament. Other responses of the sort which Hölderlin and Heidegger supply prove to be inadequate insofar as they do not sufficiently resist that which is most problematic about metaphysics in the first place: that is, the monistic reduction of difference. However complex and precarious Balthasar's strategy may seem, it is, in his estimation, nevertheless both coherent and necessary. It follows quite naturally from his effort to think the mystery of prayer. His proposed revival of analogical metaphysics *within* doxology certainly requires a different assessment than has been given to those sorts of monistic metaphysical speculation, characteristic of the modern period, which have kept their distance *from* doxology (or which have compromised it through cosmocentric or anthropocentric distortions). And yet, we have seen that what is most crucial for prayer is not the concept of entity but rather the dynamic, mystery-sustaining and freedom-respecting tensions of both levels of analogy. Whereas some aspects of Balthasar's account of an objective and subjective structure of entitative truth continue to make his thought *marginally* susceptible to the Heideggerian suspicion of ontic reductionism (but only marginally, since Balthasar learns a great deal from

Heidegger about how to avoid his charges), Balthasar's phenomenologically inflected use of analogy has the extraordinary potential
both to incorporate Heidegger's postmetaphysical meditations on an
inner-worldly ontological difference and to elevate the mind to sublime adoration before the unsearchable depths of the Creator.

DOXOLOGICAL AESTHETICS

Balthasar maintains that Hölderlin, Heidegger, and various
other representatives of the modern classicist traditions to which
these two figures belong offer, at their best, only a distorted likeness
of Christian doxology. The distortion comes in part from the monistic and thus insufficiently analogical character of their thought.
But it is also a product of their reluctance to embrace the aesthetic
features of distinctively Christian prayer. According to Balthasar, in
order to address the crises of modernity we need doxology in the
fullest Christian sense: no Hölderlinian or Heideggerian approximation will suffice, however poetically rich it may be. Nor, indeed, will
the *analogia entis* suffice apart from the gift and reception of divine
revelation that gives doxology its precise christological shape and
content. Balthasar accordingly seeks to elaborate a Christian doxological aesthetics that is able to move beyond Heidegger's reliance on
a narrow, mostly de-Christianized, and politically dangerous Greco-
German poetic tradition, as well as beyond the abstract (and thus,
even in Balthasar's view, somewhat problematically metaphysical)
theory of an analogical structure of being.[24] He does this through a
wide-ranging effort of Christian *ressourcement*, which begins quite
early in his career and arguably finds its plenary expression in *The
Glory of the Lord*.[25]

Contemplation and Revelation

In terms of the early work, we shall focus on Balthasar's 1955
book *Das Betrachtende Gebet* (translated as *Prayer*), which emerges
from his extensive retrieval of Christianity's spiritual and theological

sources. In this text, he highlights the close connection between doxological contemplation and divine revelation. These are two ways of articulating the same prayerful interaction. He describes prayer as a "dialogue" in which God speaks first and we respond. Hence, prayer occurs as a reply that we make to an anterior communication of the word of God. Balthasar clarifies that, although this divine *logos* already manifests itself through creation and the covenantal history of Israel, it also reaches out to us in a unique way by taking on human flesh in the person of Christ. The incarnation demonstrates with astonishing clarity that this word is, above all, a "word of love." It is, moreover, a word that is expressed in unison with a gift of "'glory' and 'glorification' (*doxa*)," a gift of radiant presence that makes "known the wonders of the divine nature and activity" in the form of Christ.[26] The revelation that contemplative prayer presupposes must, therefore, be understood as *revelation* in a rather strong sense of the term. This sort of prayer is not merely inspired by hints or faint traces of the divine, as Heidegger suggests. On the contrary, it is elicited by the free and loving bestowal of a simultaneously verbal and experiential (hence, *doxo-logical*) disclosure of God.

The close connection between doxological contemplation and divine revelation is what enables Balthasar to argue that the practice of contemplative prayer entails "a *parrhesia* from God," which confers upon the prayerful person "the right to 'say everything.'"[27] One major implication of this idea is that theology need not be restricted to a series of hesitating and uncertain utterances. Rather, according to Balthasar, a theology that grows out of doxological contemplation can proceed with great confidence and need not succumb to the burdensome epistemological anxiety typical of modern, post-Kantian philosophers. One can speak and think freely of God because God has already, by the very act of arriving in the *logos* and *doxa* of Christ, entitled this mode of discursive reflection. Balthasar does not understate the point. He insists that *everything* can rightfully be spoken, theorized, and contemplated precisely because it has already been given out of love. Emboldened by this sense of nearly unlimited theological possibility, Balthasar discusses some of

God's most sublime mysteries (including those related to Christology, pneumatology, ecclesiology, and eschatology) precisely as they appear in the act of contemplative prayer. Two endeavors which one might in modernity be tempted to divide, namely thinking what is given in prayer and expounding the doctrines of the Christian faith, are here shown to be inseparable. Balthasar presents them as a single effort to seek greater understanding regarding our creaturely receptivity to God's free self-bestowal.

We have seen that, for Balthasar, contemplation is an act whereby we open ourselves to *receive* Christ as the word and glory of God. But it is also an act in which we *offer* ourselves as participants in Christ. Balthasar never tires of saying, in the words of Saint Paul, that we live *en Christoi*.[28] It is in this state of Christic inherence that we lift ourselves up, together with our petitions, thanksgivings, and hymns, to the Father. Balthasar contends that this sort of doxological sacrifice is especially evident in the contemplative context of the eucharistic liturgy.[29] Moreover, although he recognizes that the definitive advent of God has already been given to us in the Son, he also preserves within his discussion of contemplative prayer a strong sense of *desire* for Christ's future coming. He contends that the Christian practice of prayer "is situated between two *parousias* of the Lord," and it, therefore, demands that we wait, watch, and look "for the Lord who is to come." It is for this reason that Balthasar insists that "contemplation must be content to remain with the Son in a state of not-knowing (Mark 13:32)."[30] Although the theological discourse that arises from contemplation has a right to say everything (*parrhesia*), the fullness of the mystery about which it speaks nevertheless lies in an eschatological future and even then will not be adequately comprehended. Nevertheless, Balthasar's emphasis is certainly that grace and consolation are already available in abundance and remain only to be more fully explored and appreciated. The erotic dimension of his doxology is more invigorated by a feeling of divine presence than it is afflicted by the pangs of absence.

The revelation-saturated doxology that Balthasar articulates in his *Prayer* book radiates throughout his trilogy, appearing explicitly for the last time in a short section entitled "Spirit and Prayer" in the final volume of *Theo-Logic* (1987).[31] But already from the first volume of *The Glory of the Lord* (1967), it is clear that a prayerful practice of contemplation lies at the heart of his entire theological enterprise. One of the central arguments of this volume is that faith (*pistis*) presupposes and finds fulfillment in a particular kind of knowledge (*gnosis*). He explains that the knowledge he has in mind here is precisely the unique kind of experiential awareness that is available in the church's tradition of contemplation (*theoria*), which is determined by a humble reception of the revelation of God that comes in the "form" (*Gestalt*) of Christ. He suggests that this sort of *theoria* enables one to lay claim to "an 'aesthetic' experience of the awesome glory of divine being." He maintains, moreover, that the light provided by this experience should "control and give evidence of itself in every branch of theological speculation."[32] Hence, there can be no doubt that, for Balthasar, prayer—and specifically the prayerful and aesthetic openness to divine revelation that he calls *theoria*—is decisive for all theological understanding.

Balthasar's *theoria* is not especially vulnerable to Heidegger's critique of metaphysics. It does not reduce God to the status of a conceptual or causal foundation, which is meant to secure an ontic system of rationally demonstrable knowledge. Nor does it contradict the basic apophatic maxim regarding God's permanent incomprehensibility.[33] Most decisively, it expresses at least one particular manner in which prayer shows itself from itself. In this respect, Balthasar's *theoria* should be carefully distinguished from the forms of nonprayerful theory that characterize some metaphysical traditions and, above all, from Heidegger's prayer-contradicting construct of ontotheology.[34]

Nevertheless, it is important to consider what questions might be raised about Balthasar's way of emphasizing an experiential knowledge of God that is already accessible to the contemplative Christian. His decision to associate theology not primarily with those uncertain and unsettling possibilities of prayer which may call such knowledge, and even faith, into question, but rather with the luminous, aesthetically rich, and even *parousiacal* condition in which prayer sometimes presents itself, allows him to proceed in his far-reaching theological project with a high degree of self-assurance. There is great power in this approach: a power to declare, with confidence, that we are loved and that we are called to love; a power, moreover, to defend this assertion by appealing, as it were, to evidence (i.e., to the revealed visibility of the form of Christ). Nonetheless, to the extent that there are epistemologically troubling regions of prayer which Balthasar deemphasizes (even in his readings of Dionysius and John of the Cross),[35] and to the extent that he does this in order to lend greater credibility to a rather *knowing* account of God and the world, his proposed reintegration of prayer and thought arguably remains unfinished, and that which is problematic about metaphysics is perhaps not fully overcome. If Heidegger approaches the event of being as though it were almost worthy of the kind of acclamation that Christians reserve for God, Balthasar may risk contemplating the divine mystery as though it were nearly as evident as the event of being itself, and one may legitimately ask whether his own subjectivity becomes too exalted in this endeavor.[36]

And yet, although Balthasar therefore does not seem to supply everything that might be hoped for from a methodological engagement with the perhaps disconcertingly apophatic aspects of prayer (which we shall explore further in subsequent chapters), what he does offer is quite significant. His *theoria* gives rise to a rather generous doxological aesthetics that accommodates Heidegger's meditations on the poetic appearances of ontological beauty and difference, along with Karl Barth's (and others') determinately Christian theological considerations regarding the glorious revelation of God in Christ. Balthasar's contemplation combines these two perspectives while importantly prioritizing the latter. Moreover, it preserves an analogical relation of finite manifestation and infinite mystery within both of these spheres (the ontological and the christological), while moving beyond an abstract consideration of this relation. In a telling parenthetical comment, Balthasar counts his teacher Przywara among those thinkers whom he believes are unfortunately "following the trend toward the formless," that is, toward a forget-ting of the concrete disclosure of beauty in phenomena and of glory in Christ.[37] This somewhat mild critique of Przywara does not imply that Balthasar now wants to renounce the doctrine of the analogy of being; rather, it means that he thinks we need a sense of this analogy that is richly informed by, and situated in the context of, a Christian doxological aesthetics.

To be clear, Balthasar does not think that Barth's explicit rejec-tion of the *analogia entis* necessarily makes Barth's work antitheti-cal to doxology. On the contrary, Balthasar maintains that as long as Barth manages to safeguard some kind of analogical relation be-tween the absolutely transcendent Creator and the permanent gift of creation (which Balthasar argues that, at least by the period of the *Church Dogmatics*, he largely does), then the formal structure of doxology can remain intact.[38] Balthasar expresses strong reservations redolent of Przywara regarding Barth's early dialectical period, rep-resented by the two editions of the *Epistle to the Romans*. However, Balthasar draws particular attention to Barth's later christologically grounded notions of the *analogia fidei*, the *analogia relationis*, and "the *analogia adorationis et orationis*: God's gracious inclusion of the creature into God's own dominion, where God gives his children power over his own will and heart."[39] Thus, for Barth as well, anal-ogy has a role to play in theology and finds its highest significance precisely in prayer. When in subsequent writings Balthasar locates the *analogia entis* precisely in Christology, he effectively upholds Barth's insistence on the primacy of Christ, while simultaneously resisting Barth's condemnation of Przywara's analogical metaphys-ics.[40] But regardless of the question of where each theologian stands on the doctrine of (the) analogy (of being), and whether on this point there is any hope for further rapprochement, the fact remains that both Barth and Balthasar *primarily* seek to understand the glorious revelation of God and the prayerful engagement with this revelation precisely as they occur in Christ.[41] In an ecumenically significant ges-ture, Balthasar acknowledges that his doxological aesthetics largely depends on Barth's insight regarding the close connection between *Herrlichkeit* and beauty.[42]

Aesthetic Sources

In order to correct the trend toward "formlessness" that Przywara's analogical metaphysics seems to represent, Balthasar turns to
the poets, though not quite in the same way that Heidegger does. Balthasar argues that "the resurrection of the flesh vindicates the poets
in a definitive sense: the aesthetic scheme of things, which allows us
to possess the infinite within the finitude of form . . . is right." He
clarifies, however, that this insight does not settle matters; one still
needs to make a decision between "the conflicting parties of myth
and revelation."[43] That is, one has to choose between a more nearly
pagan and a Christian expression of doxological aesthetics. In this
regard, Balthasar's choice is clear. To be sure, he does not neglect the
Greek and German poetic canon that Heidegger esteems; he finds
retrievable material in Homer, Hesiod, Pindar, Aeschylus, Sophocles, Hölderlin, Goethe, and Rilke, to name but a few. And yet, what
sets Balthasar apart is his interpretation of Christian poetry, together
with other prayerful modes of human perception and creativity. He
reserves the place of highest honor for the "biblical aesthetics" of
the Old and New Testaments. Among the many scriptural themes
that Balthasar illuminates, the "hymnic world of theophanic images," which emerges in the poetic writings of the Psalms and the
Prophets and is subsequently incorporated into the apostolic proclamation of Christ, is especially pertinent to the present discussion.[44]
Balthasar traces the reception of this biblical experience of the divine
glory and word throughout various Christian theological and spiritual traditions and interprets many more figures than can be engaged
here. Counting only those thinkers explored in the volumes of *The
Glory of the Lord*, a partial list would include Irenaeus, Augustine,
Dionysius, Anselm, Bonaventure, Dante, Tauler, Suso, Ruysbroeck,
Angela of Foligno, Julian of Norwich, Catherine of Siena, John of
the Cross, Ignatius of Loyola, Pascal, Hamann, Soloviev, Hopkins,
Claudel, and Péguy.

   Among Balthasar's criteria for inclusion in this canon of doxological aesthetics would seem to be not only evidence of a profoundly Christian experience of the divine glory and word but also

a certain kind of status within the Euro-Mediterranean and North Atlantic "West" (including, in his case, the churches and nations of Eastern Europe). These two criteria—doxological and occidental—can be understood as deeply interrelated precisely to the extent that Christianity has historically maintained a very prominent presence not only in particular geographical regions but also in corresponding intellectual, political, and cultural-linguistic traditions, which one might (always contestably) consider "Western" and even in some sense eventually and predominantly "white."[45] However, already in antiquity, but also and especially in the modern period, Christian doxology has taken root in many cultures and in many parts of the world that do not fall within the supposed interior of the occident or the parameters of modern "whiteness"—and this Christian "outside" or "underside" is something that Balthasar leaves largely out of consideration, despite the symphonic style of his work.

To be sure, Balthasar cannot be faulted simply for falling short of the ideal of universal inclusion. In fact, he is to be given credit for avoiding a too formal enactment of this ideal, which would only result in an abstract totality and the consequent loss of any real, meaningful, and culturally rooted aesthetics. Understood sympathetically, Balthasar means to do no more than address the local—but perhaps still relatable—conditions of an occidental culture that has forgotten the original source of its promise. This promise is not to be found, as Heidegger problematically insists, merely in the event of being that provides the gravitational center of Greco-German poetry and philosophy. Rather, according to Balthasar, the promise comes forth from the incarnate and glorious mystery of God, which has been contemplated and welcomed by generations of prayerful Christian thinkers, including men and women, representing various eras, regions, and vocations within a diversified ecclesial history. Unlike Heidegger, who sets the Greek and Hebrew foundations of doxology in opposition to each other and almost completely disregards the latter, Balthasar engages thinkers who have found ways to blend the two together. In these respects, his aesthetics shows itself to be much more inclusive than Heidegger's. Furthermore, and most decisively, although Balthasar's doxology is predominantly occidental, this cultural location does not become explicitly normative for his doxology in the way that Greco-German "purity" does for Heidegger's. Balthasar argues that all poetry has already been conditioned by, and is at best an imperfect imitation of, the incomparable communication of the *doxa* and *logos* of Christ, which manifest a universally redemptive love. In short, Balthasar affirms that Christ, not Hölderlin, is the *norma normans non normata* for salvation and, moreover, that the hope we place in this salvation must exclude no one (not even those who seem explicitly to reject it).[46] To assert this in the German-speaking part of Europe in the middle of the twentieth century is at least implicitly to take a strong theoretical and political stance against the worst forms of regnant nationalist spirit.

And yet, although Balthasar avoids the most problematic aspects of Heidegger's demand for cultural purity, the fact remains that his doxology is generally untroubled by the colonial, neocolonial, and racial implications of modern Western aesthetics, which has, since the origins of modernity, been propagated as though it were universally normative. He gives little resistance to this lamentable trend. Nor does he demonstrate critical awareness of it. His doxological symphony does not include the sort of de-colonial "border thinking" that has recently been proposed by Roberto Goizueta, Walter Mignolo, and others as a necessary epistemological and ethical recourse in opposition to the violent legacies of modern coloniality.[47] Nor does he consider the doxological significance of blackness (which Cone will illuminate for us in the last chapter). The doxological aesthetics that he offers is not thereby simply invalidated, but it is revealed to be, in these ways, significantly limited as a response to the crises of the modern age. Nihilism, technology, the oblivion of difference, the diminishment of hospitality and love—Balthasar recognizes and counteracts these problems through his practice of doxological contemplation. But he also leaves room to desire a greater remembrance of difference and a broader and more rigorous performance of love and hospitality, in which one would search for the fullness of Christian doxology not only within but also beyond (and along) the disruptive borders of a "white"-dominated West.

Gelassenheit and Kenosis

Having identified this limitation, we must still examine more deeply what Balthasar's aesthetic canon enables him to theorize. Each of the figures that he considers represents a concrete way or style of beholding the *doxa* and *logos* of Christ amid the beautiful appearances of the world—but also, and crucially, amid the miserable conditions of fallen existence. Balthasar's Christian *ressourcement*, therefore, shows that the openness of one's body and mind to the divine other which the practice of doxology entails must occur not only within the somewhat sanitized realm of the *analogia entis*, that is, the creaturely domain of being that participates in a contingent way in the being of God, but also in the factual world of sin, suffering, violence, and death which, in the extremes of alienation from God, approaches the condition of nonbeing or total dissimilarity. Hence, the insight that Balthasar expresses in *Wahrheit* concerning the need for a voluntary unveiling before the absolute fullness of divine being finds here a more historically realistic and emphatically Christian mode of expression.

Moreover, and for very similar reasons, Heidegger's *Gelassenheit* toward ontological mystery gives way in Balthasar's doxological aesthetics to a specifically christological form of kenosis. The aesthetic receptivity to the mystery of God that Balthasar's collection of saints and witnesses displays leads each of them, without exception, into a deeper participation in the totality of the Son's prayerful manner of existence, including in a particular way the absolute self-emptying obedience with which he accepts the will of the Father, even to the point of agony and death. In continuity with the Gospel of John, Balthasar holds that Christ's passion discloses "'glory' in the uttermost opposite of 'glory.'" Balthasar maintains, accordingly, that it is precisely during the Son's final "hour" and the apostolically affirmed descent into hell, where every trace of the presence of God and every reason for hope seems lost, that Jesus unveils the full reach of the *doxa* of the triune God by giving himself completely, in communion with the Holy Spirit, to the Father's supremely just and compassionate plan of salvation. In Balthasar's account, therefore, glory coincides with filial self-surrender. This convergence is not only revealed by Christ's acceptance of the cross but also constitutes a pattern that must be followed by those who seek to contemplate and imitate him.[48]

However, while recommending kenosis as an essential feature of doxology, particularly in the fallen world, Balthasar does not disregard the resurrection. Indeed, his doxological aesthetics culminates not in adoration of the cross but rather in gratitude for the unfathomable gift of resurrected life, in which we are in some sense already invited to share through the grace of the Holy Spirit that is poured out upon the church. Balthasar notes that when Jesus is resurrected, the fullness of his glory remains to some extent hidden from the disciples who nevertheless see him. So too, the contemporary church recognizes and experiences some measure of the *doxa* of the Risen Lord, but this *doxa* also abides in heavenly withdrawal.[49] Thus the aesthetic play of manifestation and mystery, of phenomenal nearness and distance, which is proper to creaturely being and its *Austrag* is not undone by the resurrection but rather taken up into its distinctive manner of appearance. It is in this sort of partly deferred manner that the resurrection shapes Balthasar's doxological aesthetics even prior to the *eschaton*: that is, even in a world in which sin still reigns.

At this point, it seems pertinent to consider how Balthasar's doxological interpretation of the paschal mystery—including both cross and resurrection—stands with respect to the problematically fatalistic tenor of Heidegger's onto-doxology. As we have seen, Heidegger encourages us to receive our exposure within the fatal sway of historical being with a spirit of gratitude. For him, this sort of compliance with the destiny of being (i.e., *Gelassenheit*) is integral to an authentic mode of prayer-like dwelling as mortals upon the earth. For Balthasar, a willing participation in Good Friday and Holy Saturday (i.e., kenosis in the Son) is similarly included as a vital part of the church's doxological calling. And yet, Balthasar's contemplation of the resurrection invests his doxology with a much greater sense of eschatological hope, and this promised future is the ultimate reason for our acts of supplication, thanks, and praise. Nevertheless, both thinkers promote prayerful (Balthasar) or prayer-like

(Heidegger) dispositions which, amid the given circumstances of *this* world, would seem to be characterized largely by a posture of acceptance and perhaps, therefore, not quite sufficiently by an actively embodied spirit of resistance. Of course, Heidegger's principle of autochthony and Balthasar's ideal of Christian love greatly complicate matters; on these grounds, both thinkers protest *some* of the destructive conditions of the modern age and seek to change them. But the proposed change in both cases depends upon a releasement of oneself toward the divine (Balthasar) or quasi-divinely ontological (Heidegger) mystery that is already given even in the midst of things as they are.[50]

Granting that there is some similarity here, we must nevertheless take note of the crucial difference between Heidegger's and Balthasar's positions. The distinctively Christian form of Balthasar's kenotic doxology is highly significant in this regard. It implies a readiness to embrace suffering and death, not simply so that being might be, but rather so that the love of God might be glorified and communicated with others. This difference can be glimpsed, in one way, by looking at Balthasar's and Heidegger's rather dissimilar interpretations of Eckhart. Whereas Heidegger abstracts Eckhart's *Gelassenheit* from its Christian context, substituting *Ereignis* in the place of the divine mystery of absolute love, Balthasar is at pains to situate Eckhart more firmly in this love and the determinate revelation that communicates it. According to Balthasar, Eckhart's doctrine of *Gelassenheit* is not merely about letting things be as they are but rather about letting oneself be conformed to the self-emptying love of Christ, which is authentic only if it bears fruit in an active love of neighbor. In Balthasar's judgment, the Eckhartian tradition becomes particularly problematic only when later, de-Christianized interpreters (including Heidegger and others) begin to appropriate Eckhart's idea of a radical openness to being without retaining his properly christological aesthetics, which specifies this openness in terms of divine and human love.[51]

Balthasar recognizes that some of Eckhart's own metaphysical excesses are partly to blame for this fateful trajectory, and it is for this reason that Balthasar gravitates more toward other figures of doxological kenosis. In particular, he welcomes Ignatius of Loyola's deeply contemplative and active doctrine of "indifference" (*indiferencia*). He argues that this doctrine remains wedded to a thoroughly concrete—that is, scriptural, imaginative, personal, contextual, and practical—exercise of receiving, offering, and desiring the glory and word of God in Christ.[52] For Balthasar, "what is absolutely decisive . . . is that, though Ignatius continued the idea of abandonment in all its Christian radicalism, he did not adopt the metaphysical formulation given it by the German mystics, most notably Eckhart."[53] In other words, Ignatius, precisely unlike Eckhart, does not leave room for the kind of Heideggerian misinterpretation according to which the Christian doxological participation in the passion of Christ is distorted into some sort of generalized submission to being. Ignatius connects the prayerful practice of finding God in all things, including the most devastating circumstances, with an active pursuit of greater love and holiness. He develops a process of spiritual discernment that enables one to distinguish, within the sway of being, between various kinds of spirits and to make decisions in accord with the salvific will of God that is revealed in the totality of Christ's existence. In these ways, Ignatius's spirituality—and, by implication, Balthasar's as well—powerfully resists the rather indiscriminate passivity that is evident in Heidegger's onto-doxology.[54]

THE DRAMA OF PRAYER

As the preceding discussion of Ignatius already suggests, Balthasar's doxological theory is not disconnected from praxis. On the contrary, he insists that they are two interrelated aspects of the same prayerful interaction with God. In his *Prayer* book, he explains that the kind of contemplation that he wants to encourage "can only take place in discipleship."[55] Elsewhere, in an essay entitled "Beyond Contemplation and Action?," he argues that contemplation and action are simply different ways of expressing the one Christian task of "making room in us for the living praxis of God."[56] Balthasar develops this theme at greater length in his celebrated article "Theology and Sanctity." The central argument of this text is that theology needs to become again, as it once was among the great saints of the church, a work of holiness. With this term he means to say two things: that theology should always be "incarnated in act" and that it should "never . . . [be] separated from the attitude of prayer." He articulates this twofold idea in another way by suggesting that theology should seek to become so thoroughly integrated with spirituality that one would no longer really be able to make sense of the now widely presupposed division between the two. Just as the fathers and mothers of the church knew no such separation, neither should we. Balthasar does not intend to reduce theology to the modern sense of the term "spirituality," which, because it has already been constructed in opposition to theology, can quickly degenerate into a merely "subjective art of describing inner states." Instead, he advocates a vibrant form of prayerful thinking and living, which is able to seek greater clarity regarding the revealed glory and word of God while embodying these most sanctifying gifts in the world.[57]

Balthasar, therefore, makes it clear that we are supposed to incarnate theory—that is, theology, doxology, contemplation—in concrete acts of love and holiness. However, what this means above all is that we are called to open our lives to the sovereign action of God that alone promises to save us. Prayer becomes active, then, not only through what we can and ought to do in light of it, but also and more fundamentally because it lets us participate in what God has already done and continues to do salvifically for us. In the final analysis, *God* is the one that overcomes with supreme love the many forces of evil that inhabit the world and, by the power of this same love, restores all things to a newness of life. This soteriological act is far from something that fallen humanity, left to its own devices, has the capacity to achieve, despite the pretensions of certain modern philosophies of history. Nor, however, is it something that God accomplishes at the expense of created freedom. By virtue of the fact that it is not abolished, the freedom of human beings must retain an active (albeit secondary) role; must continue to move as a real player on the stage of world history; and must, therefore, take part in what can henceforward be conceived only as a *drama,* precisely because the end of this interplay of freedoms remains at least somewhat in suspense.[58]

Such is arguably the central contention of Balthasar's aptly named *Theo-Drama*. In the second volume (1976), he argues that we will not be able to reintegrate theology and spirituality "so long as we fail to include the dramatic dimension of revelation, in which alone they find their unity."[59] When Balthasar speaks of the "dramatic dimension of revelation," he can be taken to mean precisely that aspect of God's revealed relationship with us that is unintelligible and unrealizable apart from our active involvement with it— that is, apart from prayer in the broadest sense. A reduction of this relationship to a merely epic, objective, nonspiritually "theological" narrative produces one kind of distortion; a reduction to a merely lyrical, subjective, nontheologically "spiritual" expression produces another. Prayer is not confined to the lyrical side of these dialectics; rather, it names the drama that constitutes them. This drama has many aspects and historical embodiments which can make it appear in any given instance more contemplative or active, more theological or spiritual, more epic or lyrical, and so on, but the central tension remains the same: infinite and finite freedom come together asymmetrically, but also reciprocally, for the sake of a still (for us) unforeseeable consummation of peace and love, which is to say, salvation.

Balthasar's discussion of petitionary prayer in the same volume sheds a particularly clear light on the dramatic interplay of freedoms that shapes prayer in all of its forms. Balthasar argues that we will be able to avoid thinking of petitionary prayer too philosophically (i.e., as having no possible effect because God is immutable) or too mythologically (i.e., as directly manipulating the divine will), and thus in either case not sufficiently dramatically, only if we recognize it as a participation in the Son's humble yet irresistible prayer to the Father, in which we are included by the grace of the Holy Spirit.[60] The philosophical one-sidedness tends toward the epic; the mythological one-sidedness tends toward the lyrical; in the center there is the divine-and-human prayer of Christ in which our own prayers and God's loving intentions for us are brought together without contradiction or erasure.

On the one hand, therefore, Balthasar clearly understands prayer as a work of God, precisely of the Trinity. In the final volume of *Theo-Drama*, he clarifies this point. He refers to the "absolute quality of prayer" as an act of worship occurring among the three divine persons: "When God stands before God we can say 'that God shows honor to God' 'in a reciprocal glorifying'; 'in an eternal reciprocal worship.'"[61] In the economy of salvation, he suggests, this intra-Trinitarian prayer takes on a petitionary form, in which the Father, the Son, and the Spirit make loving requests of one another.[62] On the other hand, however, Balthasar avers that our creaturely freedom is welcomed into this mystery. As he puts it: "There is no way that finite freedom can realistically be understood to 'influence' infinite freedom except in the context of the realization of the historical Covenant relationship, where ultimately God's trinitarian mystery is revealed."[63] The perhaps too-easily overlooked yet radical implication of this statement is precisely that finite freedom *can realistically* influence infinite freedom, provided that it consents to do so in the midst of the Trinitarian economy of salvation, in which the loving relationship of Father, Son, and Spirit is ultimately decisive.

What exactly our petitions might achieve is not something that Balthasar dares to specify in this context, but—and this remains a remarkable decision—he takes it for granted that they do not do nothing. In this way, he respects the dignity of even the most basic practice of prayer, which would involve no more than making a simple request of God. He understands this work of supplication not only as an instructive or illuminative practice that indirectly encourages us to engage in other sorts of necessary worldly action but also as a meaningful act in its own right. He treats it as a precious mode of divine and human dialogue that is mysteriously wrapped up in God's own interior colloquy and, thereby, in the fullness of redemption. This is not to say that he thinks petitionary prayer (or, for that matter, doxological contemplation) is the only kind of action through which the finite creature can participate in the salvation of the world; additional works of love and holiness are indispensable to this participation—though one might legitimately ask whether Balthasar needs to give these more overtly active elements of Christian praxis a place of greater prominence in his understanding of the drama of prayer.[64]

All in all, Balthasar's doxological theory is not just theoretical (as metaphysics would typically appear to be); rather, it involves various free actions and interactions of the Trinity and creation. Nevertheless, there are certain respects in which even the most explicitly dramatic aspects of his project remain connected with metaphysics. In this regard, one should recognize that Balthasar's *Theo-Drama* develops in conversation with Hegel, a thinker whom Balthasar credits with profoundly seeking, though not with attaining, a compelling theo-dramatic theory.[65] Heidegger, who also confronts Hegel in "The Onto-Theo-Logical Constitution of Metaphysics," would encourage us to scrutinize this aspect of Balthasar's thought. To be sure, Balthasar resists Hegel's dialectical metaphysics of identity with assistance from the *analogia entis*[66] and corrects Hegel's distorted treatment of Christian revelation by rooting his own thought much more firmly in the concrete aesthetics of Christian scripture and tradition, which provide the content for distinctively Christian contemplation.[67] In these ways, Balthasar's theo-drama is crucially distinct from the one that Hegel constructs. Balthasar nevertheless thinks about the Trinity in a manner that is perhaps too certain even while remaining speculative; perhaps insufficiently reticent before the enigmas of God and the world; perhaps, therefore, intelligible only within those regions of *theoria* that have been partially modeled after metaphysics or, then again, perhaps only in that area of metaphysics which lies just beyond the limits of what *theoria* authorizes one to think.

One might consider, for instance, the following passage from the fourth volume of *Theo-Drama* (1980), in which Balthasar—in a simultaneously Hegelian and anti-Hegelian gesture—interprets the immanent differentiation between Father and Son as the ground of all worldly separation:

> The action whereby the Father utters and bestows his whole Godhead, an action he both "does" and "is," generates the Son. This Son is infinitely Other, but he is also the infinitely

> Other *of the Father*. Thus he both grounds and surpasses
> all we mean by separation, pain and alienation in the world
> and all we can envisage in terms of loving self-giving, inter-
> personal relationship, and blessedness. . . . This [the Son's
> substantial divinity from the Father] implies such an incom-
> prehensible and unique "separation" of God from himself
> that it *includes* and grounds every other separation—be it
> never so dark and bitter. This is the case even though the
> same communication is an action of love.[68]

Balthasar argues that his way of speaking about the differentiation
between Father and Son as foundational to every type of worldly
separation (whether devastating or life-giving) enables one to avoid,
on the one hand, the rather abstract nature of Karl Rahner's transcendental reflections on the Trinity and, on the other hand, the
Hegelian immanentism of Jürgen Moltmann's Trinitarian theology, in which the God-world distinction becomes problematically
blurred.[69] And yet, granting that Balthasar steers clear of these dangers, it is important to recognize that the quasi-explanatory style
of his discussion remains questionable. His Trinitarian "grounding" of separation, pain, and alienation does not function exactly
as a theodicy—understood, at least since Leibniz, as a purportedly
rational defense of God in the face of the world's injustice. But it
does reduce an expansive array of phenomena, including the excessively opaque phenomena of suffering, to a unitary and foundational
structure (namely, the hiatus between Father and Son) and thereby
imitates, even while deconstructing, Hegel's metaphysical account of
negation. Hence, one cannot avoid asking whether Balthasar's Trinitarian doctrine, though informed by prayer, offers in this respect
insufficient resistance against the dangers of metaphysics, which
would include in this instance not only the general drive for too
much conceptual mastery but also the particular problem that comes
with attempting to give any kind of abstract theoretical foundation
to the enigmas of worldly anguish.

Balthasar undoubtedly provides some resistance against these
dangers. In a striking remark, he asserts that "suffering occurs when

the recklessness with which the Father gives away himself (and *all* that is his) encounters a freedom that, instead of responding in kind to this magnanimity, changes it into a calculating, cautious self-preservation."[70] Thus the transition from the primordial, loving drama of the Trinitarian persons to the suffering of the world is not something that occurs automatically and mono-genetically (like a Platonic emanation), even though Balthasar says that the latter is "grounded" in the former. Rather, this transition happens only when the absolute disposition of prayer and kenosis which the Trinity exemplifies is refused in favor of a technological ("calculating"), self-preserving, and ultimately self-contradictory attitude on the part of creation. If there is an explanation of suffering here, it rests largely on humanity's in some sense dispositionally "metaphysical" rejection of the proper manner of Trinitarian distance: that is, freedom-as-love.[71] In light of this sort of clarification, a case can be made for Balthasar's consistency. It could be argued that prayer remains in this context much more decisive than Hegelian metaphysics is for any kind of God-world relation that Balthasar would affirm. The distortion of freedom into a defensive form of self-securing rationality that ultimately threatens prayer and leaves no room for self-giving relationship is precisely what Balthasar attempts to overcome. He believes that this hubristic tendency, not Trinitarian distance, lies at the root of the world's problems. But the connections with Hegel's dialectic that are evident keep this from being an easy argument to make without possible rejoinder. And we do not find here the sort of questioning or lamenting outcry in the face of suffering that many thinkers of prayer (such as Metz) would recommend in contrast to Balthasar's quasi-explanatory treatment of the *mysterium iniquitatis*.

Heidegger's critique of metaphysics does not only raise certain questions about Balthasar's engagement with Hegel's metaphysical speculation; intriguingly, it also enables Balthasar to position his *Theo-Drama* against various modern alternatives that both he and Heidegger would consider dangerously metaphysical (including but not limited to Hegel's project). In the fourth volume in particular, but also in a related essay entitled "Liberation Theology in the Light of Salvation History" (1977), Balthasar uses Heidegger's critique of metaphysics to diagnose the crises of modernity. At the same time, he coordinates this critique with another line of analysis that draws on Henri de Lubac's critical assessment of modernity in view of the secularizing legacy of Joachim of Fiore and the rise of atheistic humanism. On the one hand, in harmony with Heidegger, Balthasar contends that, from Francis Bacon, to Kant, to Hegel, to Marx, modern metaphysics builds up a "technological notion of progress," which, despite its benevolent pretenses, results in a "naked power struggle between superpowers using naked technological means of annihilation."[72] Thus the development of metaphysics in tandem with technology results in the concrete nihilism of the arms race, and everything is effectively reduced to the machinations of power. On the other hand, in unison with de Lubac, Balthasar laments the modern "secularization and rationalization of salvation that [first] occurred within Christianity itself (Joachim of Flora)."[73] Here Balthasar alludes to the thesis (substantiated more thoroughly by de Lubac) that Joachim's transposition of Trinitarian doctrine into three separate ages of world history is a crucial part of the background for Hegel's distorted theo-drama, as well as for the analogous proposals of many other thinkers who have identified the age of the Spirit with the rise of some sort of post-Enlightenment anthropocentric freedom.[74] The respective dangers identified by Heidegger and de Lubac come to light as two aspects of the same phenomenon: the dangerous self-glorification of human subjectivity.

This simultaneously Heideggerian and de Lubacian view of the modern situation is one of the most decisive, though not sufficiently recognized, motivations for Balthasar's critical evaluation of liberation theology. Indeed, his primary complaint is that liberation theology seems to do precisely what Heidegger and de Lubac have argued that modernity does. He suspects that it has not broken all ties with the "will-to-power," and he contends that the goods which it seeks to deliver to the poor "originate in that very realm of technology that is characterized by an insatiability and a mass culture . . . that are destructive of the person."[75] Moreover, he fears that it may change the "Cross of Christ . . . into a 'tactical' instrument in issues that are purely this-worldly" and thereby re-inscribe the "secularized theological analyses" which have been propagated among the modern progeny of Joachim.[76] In these ways, liberation theology seems, in his view, to give more weight to humanity's own strivings in history than it does to the more urgently needed work of prayerfully opening oneself to the vertical, apocalyptic action of God.

Despite these strong reservations, Balthasar does not entirely disregard the concerns of liberation theology. He declares that "we have a strict Christian duty to fight for social justice on behalf of the poor and oppressed" and that "the Church . . . must by preference side with the poor."[77] Moreover, while reflecting on Job, Balthasar explicitly rejects any theodicy that would entail a "domestication of suffering."[78] Nevertheless, these points in favor of liberation theology and its pathos for the poor are not what receive the most emphasis in Balthasar's dramatic soteriology. Instead, he concentrates on retrieving a biblical and traditional view of the redemptive sacrifice of Christ, in which Jesus takes our place and bears our sins in order to free us from sin and death; on affirming the gift of the Holy Spirit, which enables the church to participate in the paschal mystery, including simultaneously both cross and resurrection; and on resisting Hegel's philosophically reductive speculations regarding a constitutive relation between the economic and immanent Trinity.[79] In other words, he wants to leave no room to doubt that the drama of salvation proceeds as a *Christian theo*-drama, which, even though it incorporates our prayers and our lives, is definitively a sovereign act of kenotic love performed by the Father, Son, and Spirit. His critiques of liberation theology likewise serve this end.

But to what extent are these critiques convincing? Although *some* formulations of liberation theology may lend a measure of credibility to Balthasar's suspicion, the fact remains that he does not adequately clarify which formulations in particular are especially worthy of it and conversely, therefore, which ones are much less so. He provides no thorough reading of the diverse range of liberation theologians and instead treats this conversation nonrigorously as one monolith. In this case, he does not replicate the interpretive care and the sympathy that he typically shows other figures of Christian theology and spirituality, as well as various aesthetic and philosophical sources of occidental culture. Nor does he make any attempt to discover in what ways the drama of prayer might be embodied and the crises of metaphysics powerfully resisted precisely in this liberating form of theology and its historical praxis. Heidegger's critique of metaphysics (which Balthasar supplements with a de Lubacian critique of secularized soteriology) seems to lead, once again, to an overhasty judgment of a Christian tradition and, consequently, to a concealment of the mystery of prayer that it shelters. At the same time, however, Heidegger's and de Lubac's analyses of modernity remain pertinent. Therefore, the task must be—and Balthasar attempts only the first part of it and does so only superficially—to explore in what ways these analyses of the larger phenomenon of modernity *do* and *do not* apply to the highly differentiated discourse of liberation theology, which in its pursuits of integral freedom maintains various complex relations with prayer. In the fifth and sixth chapters, we shall see how Balthasar's efforts to integrate doxological theory and praxis are mirrored, concretized, and in some respects significantly enhanced by the doxological spiritualities of certain Christian liberation theologians.

CODA: CHARLES PÉGUY

The many aspects of Balthasar's thought that we have explored (without being able to delve into their full complexity) converge nowhere more clearly than in his reading of Charles Péguy in *The Glory of the Lord*, volume 3.[80] Péguy comes to light as a poet within modernity, who differs from Hölderlin but nevertheless serves a similar function: his writings open up a richly aesthetic doxology by means of which thought can begin to move out of the technological and nihilistic edifice of modern metaphysics. At the same time, however, Péguy is (eventually) a Christian poet, which means, for Balthasar, not only that he upholds the distinction between God and creatures that the *analogia entis* is meant to protect, but also that he cares deeply about prayer and understands it as a participation in the gifts of Trinitarian revelation and salvation. Péguy, then, seems suitably positioned to provide something like what Heidegger wants from Hölderlin (though not the Germanness) but also what Balthasar wants from Christian thought and life in general. Péguy does both of these things while simultaneously embodying a profound political solidarity with the poor and the outcast, particularly the Jewish people.

Throughout Balthasar's account, he enables one to see how Péguy takes up themes in his poetry and in his other writings that resonate deeply with Heidegger's turn away from metaphysics and toward doxology. This resonance may have something to do with the influence of Henri Bergson's philosophy, which, according to Balthasar, encourages Péguy to keep his distance from thinkers who "desire to capture reality and to offer an exhaustive representation of it."[81] Péguy consequently avoids putting too much stock in the metaphysically implicated traditions of scholasticism, Kantianism, Hegelianism, and modern objective science. Furthermore, like Bergson, but also like Heidegger, Péguy resists the post-Enlightenment myths of evolution and progress and instead prefers to tell a largely declinist narrative of the modern world, in which he specifically associates the downfall of the West with the rise of modern technology.[82] On the positive side, Péguy suggests that one must recover an aesthetic approach to the inexhaustible excess of being, in which one receives it with wonder (Greek: *thaumazein*) and remembers the classical sources of culture and thought that have most originally and essentially brought it to light.[83]

No less than Hölderlin, Péguy attempts "to abide in and hold to the power of the source."[84] On the one hand, this abiding has dubious political implications. Péguy emphasizes the "value of the homeland," of "native soil," of "the French soil," and thereby appears to inscribe, only in a different location, a problematic rhetoric of national purity that is very similar to the counterpart that we have encountered in Hölderlin and Heidegger.[85] On the other hand, however, Péguy's commitment to rootedness, autochthony, *enracinement* does not only entail a concern for national identity but also and more importantly a profound respect for the phenomenally manifest conditions of life and existence. In particular, Péguy wants us to accept "the consecrated status that mortality bestows," without, however, forgetting that "the earthly . . . can find no ultimate measure in itself."[86] Here Balthasar, without explicitly arguing for it, has discovered in Péguy the bases for something very much like Heidegger's fourfold. The mortal and the divine, the earthly and the heavenly, disclosed together in proper proportion and relation, constitute the primordial context in which Péguy, like Heidegger, believes we are meant to be rooted and to dwell.

However, although something like Hölderlinian autochthony has a place in Péguy's work, it nevertheless does not predominate. Balthasar discovers many of the major threads of his own analogical, aesthetic, and dramatic contemplation woven into Péguy's later plays and poems, which Balthasar characterizes as "immersed in, impregnated with prayer." According to Balthasar, Péguy not only affirms the *analogia entis* in these texts; he also locates it precisely in Christology. Similarly, the event of being (*Ereignis*) ultimately proves less foundational for Péguy than does the event of Christ's passion, for he believes that "upon this event the world rests absolutely." In the end, the original source that Péguy seeks to recollect (*andenken*) is not so much the divine fire of the Greeks as it is the "truth that rests in the bosom of Trinitarian communion."[87] Like Balthasar, Péguy takes the insights of a philosophical openness to being and divinity and embeds them within a decisively Christian doxological contemplation.

Balthasar draws particular attention to a meditation that Péguy develops regarding the Our Father, which appears in his late poetic work *The Mystery of the Holy Innocents* (*Les mystère des saints innocents*). Here Péguy portrays the Father as one who is completely overcome by the irresistible supplication of the Son, in which Péguy says we participate through our own prayers. Thus Péguy represents poetically not only the glorious compassion of God but also the dignity of human acts of petition, which both he and Balthasar contend become efficacious in Christ. Moreover, Balthasar argues that Péguy's interpretation of the Lord's Prayer presupposes "the necessary humility, simplicity and *parrhesia*, boldness, from the Holy Ghost," which is constitutive of Christian *theoria*. And, indeed, Péguy's discourse is bold: he lets his own words be attributed to the Father and thereby dares to express the thoughts of the most unsearchable origin of the Trinity. In this way, Péguy clearly seems to have been granted the confidence to "say everything." Finally, anticipating the arguments of his *Theo-Drama*, Balthasar suggests that, while Péguy preserves the dramatic dimension of prayer by respecting the significance of our creaturely involvement, he also acknowledges its absolute quality by articulating it in the "form of 'theology as Trinitarian conversation.'" Balthasar concludes that, in this respect, Péguy's account of prayer is "infinitely far from Hegel, yet it is the truth in what Hegel says transferred into the sphere of the reciprocal freedom of love."[88] Therefore, in many ways, Péguy powerfully exemplifies Balthasar's multifaceted doxological theory.

But there is even more to Péguy's exemplarity: he incarnates this theory in praxis. This means not only that he thinks and prays in solidarity with the most impoverished and marginalized members of society, which he does, but also that he *struggles to realize* that for which he thinks and prays. The central goal of his intellectual, spiritual, and political work is precisely to draw us closer to a society of divine and human love from which none would be excluded: a heavenly and earthly kingdom of limitless hospitality. Expressed negatively, the hope that propels him forward is that no one will have to endure the "living death" of hell. For Péguy, the question of hell is not only a question of an eschatological state of perdition—which he, like Balthasar, dares to hope that God's love has the power to overcome.[89] It is also and largely "a question of the immanent Hell of the wretched of this earth, a question of the sharp demarcation between poverty (with the minimum necessary for life) and *misère* (with less than the minimum necessary for life)." In order to resist the hellacious conditions of exile and misery that he sees everywhere in the modern world, Péguy insists that contemplation and action—or, in his terms, *mystique* and *politique*—must be enacted in unison. According to his judgment, a life of prayer that would do without concrete social and political praxis is insufficient. Balthasar sums up Péguy's perspective in rather stark terms: "The eternal battle against Hell must be fought on earth. Praying alone, in place of acting, is cowardice."[90]

Balthasar indicates that Péguy's solidarity extends in a particular way to the Jewish people. In this respect, Péguy's—and, therefore, Balthasar's—thought differs considerably from that of Hölderlin and Heidegger. Balthasar takes note of Péguy's vigilant awareness of "the fact that Jesus was a Jew, in solidarity with his people and their destiny." He calls attention to Péguy's mindfulness regarding the "fifty centuries of wounds and scars" that the Jewish people have suffered. And he notes that the prophetic tradition of Israel was, for Péguy, of central importance. But the greatest sign of Péguy's solidarity is that he "saw his fate as an exile side by side with the Jewish destiny, especially that of the poor Jews who in the *monde moderne* are cut off by the same horizontal dividing line from the wealthy world above them and are thus doubly destitute and exiled by their religious destiny." What matters, then, is not only that Péguy affirms the validity of the Jewish covenant in traditional Irenaean fashion, while still understanding it as recapitulated in Christ. This is the very least that one can ask of a Christian thinker. What matters is that Péguy identifies himself with the plight of Jews living at the present, in his midst, many of whom were his personal friends and companions.[91]

And yet, for Balthasar, the most decisive point in Péguy's favor is that, at least by the time that he recovers his Christian faith, he maintains his active solidarity with the poorest of the poor and with the marginalized Jewish community precisely in the context of an orthodox Christian theo-drama. Balthasar contends that the "socialist hope" that Péguy articulates in his early writings becomes part of the "comprehensive theology of hope" that emerges with his later doxological works. His final vision is not limited to this world, nor to what humanity alone has the capacity to accomplish, but rather ultimately rests on the infinite promise of Trinitarian freedom and love. He trusts that the Father will hear Jesus's cry and have mercy on all those gathered into it.[92] In short, Péguy's hope is theocentric. Nevertheless, this does not change the fact that it presupposes and remains continuous with the hope and the work that are necessary for the historical world in which we presently dwell, which Péguy already promotes through his early forms of political advocacy. To his credit, Balthasar appears to recognize the necessary continuity here. It seems, therefore, that Péguy can be treated as a powerful representative of Balthasar's own positive form of simultaneously prayerful and political theology.

In all of these ways, Péguy may very well constitute the most synthetic, most startling, and most promising icon of Balthasar's rather complex doxology, together with its somewhat extraordinary theoretical and practical implications. We shall, therefore, leave Balthasar behind at this approximately maximal point. Several questions remain open for further consideration: Does Balthasar differentiate his doxological theory sufficiently from that which is problematic about the metaphysical tradition on which it nevertheless relies? Having incorporated certain elements of Heidegger's thought into his doxological theory, does he do enough to overcome its many dangers? Finally, are there aspects of the mystery of prayer which, especially in the midst of the crises of modernity, warrant more attention, or a different kind of attention, than he gives them? These questions point toward necessary discussions that are to come.

However, before we pursue them, it seems important to recall, once again, the great significance of Balthasar's achievement. He critically engages Heidegger and other great figures of contemporary intellectual culture and thereby sheds fresh light on some of the most pressing dilemmas of our age. At the same time, his thought is deeply saturated with prayer, and he endeavors to make known nothing other than that which prayer brings to light. By thinking through various presuppositions and dimensions of his own experience of doxological contemplation, together with those of countless generations who have preceded him, Balthasar seeks to understand above all precisely what it would mean to love and to be loved. Henceforward *love* will secure a purer thinking of prayer than that which is available within the event of being alone: precisely, a Trinitarian-and-creaturely love that presupposes a dynamic interaction of freedoms and a respect for difference. Some sense of theological analogy, aesthetics, and dramatics will likewise be unavoidable. Although the questions that remain may require us to rethink many details of Balthasar's project, they will not fundamentally alter this basic constellation of terms. In short, Balthasar demonstrates not only *that* but also largely *how* prayer unveils its significance amid the crises of modernity. The doxological character of his thought distances it from the perilous trajectory of modern metaphysics, and the integration of his doxology with prayerful and worldly action lays the groundwork for effective Christian resistance against the structures of modern violence. In his doxological theory, there is abundant freedom for the creature apart from any merely secular rejection of prayer. And in this theory, as well, theology and spirituality are one.

CHAPTER 3

DOXOLOGICAL SUBTLETY
On the Intersections of Prayer and Phenomenology

The critical discussion between Heidegger's and Balthasar's doxological alternatives to metaphysics, which Balthasar begins in his own work, continues among those who follow after them. Here we shall take up the next generation of the debate. It can be analyzed broadly in terms of two contrasting approaches. On the one hand, there are several thinkers who, though they remain much closer to Heidegger than to Balthasar, and do not directly appropriate or even engage Balthasar's theology, nevertheless seek to purify Heidegger's thought by drawing selectively on various traditions of Jewish and Christian prayer that Balthasar would recognize as at least partly constitutive of his own doxological theory. One thinks especially here of the sequence of receptions and refusals of Heidegger that runs from Emmanuel Levinas, to Jacques Derrida, to John Caputo. Along this post-Heideggerian trajectory, the event of being comes to be translated and disrupted by the advent of the other, which arises in connection with the law and the prophets of the Jewish covenant and the Christian-Platonic traditions of negative and mystical theology.

The greatest strength of this post-Heideggerian tradition has to do with its clear prioritization of hospitality and its concomitant overcoming of certain dangers of Heidegger's highly autochthonous onto-doxology. However, the welcome that these three thinkers extend to prayer remains, like Heidegger's, significantly restricted both by a sweeping disqualification of metaphysics and by a very minimal retrieval of prayer's traditional sources. Moreover, in what can only be counted as a radical departure from Heidegger, which comes with its own serious difficulties, they emphasize a largely nondoxological mode of prayer. They avoid doxology in both its Christian and Heideggerian forms precisely because, and insofar as, it seems to them to be inseparable from metaphysics. They recognize that doxology, whether oriented more toward God or toward being, promises determinate access to some sort of absolute (albeit paradoxical) presence, and they believe that in this respect it claims too much. Prayer is accordingly allowed to appear in this strand of postmetaphysical thought only on the condition that it consents to a more or less maximal degree of apophasis. Although Levinas and Caputo (and perhaps even Derrida) sometimes display a marginally doxological kind of reflection, they nevertheless subordinate it to a rather prohibitive discourse of hyperbolic indeterminacy. All in all, the post-Heideggerian tradition uniting Levinas, Derrida, and Caputo involves a significant degree of (typically modern) inhospitality toward prayer, even while it reflects a desire to transcend inhospitality of every sort and manages to embrace prayer in a few narrow respects.

On the other hand, there is a small set of contemporary Catholic thinkers who have come to be classified as proponents of a "theological turn" in French phenomenology. This group is represented by Jean-Luc Marion, Jean-Yves Lacoste, and Jean-Louis Chrétien.[1] Although they have not written much about Balthasar and although they often present themselves more nearly as philosophers than as theologians, they nevertheless do not conceal the considerable debts that they owe to Balthasar's thought.[2] Their major works re-inscribe the analogical, aesthetic, and dramatic features of his doxology, as well as the complexity of his relationship with Heidegger, including both critique and appropriation. Whether these convergences are a result of direct influence or merely a shared commitment to Christian *ressourcement*, the fact is that these three thinkers—in contrast to Levinas, Derrida,

and Caputo—address the question of prayer in a manner that is ultimately more Balthasarian than Heideggerian.

And yet, this Balthasarian profile does not prevent them from
being more Heideggerian than Balthasar. Indeed, the novelty of
their work comes to light precisely in their effort to think doxology
without any perilous metaphysical entailments. By seeking a more
complete break from metaphysics than Balthasar thought possible,
Marion, Lacoste, and Chrétien strive to eliminate the grounds for
Heideggerian suspicion that remain somewhat discernible in Balthasar's project, while retaining his thoroughly Christian doxological
orientation. Their approach thereby exhibits a very particular kind
of *doxological subtlety*. The distinction that these thinkers allow us
to draw between metaphysics and doxology, though clear and decisive, is nevertheless rather fine-grained. There is an art to perceiving
and maintaining it. It does not hang on this or that word (not even
"being," not even for Marion). Rather, it depends on an easily overlooked yet highly consequential disparity between two complex and
often complexly interrelated ways of thinking. Many postmodern
thinkers do not hesitate to elide metaphysics and doxology because
of their closely related histories. Moreover, even though Balthasar by
no means simplistically conflates the two thought-forms, he does not
always sufficiently differentiate them. Thus what Marion, Lacoste,
and Chrétien uniquely contribute is a very careful disclosure of doxology's postmetaphysical appearance.

That these three thinkers work as phenomenologists is no accident. Instead of setting up or presupposing a comprehensive system
of a priori concepts (of being, causation, etc.), they hold themselves
accountable to the subtle ways in which phenomena, and particularly the phenomena of prayer, give themselves. At the same time,
there is also a reason why they never seem to be merely phenomenologists. They endeavor to think doxology on its own terms, and
this means in the final analysis that they are committed to thinking not only about doxology but also *doxologically*. Hence, to speak
of an intersection of prayer and phenomenology here is to speak of
a mutually inclusive arrangement in which each of these thinkers
aspires to the best of both. However, the primary concern of this

post-Balthasarian contingent is not to follow all of the written rules of phenomenology as a historically constructed discipline (which are, therefore, not static in any case) but rather to respect the given determinations that are proper to doxology itself, even if this means testing the very limits of phenomenology and perhaps in some respects passing beyond them. In general, they seek to question or adjust phenomenology's methodological expectations mainly to the extent that these constraints restrict access to the mystery of prayer. Conversely, they suggest that any transgressions of phenomenology that better disclose this mystery can be somewhat justified by phenomenology's core commitment to the things themselves. In other words, they show some fidelity to phenomenology's contemplative and hospitable spirit, even when deviating from its letter.

To some theologians, the innovation represented by Marion, Lacoste, and Chrétien will not appear obviously or entirely positive. Especially among those who believe that Balthasar has already done enough to meet the challenges posed by Heidegger, any attempt to do more than Balthasar has done may seem superfluous. Moreover, and more strongly, some might suspect that too much will be conceded to Heidegger and the post-Heideggerians in the process, at the expense of the Christian theological tradition.[3] However, these doubts should be alleviated by the recognition that fidelity to prayer is the supreme criterion of Christian theology and the final measure of its authority. The core of any Christian theology that stands a chance of avoiding idolatry will be nothing other than that which prayer—the love-oriented interaction of Trinitarian and creaturely freedoms—gives to be thought. Admittedly, there is something uncertain in the search for a postmetaphysical doxology. But there is also, correlatively, the hope for a more dramatic and salutary style of thinking, in which one would be willing to risk everything for the sake of prayer and venture, without reserve, into a free and reflective contact with the glory and word of God. The challenge will be to perform this feat not only without the supposed security of metaphysics but also without losing touch with those vital aspects of prayer which the traditional way of incorporating metaphysics into doxology has already disclosed.

Other doubts might be raised from the opposite direction. It certainly remains possible to suspect, in a post-Heideggerian manner, that some kind of metaphysics continues to inform the doxological thought of the post-Balthasarians, despite their best efforts to overcome it. But, even if noticeable traces remain, the most important question is more precisely whether they effectively counteract that which is most problematic about metaphysics, that which has made it synonymous with modern crisis, that which implicates it directly in the nihilistic fate of technological reason, in the concealment of the eventful mysteries of being and of God, and finally in the forgetting of prayer and the prayerful exercise of hospitality. With respect to these issues, the post-Balthasarians' openness to doxology gives them a significant advantage over the post-Heideggerians, whose uncompromising apophasis reflects a desire for certainty that cannot be entirely disentangled from the negative effects of modern metaphysics. All in all, Marion, Lacoste, and Chrétien develop a mode of thought that constitutes a promising alternative not only to metaphysics, not only to Heidegger's Hölderlinian doxology, not only to Balthasar's still somewhat metaphysical answer to Heidegger, but also to the rival tradition of only selectively prayerful postmodern thought that has arisen in Heidegger's wake.

Although Marion, Lacoste, and Chrétien share this distinction, and are in this respect involved in a common endeavor, the differences between their doxological proposals are also noteworthy. Of the three, Marion's has received the most scholarly attention.[4] And yet, Chrétien's is the one that appears most decisive for the question of prayer. Chrétien's exemplarity is attested by the breadth of his retrieval; by the poetic dimensions of his thought; by the leave that he takes from the somewhat problematic constraints of Husserlian phenomenological method; by the rich connections that he draws between prayer, responsibility, and hospitality; and by many subtle arguments that are unique to him. For these reasons, we shall conclude with Chrétien. However, first, we shall examine the diversity of postmetaphysical approaches to prayer by considering Caputo's turn to radical apophasis, Marion's hymnic transcendence of ontology, and Lacoste's reflections on preparousiacal liturgy.

THE DIVERSITY OF POSTMETAPHYSICAL PRAYER

A Certain Apophasis: John Caputo

We begin with Caputo not only because he summarizes the tradition leading from Heidegger, to Levinas, to Derrida but also because he develops the most explicitly prayerful and most nearly Christian formulation of this tradition. His early works constitute a somewhat auspicious beginning but also give some indication of the difficulties that are to come. In *The Mystical Element in Heidegger's Thought* (1978), Caputo examines Heidegger's nontheological appropriation of Eckhartian mysticism and concludes that "there is nothing in Heidegger's '*Ereignis*' to love and much to fear."[5] Caputo argues, in effect, that *Gelassenheit* becomes fatalistic unless it continues to be understood within the prayerful context from which it initially emerged. In this respect, he basically mirrors Balthasar's response to Heidegger, even though he appears to give somewhat greater credence to Heidegger's concerns. In his next major work, *Heidegger and Aquinas: An Essay on Overcoming Metaphysics* (1982), Caputo embraces Heidegger's "destruction" of metaphysics and contends that Heidegger is right to implicate Aquinas in it. At the same time, however, Caputo suggests that the inspiration for Heidegger's somewhat Eckhartian "alethiology" could have come, almost just as well, from the "mystical life" that hides behind Aquinas's ostensibly irredeemable scholastic system. Thus Caputo seeks to recover Aquinas largely in spite of the ontological and theological theory that Aquinas actually articulates, whereas the Balthasar of *Wahrheit*, by contrast, integrates a Thomistic and Heideggerian perspective without quite so sharply dividing Thomas against himself.[6]

After these early texts, Caputo's work begins to be characterized by a Levinasian and Derridean purification of Heidegger's thought, which ultimately yields a form of prayer that is idiosyncratically Jewish, Greek, and Christian; weakly theological; postethically ethical; at best, only marginally doxological and thus maximally apophatic. The development of this unique style of thought occurs in several steps. In *Radical Hermeneutics: Repetition, Deconstruction, and the*

Hermeneutic Project (1987), Caputo repeats his call for a releasement to mystery, grounds this disposition in Eckhart and Heidegger, but adds an explicit concern for the suffering face of the other which he gleans from Levinas, and then recommends a somewhat Derridean form of indecision between "religious" (Abrahamic, Augustinian) and "tragic" (Nietzschean) interpretations of this suffering. The absolute mystery that Aquinas thinks as God and Heidegger thinks as *Ereignis* is translated by Caputo's radical hermeneutics into a strictly indecipherable *other*, which may finally approximate one or the other, or neither of these two. Caputo argues that the "identity" of this other must remain undecided. Neither ontology nor theology convincingly captures it. Drawing on Eckhart's famous prayer for "God to rid him of 'God,'" Caputo emphasizes the profound indeterminacy of our discourses and interpretative frameworks. Although he had once associated Eckhart closely with Aquinas, now he reads him more as a prefiguration of Derrida.[7]

Caputo's *Demythologizing Heidegger* (1993) presents a critique of Heidegger's dangerously mythological and discriminatory Greco-German doxology. However, the goal of this critique is precisely to discover "another Heidegger, a Heidegger against Heidegger, a Heidegger who represents all that Heidegger fought against." The sources for this other (of) Heidegger are primarily Levinas and Derrida, but more the latter than the former.[8] Caputo deeply appreciates Levinas's sense of radical responsibility for the other, which stems largely from the tradition of Jewish law and prophecy that Heidegger unjustly excludes. But, as Caputo clarifies in *Against Ethics: Contributions to a Poetics of Obligation with Constant Reference to Deconstruction* (1993), he likewise objects to Levinas's appeal to "the glory of the infinite," arguing, in Derridean fashion, that it seems to imply some sort of metaphysically (hence, illegitimately) secured hyperousiological presence.[9] In short, Caputo departs from Heidegger and Levinas by bracketing their respective forms of doxology, but he also rehabilitates versions of Heidegger's *Ereignis* and Levinas's asymmetrical responsibility in a more indeterminate Derridean mode.

Caputo's *The Prayers and Tears of Jacques Derrida: Religion without Religion* (1997) offers a sustained defense of the idea that prayer can endure—and even be thought more rigorously—without doxology. Because doxology, even as it appears within certain Christian and Heideggerian forms of "negative theology," seems to depend on a perhaps illusory, strictly unverifiable, and politically exclusionary promise of presence, Derrida and Caputo are inclined to discount it as part of metaphysics and as part of the metaphysically supported history of Western violence. For both thinkers, then, a more authentic passage beyond metaphysics requires that one abandon any appeal to a grounding presence or determinate destination of discourse—whether this is identified with the event of being, in the case of Heidegger, or with the God who lies beyond being, which one finds in the mystical theological works of Plotinus, Dionysius, Eckhart, Angelus Silesius, and more recently Levinas and Marion. Derrida and Caputo suggest that all of these forms of doxological thought need to be surpassed by an unrelenting desert of thought, a "general apophatics" undergirded by a thoroughgoing nominalism. They maintain, moreover, that it is only in this way that a radically inclusive, counterviolently democratic, and impossibly possible community of friendship can be prepared.[10]

In a rather broad sense, prayer survives in this desert as a request made of the other, anyone at all, any singularity ("God" here is but one example among many, and perhaps not even a legitimate example). But prayer also takes on the apocalyptic and affirmative form of an invitation to come (*viens!*), offered to whatever or whoever the arriving other may be. Caputo approves this other in advance, without knowledge, through the words of an indiscriminate and ostensibly nondiscriminatory multilingual refrain: yes, *oui, Ja, Amen.*[11] One senses here—in this exercise of praise without praise or apocalyptic without apocalyptic—the specter of Heidegger's "last God," purged of its deadly nationalism, but nevertheless characterized by a similarly problematic emptiness. It seems one can say "yes" only to indeterminacy.

Caputo likewise highlights Derrida's deconstructive reading of Augustine's *Confessions*, in which Augustine is prized for a question that he asks but not for any of the doxological responses that he provides for it: "What do I love when I love my God?" For Caputo, to leave this question open is to begin to pray in the most authentic sense, that is, agnostically. Left unanswered, Augustine's question constitutes a desire, a passion, a "pure" prayer for something unknown. The saying of this prayer promises the other; it calls from and to the other; and it is wounded by the other. Caputo takes Chrétien's expression as his own: this Derridean prayer is a "wounded word."[12] But the other that is addressed by such a prayer has given no trustworthy access to itself and does not authorize any kind of doxology. This other, therefore, has no approachability—not even one that would remain mostly veiled or incomprehensible, not even one that might be expressed confidently as goodness or mercy or salvation.

In the end, the hard-won abstemiousness of Caputo's Derridean prayer is not as hospitable to the other as it purports to be, at least if God and those who pray to God are allowed to count as others. Caputo's promotion of cultured indecision indicates a decision in favor of substituting something else in the place of God. The replacement is not Heidegger's *Ereignis* but nevertheless something very much like it. This point is confirmed by Caputo's *The Weakness of God: A Theology of the Event* (2006). Although Derrida's deconstruction continues to be evident in this work, Caputo also passes beyond it in certain respects by appropriating more elements of Christian scripture and theology, albeit in changed form. He styles the second half of the book as a commentary on the Our Father and the final chapter as an act of thinking prayer, with significantly more conviction than Derrida seems to allow himself. Caputo declares: "I am trying to think while praying, to pray while thinking, praying like mad—for theology, for theology's truth, for the event." He goes on to say that he is praying "with both hands": on the one hand, with the name of God, that is, theologically, in the most explicit way since his first works; but also, on the other hand, with absolute deference given to "the event." This is a name that he opposes to all other names; a name that he does not name as a name (at least not in the same way that he constantly names God as a name); a name that, therefore, enjoys a kind of unquestioned preeminence or authority.[13] It is *as though* the event and it alone (certainly not God) constitutes an exception to the rule of nominalism. The first hand holds a signifier, the second draws close to a signified. As in Heidegger's thought, so too here, the event, the mysterious and indefinite happening of all things to which phenomenology has a more reliable access—of which it can be more certain—proves more decisive than the mystery of God, and of divine love, around which there remains a cloud of suspicion.

And yet, intriguingly, Caputo partially defrays the costs to prayer through the still rather hesitant recovery of doxology that he offers in this text. He now concretizes his "yes" with a biblical meditation on the lilies of the field: "Listen to the lilies of the field, listen to their 'yes,' the *parole soufflé* that breathes the breath of 'good' through things. . . . The lilies of the field live for free, gratuitously, almost by chance, like a gift, an-economically; and behold how gloriously they are arrayed." Caputo suggests that the *logos* and *doxa* of the lilies communicate the benediction of Elohim; they express the blessing of God upon the natural world; they indicate that the event is good. Jesus also makes an appearance in Caputo's account and bears witness to the goodness of the event, precisely in his weeping for the death of Lazarus. Caputo proclaims that Jesus's tears are the "tears of God," which disclose the "compassion, the healing, the restoration of lost life." Unfortunately, however, the part of the story where Lazarus comes out of the tomb is allegorized away: to resurrect, in Caputo's partial reading, is finally nothing other than to weep for another. His retrieval of certain aspects of Christian doxology is very selective and significantly impaired from the start by his uncompromising rejection of divine sovereignty, which leaves God without the power to create or to save, and which leaves prayer without much realistic hope.[14]

The consistent problem with Caputo's approach to prayer is that it tends to be overdetermined by a law of indeterminacy. Even in *The Weakness of God*, which to some extent revives the doxological promise of his earliest texts, he does not let prayer come forth and show itself except in terms of a theory of the event, which, although it constitutes a considerable advance over Heidegger's similar theory, still does not do enough to accommodate the mystery of prayer on its own terms of divine-and-creaturely freedom and love. More so than Heidegger, Levinas, Derrida, and other modern and postmodern philosophers who precede him, Caputo makes a point of recommending prayer as worthy of thought. But very much like the rest, he disqualifies without sufficient warrant much that is included in the mystery of prayer, especially as it has been thought and practiced within the Christian tradition.

The warrant that Caputo seems to give for this disqualification can be expressed as follows. On the one hand, he suggests that the hyperbolic doubt pioneered by Descartes can no longer be effectively held at bay by post-Cartesian egological and ontotheological metaphysics. He further reasons that the demise of this characteristically modern way of attempting to secure epistemic certainty does not only challenge modernity; on the contrary, the ramifications of such doubt extend to premodern metaphysical and doxological traditions as well. This doubt operates in Caputo's works under the headings of nominalism, indeterminacy, apophatics, deconstruction, and so on—but now without any pretensions of a foundationalist antidote and with an explicit political valence. To deny self-grounded and self-grounding truth here means to welcome the other. On the other hand, Caputo is not content with a philosophical skepticism so thoroughgoing that it would be virtually indistinguishable from nihilism. Instead, he wants there to be desire, passion, compassion, and affirmation; he wants to say "yes" and not merely "no." Chastened by his critical perception of the generalized dubitability of discourse, he nevertheless proposes somewhat positive forms of prayer and contemplation through his early reflections on mysticism, his phenomenology of the event, and his "weak" theology (which only consents to praise a nonomnipotent god).

Two objections can be raised against this basic form of Caputo's argument. First, it is not obvious whether or why a full Christian doxology would necessarily be incompatible with his denial of apodictic metaphysical knowledge or, relatedly, with his sense of the radically questionable and incomplete nature of discourse in general. There is no contradiction between recognizing the profound uncertainty of human knowledge (even in a politically significant way) and adoring the Trinity as the incomprehensible, almighty, and merciful source of the freedom and love that creation most ardently desires. Second, it is not clear whether or why Caputo's attenuated prayerful theology would be any less susceptible than a full Christian doxology would be to rigorous nominalist suspicion. The particular theological affirmations that he makes are neither philosophically certain, nor agreeable to all those who pray (or, for that matter, who do not pray). The contestability of his theology is thus on the same order as that of any other determinate historico-linguistic tradition admitting of deconstruction, even though it does laudably encourage a disposition of hospitality. It follows that even thinkers who take Caputo's Derridean point regarding the disputability and danger of any given interpretation of presence (and this premise is itself not entirely beyond debate) are not thereby obligated to relinquish hope in Christian doxology or to settle for Caputo's idiosyncratic approximation of it. Without accepting counterfeit certainty, epistemic naïveté, or malign indifference to oppression, one can receive, offer, and desire the glory and word of God in Christ.

Praise beyond Being: Jean-Luc Marion

Marion's early monograph *The Idol and Distance* (1977) is more decisively theological than any of Caputo's texts, and the debts to Balthasar are clear. It nevertheless resembles Caputo's work in one respect, namely insofar as it proceeds as a dialogue between Heidegger and the Christian mystical tradition. However, Marion tellingly chooses to approach this tradition not through Heidegger's Eckhart but rather through a Balthasarian reading of Dionysius the Areopagite.[15] Marion promotes Dionysius precisely because Dionysius respects what Marion calls *distance*. This term does not designate an abstract and indeterminate transcendence but rather the mystery—Trinitarian, christological, and paschal, therefore revealed—of the nevertheless infinitely hidden God. This mystery is characterized both by the expression of the ineffable in the "*res gestae* of the *Logos*" and by the appearance of the invisible in the "iconic face of Christ."[16]

Whereas Balthasar prioritizes a discussion of *doxa*, Marion concentrates on the significance of the *eikon*. What he offers, therefore, is perhaps more strictly an *iconology* than a doxology. This focus preserves the Christic character of Balthasar's contemplation but shifts the accent, perhaps only slightly, but nevertheless significantly, away from what has been phenomenally given and toward what remains withdrawn or nonphenomenalized even in what is given. Whereas the term "glory" evokes wondrous and luminous presence, the icon opens a window into distance. The arguably greater measure of apophasis in Marion's iconological approach provides some resistance against the metaphysical influence that may be felt in Balthasar's more epistemologically confident account of doxological *theoria*. And yet, despite this difference, Marion and Balthasar can agree that, in some sense, distance, or the God who abides in distance, is already *given*—for Marion in *logos* and *eikon*. But this means that his iconology can also be interpreted as a *donatology*, that is, as a contemplation of the gift. In this respect, any evident dissimilarity from the kataphatic leanings of Balthasar's doxology is somewhat diminished.

Marion argues that, for Dionysius, although distance is never abolished, it gives itself to be traversed in prayer. Indeed, prayer designates precisely the "traverse of distance." This traverse involves a permanently incomplete entry into the mystery of God, through a unified practice of receiving, offering, and desiring that which this mystery gives from itself—which is nothing other than the act of giving itself, that is, "the movement of the infinite kenosis of charity."[17] In concert with Balthasar, Marion locates the paradigmatic case of this receptive self-donation in the relation of loving distance between Father and Son and similarly positions his own description of this relation against Hegel.[18] Because the exchange of gifts that takes place within the Trinity and from the Trinity throughout creation never collapses the distance that perpetually inaugurates it, and therefore never comes to rest, it remains erotic.[19] Thus prayer implies participation in a divine love that is composed not only of abandonment (or *Gelassenheit*) to and in the gift but also of desire for that which abides in withdrawal.

Marion does not spend much time specifying the concrete significance of this sort of love in the violent context of the modern world,
nor in the realm of ethics more generally, but one can extrapolate on
the basis of several passages that that significance is not minuscule.[20]
Marion's Dionysian doxology reaffirms, in the Christian idiom of
grace and sacrament, the indispensable aspect of Levinas's quasi-
doxological ethics, namely the mediation of infinite glory in the solidarity and responsibility that one shows for the other through the
face-to-face encounter. Thus for Marion, as for Levinas, hospitality
becomes thinkable not only as an entailment of, but also even as a
definitive manifestation of, the life of prayer. At the same time, however, much more clearly than Levinas, Marion thinks prayer starting
from itself and, therefore, not merely as a synonym for ethics. In
short, Marion argues that it is only through a genuinely prayerful
form of doxology that we can welcome from the divine other, and
can thereby mediate for other others, that which both he and Levinas agree is only in this mediation finally welcomed: the gift of self-
giving love.

In his own way, then, Marion continues Balthasar's effort to
highlight the doxological features of the Christian tradition and particularly emphasizes their crystallization in love. He focuses on one
figure (Dionysius) rather than many, but the one here stands for the
many. He follows Balthasar in distinguishing the Areopagite's theology from the context of specifically Neoplatonic metaphysics that
nevertheless informs it. However, he is also more eager than Balthasar to deemphasize, wherever possible, any such influence—and
in this respect he displays the innovative, but also more selective,
character of his retrieval. Whereas Balthasar holds that Dionysius's
discourse is more prayerful than metaphysical and seems willing
to affirm both aspects in what he considers their proper relation,[21]
Marion suggests that it is prayerful and therefore *not* metaphysical
(at least according to Heidegger's standards). By Marion's account,
the terms *aitia* (cause) and *arche* (source/ground), which would seem
to secure Dionysius's affiliation with ontotheology, actually sub-
vert it. Marion contends that *aitia* is more adequately translated as
"Requisite": that is, as the distance beyond all positive and negative

predication to which the requests of the "requestants" are voiced. Despite superficial appearances, the Dionysian God would be specified neither as *causa sui* nor even as *causa prima*, but rather as the nonpredicable, incomprehensible addressee of prayer.[22] Similarly, Marion presents the Dionysian use of *arche*—embedded in the treatments of thearchy and celestial and ecclesiastical hierarchy—as diametrically opposed to "the Plotinian model of an emanation in loss." Marion argues that the gift that is transmitted through these orders is magnified, not decreased, in the redundancy of its giving; furthermore, he stresses that it is a gift of love and, therefore, not simply a dynamism definitive of the totality of being.[23]

These novel interpretations, which uncouple Dionysius from metaphysics, are arguably more faithful to that which is most promising in his doctrine, but they require one to apply a particular kind of hermeneutic to his texts and to other similar texts in the Christian tradition—a hermeneutic that allows one both to recover them as sources for the postmetaphysical style of prayerful thought that seems most necessary in the aftermath of modernity and to treat as nonnormative the historical connections between doxology and metaphysics that have been forged within such texts. At a certain point, the question becomes not merely what Dionysius or others thought in the past but what they enable us to think now. In this light, the promise of Marion's innovative reading would seem to gain strength precisely from its strategic departures from conventional exegesis. These departures importantly occur within a space that is opened up by the texts themselves and, therefore, cannot be easily dismissed as violations. They are better understood as timely and purificatory elucidations of the prayerful core of Christian doctrine.[24]

This type of hermeneutic and the particular interpretation that it allows of Dionysius are also operative in Marion's limited engagement with Thomas Aquinas in *The Idol and Distance*. Not unlike Caputo's, Marion's early assessment of Aquinas is mixed: insofar as Thomas's thought is metaphysical, it proves questionable along Heideggerian lines; and yet, insofar as it carries forward the Dionysian and, hence, prayerful doctrine of divine names, it admits of retrieval in a way that the modern metaphysical projects of Descartes,

Leibniz, Kant, Hegel, and others do not.[25] And yet, Marion does not hesitate to warn his readers against the dangers of a Thomism that would (after Cajetan and Suarez) forget its Dionysian inspiration, subordinate doxology to a general philosophical theory of analogy, and thereby draw perilously close to the most problematic tendencies of modern metaphysics. In a remarkable departure from Balthasar, Marion refuses to give any straightforward endorsement to the *analogia entis*, precisely because he largely shares Heidegger's suspicion of this term.[26] His account of prayer as a (finite) traversal of (infinite) distance protects the measure and greater dissimilarity between God and creation that the *analogia entis* is meant to safeguard, but it omits the metaphysically implicated notion of entity from the realm of normative possibilities.

Marion argues that, from now on, theology—indeed, thought as such—needs to occur within a postmetaphysical *discourse of praise*. This unique type of discourse reveres distance by aiming at God through an endless array of biblical and creaturely names, both conceptual and symbolic, both positive and negative. It does so, however, without strictly affirming or denying any of them in a categorical act of predication. Instead of saying, with the verb "to be," and hence in the realm of ontology, that God "*is* or *is not* p," where "p" is a predicate adjective or predicate noun, Dionysius and Marion would have us praise (*hymnein*) God "*as* and *as not* g," where "g" refers to any gift from distance through which we are enabled to traverse but not abolish it.[27] Thus Marion's principal criterion for the overcoming of metaphysics, like Caputo's, proves to be prayer. But it is precisely prayer as praise; prayer as iconological and donatological doxology; prayer as disclosed within the origins of Christian theology and not merely in various tangentially Christian or postmodern forms of mysticism and apophasis; prayer that is, in these ways, thought more rigorously and fully as it gives itself from itself.

Like Caputo, Marion carefully considers the shifts that have occurred in the tradition leading from Heidegger, to Levinas, to Derrida. However, his assessment is ultimately more critical than Caputo's. His recovery of distance both subverts and transforms the logic of *Ereignis*, *l'autre*, and *différance*. The subversion is accomplished through an analysis of the varied sorts of conceptual idolatry that these terms represent. Marion contends that Heidegger's is a mostly kataphatic idolatry of being, which, although it escapes metaphysics, nevertheless similarly domesticates God within the horizon of phenomenological ontology; Levinas's is a "residual" idolatry, which seeks to overcome the neutrality of Heideggerian being by obligating one unconditionally to beings (i.e., the neighbor) but, thereby, continues to permit Heidegger's ontic-ontological difference to regulate the arrival of transcendence; Derrida's is an apophatic idolatry, which abstracts Heidegger's difference from ontology and from any determinate *doxa* or *logos*, but retains the problematic neutrality that characterizes Heidegger's *es gibt*.[28]

In addition to subverting these Heideggerian and post-Heideggerian modes of thought, Marion also hopes to transform them. As he puts it: "At issue is the conversion of the idol into icon."[29] Through a kind of "double reading," which he might have learned just as well from Balthasar as from Heidegger, Marion seeks to uncover the ways in which divine distance is obliquely indicated or partly phenomenalized even in Heidegger's, Levinas's, and Derrida's largely immanentizing discourses. He contends that, insofar as Heidegger's *Ereignis* involves a withdrawal that both transcends and gives being, it can be approached as an icon of distance. He similarly affirms Levinas's and Derrida's efforts to move beyond ontology and insists that what ultimately speaks in Levinas's thought is "not being, nor phenomenology, but, through them, the word of the prophets and the revelation of the Law"—that is, crucial voices of biblical doxology.[30]

Marion gives an analogous double reading to Nietzsche and Hölderlin: two of Heidegger's most privileged sources. In Nietzsche's poetic portrayals of Ariadne in *The Dithyrambs of Dionysus*, Marion detects a somewhat christological profile of receptivity to divine distance. Thus, although Nietzsche's earlier Zarathustran manner of saying "yes" to all things seems to fulfill modern metaphysics (as Heidegger controversially maintains in his lectures), Marion suggests that it ultimately gives way to another kind of affirmation which, for Nietzsche himself, may be more decisive, namely a releasement toward the overwhelming presence of God. In a similar way, Marion understands Hölderlin to authorize not only a poetic dwelling upon the earth, hence within the fourfold of being theorized by Heidegger, but also a poetic dwelling in the condition of filial distance: that is, within the measure that is given in the gloriously crucified and resurrected Son of the Father.[31] All in all, Marion shows that the most powerful inheritors and progenitors of Heidegger's conceptual idolatry admit, without exception, of iconic re-inscription. The decisive point against Caputo is precisely that they *need* it. The import of Marion's post-Balthasarian reading of Dionysius is determined largely by the fact that it provides the prayerful context within which such a conversion from idol to icon can occur.

Marion reiterates his Dionysian-Balthasarian response to Heidegger in *God without Being* (1982) but does so with several adjustments. He identifies the problem of idolatry more specifically with ontology. Accordingly, he locates the danger more in Heidegger than in the post-Heideggerians and lets Aquinas's account of divine *esse* (and not merely its later reception) take on a greater proportion of the blame.[32] Moreover, although his proposed iconological and donatological alternative to ontology continues to have explicit ties with Dionysius, he now articulates it, on the one hand, with more copious reference to scripture and to the Eucharist and, on the other hand, with more overt concern for phenomenological rigor.[33] Many of these adjustments can be understood as enhancements, but the intensified focus on ontology and phenomenology presages future difficulties.

It suffices to note, without extensive textual citation, that Marion's alleged "theological turn" in phenomenology begins, and then develops partially in reaction to the provocation of Dominique Janicaud, precisely as a "phenomenological turn" away from theology: that is, away from prayer as the sine qua non of postmetaphysical thought.[34] One can sense the burgeoning possibility for such a movement in some of the decisions that Marion makes in *God without Being*: if ontology is the name of the crisis, and if a phenomenology of the icon and the gift can be performed outside the limits of ontology, then ultimately a well-executed non-ontological phenomenology may accomplish what needs to be accomplished for thought. This is the logic that will guide many of Marion's subsequent texts. Whereas *God without Being* points in this direction only while remaining a work of explicit Dionysian doxology and *Prolegomena to Charity* (1986) keeps silent about Dionysius only while not forgetting the doxologically and liturgically constituted traversal of distance,[35] *Reduction and Givenness* (1989), *Being Given* (1997), *In Excess* (2001), and *The Erotic Phenomenon* (2003) are intentionally, but not for this reason unproblematically, delimited by a philosophically motivated suspension of distance and, simultaneously, of prayer.[36]

One could argue that important elements of a "phenomenology of prayer" emerge in these studies of givenness, saturation, and eros.[37] However, the promise of this approach is limited by the separation that it allows between the manner of reflection (phenomenology) and the matter (prayer). Although Marion streamlines, inverts, and innovates the methodological requirements of the former, he nevertheless does not keep them from forestalling in principle the intellectual agency of the latter. In other words, Marion seems to analyze prayer as a phenomenon—in the limits of phenomenology alone—only while ceasing to promote it as a finally decisive hermeneutic. Although prayer is perhaps never far from Marion's mind, for a considerable period of time he allows his arguments to be defined more by the strategy of bracketing than by the discourse of praise.

One might question whether Marion's return to Dionysius in the final chapter of *In Excess* constitutes a deviation from this trend.[38] And yet, although this text seems more equipped than any other to challenge the thesis that Marion's thought departs from prayer, it also ultimately confirms it. Marion offers the discourse of praise—here renamed "de-nomination"—as an answer to the Derridean objection that Christian apophasis involves a surreptitious hyperextension of the "metaphysics of presence." The debate between Marion and Derrida disintegrates under the pressure of several equivocations: Marion defines "metaphysics," "presence," and "predication" more narrowly than Derrida, narrowly enough to render the doxological tradition exempt (including not only Dionysius, but also Aquinas),[39] whereas Derrida interprets these terms broadly enough to implicate this tradition as a whole. As a result, the two thinkers quickly begin to talk past one another. Even still, one point seems clear: Marion's proposal has in its favor a greater openness to prayer. It is on such grounds, and not by means of any futile attempt to satisfy Derrida's maximally apophatic criteria (a tack which Marion sometimes seems tempted to pursue), that his thought outpaces deconstruction.

However, Marion's recasting of divine distance as the "saturated phenomenon *par excellence*" seems to jeopardize the advantage that he has gained.[40] According to Marion, a phenomenon is "saturated" when the intuition (givenness, self-showing, phenomenalization) of it exceeds the intentionality (conceptualization, interpretation, predication, nomination) through which we seek to understand it. He argues persuasively that Dionysius attests, together with several other representatives of Christian doxology, that the phenomenality of the de-nominated and glorified God of mystical theology satisfies this definition of saturation in an exemplary way. The problem is that Marion now refuses the crucial question of the ever greater non-phenomenality of God—the question precisely of God's distance, which he had formulated in his earlier works. In short, there is no longer any serious discussion of a divine excess that would not be immanent to the phenomenologist's consciousness (which does not, for Marion, mean adequately comprehended by it).

Indeed, a genuinely prayerful traversal of distance becomes unthinkable precisely to the extent that Marion locates thought within the language game of apodictic phenomenology. This language game is governed by principles designed to achieve epistemic certainty—in Marion's case: "as much reduction, as much givenness."[41] Whether or not this is his intention, by insisting on such principles he effectively suggests that Dionysian discourse attains its intellectual rigor only by allowing itself to be situated in a characteristically modern tradition of philosophical "indubitability" proceeding from Descartes, to Kant, to Husserl, and finally to Marion himself (Heidegger's "turn" makes his inclusion here questionable). Admittedly, Marion seeks to minimize the costs of this tradition's (self-)certificatory methods and to eliminate its previous metaphysical entailments. His efforts in this regard are without equal. But his limited affiliation continues to come with a price: it leads him to hold that, even insofar as it is given, the excess of God must be treated only as a "formal possibility." He maintains that the transcendence of the Requisite must be suspended, not for the sake of objectivity (Husserl) or ontology (Heidegger), but nevertheless in order to secure an immanent sphere of givenness that neither entails nor denies the reality of any giver.[42] As a result, prayer's unique manner of interpretation must likewise be put into parentheses, at least insofar as prayer dares to address and thereby place trust in the infinitely hidden actuality of God.[43]

The Erotic Phenomenon takes Marion's technique of dismantling and reconstituting the post-Cartesian tradition perhaps as far as it can go. In Descartes's search for epistemic certainty, Marion discovers the question of love, precisely the passive question of whether I am loved, and then seeks to show with phenomenological rigor that I am *assuredly* loved—that is, that my exposure to the vanity of being (which fuels the nihilistic course of modern metaphysics) is necessarily refuted by the love of another, *any* other. This argument differs strikingly from the one that Marion advances in *God without Being*, in which he identifies the "reverse of vanity" exclusively with the prayerful openness to the loving counterintentionality of God that is given in the icon and in which he likewise treats other experiences of eros as vulnerable to vanity's sway. By contrast, in Marion's later "erotic reduction," he approaches the distance of divine love as no more than a formal possibility—that is, as one hypothetical eventuality among others. He indicates that this possibility is bestowed (if ever) upon us by something very much like *Ereignis*; Marion calls it "the anonymous event"; it—precisely "it"—operates as the neutralized giver of givenness that is not known or praised as a giver, that is, as love, as God.[44] Marion displays here a remarkable closeness with Heidegger and Caputo, but precisely on a point where he could (and arguably should) differ.

Marion's *Au lieu de soi: L'approche de Saint Augustin* (2008) reverses the trend of the last several works by making an explicit return to prayer.[45] Marion disguises this text as a summation or application of his innovative phenomenological analyses, and at one level it does admit of this sort of reading, but it is more deeply constituted by the language game that Augustine—and not phenomenology—demands, and this is precisely the *discourse of confession*. Marion characterizes confession as the self-implicating communication to God of one's own and of our (humanity's, creation's) sin and praise. He argues that, like Dionysius's hymnic speech, Augustine's *confessio* "predicates nothing of God," does not think God as *causa sui*, and does not finally assimilate God to ontology (*idipsum*, he suggests, is not being).[46] At the same time, Marion does not reduce confession to apophasis but rather treats it as a positive response to the word and beauty of God, which it incessantly receives, offers, and desires.[47] In these crucial respects, Augustine's confession comes to light as a vital wellspring for postmetaphysical doxology.[48]

From Marion's discussion, it becomes clear that Augustinian confession differs most overtly from Dionysian prayer in its direct involvement of a self (*soi*)—precisely Augustine himself—who, though singular, nevertheless speaks to us, with us, perhaps even for us, in company with the whole of creation. Marion contests Descartes's *ego* and Heidegger's *Dasein* at several places in the text, in order to disclose Augustine's nonsubjective, non-ontological, deeply enigmatic and prayerful alternative. According to Marion, the Augustinian self is not its own or anything else's foundation (*subjectum*) and lives without proper essence. But it is not for this reason devoid of positive significance. Rather, it is constituted from time immemorial, and throughout the temporal *différance* of life, as a Christic and Trinitarian icon of the invisible God. Its life in the world is narrated as one of repentance and conversion: that is, as a search for holiness that is responsive to the call of the divine will (thus it serves as a figure of responsibility).[49]

Most remarkably of all, this self is defined by prayer. As Marion puts the point: "I do not say my confession; I am my confession."[50] Marion argues that, for Augustine and for those (such as Marion himself) who wish to put themselves in the place of Augustine's self, confession necessarily functions as the "sole rule of appearance" for questions and phenomena and, moreover, occupies the place of thought's principle of principles, which Marion calls here "the first thought (*la première pensée*)."[51] Hence, although the confessional self is given, saturated, and erotic, these structures of phenomenality, on their own, do not adequately disclose it. At some point, it is necessary to pass beyond not only metaphysics, not only objective phenomenology (Husserl) and ontological phenomenology (Heidegger), not only prephenomenological ethics (Levinas) and postphenomenological deconstruction (Derrida and Caputo), but also non-ontological phenomenology (the "middle" Marion), in order both to think this prayerful self and to think *as oneself* a prayerful self.

This eminently prayerful conclusion gives some a posteriori justification to Marion's strictly phenomenological studies, which can now be read precisely as preparations for the thinking of prayer. Their promise as a response to the grave dilemmas of our contemporary age is greatly amplified by this confessional recontextualization, which mirrors Marion's earlier transformative "double reading" of pre- and post-Heideggerian thinkers, along with Heidegger himself, in *The Idol and Distance*. Here his *own* thought changes from idol to icon. With Dionysius and Augustine, Marion gathers together, by way of synecdoche, an enormous doxological tradition, both East and West, and demonstrates not only its abiding but also its renewed pertinence. This tradition enables Marion to resist the dangers in the very philosophical practices that, nevertheless, also help him to think it with fresh insight. Hence, from the perspective of the final destination, the detour in the middle of his itinerary proves productive, even though, were the return route to prayer left unfinished, it would have meant another typically modern exile.

Liturgical Anticipation: Jean-Yves Lacoste

In comparison with Marion, Lacoste does not tend to risk the same sort of philosophical deferral. Although he sometimes approaches prayer through a phenomenological reduction, he nevertheless calls the sufficiency of this procedure into question by performing what he names a "theological reduction" (*réduction théologique*), which brackets many (but not all) claims that have supposedly been certified by previous acts of bracketing.[52] In general, he allows phenomenological method an important place but also turns to prayer as the source for a more definitive hermeneutic. In *Note sur le temps* (1990), he specifies the analogical character of this methodological arrangement. He offers a largely (but not exclusively) Heideggerian account of being-in-the-world and then reaffirms, adjusts, and ultimately transgresses it through a creaturely, paschal, and eschatological description of being-prayerfully-before-God.[53] The latter mode of understanding develops both *in* and *beyond* the former.[54] In short, the riddle of the proper relationship between philosophy and theology finds in Lacoste the rather traditional answer of analogy. His sense of philosophy is more phenomenological and Heideggerian than Balthasar's, and this sets him apart; his view of theology, however, is no less prayerful.

The complexity of Lacoste's engagement with Heidegger comes to light in his two major monographs, which provide an abiding foundation for his later articles. In *Note sur le temps*, he focuses his energy on Heidegger's analysis of temporality in *Being and Time*. Whereas Heidegger constructs an "eschatology of meaning" out of *Dasein*'s being-toward-death, Lacoste takes the temporal finitude (and, hence, mortality) of *Dasein* as a sign that we are not yet in possession of the *eschaton* and, therefore, not yet privileged to know with phenomenological certainty the final significance of our existence. In other words, Lacoste accepts Heidegger's description of facticity (death as existentially constitutive) but rejects, on both phenomenological and theological grounds, Heidegger's prematurely apocalyptic assessment of it (death as absolutely definitive). For Lacoste, the condition of temporality is a condition of provisionality, incompletion, and nonknowledge concerning the essential truth of our being, and phenomenology can appropriately claim no more than this.[55] Theology, too, has to remain somewhat reticent. At most, our temporally limited condition allows for a sense of theologically informed promise, inchoation, or anticipation, which nevertheless respects "the eschatological *reserve* of the ever greater God." As Lacoste says in the final lines of the text, "until the hour of our death, we can watch, and pray."[56] That is all. Theology cannot give more than prayer—which is to say, for Lacoste, hope. Any other manner of being either denies our temporality or, which amounts to the same thing, absolutizes it.

Lacoste's debate with Heidegger becomes somewhat more complex in *Experience and the Absolute* (1994), insofar as he gives more attention to the influence of Hölderlin. And yet, his argument is very similar. According to Lacoste, Heidegger's discussion of the fourfold event of being seems, if anything, only to obscure more greatly the preeschatological condition of humanity and, hence, the genuine possibility of prayer.[57] On the whole, Lacoste's assessment of Heidegger's Hölderlinian doxology echoes Balthasar's protest against a hidden identity-philosophy and Marion's warnings about the horizon of ontology but translates these critiques into the terms of time and experience—that is, into a conversation focused primarily on the constitutive features of human existence (the "*disputatio de homine*"). This anthropological locus adds important existential texture to the post-Balthasarian critique of Heidegger.

Lacoste develops his interpretation of prayer more extensively in *Experience and the Absolute* than he does in *Note sur le temps* and gives prayer a technical name: *liturgy*. He defines liturgy as "the logic that presides over the encounter between man and God writ large."[58] This definition clearly broadens the use of the term beyond the limits of ritualized collective worship but nevertheless encourages one to treat this more narrowly liturgical context as paradigmatic of the divine-human relationship as a whole. Lacoste suggests that the paradigm of liturgy helps us to think of this relationship in a manner that respects eschatological distance. Without factually exempting us from being-in-the-world and dwelling-upon-the-earth, liturgy brackets these conditions, questions their ultimacy, and exposes us, usually without immediate experiential confirmation, to the infinitely hidden presence of God, for which we must wait in vigil. Liturgy, therefore, has a nocturnal character. Any overwhelming experience of the daylight of God in the present—attested by the mystics, for instance—remains exceptional and constitutes no more than a foretaste of the *eschaton*.[59]

Lacoste's argument against Heidegger redounds to modern metaphysics as a whole.[60] He indicates that this intellectual tradition finds itself in crisis, not so much because it is ontological (as Marion suggests), but more exactly because it reduces the absolute to something that can be experienced adequately or known apodictically in history. Friedrich Schleiermacher's doctrine of religious experience—which, whether one counts it as metaphysical or not, certainly manifests a considerable closeness with metaphysics—comes under Lacoste's scrutiny insofar as it construes the absolute as always already accessible to feeling.[61] Lacoste maintains that Hegel, the modern metaphysician par excellence, exhibits a more complicated but nevertheless deeply related form of the same problem: for the Hegelian "sage," who already supposedly lives at the end of history, the "absolute future *is* the present reality."[62] In short, Heidegger, Schleiermacher, and Hegel—together with other figures of the tradition of contemporary philosophy that they represent—run into serious difficulties precisely by forgetting liturgy and its "preeschatological site."

Lacoste interestingly argues that the recovery of liturgy cannot occur without ontology—albeit of a particular sort. In this respect, he moves against the current of Marion's thought and positions his own project in a different relation with Levinas. Against Levinas's hyperbolically preontological rhetoric, Lacoste maintains that "our openness to the good is . . . held in the ambiguity of our being." Thus, although the infinite calls us outside of ontology—that is, in Lacoste's idiom, beyond the chiaroscuro of worldly existence—he insists that we receive this ethical call and must respond to it precisely within the manifest limits of this existence, which Heidegger's phenomenological ontology more or less persuasively articulates. And yet, in deference to Levinas, Lacoste is willing to embrace Heidegger's ontological analysis only if, on the one hand, it can be restricted to a discourse concerning the "atotality" (*l'atotalité*) of temporal being and if, on the other hand, it can be situated within a liturgical anticipation of the kingdom of God which sheds light on our ethical duties in the here and now.[63] In short, Lacoste retrieves Levinas's infinite from its anarchical place before being and rearticulates it as an eschatological vocation that becomes audible to the greatest extent only in liturgy, which, though it symbolically subverts the logic of the world, does not factually escape it. Thus, in keeping with the analogical structure of his thought, Lacoste locates liturgy, together with the requisite responsibility and hospitality that it illuminates, both in and beyond being.

If Lacoste's proximity to Przywara on the question of analogy supplies an elegant solution to the problem of the relationship between phenomenology and theology, another feature of Przywara's thought that Lacoste emulates has a more ambiguous status. To wit, both Przywara and Lacoste display a preference for a highly conceptual and formal style of discourse, in which a general account of the structure of something is prized over a more poetically rich or experientially eventful construal. To his credit, Lacoste approaches God as an actuality but nevertheless, largely, as a *formal* actuality: that is, as "the absolute." The abstractness of this term does not prevent it from doing the work that Lacoste needs it to do in his debates with Heidegger, Hegel, and other insufficiently liturgical thinkers. Moreover, the term provides the basis for a kind of "elementary grammar,"[64] or set of discursive boundaries, without which a more concrete depiction of the divine mystery would not be as doxologically rigorous. The promise of Lacoste's project is nevertheless limited in comparison with Balthasar's by its more streamlined mode of aesthetic retrieval. Lacoste alludes to various prayerful figures in the Christian tradition (e.g., Augustine, Benedict, Francis, John of the Cross, and Kierkegaard) but does not supply the sorts of dense and evocative readings that Balthasar offers.

What might seem to be no more than a stylistic difference in this case indicates a more substantive divergence: whereas Balthasar positions his aesthetic contemplation between "two parousias of the Lord" and accordingly gives considerable eschatological weight to the various historically situated perceptions of divine glory that he interprets, Lacoste indirectly but clearly encourages us to interpret these perceptions with a greater sense of their preparousiacal and, hence, merely provisional character. His more or less formal analysis of temporal and experiential finitude decreases the incentive to plumb the Christian tradition and other traditions in search of wondrous disclosures of the living God. For Lacoste, liturgy is important mainly because it requires us to recognize that we are not yet conscious of that which is definitive, *not* because prayer is already overflowing with the manifest glory of the definitive. Hence, those encounters with the divine majesty that doxology has historically brought to light would appear to be somewhat diminished in significance by Lacoste's appeal to an obligatory liturgical patience. Balthasar, for his part, does not dispute the necessity of some sort of eschatological reserve. However, he strives to highlight the often-underappreciated experiential and epistemological richness of prayer's poetic, imaginative, and sensorial possibilities, which Lacoste seems, by contrast, more inclined to question.

This disparity between Balthasar and Lacoste can be taken in different ways. On the one hand, Lacoste's approach arguably retains some measure of the modern or postmodern skepticism, which Derrida and Caputo promote in a much more extreme way, concerning the meaningfulness of temporally given forms of thought and experience. In other words, his particular way of insisting on the gap between presence and parousia involves a kind of apophasis that is not entirely disconnected from the post-Cartesian desire for—and methodological pursuit of—certainty. On the other hand, Lacoste can be read more sympathetically as providing an important corrective to Balthasar's perhaps overly parousiacal interpretation of aesthetic contemplation, which, as we suggested in the last chapter, might bear traces of a problematic metaphysical influence. In short, Balthasar's "already" counterbalances Lacoste's "not yet" and vice versa. Between the two, a middle way emerges for the thinking of prayer in which one would be prepared to resist more rigorously the distinct metaphysically related pretensions of negative certainty and definitive experience to which Lacoste and Balthasar, respectively, are somewhat connected.

Although Lacoste's general attitude toward doxological aesthetics is appreciably distinct from Balthasar's, he nevertheless develops his interpretation of prayer in close contact with Balthasar's doxological aesthetics. At the beginning of *Note sur le temps*, he declares that "it is above all to the influence of Hans Urs von Balthasar that I owe that which in this book manages to be theological."[65] Elsewhere in the text, without ceasing to emphasize the need for an eschatological reserve, he contends, in harmony with Balthasar, that the covenantal word, incarnate life, crucial hour, and gloriously resurrected appearances of Christ have already been given in history, not exactly as parousia, but nevertheless as irrevocable inchoation and promise. According to Lacoste, our task is to receive, remember, and interpret these kairotic gifts in anticipation of the final manifestation of the God whose mysterious presence is already mediated sacramentally through them.[66] In *Experience and the Absolute*, Lacoste gestures toward the doxological character of his thought when he asserts that "we pray, of course, in order to praise." Arguing, by implication, against the Derridean approach to prayer, he clarifies that liturgy is not oriented toward an "absolutely other," which would have to be pursued or awaited without any knowledge whatsoever, but rather toward the absolute God who has already become known as worthy of praise, particularly in the events of Good Friday and Easter. In short, the one who prays "thinks of God and has something to think."[67] The eschatologically apophatic character of Lacoste's account of liturgy is, therefore, held in check by his kataphatic, anamnestic, laudatory, and specifically christological reception of the divine mystery. In these respects, without directly reiterating Balthasar's doxology, Lacoste demonstrates his deep sympathy for it.

All in all, Lacoste's work clearly belongs to a post-Balthasarian field of prayerful discourse. Like Marion, he treats Heidegger, Levinas, and other figures of postmetaphysical thought with greater seriousness than Balthasar but also seeks to move beyond these thinkers with considerable support from Balthasar. At stake in this complicated intellectual endeavor is precisely the rigorous thinking of prayer among the crises of modernity. In comparison with Caputo's deconstructive texts, Marion's and Lacoste's studies are much more compliant with the mystery of prayer as it gives itself in the Christian tradition. To be sure, less costly forms of the abstract philosophical apophasis that characterizes Caputo's approach also arise for Marion and Lacoste in connection with their respective reformulations of phenomenological method. Even though greatly modified, this method still leads Marion to cast God as a "formal possibility" and Lacoste to construe human experience as somewhat structurally atheological. And yet, both Marion and Lacoste largely overcome what is problematic about these positions through their reflections on praise, confession, and liturgy. They thereby lay the groundwork for a postmetaphysical doxology, which is significantly less restrictive than Caputo's apophatic prayer, still resistant against Heideggerian suspicions and dangers, and deeply informed by the *doxa* and *logos* of the Christian tradition.

THE EXCESS OF INTIMACY: JEAN-LOUIS CHRÉTIEN

A poet, a thinker—perhaps necessarily in this order—Chrétien does not merely theorize prayer; he lets it appear. His texts of prose, like those of John of the Cross, are haunted by his poetry, as by a dazzlingly dark shadow. That which he endeavors to think in them is nothing other than that which he writes elsewhere in a "subtler language."[68] The dialogue between thinker and poet, which Heidegger pursues principally in remembrance of Hölderlin, takes place in Chrétien's work almost as a soliloquy: in a sense, he occupies both roles. A moment's reflection reveals, however, that the inseparably poetic and prosaic word of Chrétien is far from solipsistic. It is best understood not as the expression of an individual but as the echo of a chorus. A multitude of voices, a multitude much greater than Heidegger's highly selective conversation allows, resounds in the textured and intertextual unity of Chrétien's voice. The deepest meditation on Chrétien's thought would need to consider his poetry as such; however, we shall have to restrict ourselves here to a preliminary exploration of the polyphonic discourse that he pursues in tandem with it.

Postmetaphysical Phenomenology and Theology

First, it is necessary to specify in what sense Chrétien's thought qualifies as postmetaphysical. In his "Retrospection" (1999), he explains that religious and mystical thought and speech have frequently seen and spoken higher, farther, and otherwise than metaphysics in the form that Heidegger has defined for us. And it is necessary to hear their promises. For they are not obsessed and blinded by the human project of total self-assurance and self-understanding as we truly are (to paraphrase St. Paul), in transparency: they are rooted at each instant in the hearing of an other Word that wounds body and soul, and which they know that, if it wounds completely, could never be completely understood—not even in eternity.[69]

Although Chrétien accepts the point that metaphysics, in Heidegger's sense, constitutes a threat, and particularly for the contemporary world, he questions the extent to which this classification comprehends what is actually at stake in many intellectual traditions, including both pagan and Christian, which he suggests are characterized by a prayerful vulnerability to a divine word. Already in *Lueur du secret* (Glimmer of the secret, 1985), he does not dispute the continuity between Dionysius the Areopagite and non-Christian figures of Neoplatonism (such as Proclus), as Marion does in *The Idol and Distance*, but rather understands both as supporting a spiritually fruitful "hermeneutic of obliquity," which does not intend to comprehend or master the "most high" but instead only to approach it reverently and paradoxically through the "apparent forms of the lowest beings." The Christian tradition has in its favor a recognition of the cross as the dissimilar symbol par excellence, and this christological insight sets that tradition apart in a decisive way, but it does not warrant, for Chrétien, the dismissal of non-Christian forms of the hermeneutic of obliquity as though they were easily assimilable to Heidegger's account of metaphysics.[70] In this respect, his approach seems closer to Balthasar's than to Marion's; and yet Chrétien, more clearly than Balthasar, finds a place for Neoplatonism not insofar as it is metaphysical but insofar as it is prayerful. In effect, he reads this philosophical tradition the way Marion reads Dionysius, which is to say, for the most part, in prayerful opposition to metaphysics.

A similar style of interpretation appears in several other texts. For example, in *L'effroi du beau* (The shock of the beautiful, 1987), drawing especially on the myth of the *Phaedrus*, Chrétien presents Plato as a thinker of the erotic—and finally pious and cultic—relationship between the human lover and the permanently ungraspable divine beloved. Although he maintains that "Platonic love is not as cordial as the love revealed by the Bible," he nevertheless contends, against conventional metaphysical exegesis, that it is "given above all as nonknowledge" and as "praise." Plato does not ultimately leave us with an apodictic account of being as such and as a whole but rather with a mythologically sheltered question: "How to think the act of praise, if it is essentially required by the encounter with beauty, and as included in this very encounter?" Chrétien's search for a promising response to this question takes him beyond Plato to an elucidation of Christian, and more exactly "Christic," prayer, but the intriguing point at the moment remains that he invites Plato into the conversation without endorsing metaphysics—indeed, precisely in order to resist it.[71]

Chrétien's argument in *The Unforgettable and the Unhoped For* (1991) does not depart from this pattern. He contests the "purely rational" (Leibnizian, Kantian, and Hegelian) interpretations of Platonic recollection that have reduced Plato's sense of the immemorial—that is, the excess that always already precedes human consciousness—to the modern metaphysical doctrine of the a priori which human reason would universally and necessarily possess. Plotinus confirms and augments Chrétien's nonmetaphysical recasting of this ancient philosophical tradition. Chrétien summarizes his analysis in this way: "With respect to the Good, Plotinus is not so much a thinker of 'total presence' as a thinker of immemorial presence, which is an entirely different thing." In other words, for Plato, and for Plotinus as well, the anamnestic mind is not endowed with complete foundational access to that which it seeks to understand but, on the contrary, must acknowledge that its own sphere of awareness remains forever posterior to an infinite other that it cannot recuperate. This particular line of interpretation enables Chrétien to argue that Heideggerian self-forgetting and Levinasian diachrony—two influential examples of postmetaphysical thought—are anticipated by a Platonism other than that which moderns tend to remember, a Platonism that has already in some sense begun to pray.[72] In short, even in those places where Chrétien speaks in harmony with thinkers that one might quickly classify as metaphysical, he does so only while combating, more rigorously than Heidegger and somewhat more overtly than Balthasar, the self-assured, totalizing *noesis* and concomitant antipathy toward prayer which constitute the crisis of modern metaphysics.

The relation between Chrétien's thought and phenomenology is no less subtle than its relation with metaphysics. He seems to insist on his inclusion in the phenomenological tradition by mentioning it in the titles of several of his texts, and Janicaud critiques him on precisely these grounds.[73] In contention, of course, is the precise meaning of "phenomenology." The particular style of thought to which Chrétien affixes this term does not entail the typical demand for epistemic certainty, does not concern itself exclusively with immanence, does not limit phenomena to the status of formal possibilities, does not necessitate a primarily formal account of actual structures, and does not take for granted the adequacy of previous phenomenological horizons (objectivity, being, *Ereignis*, the other, *différance*, givenness, etc.).[74] At the same time, Chrétien is deeply informed by and remains conversant with many of the greatest representatives of the phenomenological tradition and embraces their commitment to the task of attending patiently and rigorously to that which, insofar as it allows itself to be accessed, calls for this sort of attention (i.e., "the things themselves"). If his phenomenology has a horizon that universally conditions what appears, it is that of a vocative and radiant excess, which is opened up ever again with the endlessly diverse and intimate arrival of speech and phenomena. The question about the legitimacy of his phenomenology as a phenomenology can be addressed only by considering to what extent this horizon without horizon lets things show themselves from themselves. Arguably it does so better than many alternatives.

The excess that saturates and transcends Chrétien's thought withdraws infinitely into the mystery of God and, therefore, demands to be interpreted not only phenomenologically but also theologically (which is not to say that these two can be sharply demarcated in his works). Although, as we have seen, Chrétien welcomes some non-Christian thinkers (mainly Platonists but also others) into his theological discourse, he ultimately favors a distinctively Christian mode of speech, at once ecumenical and Catholic, composed of a symphony of voices numbering in the hundreds, including doctrinal giants such as the Cappadocians, Augustine, Aquinas, Luther, and Calvin, but also many other figures: women and men; religious and lay; saints, monks, philosophers, theologians, mystics, poets, artists, and novelists; from the first century to the present; dwelling throughout the Mediterranean and Eastern and Western European worlds; some almost entirely unknown to modern readers; each treated with great care and sympathy, though not without the sometimes necessary nuance or correction; a host of witnesses rivaling and perhaps nearly surpassing Balthasar's. Chrétien deepens this impressive recovery of the Christian tradition with copious references to sacred scripture, which he, like Balthasar, recognizes as the inspired source of Christian contemplation.[75] Chrétien's almost exclusively occidental canon shares the strengths and limitations of Balthasar's. On the one hand, it allows for an extraordinarily rich anamnesis of Christian doxological aesthetics; on the other hand, it shows little awareness of, and consequently provides insufficient resistance against, the racial and colonial dynamics of modernity, which are inseparable from questions of aesthetics. However, what must be emphasized at the moment is that, without ceasing to think phenomenologically, Chrétien also thinks theologically. He does not treat excess as an abstraction. Instead, he receives, offers, and desires it as the glory and word of God.

Excess in Glory and Word

Chrétien develops each facet of his phenomenological and theological doxology with great originality. In "La beauté comme inchoation de la gloire (sur Hans Urs von Balthasar)" (Beauty as inchoation of glory [on Hans Urs von Balthasar], 2005), Chrétien appropriates

Balthasar's understanding of the glory of God as both inchoately present within and definitively transcending the beauty of creation.[76] At the same time, he adds his own nuance by parsing this relationship in terms of *call* and *promise*, two themes that are central to his distinctive style of prayerful reflection. In order to understand how he connects *doxa* with the call, one may consult his earlier text *The Call and the Response* (1992). Here he offers a simultaneously Platonic and Heideggerian account of the Greek etymological, but also in his view conceptually decisive, link between the beautiful (*kalon*) and the act of calling or naming (*kalein*). In light of this Greek sense, he argues that beauty is not a static property of entities but rather a mode of appearance that moves us toward what we love. He likewise explains that, in Judaism and Christianity, "the call takes on its biblical meaning of election"; it comes forth as a sovereign voice from God that both creates and saves. Quoting the Jewish philosopher Philo of Alexandria, Chrétien continues to associate this biblical call with the realm of worldly appearance: "God's voice is truly visible. Why so? Because God's every utterance is not made up of words but of deeds that are better witnessed by the eyes than by the ears."[77] The acts of creation and redemption through which the biblical God calls out to us are, therefore, given to be seen.

Although Chrétien defends a certain degree of interplay between the beauty desired by Greek antiquity and the visible activity of God attested by scripture, he does not thereby endorse a primarily optic construal of *doxa*, according to which visibility would be its most important characteristic. On the contrary, he contends that the double call of beauty and glory is addressed to the entirety of human flesh and spirit, including all of the carnal and spiritual senses (which he maintains are deeply interrelated). On the last pages of *The Call and the Response*, he meditates on the words of John of the Cross, who, speaking of his experience of "'God's touch' (*toque de Dios*) . . . describes indeed how this supernatural touch is able to radiate into bodily glory, into the glory of the whole body."[78] In the advent of Christ, the glory of God has not only appeared before our eyes but has also come into intimate contact with all of the sensitive, affective, and exposed aspects of our bodily existence. Chrétien's

Symbolique du corps: La tradition chrétienne du "Cantique des Cantiques" (Symbolism of the body: The Christian tradition of the Song of Songs, 2005) makes this point irrefutable: not only the eyes and the ears, but also the teeth, the nose, the lips, the neck, the cheeks, the hair, the breasts, the stomach, the navel, the fingers, the legs, and the feet (to mention only those parts to which Chrétien devotes distinct chapters) are naked before the call of the divine lover, vulnerable to this lover's caresses, and cherished without end in their every detail.[79]

In "Does Beauty Say Adieu?" (1998), Chrétien argues that the conventional aesthetic determinations regarding beauty and ugliness that are propagated by both popular and high philosophical culture must be entirely rethought in light of Augustine's recognition that the beauty of Christ is not constituted by his "physical appearance" but rather by "the radiance of his justice." We accordingly participate in this beauty not by virtue of any external characteristics but rather only insofar as we seek to embody "the glory of . . . [his] Spirit." Chrétien concludes that every time a face appears, in any form, however it might be judged according to the world's quite arbitrary regimes of taste, it calls for "an almost prayerful kind" of attention, as though one were preparing to make a portrait of God. In Christ, he says, all faces have become "theophanic."[80] At this point, Chrétien's doxology draws very close to Levinas's, insofar as it locates the glory of God in the face of the other, any other.

If Chrétien understands glory as a call that beckons the whole body and every-body, he also interprets it as a promise, precisely as "God's promise [which] unites the immemorial, the unforgettable, and the unhoped for." We have already encountered the immemorial as an excess of anteriority that remains permanently irrecoverable for consciousness. Here we must take note of the fact that Chrétien also defines it as "the glory of what is lost." The immemorial promises a glorious parousia that is now inaccessible to us. By contrast, the unforgettable corresponds to a parousia that, though still exceeding all human capacities for comprehension, has nevertheless made an indelible impact on us. Chrétien expresses this aspect of his doxology with characteristic elegance: "To call God unforgettable is to say that we are forever, at the most inward part of ourselves, transpierced by his light." He suggests that this luminous, wounding excess of divine presence takes on diverse forms throughout history and at different moments in our personal narratives, appearing sometimes more hidden than disclosed, sometimes more painful than joyous, but it remains throughout all of these permutations something inescapable. We cannot fathom it, but we can sense the immensity of its promise.[81]

Finally, Chrétien approaches the promise of divine glory in relation to what is unhoped for in it. He explains that "the *unhoped for* is what transcends all our expectations." Even when we hope for divine glory, we must say that we do not know we are hoping for. His discussion of this futural excess does not suffer from the same emptiness that jeopardizes the promise of Heidegger's "last God" and Derrida's messianism without messianism. Positioning his thought against these sorts of perspectives, Chrétien contends that "the unhoped for has been given, it has a place and a date"; it is identifiable as the "divine *philanthropia* [that] gives itself, . . . completely and in all suddenness, in the Incarnation."[82] Hence, the unhoped for emerges from the unforgettable and the immemorial, and is not thinkable without them. As figures of excess, these three cannot be adequately constituted for consciousness. And yet, as moments of an incarnate divine promise, they belong to the christological revelation of glory and, moreover, specify its temporality.

Chrétien's interpretation of glory intersects constantly with his understanding of the word. To approach the two as separate modes of excess would be to treat them artificially. For, as he says, "splendor itself is vocal."[83] The call and the promise are articulations of the *logos* as much as they are disclosures of *doxa*, and they are both at once. Having reflected on the one, we must still attend to the other in order to bring out its distinctive aspects. In *The Ark of Speech* (1998), Chrétien makes the phenomenological observation that "the voice . . . does not belong to itself." Speech is not possessed or invented by anyone in particular but rather "circulates and is transmitted from one voice to another and from one life to another, consuming and consummating them on the wing."[84] He notes, in another essay, entitled "Ce que la parole ne cesse de promettre" (What the word does not cease to promise, 2004), that this excess of speech that precedes our own vocal acts has already been recognized by Heidegger in the *Letter on Humanism*, precisely in his description of language as "the house of being."[85] However, Chrétien maintains that, like beauty, which is given and surpassed by glory, the human language that houses being mediates the divine *logos*, to the extent that it does, only while remaining infinitely exceeded by it. As he argues in *The Ark of Speech*, "God has already addressed man, has already spoken to him before he starts to speak." In the first pages of Genesis, God calls on humanity to name and to safeguard the animals and, thereby, to provide with an already posterior language something not unlike a house for being but nevertheless more radically soteriological in its significance: "the *first ark*" for creation.[86] In human speech, there is an excess not only of onto-logy but also of theo-logy.

Chrétien draws attention to the specifically biblical character of this doubly excessive word in his *Sous le regard de la Bible* (Under the gaze of the Bible, 2008). Although he insists that God "does not only speak to us in the Bible but in a thousand other exterior and interior ways," he nevertheless maintains that "God speaks to us in the Bible with an incomparable light and authority." The sacred scriptures expose us to the "living Word of God," which comes to us ever again in order to read and critique us (along with our "biblical criticism"). One should not be surprised to find that Chrétien cites Barth and Balthasar in support of this view. To be clear, his point is not to encourage an uncritical reading of the Bible. He acknowledges that much depends on what use we make of it, and he warns that this usage can be harmful. The implication is that great care must be taken with interpretation. What he does want to emphasize, however, is that we should approach the holy book not merely in the mode of a critic ready to dissect an inert body of text but rather in the nudity of prayer—that is, in a disposition of openness to the at once welcoming and demanding call that resounds within it.[87]

The word that calls is also a word that promises. Chrétien's argument in "Ce que la parole ne cesse de promettre" verifies this claim. In a move that effectively, if only implicitly, brings his work into conversation with Metz, Chrétien appropriates several crucial features of Walter Benjamin's analysis regarding the dangerous memory of the vanquished voices of the past, focusing in particular on Benjamin's sense that these voices promise a future in which they will be revivified. In opposition to Benjamin's Marxism, Chrétien declares that "our words cannot hold, or attempt to hold, *all* the promises of the words of the past such that these promises would form the steps of one and the same unique promise, such that humanity would be completely unified in one and the same unique axiological and normative history, and such that we would be in one way or another at the end of history."[88] On the contrary, Chrétien argues that the ultimate apocalypse of meaning, which would redeem the hopes voiced by those who have been lost to the violence of history, is not conceivable except as a work of the divine word in which all of our words can be gathered. The promise of language is attributable, in the final analysis, not merely to the excess of worldly speech, which already surpasses our comprehension, but to the excess of the immemorial, unforgettable, and unhoped-for *Logos*, who not only speaks to us but also hears and responds to our cries.[89]

The somewhat kataphatic tone of Chrétien's discussions of glory and word is gracefully supplemented by his more nearly apophatic meditations on the night and silence. In *L'antiphonaire de la nuit* (The antiphonary of the night, 1989), he supplies poetic evidence to support his phenomenological account of the mutuality of light and darkness, which are joined together by the crepuscular, transitional, and shadowy arrivals of morning and evening.[90] Along similar lines, he suggests that we are exposed to the glory of the infinite not only as to the rays of a blazing sun, which he thinks elsewhere precisely as a cleansing and mystical fire; but also as to a vast nocturnal stillness, a night hidden in the night, which nevertheless has its own exceedingly subtle forms of visibility; and finally, therefore, as to a mysterious and dynamic intermingling of the two.[91] Chrétien makes an analogous point in "The Hospitality of Silence," in which he argues that "speech and silence belong mutually to one another, and are devoted as if fraternally to one another."[92] With reference to John of the Cross, he characterizes the silence that pertains to the divine word as a "loving silence . . . of union with God." It is not defined by the mere absence of discourse but rather by the paradoxically "'silent music,' *música callada*" of nuptial encounter.[93] The play of the "theophanic" and the "theocryptic," which Chrétien identifies in his early work *Lueur du secret*, resurfaces in his subsequent analyses of the reciprocally luminescent and obscure appearances of glory and the reciprocally audible and inaudible expressions of the word.[94] Far from categorically affirming or negating "negative theology," Chrétien thinks doxology in compliance with the subtle kataphatic and apophatic manners in which it gives itself.

Responsorial Thought

The glorious, verbal, calling, and promising excess that reverberates throughout Chrétien's discourse does not overwhelm it, as an infinite torrent which would submerge and obliterate everything finite. Rather, this excess comes into his thought and into our thoughts in order to elicit from them a response—or, to be more exact, a panoply of responses. The drama of Chrétien's doxology is protected by his insistence on the importance of our act of responding, which he permits us to think not only as a prayerful practice of receiving, offering, and desiring, but also as an ethically and socially significant labor of responsibility and hospitality.

The first mode of response to consider is that of receptivity. *The Call and the Response* presents it as a kind of listening, which involves not only the ears but also the eyes and the entire body. This text suggests that we are meant to welcome the other not merely aesthetically but synesthetically, that is, with the interlaced attention of our whole fleshly and spiritual sensorium.[95] In *The Ark of Speech*, Chrétien develops a phenomenology of listening. He argues that "when I really listen *with* the other to what he himself, as he speaks, is listening to or has listened to, then it is really he to whom I am listening," for I am striving to understand the "unheard-of" that he deeply wants but is perhaps barely able to say. In this way, Chrétien locates our receptivity to divine excess precisely in the moment of respectful and patient encounter with the words of another. Chrétien clarifies that in order to listen, it is necessary to speak and to reply or, as he puts it, to make of one's voice a "luminous monstrance" for the meaning of the words and cries of another.[96] Chrétien develops this line of reflection in *Saint Augustin et les actes de parole* (Saint Augustine and the acts of speech, 2002), arguing that "listening forms for Saint Augustine the very locus of the humanity of the human being." Listening gives rise to all the other acts of speech, including the crucial act of confession (which, as we have seen, Marion also considers in great detail), but also eating, drinking, chewing, and belching (*éructer*: for Augustine, we truly nourish ourselves with the word), questioning, translating, reading, remaining silent, teaching, thinking, witnessing, crying, blessing, requesting, granting, recalling, pardoning, baptizing, groaning, and rejoicing. According to Chrétien, each of these modalities of the human voice is made possible by an actively cultivated receptivity to other voices.[97]

Chrétien offers a subtle interpretation of the episode in Luke 10:38–42, in which Martha and Mary receive Jesus into their home, in "La double hospitalité" (The double hospitality, 2002). This text must be counted as one of his most decisive and significant treatments of the theme of receptivity. After gathering together and commenting upon a diverse exegetical tradition uniting Origen, Cassian, Augustine, Gregory the Great, Aelred of Rivaulx, Aquinas, (a very non-Heideggerian) Eckhart, Teresa of Ávila, Pierre de Bérulle, Louis Chardon, and Jerome Nadal—one of the first followers of Ignatius of Loyola, who gives us the phrase "contemplation in action"— Chrétien concludes:

> It does not suffice, therefore, to be Martha and Mary; it is necessary to be Mary tending toward the better of Martha, Martha tending toward the better of Mary, in order to have a listening which acts and hands which listen. The unity of the two does not form the synthesis of two concepts but the convergence and the encounter of two possibilities of existence, in which each attains its incandescence only by letting itself by disquieted by the burning of the other.[98]

The particular sort of unity that Chrétien perceives between contemplation and action is not only quite strong; it is also dynamic: each form of existence is meant to move toward what is best in the other and be constantly unsettled by it. The implication would seem to be that, regardless of our diverse states of life (whether religious or lay, monastic or apostolic), and indeed precisely within them, we have been called, as much by this gospel pericope as by the history of its reception, to cultivate a practice of active and embodied listening, which prepares us not only to hear the unheard-of in what the other says but also to pay attention to and address his or her bodily needs. This sort of listening forms the basis of a double hospitality, extended as love to both God and neighbor, and—as Matthew 25 reveals and Chrétien remembers—in many cases extended to both precisely at the same time. Far from merely signifying a general philosophical discussion about the concepts of theory and practice, the Christian tradition of Marian-and-Marthan hospitality is, in Chrétien's judgment, concerned more specifically with the question of what it means to welcome, to embrace, and to love the other.

Chrétien leaves no room to doubt whether the sort of corporeal, vocal, obediential, and hospitable receptivity that he recommends will be challenging. He interprets it in *Hand to Hand: Listening to the Work of Art* (1997) precisely as an agonic struggle, prefigured for the remainder of history by the unforgettable battle between Jacob and the angel, in which Jacob not only receives a wound (*blessure*) but is also blessed with a new name, Israel.[99] Chrétien cites this scene as the inspiration for his now well-known description of prayer as a "wounded word" and returns to it again in "La prière selon Kierkegaard" (Prayer according to Kierkegaard, 2000). Here he explains that, for Kierkegaard, it is precisely our proximity to God in prayer that provokes the fight; this proximity forces us to confront, and always with "fear and trembling," the decisive question of who we are. The hope is that the resulting combat of freedoms will bring about a change not in God (who interacts with us from eternity) but in ourselves—a conversion through which pain and anguish might give way to tears of repentance and finally to tears of thanksgiving and adoration.[100]

Insofar as it culminates in this sort of eucharistic and doxological conversion, the receptive aspect of response becomes almost indistinguishable from another aspect: offering. In *L'effroi du beau*, Chrétien describes the act of offering not only as a "sacrifice of praise" but also and more exactly as a "sacrifice of humility," in which we "offer to the one whom we love our very inability to love, give our inability itself as a gift, carry into the word of praise our suffering from not being able to praise." When we respond to God with an offering, what we can and must give is nothing other than the condition of nudity, frailty, incapacity, and pain in which we find ourselves. It is for this reason that Chrétien avers that "all praise is plaintive." In his judgment, suffering must be included in doxology, not because it would thereby be justified (as by some sort of Panglossian theodicy), but rather because it is integral to that which we have to offer to God, namely our concrete experience of ourselves.[101]

Although Chrétien argues that praise cannot be offered without suffering, he does not thereby discount the distinctively Christian experience of joy. He concludes *Saint Augustin et les actes de parole* with a meditation on the act of rejoicing, in which we "return to God that joy in us which comes from him" and lift up "our jubilant song" as a sacrificial offering.[102] In an early article, "La joie d'être" (The joy of being, 1980), the question of joy becomes a crucial point of contention in a debate with Nicolas Malebranche, who, in a quintessentially metaphysical and, therefore, proleptically nihilistic decision, neutralizes being and construes the good exclusively in terms of the values of the will. Against this position, Chrétien recalls the voices of Augustine, Aquinas, and Eckhart in order to announce that being itself is a gift from God and, therefore, properly an occasion of joy.[103] His study *La joie spacieuse: Essai sur la dilatation* (Spacious joy: An essay on dilation, 2007) expands this idea into a contemplation regarding the ever greater expansiveness of the mystery of divine joy and of the heart that is opened to it.[104]

Chrétien clarifies in *L'effroi du beau* that it is not only one's own sorrows and joys that must be raised up to God in praise but also those of countless others: "When I praise, I never do it with a single voice but instead let my voice be absorbed into all the voices of the world." The act of offering, therefore, has a "polyphonic" and "choral" character.[105] He confirms this point in "The Offering of the World" (1998). The intimate exchange between a solitary and a collective form of offering does not, in Chrétien's judgment, devalue the singularity of one's voice, nor that of any other, but rather preserves each as an unrepeatable gift. He insists that all voices, including especially those silenced by the violence of history, but also those speaking through the many beautiful things of creation (as in Francis's canticle), must be regarded as "irreplaceable offerings."[106] In this way, Chrétien supplies the warrant not only for his own choral discourse but also for other efforts that might be made to transcend his mainly Eurocentric canon. He also sheds light on the ecological significance of his doxology, which approaches the world not as raw material (*Bestand*) but rather as a song to be sung. Chrétien owes this insight, at least in part, to Balthasar's account of Maximus the Confessor's "cosmic liturgy."[107]

The simultaneously cosmic and cosmopolitan hymn that humanity is called to sing to God is understood by Chrétien not only as a form of response but also and more specifically as an act in which we "take responsibility for the world."[108] Hence, for Chrétien, as for Balthasar, prayer is not a matter of mere passivity but rather a highly significant way in which we freely and actively participate in the historical and eschatological drama of salvation. By offering ourselves and our world in a necessarily plaintive prayer, we begin to fulfill our obligation to do what we can to right the wrongs of history. Moreover, this prayer has a constitutive relation with the ethical acts through which we offer ourselves in the world for the sake of another.

Chrétien develops this argument in his Gilson lectures, *Répondre: Figures de la résponse et de la responsabilité* (To respond: Figures of response and responsibility, 2007). In the fifth lecture, he critiques the modern ethical tradition of "auto-responsibility," which he associates with thinkers such as Kant, Hegel, Nietzsche, Husserl, Sartre, and paradoxically Levinas (who, despite emphasizing alterity, continues to locate responsibility in the constitution of the "abstract individual"). Although the precise meaning of auto-responsibility varies from one philosopher to the next, Chrétien highlights one consistent problem: this tradition pays insufficient attention to the *finitude* of the responsible agent. It does this in one way by presupposing a correlation between "ought" and "can"—that is, between all of the ethical demands that press upon us and what we actually have the power to accomplish. What he has in mind here is the danger of a "properly Pelagian pride," which distorts the drama of salvation into something that would be entirely contingent on human efforts. The tradition of auto-responsibility conceals finitude in another way by appointing human reason or the human will as the final judge concerning what counts as responsibility. Chrétien protests: "That I would be my own judge, or that humanity would judge itself, does this not amount to the same thing, that is to say, a parody of justice?" In this respect, Nietzsche proves exemplary, if only because his discourse is intentionally parodic: he preaches what he calls a "new gospel," whose message is that we are already innocent, and guilty only by our own arbitrary judgments. These two ways of forgetting finitude amount, finally, to "the adoration of humanity by itself."[109]

Although Chrétien rejects the doctrine of "auto-responsibility," he nevertheless promotes a rigorous sense of "omni-responsibility." His hero, in this respect, is Dostoyevsky, who recognizes in *The Brothers Karamazov* that each is responsible for all but who situates this idea precisely "in the context of the *imitatio Christi*" and defines it strictly in terms of "the acts of prayer, of humility, and of charity." Chrétien argues that our responsibility for the other is unlimited both with respect to our potential obligations and with respect to the potential consequences of our actions. In a move redolent of Derrida's analysis concerning the sacrifice of Isaac in *The Gift of Death*, Chrétien concludes that the finitude of all of our attempts to meet the requirements of this twofold condition of omni-responsibility implies an inescapable element of "irresponsibility." In the effort to do everything that we should or could do, there is a sense in which we will have always already failed.[110] At the same time, he draws attention to the many evitable forms of our "co-responsibility," in which we, perhaps even without intention or active involvement, culpably do much less than we both could and must do. In particular, he reflects on the Second World War, "the massiveness of the destruction of the bodies, of the souls, of the things, of the places, of the truth," and suggests that we have always already been implicated in the injustice of such horrific situations "before becoming ourselves the agents and the propagators of it."[111]

The question of responsibility is, for Chrétien, no less than for Derrida, inseparable from a meditation on sacrifice. It is a question about who will offer what to whom and in what way. Chrétien suggests that we become responsible—to the extent that we can, and hence without renouncing our finitude—precisely by offering ourselves and our world to God in prayer and by simultaneously offering all that we can to our neighbors, whoever they might be, through acts of justice and hospitality. In the sixth and final lecture, "Le Répondant plus fort que nos questions et que nos crimes" (The respondent stronger than our questions and our crimes), he adds an important theological clarification. Citing Balthasar, he contends that "this circulation of prayers, of intercessions, and of works of justice . . . is founded on the substitution and the sacrifice of Christ." This supreme christological and Trinitarian gift—which Chrétien describes as a singular event occurring at a specific moment in history but also as a happening that is embodied collectively and trans-historically in the communion of saints (i.e., as the *totus Christus*)—accomplishes what we cannot accomplish by ourselves, namely the effacement of "injustice as such." It nevertheless includes our response and responsibility as indispensable modes of participation. With Balthasar, Chrétien emphasizes "the 'yes' of Mary as the clearest figure of this inclusivity." He affirms, moreover, that we can lift up our prayers in Christ to the Father with confidence that they will be heard and that someone with greater responsiveness and responsibility than us—infinitely greater, because infinite—already welcomes them.[112]

Chrétien's belief that the divine excess that calls and promises has already responded decisively to our prayers does not prevent him from seeking and desiring it. On the contrary, as "Trouver et chercher" (To find and to seek, 2004) demonstrates, there is a sense in which the search for God grows in direct proportion with the discovery of God. Chrétien embraces Gregory of Nyssa's doctrine of infinite desire (*epektasis*) and finds a similar view expressed in Augustine's *De Trinitate* (15.2.2). On the basis of these and other sources, he concludes that "never ceasing to seek that which we have already found (under another mode, certainly, than that wherein one discovered it, but a mode that is no less urgent) is the condition for not losing it, nor being lost." The search must continue without end precisely because that which is found and sought is not an object of comprehension or control but rather the very "growth of an amorous and luminous intimacy," which abides as what it is only in a perpetual play of mutual longing and belonging.[113]

Chrétien draws particular attention to Angelus Silesius—not, however, like Heidegger, simply to make the point that the rose blooms without why (which Chrétien nevertheless does not fail to affirm), but rather in order to shed light on Silesius's Trinitarian reflections regarding the Lucan parables of the lost sheep, the lost coin, and the prodigal son. Chrétien quotes *The Cherubinic Wanderer* (1:277): "The Holy Trinity comes and seeks me in every hour: the Spirit finds the money, the Father receives the Son, the good shepherd Jesus carries the sheep. You see how I am three times lost and found." As Chrétien reads him, Silesius teaches us that in the erotic drama of prayer it is not only we who yearn for God but also God who yearns for us. Divine desire precedes and elicits our desirous response.[114] But it is, therefore, necessary to think of this response not only as an act in which we strive for greater intimacy with a divine beloved but also as an act in which we learn to perceive ourselves as loved, passionately and tirelessly, by a divine lover— that is, by love itself.

We shall let Chrétien's final word to us be perhaps the most intimate of all: breath. *Pour reprendre et perdre haleine: Dix brèves méditations* (In order to catch and lose [one's] breath: Ten brief meditations, 2009) is one of his most prayerful and strictly spiritual works. Each meditation unfolds the meaning of a specific word that he holds dear: breath, path, temptation, attention, recollection, benediction, peace, sweetness, abandon, and wound. The first, "Souffle" (Breath), sets the tone for the rest. After inviting his readers to take a breath, to inhale and exhale, he explains that "breath is the site and the agent of an incessant communication, even communion, between the interior and the exterior, between the world and us; as well as, by the words and the songs that it permits us to form, between human beings; and when these words are absorbed into hymn or prayer, between human beings and God." Alluding to Paul Claudel, Chrétien reminds us that breath circulates and is continually exchanged throughout the cosmos and is the primary medium of God's acts of creation and re-creation. He avers that it is an indispensible divine name, a name that opens us to the "active, free, and sovereign" presence of God that blows wherever and however it wills; a name that requires us to listen for God, with Elijah, even in the gentlest breeze; and a name that beckons the third person of the Trinity, as in the Latin hymn *Veni, sancte Spiritus* (Come, Holy Spirit!). Chrétien contends that this "invisible and ineffable Breath passes in human breaths and acts through them." He says that we are called to "let it enter, arrive in, and inhabit us" so that we might manifest it in the world. These fragile, carnal, mortal lives of ours—which, as the Psalms and Job maintain, are no more than a breath—are thus invited to become, through the inspiration and respiration of God, channels of historical and eschatological peace.[115]

Chrétien discusses this universal spiritual vocation at greater length in his seventh meditation, "Paix" (Peace). Against certain negative definitions of the term, which imply nothing more than the temporary cessation of violence, he proposes a positive interpretation characterized by "the integrity and the accomplishment of corporeal and spiritual life." Moreover, glossing Augustine's discussion in *The City of God* (bk. 19), he maintains that peace can be reached only through the "tranquility of order," by which Chrétien means the simultaneous achievement of justice and reconciliation in our relations with God, with others, and with ourselves. This sort of integrally tridimensional peace, so rare in human history, could seem to be no more than an eschatological hope—and, indeed, Chrétien believes that it will be perfected only in eternity. And yet, he insists that eternity begins here and now. Although this peace is "not the fruit of our own spirit," he argues that it is nevertheless a "daily and quotidian task" which we are empowered to enact as blessed peace-makers (in fidelity with the beatitudes), living and breathing in our bodies the very life and breath of God.[116] Breath, of a certain sort, would therefore bring about the transformation of the world.

Thus Chrétien's doxology gives itself to be thought not only as a postmetaphysically prayerful reflection but also explicitly as a *spirituality of peace in a world of violence*. This aspect of the significance of prayer is not foreign to the works of the other thinkers considered here (even Heidegger, despite sundry problems, envisages a peaceful dwelling of mortal humanity between earth and sky), but it finds in Chrétien's voice the most subtle, most striking, and most palpable articulation. The stakes of an excessive intimacy—the stakes, precisely, of a divine and human love that would permeate every dimension of phenomenality, hermeneutics, and life, should we let it—are enormous, greater than can be conceived, but Chrétien nevertheless helps us to see them and to understand them, and it is for this reason above all that his work deserves much greater attention than it has hitherto received.

In the first three chapters of this study, we have tracked a complex series of itineraries from metaphysics to doxology (though, in Caputo's case, we instead glimpsed a radically apophatic and thus minimally doxological alternative to both, which in its still philosophically regulated diminution of prayer remains perilously close to the dangers of metaphysics). Although Heidegger's doxology helpfully inaugurates the debate, it suffers from several ontological, cultural, and political distortions that have been corrected by both his more nearly doxological and nondoxological followers. Balthasar's work proves to be foundational on the Christian doxological side, but this does not mean that it is unsurpassable in every respect; we have seen where there may be room to raise questions regarding both his susceptibility to and proximity with Heidegger. In the present chapter, Caputo enabled us to discern what is at stake in, but also not entirely satisfying about, a post-Heideggerian, post-Levinasian, and eventually even post-Derridean mode of deconstructive prayer.

The limitlessly hospitable and avowedly uncertain promise of this desert of thought seems, in fact, to exclude unnecessarily many doxological traditions and communities and to rely too apodictically on God's supposed nondisclosure. By contrast, the innovative intersections of prayer and phenomenology that appear in the writings of Marion, Lacoste, and Chrétien allow one to think doxology and doxologically while avoiding the technological, nihilistic, and difference-concealing dangers of metaphysics; the impurity of Heidegger's poetic thinking; the still somewhat questionable metaphysical features of Balthasar's theory; and the still somewhat exclusionary hyperbolic doubt that continues to fund Caputo's project.

Among the doxological phenomenologists, Marion retains the most problematic ties to typically modern phenomenological principles of epistemic certainty that are not well disposed to accommodate the distinctive mystery of prayer, but his reflections on Dionysius and Augustine demonstrate that doxology was initially and still remains his primary concern. Lacoste more clearly situates each of his phenomenological reductions in a decisively theological and, indeed, liturgical reduction, though one may still question the degree to which his work remains largely schematic and, thus, somewhat distanced from the promise of a doxological aesthetics. Of the three representatives of this emerging intellectual and spiritual tradition, Chrétien does the most to translate phenomenology into a doxological idiom. He gives comparatively less weight to formal possibilities and abstract existential structures, preferring instead to develop a richly textured symphonic discourse, including postmetaphysical interpretations of many of the sources that inform Balthasar's trilogy. Without losing touch with the Creator-creature distinction, the sense of wonder at being, or the greatest minds in the Western metaphysical canon, Chrétien models a significantly new kind of contemplation. He follows Heidegger's poetic turn away from the illusory ideal of an apodictic phenomenological science, but he also thoroughly Christianizes this turn and reorients it toward the ongoing drama of divine and human freedom and love. He, therefore, does phenomenology in his own way but not in an incoherent way. He turns this discipline into a practice of receiving, offering, and desiring that which promises, and calls us into, the excess of intimacy. His prayerful discourse responds and corresponds to the simultaneous distance and nearness that are given together in the appearances and words of the things themselves.

Throughout this chapter, we have seen that the twofold effort to overcome metaphysics and to rectify Heidegger's way of overcoming it has been motivated, to some extent, by a sense that these measures are ethically necessary. With metaphysics and with *Ereignis*, there is violence against the other. This is a point that Levinas makes with great forcefulness (notwithstanding his ethical recuperation of the term "metaphysics") and that no thinker who follows after him, whether more or less doxologically oriented, can afford to forget. Like their deconstructive peers (Derrida and Caputo), the three phenomenologists we have considered (Marion, Lacoste, and Chrétien) remember this Levinasian insight. However, instead of opposing it (as even the *somewhat* doxologically inclined Levinas seems to do) to a full theocentric doxology, they show how it flows from such a doxology and even depends on it. Marion emphasizes the solidaristic redundancy of the divinely originate gift, and Lacoste highlights the ethical implications of the liturgical anticipation of the kingdom of God. But, once again, Chrétien's project seems to be the most developed in this area, insofar as he offers extensive meditations on the prayerful bases and concrete phenomenalities of both responsibility and hospitality. Nevertheless, even Chrétien's doxology leaves room to desire a more concrete and historically rooted confrontation with the multifaceted violence of modernity. In general, it seems that however far removed phenomenology becomes from metaphysics, and however deeply it ventures into the mystery of prayer, it will not supply a maximally adequate response to the crises of modernity unless and until it learns to prioritize the prayerful perspectives of the poor and the outcast who dwell on the undersides of history.

PART 2

SPIRITUALITY IN A WORLD OF VIOLENCE

CHAPTER 4

POVERTY OF SPIRIT
Johann Baptist Metz

Already we have considered numerous efforts to bring forth some sort of spirituality as a healing balm or powerful source of change amid the structural violence of modernity. But we have not yet done all that we must do to think through this crucial, life-affirming possibility. The debates surrounding metaphysics and doxology that we have been addressing are relevant to this endeavor, but they do not exhaust it. We must also study other traditions of thought rising up from the anguished depths of modern suffering and injustice in order to glimpse prayer's full counterviolent potential. To this end, the following three chapters shed light on the forms that Christian spirituality takes within several interconnected traditions of political, liberation, and black theology. These chapters demonstrate that the consistent prioritization of the prayerful perspectives of the victims of history which one finds in these critical theological traditions is congruent with—and in some cases already includes its own versions of—a phenomenologically and poetically refined postmetaphysical doxology comparable to those presented above. Nevertheless, these chapters also show that there is room for some mutual enhancement between these two broad sets of approaches to prayerful Christian thought.

On the one hand, the arguments of the previous chapters help one draw out postmetaphysically doxological possibilities from the traditions of political, liberation, and black theology that might otherwise be neglected; they connect these possibilities with a more extensive *ressourcement* of the Christian doxological tradition; and they give greater specificity to the distinction between doxology and metaphysics, which is integral to the unique promise that prayer displays amid the crises of modernity. Of these three enduring benefits, the specificity of the distinction between metaphysics and doxology is perhaps especially important, and not only for theoretical reasons. This distinction comes with some practical implications, precisely insofar as the fate of metaphysics in modernity remains somewhat connected to the structural violence that is also characteristic of this age. Therefore, the ability to think doxologically in a way that resists the dangers of metaphysics (along with the related dangers of certain largely nondoxological ways of attempting to overcome metaphysics) has value not only for prayerful thought but also for the counterviolent actions that flow from it.

On the other hand, the purpose of these chapters is primarily to clarify in what ways the Balthasarian and post-Balthasarian style of doxological contemplation needs to be supplemented and in certain respects significantly modified by the types of prayerful spirituality that have developed in direct opposition to the structural violence of modernity. These traditions of counterviolent spirituality make several weighty contributions to the foregoing discussion: they consider what happens to doxology when it is disrupted by the prayers of questioning and lament that arise in the midst of unjust suffering; they specify the connections that ideally should and actually do exist between prayer and certain Spirit-filled struggles for justice and liberation in history; they offer vastly underappreciated treatments of the aesthetics and dramatics of prayer which, though located on the supposed margins of modernity, manifest a transformative power that is by no means marginal to the significance of prayer itself; and they facilitate critical awareness of the dangers of prayerful theories that do not sufficiently exhibit these other characteristics. Thus many of the limitations that we have noted in previous chapters—particularly with respect to the disconcerting conditions of worldwide suffering, the urgency for real historical action, and the neglected viability of non-Eurocentric sources—begin to be remedied here.

These spiritual traditions associate the hospitality that is required by prayer with concrete (and sometimes profoundly costly) forms of solidaristic commitment to the poor and oppressed. The practice of listening that is exercised by these traditions is primarily oriented toward the cries of those who needlessly endure the most devastating consequences of politico-economic and identity-based violence. And yet, these traditions do not forsake the universal character of prayerful hospitality but rather give it a more realistic, because less abstract or timeless, articulation. They take on the challenge of actually overcoming, and not merely ignoring, history's many deeply entrenched friend-enemy distinctions, but the promised gift of divine-and-human peace remains their ultimate goal and presupposition.

Moreover, the sense of responsibility that is entailed by prayer as an act performed *coram Deo* is not diminished by these traditions but rather given sharper focus by them. In the light of God's counter-intentionality, these traditions ask us to consider the many ways that we have perhaps failed to show compassion to our neighbors and, thereby, participated in the historical falsification of spirituality and the sometimes-horrifying contradictions of its promise. The stronger emphasis on suffering that is found in prayerful forms of political, liberation, and black theology does not erase the questions of sin and guilt but rather provides clearer criteria for their discernment. Furthermore, prayer becomes a crucial source of insight concerning the kinds of Christoform and kingdom-directed lives that we ought to lead. In short, the references to hospitality and responsibility that we have already encountered in the context of postmetaphysical doxology do not disappear within but are rather invigorated by these various forms of counterviolent spirituality.

It is true that the proponents of political, liberation, and black theology interact with critical theorists and social movements that are in some cases avowedly secular (in the sense that their aim is to analyze and change the world independently of God or perhaps with help from some significantly diminished sense of "God," reduced largely to the status of a trope or a mere practical ideal conducive to anthropocentric progress). Nevertheless, we shall see that many of the major representatives of political, liberation, and black theology distinguish their projects from those of their more secular counterparts precisely by turning to prayer. Moreover, the doxological character of their prayerfulness allows them to avoid promoting any excessively apophatic (and in this sense constitutively weak or empty) forms of messianism, in which one would pray, if at all, only for and to a mostly indeterminate event. The best versions of political, liberation, and black theology do their thinking on the basis of the prayers that various suffering communities regularly offer for and to the living God who has already entered into history through the *doxa* and *logos* of Christ. The historical and eschatological hope of these traditions takes root in particular cries, supplications, and prayerfully informed actions that are always in some sense oriented toward the possibility of praise and, therefore, the perpetual giving, receiving, and desiring of divine love. One can thus legitimately locate political, liberation, and black theology under the heading not only of prayer but also of doxology.

Nonetheless, we shall approach these traditions here mainly as examples of *spirituality*. We shall do this not in order to deemphasize their constitutive relation with prayer and doxology but rather in order to bring out their most striking achievement: connecting prayerful thought and doxological contemplation unmistakably with a real, historical, and active affirmation of life—as demonstrated particularly by their compassionate attention to the lives of the most vulnerable and forsaken. To be sure, insofar as the figures in part one also think in a manner that is conducive to spirituality's enlivening embodiment of divinely given freedom and love, their works must also be considered life-affirming in a very true sense. But there is a marked intensification of the prayerful affirmation of life (i.e., of spirituality) that comes only through overt struggles against particular structures of violence and only through intimate, cooperative relationships with those whose lives are regularly impeded and destroyed by such structures.

The first spiritual thinker we shall consider in this regard is Johann Baptist Metz, the student of Karl Rahner who has become well known as the major proponent of a new approach to Catholic political theology. Metz's prayerful thought is worthy of attention in the present argument not only insofar as it takes leave from metaphysics but also, and especially, insofar as it directly counteracts the socioeconomic and culturally exclusionary violence of modernity. We shall study his approach first for both historical and substantive reasons. His politically significant way of thinking prayer partially predates and influences some of the others we shall engage. Furthermore, he makes points about the constitution of human freedom in dynamic relation with the freedom of God, the integration of doxological contemplation with both critical theory and solidaristic action, and the significance of prayers of extreme suffering that will provide helpful bases for comparison and analysis in subsequent chapters.

The spirituality that animates Metz's theology is shaped by his multistaged interpretation of "poverty of spirit" or "poverty in the Spirit" (*Armut im Geiste*). Appearing in the Matthean beatitudes, then becoming deeply ingrained in the Christian doxological tradition, the doctrine and practice of spiritual poverty receives in Metz's thought a contemporary reformulation, which discloses its extraordinary relevance in the midst of the crises of our age. For Metz, spiritual poverty is expressed nowhere more decisively than in prayer. At the same time, he understands spiritual poverty to be deeply rooted in the life—that is, the historical, social, actively embodied, and radically vulnerable existence—of those who pray. Moreover, the spiritual poverty that he recommends does not only take place "in the Spirit" but also as an intentional practice of following Christ. Hence, there can be no question that we are dealing here with a Christian spirituality exhibiting the essential traits outlined in the introduction (the unity of prayer and life and participation in the salvific missions of Christ and the Spirit). The purpose of the present chapter is to illuminate the promising features of this particular Christian spirituality.

Metz's prayerful thought develops in three stages: an early stage in which he employs the poverty of spirit in order to critique and partially appropriate Heidegger's existential phenomenology; a middle stage in which, having begun to reflect on the political significance of theology, he reframes the poverty of spirit as an indispensable foundation for and delimitation of politics; and a later stage in which the poverty of spirit becomes a key symbol for the sort of prayer that he believes continues to be legitimate and necessary after Auschwitz. We shall examine each of these stages in turn.

In the first stage, we shall see that Metz does not simply embrace the foundational subject of modern metaphysics, nor Heideggerian *Dasein*, but rather a christologically inscribed subject that is constituted by a prayerful openness to the freedom and love of God. In short, he proves that it is not enough to be for or against subjectivity in general; instead, one must seek its proper doxological configuration. In the second stage, our aim will be to understand the metamorphosis of this prayerful subject into a political actor in the world. A consideration of Metz's political theology in relation to the more secularized alternatives of the Frankfurt School and Carl Schmitt will enable us to grasp just how decisive prayer is for Metz's approach. In his judgment, a prayerful poverty of spirit not only more successfully maintains a subject that is oriented toward necessary forms of transformative action; it also importantly reminds us that we are not the masters of history but rather, at most, servants of the apocalyptically awaited God of the living and the dead.

Finally, we shall consider how Metz's confrontation with the Shoah intensifies his account of spiritual poverty and connects it with prayers of extreme suffering. It is at this point that his relation to the doxological tradition becomes most strained. And yet, as we shall see, he does not seek to dismiss this tradition but rather only to let it become unsettled by the particular kinds of prayer, lamentation, and questioning that have arisen in the midst of, and in remembrance of, the concrete horror of the Nazi death camps. Situating Metz's retrieval of Nelly Sachs in relation to Derrida's analogous reading of Paul Celan will enable us to specify the extent to which Metz's prayerful thought remains indebted to doxology. Moreover, a Chalcedonian argument regarding the christological unity of suffering *in* and *unto* God will help us work through certain tensions between

Metz's post-Auschwitz theology and Balthasar's theo-dramatic so-teriology. In the end, Metz's spirituality occupies a unique place in between the more nearly doxological and nondoxological correc-tions of Heideggerian doxological impurity that we encountered in the last chapter. At the same time, his approach remains notice-ably closer to the former than the latter and seems to surpass both in terms of historically situated counterviolent potential.

AFFIRMING THE HUMAN SPIRIT

The first task will be to think through the implications of Metz's early phenomenological and theological anthropology (which ap-pears in the 1950s and early 1960s), focusing in particular on the complex relationship that it maintains with Heidegger's thought. Throughout this period, Metz draws selectively on Heidegger in order to develop his own unique take on Karl Rahner's doctrine re-garding the direct (thus not inverse) proportion that abides between our openness to God's self-communication and our authentic fulfill-ment as human beings, a doctrine that is crystallized by Irenaeus's saying *gloria Dei vivens homo* (the glory of God is the human being fully alive).[1]

Metz makes sense of this Rahnerian "direct proportion" by as-sociating it with the twofold significance of a prayerful (and, indeed, doxological) poverty of spirit. On the one hand, against various secu-larizing forms of modern subjectivity (including even Heidegger's early anti-idealist reflections on being-in-the-world), which inter-pret the essential meaning of human existence apart from any explicit humble receptivity to God, Metz argues that we need a Christian theological anthropology formed by a humble practice of recollect-ing, anticipating, and adoring the glorious advent of God in Christ. This is largely what he means by spiritual poverty. On the other hand, against the Western philosophical tradition's ancient meta-physical "cosmocentrism" and implicitly against various contempo-rary forms of apophatically postmodern and theologically kenotic self-effacement (which are perhaps not sufficiently resisted by all of the examples of postmetaphysical doxology considered in previous chapters), Metz passionately affirms the ontological and theological dignity of the human spirit. In the process, he critically appropriates certain features of Heidegger's existential anthropology, while integrating these features into a christologically situated account of the human subject of prayer. This is part of his understanding of spiritual poverty too. Poverty of spirit is Metz's preferred way to hold together, and indeed to unite in a single concept, the only-seemingly-opposed phenomena of humanity's worshipful dependence on God and humanity's full self-realization. Poverty of spirit names this one inseparable meeting of divine-and-human freedom. All in all, the key insight of this stage of Metz's thought, which he emphasizes more strongly than any thinker we have studied thus far, is that our human spirit (together with its constitutive freedom) remains an irrevocable and inestimable gift even—and precisely—in the midst of prayer.

In his first major monograph, a dissertation in philosophy that he wrote under Emerich Coreth, Metz seeks to combine a Thomistic analogical ontology that resists Heidegger's monism with an existential account of human facticity that draws significantly on Heidegger's early phenomenology. Like Balthasar, Metz contends that Heidegger's lingering attachment to modern identity-philosophy needs to be corrected in view of the more adequate theory of difference that Przywara formulates in his analogical metaphysics. However, unlike Balthasar, Metz is not primarily interested in developing a Christian alternative to Heidegger's poetic doxology but rather in affirming Heidegger's reflections on the conditions of human finitude, particularly time. Metz's argument here is very close to Lacoste's: there is something valuable to be retained in Heidegger's exposition of the temporal and mortal structure of *Dasein*, provided that this analysis is limited to a question of anthropology and is not allowed to settle the question of being itself (in Lacoste's terminology, the absolute), which must be approached with reference to the mystery of God and not merely human experience.[2]

Metz's qualified support for Heidegger's anthropology begins to wane as his own theological perspective develops. Following his first dissertation, he starts to distance himself from any "transcendental metaphysics"—including, in his judgment, Heidegger's existential philosophy—which refuses to receive the free word of God that is communicated in history itself. At this point in his career, Metz continues to embrace Rahner's idea that such transcendental metaphysics can helpfully elucidate the conditions under which human beings become "hearers of the word." However, he also insists that, without historical revelation, this sort of metaphysics tends to distort thought into a form of "mythological gnosis" and reduce the "whole of history into a mere anthropophany, in which the human being only ever sees itself."[3] In short, Metz argues that the transcendental tradition of modern philosophy is seriously jeopardized by the very trait that distinguishes it most clearly from Christian theology: that is, by its aloofness from historical revelation.

The dissertation in theology that Metz completes under Rahner's direction sheds greater light on what he is and is not willing to appropriate from Heidegger. Having already rejected Heidegger's monistic conflation of phenomenology and ontology in his first dissertation, Metz now defends the practice of letting phenomenology inform, and be informed by, ontology. Thus he allows a certain kind of reciprocity between the two without accepting any strict identity. It is in this respect that Heidegger's *Being and Time* continues to influence Metz's project, even while not violating its analogical precautions. Heidegger's influence is particularly evident in Metz's call for an "anthropocentric thought-form," which can be defined as a way of thinking being itself primarily in light of categories that are appropriate to human experience: that is, "the peculiar manner-of-being of the human, subjectivity." Here Metz is clearly not far from Heidegger's method of thinking *Sein* on the basis of *Dasein*.[4]

However, in contrast to Heidegger, Metz locates the real problem of occidental thought not with the ontotheological constitution of metaphysics (or any other general account of metaphysics), but rather with the "cosmocentrism" and "objectivism" of ancient Greek metaphysics. Moreover, Metz contends somewhat provocatively that Aquinas (a figure whose relation with metaphysics we have seen Balthasar, Caputo, and Marion grapple with in different ways) subverts this problematic thought-form. Metz's central point is that, for Aquinas, the whole of reality is shot through with free-dom. While granting that Thomas borrows some cosmological terms from the Greeks, Metz argues that Thomas does not understand being originally and essentially as some sort of massive *physis* gov-erned by universal and necessary laws but rather as an intrinsically spiritual reality that is ordered above all by a dynamic interplay of divine and human knowledge and love (i.e., subjectivity). According to Metz, Aquinas's "anthropocentrism" emerges from the scriptural portrayal of a "real dialogical relationship" with God (i.e., prayer). This relationship takes on its greatest concreteness in Christ, who enables us to interact with God in an accessible human form and likewise to perceive our human existence as capable of representing something crucial about the divinely originate structure of reality as such.[5] Although Metz suggests that this kind of theological an-thropocentricism appears in the Christian tradition before Aquinas, he maintains that Aquinas makes it graspable as never before by bringing it into the mainstream of Western thought as a new formal paradigm.[6] In short, Thomas gives ontological intelligibility to the christological form of prayerful encounter with God.

Having traced Aquinas's "anthropocentrism" back to scripture, and specifically to prayer and Christology, Metz also traces it for-ward to the modern age. He explains that Aquinas's thought-form begins to be developed in unforeseen directions by the many meta-physical accounts of subjectivity that arise in Descartes, Cusa, Male-branche, Berkeley, Leibniz, Pascal, Kant, Fichte, Hegel, Schelling, Kierkegaard, Nietzsche, Husserl, and Heidegger. There is then, in Metz's view, a genealogical connection between Aquinas and Hei-degger, which shows that the latter's insights regarding the ontologi-cal expressivity of human experience have Christian roots. To be clear, Metz does not maintain that the particular forms of modern subjective metaphysics from Descartes through Heidegger are un-problematic simply because they are at some level foreshadowed by Aquinas. On the contrary, he contends that they are valid *only in-sofar* as they can help us think that which Thomas makes thinkable: that is, a christologically and prayerfully specified account of divine and human freedom and love. He observes, once again, that insofar as this transcendental philosophical tradition loses touch with historical revelation, it will always be in danger of degenerating into a "system of modern gnosis."[7] In short, Metz's sympathy for modern subjective philosophy has clear limits, and Aquinas's thought-form (at least purportedly) remains for him the surest standard of legitimacy.

And yet, Metz's assessment of modern subjectivity is much more positive than negative. He wants his readers to reflect on the possibility that something like Heidegger's ontological analysis of *Dasein* could be welcomed, with some important adjustments, as congruent with the type of anthropocentric thinking that is authorized by a christological understanding of prayer. Conversely, he suggests that the greater threat has to do with a kind of theological reasoning that would remain insufficiently critical of Greek metaphysical cosmology and thereby conceal the very relationship of divine and human freedom that is Christian theology's own innermost possibility. Thus, in a complicated way, Metz becomes a kind of apologist for the modern subject while simultaneously preparing the way for a return of a distinctively prayerful spirituality as an alternative to both the Hellenistic roots and modern idealist excesses of Western metaphysics.

The conceptually dense, phenomenological and theological anthropology that Metz articulates in his two dissertations and various early scholarly articles takes on a more accessible and arguably more compelling form in two short spiritual works that he writes around the same time. In the first of these, *The Advent of God* (1959), he offers a doxological critique of contemporary culture. On the one hand, he implicates Heidegger in this critique by suggesting that Heideggerian *Angst* is actually a symptom of our refusal to be open to God's historical advent. On the other hand, in harmony with Heidegger, Metz questions the unchecked drive for safety, security, and technological dominance that seems to characterize our age. Nevertheless, he departs from Heidegger once again by specifying that what is endangered by this drive is not merely our readiness for the destiny of worldly being but rather our openness to "a mysterious destiny that can only be explained by God."[8]

Although one could perhaps classify the theology of this text as Thomistic, this classification would be somewhat imprecise. Metz's most obvious source here is not Aquinas but rather the church's liturgical celebration of Advent and Christmas. He stresses that these seasons are not only about reflecting on the mystery of the nativity but also about waiting, in light of this event, for the arrival of God that is still to come: the glorious appearance of God "in all the naked splendor of His fiery holiness and divinity." Metz gives particular emphasis to the last sentence of scripture, which takes the form of a prayer: "Maranatha, 'Come, Lord Jesus!' [Rev. 22:20]."[9] His advent theology is, therefore, an apocalyptic theology. To be exact, it is an apocalyptic doxology. He seeks to counteract the forgetfulness, anxiety, and will-to-power of the modern subject not only by meditating on the incarnation but also by embracing the final prayerful words of the Bible through which we ask the Lord to come again in glory.

Metz treats this apocalyptic doxology as a crucial element of the spirituality that he believes will help the human spirit affirm itself in the right way. Against the modern subject that strives to control its own future and thereby shelter itself from the advent of God, Metz gives voice to a subject that has learned to await God with an "authentically evangelical 'poverty of spirit' [Matt. 5:3]." He concludes his argument with an account of spiritual poverty that strikes an unmistakably doxological chord:

> When we become the hope-filled poor of which the Gospel speaks, when we dare to embark upon the great adventure of God's coming, then we shall begin to taste some of the happiness that comes with advent existence. . . . Then we will be able to raise our weary heads and sing our songs with joy, listening for the accompanying voice of Him who is our future: God Himself.[10]

Metz is very clear: to be poor in spirit is not to drown in the sorrows of life but rather to let oneself be open to the "happiness," "love," and "joy" that belong to God's coming. Spiritual poverty is expressed not in words of despair or self-deprecation, but rather in jubilant "songs." It is not a negation of the human spirit but rather an affirmation through which "our full self will be given to us." It is an affirmation, however, that departs radically from the modern dream of self-sufficiency and replaces this with an act of "listening" to God's voice, an act that lies very close to the Christian traditions of kenosis and *Gelassenheit* that saturate Balthasarian and post-Balthasarian doxology.[11]

Metz develops his interpretation of the poverty of spirit at greater length in the book (from 1962) that bears its name—a book which, despite its brevity and mostly homiletic quality, can be read as the pièce de résistance of his early thought. Here the connection with the kenotic tradition becomes explicit through the many references that he makes to the Philippians hymn, along with other relevant passages from scripture (especially the Gospels).[12] Although Metz seems to interpret poverty of spirit in this text more in relation to the trials of Lent and Good Friday than the joy of Advent and Christmas, his understanding of it remains profoundly positive. Christ's kenotic movement does not efface the human condition but rather embraces it absolutely. Metz argues that, in emptying himself, Christ "professed and accepted our humanity, . . . struggling with his whole heart to have us say 'yes' to our innate poverty." Far from the hatred of self, poverty of spirit therefore entails a christologically grounded "love of self." Metz explains, moreover, that poverty of spirit is for this very reason deeply connected with our ability to love the neighbor *as ourselves* and, simultaneously, as a sacrament of Christ (Matt. 25:40–45).[13]

Hence, Metz's attention continues to be directed toward the meaning and value of the human subject (including importantly oneself and others). His complex engagement with Heidegger's early existential thought reemerges here as an indispensable dimension of his theological anthropology. In particular, Metz's definition of human existence as "the *ecstatic appearance of Being*" confirms his ongoing commitment to an analogically conditioned reciprocal relationship between ontology and phenomenology. Moreover, his contention that our existence is constituted by temporality, finitude, and death likewise remains close to Heidegger's analysis. Metz gathers the features of his own theologically re-inscribed account of *Dasein* together in his concept of humanity's "innate poverty." This innate poverty should be carefully distinguished from the poverty of spirit that he recommends as a vital mode of *imitatio Christi*: whereas the former is always already given as the phenomenologically evident condition of our being, the latter is an intentional spiritual practice through which we accept this condition with our hearts open to God. Thus, although Metz basically endorses Heidegger's description of human facticity, he replaces Heidegger's prescriptive appeal to anticipatory resoluteness (or, for that matter, poetic dwelling) with his own normative theological discussion of a central evangelical virtue. Metz implies that, in order to become who and what we are called to be as ecstatic manifestations of the truth of being, it is not enough to face death with firm resolve or live as mortals in the fourfold; rather, we must release ourselves to the mystery of God's incarnate love.[14]

This subject-affirming poverty of spirit finds its most definitive expression in prayer and worship. Metz concludes his text by declaring that

> It is when we, in the poverty of our worshipping spirit, tread before the face of God's freedom, into the mystery of that impenetrable "Thou"—it is then that we find access to the depths of our own Being and worth. Then we really become fully human. In worshipping God we are brought totally before ourselves and to ourselves. This is the case since we are, after all, given to ourselves, called and gathered into the depths of our personal Being, by the address and the appeal of God.[15]

In short, he says, "prayer is the ultimate realization of humanity." There are two sides to this claim. On the one hand, it implies that our access to being depends entirely on God. In our worship and in our very existence, we are impoverished and thus ever at the mercy of God's gratuitous love. We, therefore, have no power to ground ourselves (whether by reason or sheer force of will). This lesson of humility, which counteracts much ancient and modern philosophical hubris, is a significant part of Metz's understanding of spiritual poverty.

On the other hand, Metz indicates that an ontologically expressive human subject *does* emerge in this doxological encounter. He emphasizes this point more than any of the doxological thinkers we have encountered thus far. Although each includes some sort of anthropological figure, they tend not to make this the focal point of their arguments in the way that Metz does, and when they do address it directly they generally exhibit a greater distrust of the modern tradition of subjectivity leading up to and including Heidegger. Like Metz's *Poverty of Spirit*, Marion's *Au lieu de soi* defines the authentic self as the prayerful self. However, whereas Metz's ontological discourse maintains a positive connection with Heidegger's existential thought, Marion's adamantly non-ontological reading of Augustine seeks to break this connection. Insofar as Lacoste's account of liturgical existence incorporates some aspects of Heidegger's phenomenological ontology, it may exhibit greater affinity with Metz's approach. And yet, Lacoste seems to be more wary than Metz of Heidegger's parousiacal pretensions and, therefore, continues to emphasize kenosis more strongly than self-realization. In the case of Chrétien, who draws attention to the response and responsibility of the creature, there is perhaps more affinity still, but the accents are in different places. The gravitational center of Chrétien's thought is the excess that occasions the response, not the response itself—though the latter is highly significant for him. Even Balthasar, whose still somewhat metaphysically constituted subject would seem to offer the most substantial basis for comparison, remains considerably more antagonistic to modern anthropocentrism than Metz.[16]

It is possible to think that Metz has gone too far and risked too much with his use of the admittedly dubious term "anthropocentrism," especially since he employs this thought-form only as the corollary of a particular sort of theocentrism, which he should probably have made more terminologically explicit. Moreover, with Marion, one might at this point in the history of philosophy prefer to do without such heavy ontological claims. But whatever one's final assessment might be, Metz at least gives us reason to believe that the human spirit has an appreciably positive mode of appearance in prayer, and that this positive mode of appearance should not be construed as contradicting the human spirit's radical dependence on God. He importantly specifies that the only spirit, the only *Geist*, worthy of our collective and individual investment is one that knows its own poverty, has accepted it, and has dedicated it to the glory of God. But this specification does not require, or even strictly permit, the sort of skeptical distance from the very idea of the subject that has become common currency in much postmodern secular and Christian discourse. The primary message of Metz's early period is that we do not need to make a fateful choice between modernity's technological, self-aggrandizing, and mythologically gnostic subject, on the one hand, and its mere deconstructive or theopanistic erasure, on the other. Rather, precisely in remembrance and anticipation of Christ, we can explore the deep connections that prayer sustains between the (innate and intentional) poverty of the human spirit and its full doxological realization.

A NEW POLITICAL AND PRAYERFUL THEOLOGY

From the middle of the 1960s through the 1970s, Metz articulates the central ideas of the new approach to political theology with which his name is now primarily associated. His approximately Rahnerian brand of Heideggerian Thomism gives way to a very different theological framework constructed in critical dialogue with post-Enlightenment practical philosophy, particularly the critical theories of the Frankfurt School. His affirmation of the human spirit now takes on an explicitly political significance. He ceases to be concerned primarily with the question of the subject's authenticity, or ontological self-understanding, and becomes more interested in questions about how to specify and work toward a political vision of freedom and justice for all subjects. In the process, he retains and deepens his christological perspective. His recourse to history and society is by no means a merely secularizing move.[17] On the contrary, its most significant presuppositions and implications are unmistakably theological and, moreover, deeply connected with prayer. In fact, prayer is, if anything, more crucial to his thought after his political turn than it is before. His practical fundamental theology is virtually indistinguishable from the particular spirituality that appears everywhere within it: precisely, the prayerful practice of spiritual poverty that animates every stage of his work.

Many readers of Metz have discussed his reorientation of theology in a political direction and have treated this as one of the most interesting aspects of his thought, and certainly it is.[18] However, his prayerful riposte to much contemporary politics and critical theory is no less important. In other words, it is necessary to appreciate not only how he moves beyond his initial Heideggerian-Thomist paradigm in order to bring out the political stakes of theology but also how he contests many of the problematic positions of his new critical interlocutors precisely on the basis of prayer. This contestation can be analyzed in terms of two major ways in which Metz argues that prayer responds effectively to the violence of the modern age. On the one hand, he suggests that prayer forms a spiritually poor, solidaristic subject that is capable of the needed sorts of concrete transformative action on behalf of the most vulnerable members of society. Prayer, therefore, undergirds human responsibility in a way that other potentially subject-negating foundations of political theory do not. On the other hand, Metz clarifies that prayer encourages us to recognize the finitude of this responsibility (as Chrétien would call it): that is, the finally inescapable poverty of our human strivings. It does so by eliciting our hope in the God of universal justice and love who alone can answer our deepest longings for salvation, especially for the dead. These two aspects of prayer's efficacy—which largely correspond to the human-historical and divine-apocalyptic dimensions of Balthasar's theo-drama—are confirmed not only by *Faith in History and Society* (1977), arguably Metz's most important work of political theology, but also by two more overtly spiritual texts that he publishes in the same year: *Followers of Christ* and "The Courage to Pray." We shall consider each text in turn.

In *Faith in History and Society*, Metz tracks two distinct philosophical genealogies stemming from a specifically Kantian version of *Aufklärung*: an "idealistic" tradition passing from the *Critique of Pure Reason* through German Idealism up to the twentieth-century schools of phenomenology, existentialism, and personalism that Metz engages in his early work, and a primarily "practical" tradition that begins with the *Critique of Practical Reason* and is then developed in a more radical form by Marxism and later revisionist interpreters of Marx.[19] Metz's critical engagement with this practical tradition has two major fronts, roughly corresponding to the two fronts of the then dominant Cold War political landscape: the liberal West and the socialist or communist East (but, to be clear, he mostly approaches the latter indirectly through a conversation with members of the "Western Marxist" Frankfurt School who remained, on the whole, very dissatisfied by the policies of the Soviet Union).[20] There is also a third front, which is neither liberal nor Marxist, namely the so-called old form of Catholic political theology that, as we shall see in the case of Carl Schmitt, has a very questionable way of refashioning itself in modernity. The point of departure for Schmitt is not so much Kant as Hobbes: the modern theorist of the sovereign ruler. The prayerful foundations of Metz's critique are essentially the same in each of these three contests—which can, therefore, be understood precisely as debates about the status of prayer in modernity.

Contesting the Frankfurt School

At first glance, it would seem that Metz is most concerned with challenging the stereotypical subject of the West. He classifies it, precisely in a Marxian classist sense,[21] as the "bourgeois subject" (*Bürger*): the infamous privatized and propertied individual that remains largely ignorant of, and blithely indifferent to, the negative implications of its particular historical and social manner of being. This sort of person is the privileged target of the ideology critiques that Metz appropriates from his conversation partners in the Frankfurt School. In particular, he adopts Max Horkheimer and Theodor Adorno's theory regarding the "dialectic of Enlightenment" in order to argue that the bourgeois subject's apparent emancipation from tradition and authority has a grim underside, related to the "calculating reason" that it uses to make profits and exert uneven levels of control within a supposedly free and fair market. Moreover, at least partly under the influence of Ernst Bloch's and Walter Benjamin's messianism, Metz objects to this subject's presupposition of an empty continuum of evolutionary time, which tends to encourage an apathetic acceptance of the supposedly normal course of events (the status quo). Finally, Metz employs a fairly standard Hegelian and Marxian argument that the bourgeois subject's Kantian morality is insufficient to the extent that it does not emphasize the constitutively social or political dimensions of praxis.[22]

Metz maintains that these interconnected aspects of bourgeois subjectivity—namely, its technical market-driven rationality, untroubled progressive view of time, and individually focused morality—have, notwithstanding some potential merits, a largely negative set of consequences. The natural world, as Heidegger also warns, begins to be reduced to raw material; the majority of human beings, especially in the global South, are largely excluded from the economic and political freedoms and other benefits that such a system is meant to provide; and the bourgeois subjects themselves become alienated from the deepest theological and communal sources of their subjectivity. With the last point, Metz recalls the problematic of the "death of man" upon which Heidegger and several other post-Nietzschean thinkers have commented in connection with the "death of God" (he mentions Adorno and Foucault in this context). Precisely there, where the human being would seem to posit itself absolutely by ridding itself of all external authority, including that of God (now "killed"), it finds itself downgraded to the status of an exchangeable element in the supposedly smooth operations of a techno-economic world order.[23]

It is important to realize here that, although Metz draws on a critical tradition that resonates with Heidegger's declinist narrative of modernity, which culminates in this sort of nihilistic diminution of the subject, Metz's sources—and, by implication, Metz himself— count Heidegger as part of the problem. Adorno's scathing ideology critique of Heidegger in *Negative Dialectics*, to which Metz briefly alludes, represents another way (beyond those we have already considered) of challenging the idea that Heidegger's poetic ontology offers anything like a sufficient or even acceptable response to the crises of our age. According to Adorno, Heidegger uncritically promotes his own bourgeois subjectivity and, what is worse, hides this fact from himself and his readers through countless references to a vague yet supposedly definitive account of being itself, which allows no critical subjectivity or consciousness to come into play. More concretely, Adorno is concerned that this obfuscating ontology lets Heidegger remain blind to the many victims of history, including, in a way, his own history.[24] Citing *Negative Dialectics*, Metz contends: "The slightest trace of meaningless suffering in the world as we experience it gives the lie to this whole affirmative ontology and teleology [as articulated, for example, by Heidegger], and reveals them to be modernity's mythology."[25] In short, Metz endorses a form of critique which holds that Heidegger's *Gelassenheit* to the event of being does not provide the sort of resistance that is needed against the death of the subject as such, nor against the unjust suffering and deaths of innumerable people on the undersides of history. In Metz's judgment, as in those of other post-Heideggerian critics (Levinas, Derrida, and Caputo, but also Balthasar, Marion, Lacoste, and Chrétien), the apparent profundity of Heidegger's poetic turn conceals a descent into irresponsibility.

Although Metz's argument against the bourgeois subject therefore implicates Heidegger's thought, it is more directly focused on correcting certain strands of Christian theology—including Rahner's theology and Metz's own early efforts—which have promoted a theologically grounded post-Enlightenment subject but have not paid sufficient attention to its deeply questionable and even contradictory historical and social conditions. As we have seen, the Frankfurt School certainly informs Metz's decision to take theology in a more politically conscious direction. And yet, the most decisive source for this shift in his thought remains historical revelation and its prayerful subjectivity, which he now associates primarily with the exodus community of biblical Israel and with the protoecclesial praxis of discipleship that is integral to biblical Christology. His constant refrain is that the subjects disclosed in the Bible are formed not only through history, society, and praxis but also "in God's presence."[26]

For Metz, existence in the presence of God has a dialogical character, in which both human and divine agency have a role to play and in which, therefore, subjectivity is by no means negated. He explains that, in scripture,

> prayer compels the one who prays to remain a subject and not to defer one's responsibility when confronted with one's own guilt. It demands that the one who prays remain a subject in the face of one's enemies, in the face of the fear of losing one's name, one's identity, one's very self. . . . The Christian biblical idea of God . . . is an idea that forms identity, reaching down into the very roots of existence. It resists the formation of the identity that is structured by having and by possessing and constitutes the subject as a solidaristic subject.[27]

This passage merits a close analysis. The first point to observe is that Metz reaffirms the concluding argument of *Poverty of Spirit*, namely that a prayerful relationship with God does not contradict but rather definitively establishes the human subject as such. Second, he argues that the subject that is constituted in prayer manifests itself amid the conflicts of the world precisely through the ownership that it takes for its actions and the openness with which it encounters even the possibly hostile other. Exposed to the judgment of God, this subject must acknowledge its "guilt" and remain obedient in the face of "enemies" and even the potential loss of its "very self" (which, paradoxically, coincides with the act of remaining a subject). Hence, those very traits prized most highly by the Levinasian tradition of postmodern ethics—that is, radical responsibility and hospitality for the other—appear here as entailments of prayerful subjectivity. Finally, without employing the term "poverty of spirit," Metz alludes to the concept and gives it a new political significance. Resisting the association of identity with "having" and "possessing," which are

characteristic of the bourgeois subject and its attachments to con-
sumable goods, biblical prayer supports an alternative way of being
as a nonpossessive "solidaristic subject." Metz's decision to translate
the spiritually poor person as a person of solidarity emphasizes that
poverty is not an end in itself but rather a way of freeing oneself to
be in relationship with others.

Metz contends, accordingly, that the poor in spirit are not meant
to be absorbed in their own askesis but rather join together to work
for greater justice and freedom for the whole of humanity, that is, for
"*all* men and women." It is in hope of approximating this sort of universal solidarity that he argues for "an ecclesial spirituality . . . that
gives its witness and proves itself by spreading a socially critical freedom." On the one hand, he suggests that such a spirituality needs to
cultivate a serious practice of prayer in order to seek "freedom from
what is alleged to be plausible in the mechanisms and prejudices of
society, as well as the capacity for that selflessness which demands
action in the interest of others, of 'the least of your brothers and
sisters.'" In other words, Metz believes that prayer is necessary in
order to promote the kind of detachment or *indiferencia* that makes
solidarity possible.[28] On the other hand, Metz argues that prayer empowers us to make a concrete difference in society only if its spirit is
embodied in action; a "purely cultic experience," as one might find
in bourgeois religion, is not enough. Expressing the same point in
different terms, he avers that the "mystical" process of becoming a
subject in the presence of God cannot be given an authentic witness
unless one also dares to become "political" by confronting the injus-
tices that are part of one's historical context.[29]

It is necessary to recognize that, if Heidegger, Rahner, and other
representatives of the more nearly "idealistic" side of post-Kantian
thought do not do enough to promote a mystical-political synthesis
that can seriously counteract the structural violence of our age—the
violence widely perpetrated against nature, against the marginalized,
and against humanity as such—Metz thinks that the same can also be
said for many of the critical theorists who have helped him perceive
this shortcoming. He contends that the "dialectical materialism [of
the Frankfurt School] falls prey itself to a subjectless evolutionary

logic, when and to the extent that it can find no other grounds for its interests in liberation . . . than a teleology toward freedom attributed to matter or nature itself." In short, Metz maintains that dialectical materialism does not offer enough inspiration to act in the radically self-giving and other-affirming way that the exigencies of the present demand. The nondivine, despiritualized matter that determines this thought-form as its highest ground (*causa sui*) and as its most general ground (doctrine of being as such) does not, in his judgment, give adequate support to a spirituality of critical freedom that has real hope of rising above the dehumanizing forces of this world.[30]

However, it is necessary at this point to acknowledge a certain degree of complexity in the Frankfurt School itself. In the first place, as Pierre Bourretz demonstrates, it would be possible to interpret at least the figures of Benjamin and Bloch primarily as witnesses of a particular Jewish spiritual and intellectual tradition that has in the modern age become entangled with, but not simply overtaken by, Marxism.[31] Jacob Taubes makes a similar point about Benjamin, whom he contrasts with Bloch and Adorno: Benjamin seems to await "the Messiah" in a realistic sense, whereas the latter two appear to treat this scriptural term as no more than a figurative image or a Kantian regulative ideal.[32] In any case, a form of political subjectivity influenced by Benjamin's somewhat Marxist messianism, and perhaps even by Bloch's apparently more Marxist messianism, could nevertheless have as its most original source of inspiration a biblical tradition of prayer that would be very similar to that which Metz recommends. But even if one considers the spirits or "specters" of Marx himself, as Derrida does, there are at least traces of a Jewish or Christian prophetic spirituality and eschatological promise to be found here as well, both in Marx's own thought and in its effective history, notwithstanding the prevalent critiques of religion—which are, in any case, not entirely unrelated to the scriptural prohibition of idolatry.[33] And yet, the effectiveness of prayer as a constitutive feature of solidaristic subjectivity may rest to a significant extent on a more or less faithful manner of thinking it, in which one would guard against the subject-negating consequences of too high a degree of secular distortion.

Metz's critique of the subjectless (precisely because prayerless or not adequately spiritual) character of dialectical materialism is the first of his arguments against the Marxist front of his immediate political context. It correlates with his suspicion regarding the attenuated subjectivity of the bourgeois individual, which, though perhaps open to a cultic experience of prayer, does not exhibit a sufficiently active or critical spirituality. The second argument—which applies to both of these fronts and asserts not merely the importance of a reciprocal relation between politics and prayer but also the insufficiency of politics as such—is, in a way, more decisive. Whereas one can imagine a likely objection to Metz's view that prayer is crucial for the subject of liberative praxis, insofar as it seems possible to insist more strongly than he does on the significance of nonreligious proponents of very similar political ideals, the strength of this sort of objection to Metz's sense of the necessity of prayer amid modern violence is diminished if the question is precisely about the dead. With this question the problem of how best to respond to the destructive forces of history exceeds the competence of merely political reflection—including, for instance, Judith Butler's incisive thoughts regarding a politics of mourning that still hopes only for a more just treatment of present and future generations.[34] Even a prayerfully grounded account of political responsibility must give way in this circumstance to another modality of prayer in which the ability to do justice to the deceased and to fulfill their unrealized hopes is recognized as most properly belonging not to human efforts but to the sovereignty of God. Moreover, bourgeois religion's privatized eschatological anticipation must also be surpassed by a strictly universal apocalyptic longing in solidarity with all those who have suffered and died.

In other words, if we are concerned with the political sphere, which is shaped by our finite projects and struggles, then a debate can arise regarding the necessary conditions or most promising sources for the right sort of political subject, and Metz takes a position in this debate in which he emphasizes the formative significance of prayer. However, if we are troubled by the innumerable human bodies that have already been decimated in the course of natural or unnatural (i.e., possibly preventable) violence, this opens up a different sort of conversation in which one must decide whether those who have died are still called to be subjects or are irrevocably lost, however unjust this may be—and Metz again takes a position, this time in support of the more-than-political significance of prayer, understood as an insistent request for decisive *divine* action. It is in this respect that he advances his most provocatively theological and prayerful argument against both the bourgeois individual and the secular critical theorist.

For Metz, the deepest and most expansive form of solidarity implies a connection between the living and the dead in which the former remember the latter and pray for and with them to the God who is now their last and only resort—their only possibility of a new spiritual-and-corporeal life as subjects (i.e., resurrection). He argues that "this is where religion is fundamentally distinguished from any pure utopia, to which, as everyone knows, nobody prays and which also only knows about a promise for those still to come, a 'paradise for the victorious,' but nothing for those who died suffering unjustly." Against any thinker who would associate the goal of history with a merely political form of liberation (i.e., utopia), Metz insists that "God appears in God's eschatological freedom as the subject and meaning of history as a whole." Concomitantly, he argues that "there is no politically identifiable subject of universal history" which, whether appearing in the form of "a party, a race, a nation, or a church," would actually resolve all its contradictions.[35] The negative dialecticians of the Frankfurt School would agree that there can be no identifiable political subject of universal history; however, this leaves them in the position of implying that there simply is no resolution, that negativity has a sort of final—or at least never-ending—operation. Metz substitutes prayer in the place of such resignation. He turns prayerfully to God in order to preserve his hope for the dead.

Hence, although Metz's closely related anamnestic concepts of "dangerous memory," "*memoria passionis*," and "*memoria passionis, mortis, et resurrectionis Jesu Christi*" have implications for how we should act in history and society, they must also be interpreted as pointing forward to the final advent of God that promises to address,

in a definitive way, the world's negativity. These modes of historical and christological remembrance give rise to and find their most
intense expression in the quintessential apocalyptic prayer, to which
we have already seen Metz refer in *The Advent of God*: "Come,
Lord Jesus!"[36] This prayer retains, even in the midst of his political
theology, a more-than-political significance insofar as it effectively
announces the limits of our own strivings. Moreover, as Bruce Morrill indicates, the particular praxis of memory and hope that radiates
throughout Metz's work has its roots precisely in the church's celebration of the Eucharist; his theology is, therefore, not only political
but also in some sense, if only suggestively, liturgical.[37]

On these points, Metz's argument intersects significantly with
Balthasar's doxological theory. Both thinkers agree that, however much prayer undergirds human responsibility, it also leads us
to praise and worship the God of Christian revelation who is the
definitive savior of the world. The distinction between Metz's and
Balthasar's versions of a memorial-apocalyptic doxology does not
depend on the question of theological verticality, since on this issue
they are in clear agreement. Rather, the distinction stems from their
respective soteriological priorities (whether emancipation from suffering or redemption from sin) and their respective temporalizations
of the human experience of divine glory (whether mostly futural or
already significantly present).

In the first case, although Metz critiques certain secular philosophies of history for only imagining a political liberation from suffering and no redemption from sin, and although he even approvingly
cites Balthasar's *Mysterium Paschale* in support of this argument, the
fact remains that when he begins to develop his own soteriological
perspective he does so by concentrating on the hope that God will
free us from "the real and all-inclusive history of suffering." This
history certainly entails the universal condition of being a sinner,
but it also includes all of the useless anguish that has been endured
by undeserving victims throughout the ages and, in a sense, this is
main characteristic.[38] In contrast to Balthasar, Metz accents suffering
much more strongly than sin (which is not to say that either theologian entirely neglects the one or the other). The relative advantage

of Metz's emphasis is that it enables him to treat the unjust affliction that permeates this violent world as an absolutely *central* problem for theology, spirituality, and concrete historical action. At the same time, his prioritization of the history of suffering does not negate his prayerful recognition that God is the final source of its overcoming.

The second difference has to do with questions of time and experience. Both Metz and Balthasar acknowledge that the event of salvation is in various ways both "not yet" and "already" accomplished. However, whereas Balthasar interprets this event in Trinitarian terms as the historical unfolding of relationships between the Father, Son, and Holy Spirit that have already been expressed and made luminous in the paschal mystery and in the saints who have variously embodied it, Metz understands this event primarily as the still unfulfilled manifestation of God's "universal, integral justice." This hermeneutical divergence gives rise to two distinct temporalities of the creature's experience of glory. Whereas Balthasar's account makes an aesthetics of glory conceivable in the here and now, albeit one that is far from complete, Metz largely defers the possibility of any such aesthetics, precisely because unjust suffering has not ended and the dead have not been raised (at least not in any manifest way). For this reason, his doxology is primarily constituted, very much like Lacoste's, in the form of expectation—though explicitly with the "apocalyptic sting" of an always potentially disruptive and politically demanding "imminent expectation."[39]

At the same time, the weight that Metz places on the concrete memory of Christ as the basis for hope clearly distinguishes his position from the more indeterminate eschatologies that one finds in Heidegger's "last God" and Derrida's prohibitively apophatic messianicity without messianism. Hence, the anamnesis of revelation, which Metz argues is transmitted through the at least somewhat aesthetic medium of narrative,[40] has a determinative influence on his nevertheless largely "unrealized" anticipation of God's definitive salvific coming. The fact that Metz's prayerful thought seems to be less aesthetically enriched than Balthasar's indicates both a questionable limitation and a deliberate decision: the lesser degree of experiential confirmation that Metz allows coheres with his desire to remain in solidarity with those who are still trapped in the frankly inglorious and grisly suffering of history. Once again, however, this point of relative discontinuity with Balthasar leaves the verticality of Metz's theology intact.

Thus, although Metz diverges from Balthasar in certain significant respects, it is important to recognize that he still situates the human practices of memory, hope, prayer, and action (i.e., spirituality) in the context of a genuine *theo*-drama over which we do not ultimately have control. In short, Metz's new political theology must be understood, at the same time, as a new *prayerful* theology, and in two senses: prayer structures the right sort of politics by forming subjects capable of it, and prayer reveals the limits of politics by calling out in urgent longing to the God of the living and the dead, who alone promises to bring comprehensive justice to those who have suffered and died and, thereby, to give a believably positive meaning to history as a whole.

Contesting Carl Schmitt

The foregoing analysis implies, moreover, that it matters a great deal not only whether one develops something classifiable as a "political theology" but also what precisely is entailed therein and, specifically, how thoroughly it remains integrated with prayer. It should by now be clear that, for Metz, the residual "theological concepts" that appear in the dialectical writings of the Frankfurt School do not suffice.[41] In fact, the arguments that he makes against this way of incorporating theology into political reflection are not altogether different from those which Christian theologians would be advised to raise against Carl Schmitt's somewhat infamous "political theology." Although Metz does not spend a great deal of time engaging Schmitt's work, the latter deserves some attention here both because it remains a significant part of the background for Metz's political theology (which can be called "new" largely because it overcomes Schmitt's "older" approach) and because there has been a resurgence of theological interest in Schmitt in recent years which, from a Metzian perspective, must be met with some degree of suspicion.[42]

As a German intellectual who joined the National Socialist party in the same year as Heidegger, promoted an account of the sovereignty of political rulers in times of emergency that led him to support the rise of the *Führer*, and grounded the "concept of the political" in a friend-enemy distinction that could be easily turned against the Jews, Schmitt proves problematic in more ways than one.[43] He undoubtedly differs a great deal in overall political orientation from the Frankfurt School. However, a notable point of connection does appear in Schmitt's well-known claim that "all significant concepts of the modern theory of the state are secularized theological concepts," that is, concepts that "were transferred from theology to the theory of the state, whereby, for example, the omnipotent God became the omnipotent lawgiver."[44] Insofar as both Schmitt and the Frankfurt School are engaged in the deliberate secularization of theological themes, with a significant loss of the original theological meaning, Metz gives us reason to object to both and on very similar grounds.

With respect to Schmitt in particular, it is important to recognize that, although he appeals to certain figures of the modern Catholic counterrevolution, such as Bonald, de Maistre, and Donoso Cortés (whom Metz lists as representatives of Catholic "traditionalism"), what Schmitt actually proposes in *Political Theology* (1922) is not meant to be a theology at all, as he clarifies again in *Political Theology II* (1970), but rather a merely juridical treatment of the question of political (i.e., human) sovereignty.[45] Because he performs a strict politico-anthropological reduction of any "theological" or "metaphysical" ideas that he appropriates from his selective reading of the Catholic tradition (and he tellingly uses both words without clearly distinguishing the two), it seems that his proposal can best be understood neither as theological nor as traditional, but rather as post-Hobbesian.[46] Creating a space for the decisive action of the ruler, his original 1922 text has no room for the decisive action of God; instead it merely recalls this doctrine as a now mostly irrelevant precursor to, and extrinsic source of legitimization for, a questionable model of this-worldly decisionism. In other words, unlike Metz, Schmitt does not invoke divine sovereignty as such but only as an analogue to human sovereignty, and he leaves the important question of the limits of this analogical connection, which would be demanded by the greater dissimilarity of the *analogia entis*, largely unexamined.

Schmitt's thought becomes especially questionable in view of the particular kind of apocalyptic awareness that is proper to Christian prayer.[47] In *Political Theology II*, Schmitt speaks briefly about Metz's *Theology of the World* and grants that Metz is right to affirm the "eschatological orientation of the faith." However, Schmitt confuses Metz's position with that of the Frankfurt School, arguing that Metz offers no more than a "utopia on the principle of hope [a clear allusion to Bloch], the content of which is an *homo absconditus* who produces himself." But it is, in fact, Schmitt who leaves a genuinely Christian mode of apocalyptic expectation unthematized, preferring instead to focus on the preapocalyptic question of the *katechon* that is mentioned in 2 Thessalonians 2:1–12, which he interprets as a political apparatus that is meant to restrain chaos in the meantime, that is, prior to and independent of Christ's second coming.[48]

Schmitt acknowledges that his primarily historical or "this-worldly" orientation lies at the root of the theological critique of his work that Erik Peterson advances in *Monotheism as a Political Problem*.[49] According to Schmitt, Peterson's critique uses a strategically coded language that is not particularly difficult to decipher: Peterson denies the legitimacy of Eusebius's (i.e., Schmitt's) Constantinian (i.e., Hobbesian) political theology. Moreover, Peterson objects to Schmitt qua Eusebius not only because Schmitt's "political theology" is monarchical as opposed to Trinitarian—a point which Jürgen Moltmann takes in an intriguing yet problematic direction[50]—but also and primarily because it is not sufficiently informed by eschatological hope.[51] In short, Peterson accuses Schmitt of lacking the very sort of apocalyptic expectation that Schmitt eventually encounters but misconstrues in Metz. The irony is that Schmitt seems to appreciate Peterson's and Metz's arguments just enough to make it clear to us what direction his work could have taken to address their concerns (i.e., toward a more constitutive longing for a definitive future) but not enough to persuade him to move his work in this direction.

Schmitt's counterargument against Peterson rests mainly on a rejection of Eusebius's exemplarity, an awareness of the multifarious historical interconnections between theology and politics, and a paradoxical assertion of the theology-neutral validity of his own supposedly purely juridical or descriptive manner of reflection, but it therefore never actually becomes an adequately theological defense of his political thinking (which has certain characteristics that are vulnerable to theological critique). Unlike Metz, who discusses prayer frequently, Schmitt refers to prayer in his "political theology" only when he refers to the prayer that begins Peterson's book (which Schmitt mentions without quotation): "*May St. Augustine, whose impact has been felt in every spiritual and political transformation of the West, help with his prayers the readers and the author of this book!*" This prayer is made poignant by its insistence that we are in need of "help" and, therefore, not strictly sovereign in ourselves.[52] Although Schmitt clearly demonstrates that theology and politics have some sort of complex historical relationship, he does not let prayer become a major factor in understanding what this relationship ought to be. Prayer does not function as a constitutive feature of the political subjectivity that Schmitt endorses, which has the ominous appearance of a largely unrestrained authority possessed uniquely by a human ruler and, therefore, has very little in common with a divinely given exercise of critical freedom and love that is shareable by all. Nor does his work allow prayer to shape an anamnestic and apocalyptic solidarity which, including and transcending the political sphere, is especially concerned in both cases with the hopes of the most vulnerable.

Many of the profound differences between Schmitt and Metz are, therefore, closely related to Metz's prayerful manner of thinking, which is nearer to Peterson's, but also significantly more critical and politically agentive. At a conference in 1995, Metz argues that Schmitt's nearly exclusive concern with imposing some kind of order on a sinful and chaotic society keeps him from attending sufficiently to the challenge posed by the universality of human suffering—which, as we have seen, is the focus of Metz's alternative approach.[53] But the fact that Schmitt's thought has almost no place for prayer is no less important and, moreover, ultimately related. Although it is possible to imagine one occurring without the other, in Metz's case the politically active response to the suffering of others and the prayerful openness to the actions of God are mutually supportive: the latter motivates the former, while the former authenticates the latter. Schmitt does not display this dynamic. Thus, whatever merits he may have as a descriptive juridical thinker, the intellectual distance that he keeps from prayer seriously jeopardizes any theologically or politically prescriptive aspects of his discourse.

All in all, the extraordinary promise of the new political theology that Metz articulates in *Faith in History and Society* comes to light most clearly through its prayerful contestation of various liberal, leftist, and authoritarian rivals. Hence, although his theology is certainly political, it is so only in a very particular sense. In lieu of a theory of the state, Metz discusses possibilities for thought and action pertaining to the church and what one might cautiously call, in Jacques Maritain's terminology, the "body politic" (i.e., that manner of being-together which is not officially and constitutively governmental in function, but which still influences what happens in procedurally democratic political institutions).[54] In dialogue with the members of the Frankfurt School, Metz finds more to agree with politically than he does with Schmitt—and we have seen that this may be due in part to their positive relation with Judaism—but the absence in their reflection of a rigorous integration of prayer and thought remains a significant impediment, just as it does with Schmitt. In the end, what distinguishes Metz as an authentically *theological* political theologian and as a thinker who illuminates a spiritually viable way of responding to the crises of modern violence is precisely the serious and sustained attention that he gives to prayer.

Mystical-Political Spirituality

It remains to consider more deeply what sort of prayerful spirituality Metz has in mind. He develops more focused discussions of his spirituality in *Followers of Christ* and "The Courage to Pray." In both works, he reflects at greater length than he does in *Faith in History and Society* on the political and more-than-political significance of prayer, while further specifying his understanding of its constitutive connection with the poverty of spirit and foreshadowing some of the new directions that his thought will take in the next three decades. In particular, he begins to prioritize the cry of lament as a corrective to doxology and to interpret prayer in explicit opposition to the violence of Auschwitz. Together these developments set him on a path toward an intensified mode of prayerful thought that is affected ever more deeply by a passionate remembrance and awareness of the suffering of others.

Originally composed as an address to an audience of religious superiors that would give them insight into the German Synod document *Unsere Hoffnung* (1976), of which Metz was the principal author, *Followers of Christ* highlights the importance of consecrated religious life in the contemporary age. Metz argues that this way of life is "a kind of shock therapy instituted by the Holy Spirit for the Church as a whole." Those Christians who take vows and live according to a specific monastic or apostolic rule do not, according to Metz, enjoy any exclusive access to contemplative graces, nor are they exempt from concrete responsibilities in the world. They do, however, have a special role insofar as they are meant to remind the church in a particularly intense and effective way of the holiness that is its universal calling: that very holiness which is received as a free gift from the Holy Spirit and embodied in an inevitably costly *imitatio Christi*.[55] The perichoretic quality of Metz's spirituality is, therefore, very clear in this work, along with his rather balanced view of the value of religious and lay vocations in the church.

But the most remarkable elements of this text are the four "mystical" and "political" interpretations that he gives to the three evangelical counsels of poverty, celibacy, and obedience and finally to the theme of apocalyptic. Although one might assume that poverty of spirit is but one element among many here (the first one), it is in fact the guiding thread of the whole argument. Celibacy, obedience, and apocalyptic extend and specify the mystical and political dimensions of the practice of spiritual poverty that Metz begins to treat in the first meditation. In his treatment of each of these Christian virtues, he draws attention to a Christic model that we are called to imitate voluntarily, along with a parallel involuntary condition endured by many in the world, which demands the response of our practical solidarity. The involuntary aspect here is not limited to the innate (existential) poverty that Metz discusses in his early work but also crucially includes certain historically contingent situations of suffering that need not be.

Metz identifies the mystical element of the counsel of poverty with the act of following Jesus in his "poverty in the Spirit" (*Armut im Geiste*), that is, his "poverty and freedom of love." Metz argues that this mystical participation in Christ's self-emptying and self-giving poverty also requires political and material solidarity with the impoverished around the world, and especially those in so-called developing regions, who are victims of the possessive and calculative spirit of bourgeois society. At the same time, this mystical-political synthesis leaves what he calls a "specific place" for a more-than-political, but still solidaristic, practice of prayer, in which one would "pray not only for the poor but with them," that is, in their languages, in their presence, and with their concerns in mind.[56] In this respect, the evangelical call to a Christ-like poverty of spirit would not only be realized in a prayerfully inspired political praxis but also in a politically conscious act of praying—intentionally praying and not merely working or struggling—together with others.

Similarly, Metz contends that the virtue of celibacy, which he defines as the chosen state of "not having anyone," involves a particular kind of poverty: the poverty of loneliness. He suggests that celibacy should include a mystical longing for Christ, in which one refuses to let one's desire be satisfied by anything other than the coming *parousia* of the Lord. At the same time, it demands concrete acts of solidarity with those who are involuntarily isolated or alone, including the unmarried, the divorced, the young, and all those who are in some sense *socially* poor. He explains that one should strive not only to be physically and emotionally present with them, but also to give "their sufferings a language, and indeed the language of prayer."[57] Thus in the midst of mystical-political celibacy as well, prayer has a special place as a solidaristic, but not for this reason any less theocentric, spiritual practice.

For Metz, obedience is also a kind of poverty: one in which we surrender ourselves entirely to the will of God. He contends that this obediential poverty is manifest most clearly in the Son's kenosis and particularly in his cry from the cross. This cry expresses the depths of Jesus's suffering *from* and *unto* God (*Leiden an Gott*). The ambiguity of this "*an*" reflects the duality of Jesus's experience of obedient God-forsakenness: it indicates both his voluntary passivity to the will of his Father "from" whom he suffers abandonment and the questioning complaint that he directs "unto" his Father without thereby becoming disobedient or unfaithful. Metz clarifies that prayer is the act through which we participate mystically in this Christic experience of suffering from and unto God.[58] Hence, for Metz too, as for Chrétien, prayer in this instance becomes a kind of "wounded word." The wounding is real and it is not only a product of the violence of the world but also, to some extent, an effect of a simultaneous obedient and agonistic interaction with God. But exactly what sort of prayer does Metz have in mind here? If it is doxology (as it mainly seems to be for Chrétien), then it is doxology of a very peculiar sort, which would be essentially characterized by the seemingly opposed form of a passionate cry of lament. It would be a doxology largely without the perception of *doxa*, an offering of protest more than of praise, a critical act of questioning rather than a joyful acclamation.

Metz suggests that this lamenting form of prayer, in which Christ's followers participate mystically, has significant political consequences. In contrast to Balthasar, he emphasizes that it is precisely the absence of glory in Christ's passion that makes his obedience unto death concretely imitable for his followers, who must remain steadfast in their divine service even when there is virtually no consoling evidence of an already given victory in their lives. Moreover, Metz contends that the absence of glory makes Jesus's cry relevant for the victims of history who involuntarily endure similarly inglorious conditions of worldly humiliation and oppression. In order to remain in solidarity with this anguished majority of the earth's population, Metz maintains that prayer must avoid adopting "any language of over-affirmation, any artificial language of rejoicing isolated from all language of suffering and crisis."[59] Thus, in addition to highlighting the mystical and political dimensions of obedience, as a mode of spiritual poverty, Metz also makes a case against any excessively doxological construal of obedience, preferring instead to emphasize its oppositional characteristics.

The christological context of Metz's discussion is crucial for an adequate understanding of his notion of *Leiden an Gott*. This context keeps Metz from dismissing doxology altogether. In the same section of the argument, he praises Christ as "the brilliant image of God who raises up and liberates."[60] He, therefore, clearly does not want to prohibit this sort of doxology but rather merely to insist that it must remain connected with, and thus somewhat troubled by, the practice of lament. In short, his point is simply that those who voluntarily or involuntarily imitate Christ's passion are right to adopt his questioning and somewhat accusatory prayer as their own: "My God, my God, why have you forsaken me?" (Ps. 22:1; Mark 15:34). It is very striking that this almost rebellious form of prayer arises in Metz's work as a central feature of his discussion of what it means to imitate the Son's *obedience*. This extraordinary connection has been too often overlooked. It suggests that christological kenosis and *Gelassenheit* could cohere with—and even *demand*—a particular way of asserting oneself before God, in which one would not quietly accept the seemingly inescapable godlessness of the world as a paradoxical gift from being or divine providence, but rather shout out against it and call upon God to do something about it.

Metz's developing idea of the poverty of spirit reaches its high point in his discussion of apocalyptic. Once again, he cites Matthew 25 as proof that imminent eschatological expectation is linked with the need for active solidarity, and he quotes the urgent prayer concluding the book of Revelation, "Come, Lord Jesus," in order to show that much more is required to save the world than that which human effort alone can supply. By situating this apocalyptic prayer at the end of his account of the virtues of consecrated religious life, he appears to emphasize one crucial point, namely that however necessary and costly these virtues are, they do not put the fate of the world entirely into our hands. As religious or lay followers of

Christ, we are called to give ourselves completely to the Christic task of becoming poor, chaste, and obedient in spirit, but this does not mean that everything depends on our ascetical self-mastery. At the end of the day, we must entrust this world to God, not to ourselves. Metz shares this insight with the greatest saints and mystics of the Christian doxological tradition. At the same time, he adds his own distinctive accent: this sort of trust implies the need to wait and to hope for God's decisive intervention and, hence, to avoid the temptation of letting oneself become spiritually full or satisfied prematurely.[61] For Metz, therefore, the poor in spirit are those who give everything of themselves while acknowledging that God is the true savior and who do not allow themselves to rest or feel content until the glorious disclosure of this salvation is complete.

It is not difficult to see why Metz would want to describe the poor in spirit as *courageous* in prayer: they dare to wait as long as necessary for a time of rejoicing, and yet in the meantime they hold nothing of themselves back, neither in terms of spiritually motivated political commitment, nor in terms of their urgent and constant plea for the advent of God. The main point of *Followers of Christ* and "The Courage to Pray" is thus, in many respects, the same. A very similar prayerful subject comes into view in both texts. In the latter, Metz helpfully summarizes many of the ideas about prayer that he has left scattered throughout other works. He connects prayer with the realization of "subjectivity and identity." He explains that prayer, by definition, says "yes" to God, but not without "the language of pain and crisis, lament and accusation" that is found throughout the tradition of biblical Israel and particularly in Jesus's cry from the cross. He calls on us to remember the unfulfilled prayers and hopes of the dead. He argues that prayer involves "the readiness to accept responsibility" for one's wrongdoings and to engage in political action in solidarity with the most vulnerable. And he contends that prayer confronts the apathy of our technological and evolutionistic culture with imminent eschatological hope (as one might expect by now, his final words are "Come, Lord Jesus!").[62]

The primary element that we have not yet encountered which he adds in "The Courage to Pray" appears in the form of a thesis that he will reiterate several times after this point: "We can and should pray after Auschwitz because even in Auschwitz, in the hell of Auschwitz, they prayed."[63] With the word "we," he refers especially to German Christians, whom he understandably takes as his main audience, but also to all Christians and indeed to all human beings who survived or will live on after this hellacious event. With the word "they," he means primarily the Jewish people in Auschwitz and the many other Nazi death camps, who were the principal targets of the attempted genocide. *Their* prayers—the prayers precisely of *these* Jewish victims—now constitute, in his judgment, a permanently indispensable criterion of legitimacy for his *own* prayers, as well as those of his fellow Christians and theologians. This sort of radical openness to the prayers of others (in this case, very specific others), adds a further layer of intensity to his spirituality, which must now be located definitively after Auschwitz and *against* it. In what follows, we shall examine the implications of Metz's particular way of prayerfully resisting this singularly horrible manifestation of modern violence.

PRAYER, AUSCHWITZ

Having developed a largely Rahnerian response to Heidegger's insufficiently theological anthropocentrism, and having endorsed the sort of ideology critique of Heidegger's ontology that one finds in Adorno, Metz now effectively combats Heidegger's anti-Judaism and exposes this as the root cause of Heidegger's twofold inability to think prayer as it gives itself and to think prayer in a manner that actually promises to address the crises of our age—which, in Auschwitz, are condensed in a form much more tangible and inescapable than the structure of ontotheology. Violence here takes flesh. It becomes indistinguishable from the world.[64] It enters into the history of human bodies and destroys them, millions of them, millions of God's children, God's chosen people, and this is the crisis. To the extent that prayer survives in this place, and among its victims, it also implicitly defies this violence and indicates at least one essential way in which it must henceforward be continually defied.[65] In many of his texts from the late 1970s through the present, Metz devotes himself to understanding what exactly it would mean to treat the prayers in Auschwitz as normative for his own prayerful form of Christian theology.[66]

Three questions merit particular consideration here. First, exactly what sort of relationship between Jewish and Christian thought, and between Jews and Christians themselves, does Metz advocate? This question is unavoidable because, however much he wants to ground his theology in the prayers of Jewish victims, he nevertheless continues to speak as a Christian and, hence, at some remove from the immediately relevant (which is to say, non-Christian) manifestations of Judaism. However, despite this distance, he envisions a uniquely close and intimate relationship that is worthy of attention. Second, how does Metz, and how should Christian theologians, finally address the tension between prayer understood as doxology and as *Leiden an Gott*? This question compels us to sort out the contours of an implicit debate between Metz's approach and the postmetaphysically doxological and nondoxological thought-forms that we explored in the first three chapters. Situating Metz in relation to the distinctive poetic visions of Paul Celan and Nelly Sachs will help us pursue a meaningful response to this question. Finally, what about the suffering and the prayers of *other* others? Does Metz's focus on Auschwitz involve an illegitimate neglect of other devastating incarnations of modern violence, particularly outside of Europe? We shall examine some of the ways in which he guards against this danger.

With respect to the first question, Metz makes two interconnected arguments that need to be disentangled. On the one hand, he contends that Christians must take responsibility for the roles that their theology and praxis have played in the history of violence against the Jews and, moreover, remember and welcome their Jewish neighbors with the respect that is their due not only as human beings but also precisely as God's chosen people. With these changes he believes that a better relationship might be cultivated not merely between Christianity and Judaism as two different religions but more fundamentally between Christians and Jews as living, breathing subjects. On the other hand, he maintains that there is something crucial about the Jewish spirit—that is, about particular aspects of Israel's prayerful way of life, as this is disclosed not only in scripture but also throughout history and especially in the hell of Auschwitz—that must be retrieved as the heart of an authentic Christian spirituality and theology today. Although these two arguments are related, they are also importantly distinct: whereas in the former Metz approaches the Jews as someone striving to enter into solidarity with others, in the latter he reflects on their spirituality as intrinsic to his own. Each argument deserves a closer look.

In the first, Metz stresses that Christians should not let themselves be consoled by the misleading claims which some interpreters have made that the Shoah was a "purely National Socialist crime" or merely the product of a "German spirit" that might be safely separated from Christianity.[67] More generally, he insists that Christians must acknowledge all of the persecutions against Jews that are part of their history and simultaneously demand and enforce "the radical end of every persecution of Jews by Christians."[68] This recognition and cessation of active violence is only the first step. The next involves interrogating and overcoming the apathy that has historically prevented Christians and others from responding effectively to the violence occurring all around them. Metz recalls the fact that during the Nazi period, "we prayed and celebrated our liturgy with our backs to Auschwitz."[69] Prayer, in this instance, abetted the triumph of inhumanity. With the threat of this sort of deadly hypocrisy in mind, Metz concludes that the confessions of guilt and regret that Christians may make today regarding their collective inaction will become credible only if they continue to work toward a more positive relationship with Jewish people, engage in political resistance against anti-Semitism, and, perhaps most crucially of all, affirm the enduring validity of the Jewish covenant (now a normative teaching of the Catholic Church).[70] Responsibility demands at least this much.

But Metz ultimately calls for more than the overcoming of violence and indifference, more than political solidarity, and more than theological respect: he envisions an intimate relationship with Jews

built on hospitality. He encourages Christians to be physically receptive to their Jewish neighbors, striving to hear what they hear
and see what they see.[71] The hospitality of the ears and the eyes,
which Chrétien analyzes as an indispensable aspect of our doxological openness to the unheard-of excess of God, becomes concretized
in Metz's work as a vital way in which Christians are able to participate in what Emil Fackenheim calls the praxis of *tikkun olam*, the
mending of the world.[72] This praxis has to take place in the present
and in remembrance of the past. In order to pray in a manner that
promises to begin healing their deeply damaged historical relationship with Jews—in order, precisely, to pray *without* their backs to
Auschwitz—Christians must, Metz contends, not only welcome
their Jewish neighbors in their midst now but also open their hearts
to "the destroyed faces, the burned eyes," and the screams of the
Jews who were killed in the death camps and in the horrific history
of Christian anti-Jewish violence.[73] He argues that this memory of
sensible, palpable horror should disturb every blithely affirmative
practice of Christian prayer. The willingness to accept this sort of
disturbance is an important aspect of the relationship-mending hospitality that he prescribes.

Metz's second argument proceeds in a different direction, and is
concerned less with how Christians must relate to Jews after Auschwitz through responsibility and hospitality, and more with a certain kind of Jewish spirituality that he understands as intrinsic to
Christianity. He explains that "precisely as a Christian theologian
after Auschwitz, I have always asked myself this question: What is
it finally that makes Israel . . . indispensable, even for Christianity?"
His answer is "Israel's poverty of spirit" and its "mysticism of suffering unto God [*Leiden an Gott*]," especially as these are expressed
in "Israel's prayer traditions." Thus the particular account of Jewish spirituality that he seeks to retain is largely isomorphic with the
particular form of Christian spirituality that he presents in *Followers
of Christ* and "The Courage to Pray." Metz explains that the Jewish
tradition of spiritual poverty and *Leiden an Gott* is an indispensable
part of Christianity precisely because Jesus is part of this tradition.
Jesus's cry from the cross is a quotation from a psalm; it, therefore,

belongs to "the landscape of cries" (a title which Metz, following Nelly Sachs, gives to Israel). The obediential and agonistic prayer of Christ's passion, which Christians are called to imitate, does not emerge as part of the cosmological metaphysics of Greek antiquity, nor as an element within its consoling mythology; these are not its spirit (*Geist*). Rather, it comes forth from the "spirit [*Geist*] of the Jewish traditions."[74] Hence, in contrast to Heidegger's attachment to Greco-German culture and even Caputo's search for a "Jewgreek" manner of thinking, Metz advocates the recovery of a Christian spiritual practice that would be specifically Jewish and decidedly not philosophically or mythologically Greek.

To be sure, Metz's construal of "Jewishness" is bound to be controversial. He interprets Israel almost reductively as the bearer of the theodicy-question—the question of how to think about or address God in the midst of unjust suffering—and he tends to give much less attention to other important features of Israel's historical existence as a people.[75] Moreover, as a Christian thinker, he seems unable to avoid treating Israel in some sense as a prefiguration or prototype of Christ, even though he acknowledges the enduring validity of Israel's covenant. The apparent inevitability of this typological connection for Christians does not erase its dangers; one can only insist, from a Christian perspective, that it is better to recognize the deeply Jewish roots of authentic Christian spirituality than it is to forget them.[76] Finally, in order to correct an excess in the opposite direction, Metz may risk aligning Christianity so closely with Judaism that Christianity's own distinctiveness begins to be underemphasized (we shall return to this objection below). However, despite these potentially legitimate concerns, Metz's account of the Jewish spirit *within* Christianity is perhaps best understood as the attempt of a Christian theologian to take seriously the prayers of the victims in Auschwitz and the traditions from which they arose, and in this respect the effort is commendable.

For Metz, it is not only the *fact* that there were prayers in Auschwitz that matters but also and more importantly the particular *characteristics* of these prayers. He wants Christians to realize that the passionate questions and cries emerging from the Shoah are normative for their own spiritual practice, and he is able to make this case, in part, by showing that this sort of prayer is continuous with the Hebrew scriptures (Job, the Psalms, Lamentations, etc.) and, most crucially, with Jesus's lament on the cross. One can pray like Christ and against Auschwitz simultaneously.

At this point, we must turn to the second question of this section and consider how Metz's post-Auschwitz spirituality—which, as we have seen, involves a simultaneously Jewish and Christian practice of spiritual poverty and *Leiden an Gott*—not only disrupts, but also in some sense preserves, a connection with doxology. The issue here is not whether there can be poetry after Auschwitz (which was not Adorno's point in any case) but rather what sort of poetry and, by extension, prayer actually promises to resist its violence.[77] Metz gives some indication when he refers to Paul Celan and Nelly Sachs, two Jewish poets and friends who, having in different ways only barely survived the Shoah, gave voice to a deeply scarred but nevertheless in some sense abiding relationship with God.[78] Without offering any detailed readings, Metz invokes their names in a way that suggests that their poetry constitutes one of his major points of access to what it might have meant to pray in Auschwitz and, therefore, to pray legitimately after it. In a sense, just as Hölderlin informs Heidegger's rather impure doxology, so too Celan and Sachs give inspiration to Metz's thoughts regarding *Leiden an Gott*. Neither poet—not even Celan—eliminates doxology altogether. But they do deeply unsettle it. Beneath every hymnic verse that they write there is an audible or inaudible cry that carries the passion of unjust death toward God and treats it not as a gift but as a contradiction for which God must be held to account, a contradiction which appears to challenge the very divinity of God.

Celan takes the greater risk in this respect. His manner of thinking poetically and prayerfully after the Shoah approaches the largely nondoxological and almost entirely apophatic style of speech that one finds in Derrida and Caputo, in which God is not (yet, any longer, or perhaps ever) given. The connection between these thinkers can be approached in two ways: on the one hand, both Celan and Derrida remain indebted to Heidegger's (and thus Nietzsche's and

Hölderlin's) awareness of the "death" or "default" of God, even when they radically depart from Heidegger's theory in other respects.[79] On the other hand, Celan is an explicit source for Derrida's later thought. It is worth noting that Derrida quotes several lines from Celan's "Psalm": "No one moulds us again out of / earth and clay, / no one conjures our dust. / No one. / Praised be your name, no one. / For your sake / we shall flower. / Toward you. / A nothing / we were, are, shall / remain, flowering: / the nothing-, the / no one's rose."[80] Derrida explains that, in this case, "to address no one is not exactly not to address any one."[81] Philippe Lacoue-Labarthe makes a similar observation: if it simply did not invoke anyone, Celan's "Psalm" would not be a prayer in any meaningful sense; however, because it precisely invokes "No one" it remains a prayer, "a *real* prayer," indeed, "a song or a hymn in honor of . . . No one."[82] Thus we are confronted by a doxological prayer at the very limits of the possibility of doxological prayer, whose implicitly divine addressee remains anonymous, nonapparent, nonexistent.

The allusion in Celan's poem to Angelus Silesius's rose seems, at once, to applaud and indict Heidegger, who according to Celan rightly rejects Leibniz's principle of sufficient reason but is nevertheless implicated in the genocidal violence that has exposed creation as "the no one's rose." No real delight can be taken in the "whylessness" of the blooming flower because it has now been reduced to "a nothing." It lacks essence, form; "no one moulds" it again. Therefore, the doxology which would praise God in thanksgiving for all of the beautiful gifts that are radiant in creation becomes in this world of violence impossible to sing without the overwhelming sense that the infinitude and finitude of being, both sides of the *analogia entis*, have been negated. Glory has become *Aschenglorie*.[83] As a result, praise must be expressed as accusation; prayers are addressed to "You" as "Not-You" (*Aber-Du*); one speaks to God "as one speaks to stone."[84]

When Metz describes the language of prayer as "the only language without forbidden speech," as a language "in which one can also say that one does not believe," and as the "source of negative theology"—and when he maintains, finally, that it must not be reduced to a comfortable "I-You" conversation—one can begin to sense his respect for the sort of painfully apophatic discourse that Celan's poetry epitomizes.[85] However, Metz's discourse has more in common with the arguably more determinate, but no less anguished, hope in God that Sachs displays in her poetry. The difference between these two poets is somewhat clarified when Celan speaks with Sachs about "your God": that is, the biblical God that is still hers but no longer his, at least not as openly or directly.[86] The somewhat subtle but important theological difference that is signaled by this exchange also distinguishes Metz's *Leiden an Gott* from the Derridean form of radically apophatic, post-Auschwitz prayer which, as we have seen, invokes Celan as a privileged witness. In short, Metz's theology is closer to Sachs's poetry than Celan's, insofar as Metz's hope maintains a somewhat less negative relation with biblical doxology.

In "Chorus of the Dead," Sachs writes: "Withered on our bodies are the deaths done unto us / Like flowers of the field withered on a hill of sand. O you who still greet the dust as friend / You who, speaking sand, say to the sand: / I love you. / We say to you: / Torn are the cloaks of the mysteries of dust / . . . We dead of Israel say to you: / We are moving past one more star / Into our hidden God."[87] As in Celan's "Psalm," so too here, the floral quality of creation is above all a sign of vulnerability and mortality: the flowers wither and disappear into almost nothing ("sand," "dust"). The implied accusation is similar: How does your "I love you," your friendship with creation and with your people, mean anything when there is so much meaningless death, when the inexpressible "mysteries" shrouded in our embodiment are torn to shreds? However, unlike Celan, Sachs does not invoke "No one," does not address "Not-You," but rather "You." This is a prayer, sung in chorus with the dead of Israel, to "our hidden God." God hides but is still possessed ("our"), still sought and loved, even when passionately questioned and protested.

This is more the spirit of Metz's lament. His question of theodicy is not a question that considers ridding itself of God, nor even remaining indefinitely in a state of apophatic suspension, but rather a question that continues to presuppose that God is the only one who promises to save. He asks rhetorically: "Is this not a cry that 'arrives' never and nowhere? No! But why not? Because this cry is itself the expression that it has arrived." Extending the logic of Sach's poetry, Metz locates the painfully incomprehensible nearness of God precisely in the cry: "God has, in his inapproachable and ineffable divinity, drawn so near to the Israelites that they cried after him. In this cry he was 'present' to them as God; in this cry he haunted them in his godliness; in this cry is fulfilled for them what theology calls 'present eschatology,' the present event of God [*Gotteseignis*], the being-there of God [*Da-sein Gottes*]."[88] Metz could hardly be more audacious here: he claims that the prayer that arises from the depths of Israel's suffering coincides precisely with a mysterious advent of God. It is for this reason that Metz categorizes *Leiden an Gott* as a kind of "mysticism." To be sure, it is not defined by a sense of blissful absorption in divine love. Largely devoid of *doxa* (as we have seen), it also has a very tenuous connection with *logos*, at least insofar as this word implies some high degree of intelligibility in which the questions of suffering would have clear and certain answers.[89] But it is a kind of mysticism nonetheless precisely because it involves an experience of intimacy—wounded, angry, frustratingly opaque intimacy—with the hidden God.[90]

Metz does not clarify how exactly his account of the mystical character of *Leiden an Gott* coheres with his claim that Christians are not permitted to find "traces of God" in Auschwitz.[91] One potential answer would involve insisting that individuals and communities should be given space to struggle with and interpret their own experiences of suffering. Hence, Christians should *by no means* seek to explain how God is present in the horror that is endured by others, especially by Jews who are the victims of Christian anti-Semitic violence. At another level, however, we are perhaps simply confronted here with an irresolvable tension, in which it appears necessary to deny both the presence and the absence of God in the midst of suffering, while simultaneously recognizing that each is in its own way undeniable. For Metz, the only legitimate response that can be made to this aporia is to raise it up to God as a question or, as he says, "to question back" (*Rückfragen*). Thus, although a somewhat doxological (because divinely given) mysticism remains integral to

Metz's reflections on the cry, this very same mysticism (as in Sachs's poetry) has been called into question—or rather been reconfigured precisely *as* a question. Metz interrogates the encounter with God, but this interrogation is also an encounter.

The clearest difference between Sachs and Metz is that Metz discovers the unsettling closeness of God not only in the prayer tradition of Israel but also in Jesus's prayer. However, because the latter is intelligible only in the context of the former, this difference proves less momentous than one might expect. For this reason, it seems that Christian theologians must still consider whether Metz does enough to preserve a distinctively Christian mode of prayer. In Metz's later work, do Christ's life, death, and resurrection actually accomplish something radically new and decisive, which would necessarily be relevant to the meaning and practice of prayer, particularly as praise or thanksgiving? Does Christ add anything that is not already sufficiently expressed in the Hebrew scriptures? And most pointedly, is it possible to affirm this idea any longer after Auschwitz?

The main point at which Metz's theology could fare better on these questions comes to light in the needlessly stark opposition that he draws between *Leiden an Gott* and *Leiden in Gott*. The latter is his term for a Trinitarian and christological way of incorporating the world's suffering into the divine mystery of salvation—a theological stratagem that he discovers in the works of Barth, Jüngel, Bonhoeffer, Moltmann, and most notably here, Balthasar. Metz is understandably concerned about various dangers in this approach: it seems to offer "*too much* of a response, soothing the eschatological questioning of God"; it is "too speculative, almost gnostic"; it involves "too much Hegel . . . , that is, too much reduction of suffering to its concept"; and it employs an "aestheticization of suffering" which surreptitiously and illegitimately treats it as though it were actually "exalted" or "noble" (i.e., glorious). These recent representatives of Christian doxology would thus appear to be implicated in the overly consoling and amnesic cultural dynamics that are characteristic of our now "postmodern" bourgeois society—dynamics which Metz argues ultimately encourage the forgetting of concrete historical suffering.[92]

These are real threats that should not be taken lightly. However, in order to resist them through a distinctively Christian form of prayer, it seems necessary to acknowledge that Christ discloses, in himself, both *Leiden an Gott* and *Leiden in Gott*. The duality here corresponds, more or less, to the doctrine of Chalcedon: it is in Jesus's humanity especially that we see him suffer from the absence of God and cry out for God's presence; but it is precisely in his divinity that he takes up the human experience of prayerful suffering that occurs in our violent and impoverished world and brings it into the very heart of the Trinity's salvific action, as an irresistible petition addressed by the Son to the Father. What Metz successfully demonstrates is that, in contemplating the latter, we must not forget the former.

On the one hand, we must not lose sight of the fact that our prayers, our obedience, and our humanity can be no greater than Jesus's. It follows that we must not allow ourselves to be content, in some sort of quasi-Hegelian manner, with an intelligible (whether this means theo-aesthetic or theo-dramatic) reconciliation of the world's negativity with God. This sort of premature sense of conceptual or perceptual closure (which Balthasar perhaps does not wholly avoid) cannot do justice to Jesus's own cry. On the other hand, there can be no serious prohibition of the sort of doxological thought that is occasioned by the revelation of divine *doxa* and *logos* that occurs in the biblical narration of Christ and in the Christian spiritual and theological tradition (which, notably, form the heart of Balthasar's reflections). To honor these sources of prayer, it seems one must find the courage to be consoled by the glorious promise of Christ's *first* coming while at the same time courageously practicing a Christ-like poverty of spirit in urgent longing for his definitive second coming. Auschwitz cannot break the christological link between *Leiden an Gott* and *Leiden in Gott*, which is implied by the hypostatic union and more concretely by the events of Christ's life, death, and resurrection. The destructive force of Auschwitz has been immeasurably powerful but not this powerful. Such, at least, is the only hope that remains for a recognizably Christian form of prayer after Auschwitz.

Finally, there is the question of a horror in the world not limited to the Shoah—a more widely forgotten violence, not located in Europe, but nevertheless having much to do with Europe and its modern history. With this question, it seems necessary to look beyond Metz. And yet, he has not neglected it. While focusing on the concreteness of Auschwitz, he retains a sense of the universality of suffering and, particularly, a concern for the unjust suffering of the poor and marginalized wherever they might be. The Jewish-Christian encounter is not the only context for an "open-eyed," "face-seeking" mysticism of compassion. Metz makes this clear when he reflects on the many anguished faces that he witnessed while visiting several countries in Latin America in 1988 (specifically Mexico, Columbia, Peru, and Brazil). Metz contends that the will-to-power has distanced modern and postmodern European culture from the memory and the experience of this sort of suffering on the undersides of history, whereas the biblical tradition of the poverty of spirit demands precisely that we remain cognizant of this suffering, seek to resist it practically, and raise it up prayerfully as an urgent question to God.[93] One cannot say, then, that Metz focuses on Auschwitz to the exclusion of other manifestations of modern violence, even though he treats Auschwitz as a singularly decisive event.

The breadth of Metz's perspective is confirmed in another way by his insistence that, although the state of Israel must be supported (albeit not uncritically) as a safe-haven for Jews after the Shoah, this in no way authorizes one to forget the suffering of the Palestinians. On the contrary, for Metz, the practice of spiritual poverty requires that we, whether Jew or Christian, keep our eyes open "not only to the suffering of our own people but . . . also to the suffering of others, the suffering of those who have until now been enemies." This rule of hospitality, this politics of peace and friendship, obligates Israel as much as it does the church. Addressing Christians in particular, Metz argues that, like Christ, they must endeavor to see first the suffering and the needs of others, not their sins.[94] In a sense, the primary concern of Christians should be—as Jesus's was—that for which *others* pray: that hope arising in the midst of their suffering that compels them to cry out, silently or vocally, to God or to their neighbor. Here Metz implicitly, and yet radically, disputes the competence of Schmitt's categorical friend-enemy distinction. At most, this distinction would offer a provisionally accurate outline of a conflictual situation; however, in light of Metz's spirituality (which on this precise point intersects with Levinas's and Derrida's ethical affirmation of the other), the friend-enemy distinction cannot be taken as settling the prescriptive question regarding the sort of political action that should or must ensue.[95] An actively embodied attention, of the sort that Metz recommends, which would be given to the faces, eyes, and prayers of others, promises not only to forestall any future repetition of Auschwitz but also to counteract innumerable sorts of violence occurring throughout the world, including those that are perpetrated against so-called enemies.

In the end, therefore, as much as Metz is a political theologian, he is also a prayerful theologian—and, specifically, a practically oriented theorist of the poverty of spirit. This is the central idea that arises again and again throughout his works. At first, it enables him to embrace the human spirit in the form of a constitutively prayerful subject that has been largely (though not entirely) differentiated from the modern metaphysical subject. The explicitly ontological character of his early thought is perhaps, after Marion, something that one could beneficially nuance. More generally, his doctrine of anthropocentrism seems to be overstated. But the fact that Metz turns to prayer in order to resist the crises of metaphysics and, while relying significantly on Heidegger, also distances his project from certain problematic aspects of Heidegger's never-quite-theological thought is certainly noteworthy. At the very least, it should now be clear that Metz's early work cannot be easily dismissed as a merely transcendental and, therefore, unacceptably metaphysical theology. It is, on the contrary, much more thoroughly shaped by prayer, doxology, kenosis, and *Gelassenheit* than it is by any metaphysical and typically modern sense of a foundational ego. It is precisely prayer which gives Metz the courage and the resources to uphold the dignity of the human spirit in a world that, as we have especially witnessed in postmodernity, threatens to disintegrate it. In short, he declares, in a phrase that is at once doxological, theological, spiritual, and humanistic: *gloria Dei vivens homo.*

Then there is the crucial political turn that, we have seen, in no way diminishes but in fact deepens Metz's engagement with prayer and the poverty of spirit. The prayerful features of his new political and more-than-political theology—specifically, the actively solidaristic subject that is formed by prayer and the apocalyptic hope for the dead that is expressed in prayer—are precisely those features that most clearly distinguish it from various influential but problematic alternatives, especially those associated with bourgeois religion, neo-Marxist theory, and post-Hobbesian authoritarianism. Furthermore, Metz's account of the mystical-political following of Christ discloses a spirituality that is deeply rooted in the ancient Christian pursuit of holiness through poverty, celibacy, and obedience; practically oriented toward alleviating analogous involuntary conditions that are part of the injustice of contemporary society; and yet ultimately aware that the salvation of the world is not something that we can achieve through our own strivings, however virtuous, obligatory, and significant they remain.

Finally, without neglecting other manifestations of violence in the modern age, Metz turns his attention particularly to the Shoah, which he approaches in remembrance of the concrete horror of Auschwitz. As a German and Christian thinker, he advocates not only a new posture of responsibility and hospitality toward the Jews precisely as legitimately other (especially because their covenant abides), but also a retrieval of a particular sort of Jewish spirituality as integral to any sort of Christian prayer and theology that actually promises to remember and resist the violence of Auschwitz. In this regard, although he shows great respect for the radical sort of lament that appears in Paul Celan's poetry and is taken up by Derrida as a source of mostly nondoxological prayer, Metz's understanding of *Leiden an Gott* remains closer to the somewhat more determinately theological lament of Nelly Sachs and, therefore, to something like doxology. Metz's recourse to a particular sort of Christology is that which distinguishes him from Sachs but also leads him to oppose, it seems too strongly, any theory of suffering *in* God, which is to say any aesthetics or dramatics (such as Balthasar's) that already authorizes a christological and Trinitarian contemplation of God's victory over the negativity of the world. The argument here has been that, for Chalcedonian reasons, it is necessary to hold in tension the christological profiles of *Leiden an Gott* and *Leiden in Gott*, without, however, ignoring Metz's insightful analysis regarding the dangerous forms of collective apathy that tend to arise in tandem with an uncritical prioritization of the latter.

In order to rebel credibly and authentically as a Christian against the horror of Auschwitz and other horrors in which Christians have been implicated, it is necessary to let Christian doxology be disrupted by prayers of suffering, including especially the suffering of Jews and other victimized communities that may or may not be Christian. This is an indispensable aspect of a genuine poverty of spirit. At the same time, Metz's very early affirmation of the christologically grounded consolation that comes with an explicitly pneumatological practice of spiritual poverty remains thought provoking, even in the midst and the remembrance of such suffering. Can there be a joyful resilience, borne of prayer, which survives even in prayer's moments of greatest desperation?

With Lacoste, one might suggest that in Metz's work we are confronted once again precisely with a distinction between presence and *parousia*—a distinction that leaves us, in the meantime, without the satisfaction of being spiritually rich, saturated by glory, perfectly content in a realm freed from all contradiction and misery. These beatific states are not the conditions of our worldliness, nor, therefore, of any contemplation that actually occurs with open eyes in this world. And yet, after the incarnation and the sending of the Spirit, we can and must say that ours is a world already marked, perhaps almost invisibly but nonetheless unforgettably—as Chrétien would say—by the promise of transformation. However unfulfilled it remains, this promise is undoubtedly relevant to the challenge of sustaining hope in the midst of violent and useless suffering. Therefore, no longer *merely* doxological—and for important reasons— spirituality would after Metz need to retain, precisely in its critical anguish, at least something like the *possibility* of doxology. Its very hope depends on it.

In the next chapter, we shall consider the prayerful contributions of several Latin American theologians who are interested not primarily in the poverty of spirit but rather in the grace, freedom, and social healing that the right sort of spirit or spirituality has the power to confer. However, here it will be crucial to ask and carefully discern, which spirit and which spirituality? The most prayerful and doxological of these liberation theologians proclaim an experience of integral liberation constituted by an already operative Trinitarian sanctification of history, which prepares creation to receive the full glorious advent of the triune God's eschatological reign. They are not content with any merely anthropological self-emancipation, characteristic of certain rival "spirits" and "spiritualities" in the modern age. Moreover, although the cry of apocalyptic longing that sharpens Metz's reflections on the poverty of spirit does not disappear in their works, it is supplemented by a resilient conviction regarding the divine spirit's liberating actions in the here and now: in the struggles of abused and abjected peoples; in their perhaps only infinitesimal victories; and in the prayers, hymns, and contemplations that sustain them along the way. At this point we shall turn from Europe to a larger world, which many Christian theologians perhaps still wish to see as peripheral, though for Christ and the church it is certainly not. We shall draw closer to the victims of this world who are the countless, unenviable poor. We shall endeavor to hear their prayers and understand what they imply for the future of a planetary society, which may yet become more open to God's promised gifts of holistic justice, peace, and liberation.

CHAPTER 5

DISCERNMENT OF SPIRITS
On the Integrity of Doxology and Liberation

The texts and the lives of many Latin American liberation theologians can be studied together as various expressions of a
particular tradition of counterviolent Christian spirituality, which,
though largely consistent with the distinctive spirituality that forms
Metz's prayerful political theology, also deserves to be analyzed in
its own right. This tradition seeks to disrupt the systemic violence
against the poor that continues to afflict much of the contemporary
world, particularly Latin America and the global South. The best
representatives of this tradition do this by promoting an integrated
performance of doxological contemplation and historically liberative action. The now well-known doctrine of the preferential option
for the poor and the epistemological prioritizations of solidaristic
praxis and the "view from the victims" clearly underscore the latter aspect. However, what needs to be emphasized here—because
it has not always been very well understood and because it tends to
be concealed even by some of the most influential inheritors of this
tradition[1]—is that many liberation theologians have also treated the
former aspect as absolutely essential. In short, the most adequate sort
of liberation theology includes a prayerful and doxological spirituality as one of its founding principles.[2] The freedom that is promised
by God and perpetually received, offered, and desired by humanity

218

is a freedom that arises from the simultaneous affirmation of prayer and life. It is a freedom that, insofar as it overcomes the destructive powers of the world, must be recognized not merely as liberty but as liberation. This freedom is not just a gift of volition but a qualitative and social reality. It involves an ever-greater corporeal, historical, dialogical and transformative participation in the liberating presence of the glory and word of God and in the sanctifying gifts of the Spirit.

Although the primary reason to recover this spirituality of liberation has to do with its vivid attestation of Christian prayer and holiness in a violent world, a secondary reason has to do with its potential to help liberation theology address the concerns of some of its critics.[3] In particular, the Balthasarian suspicion that we encountered in chapter 2, which rests mainly on a negative construct of liberation theology as bound up with the modern world's nihilistically technological subjectivity (the Heideggerian critique) and the modern world's development of atheistic humanism (the de Lubacian critique), is powerfully resisted by the manifestly prayerful and doxological character of many of the approaches to liberation theology explored here. At the same time, although this chapter offers a rather decisive rebuttal of Balthasar's indiscriminately negative assessment of liberation theology, it does not wholly discount the issues that he believes are at stake. For the most part, these issues have to do with his reasonable distrust of strict Marxism as a prayerlessly metaphysical and secularizing tradition. We shall see that some representatives of liberation theology at least partly validate Balthasar's worries in this regard, insofar as they let these sorts of Marxist (and more broadly, modern) tendencies adversely affect their treatment of prayer. Because of this complexity, it is necessary to pass beyond the consideration of an abstract genre of liberation theology and instead pursue a much more concrete and discriminating practice of interpretation. The diverse field of liberation theology demands a careful *discernment of spirits*, through which one can make distinctions between more and less adequate (which means adequately prayerful and life-affirming) approaches.

Any suitable set of criteria for such discernment should include some sort of integrated but nonreductive relation between a prayerful openness to God and a solidaristic commitment to the flourishing and freedom of others, including especially the poor and oppressed. Analogy can serve as a basic model for this type of relation: just as the mysterious presence of God should be sought in and beyond creaturely existence (as Przywara indicates), so too our prayerful relationship with God should have some significant role to play in and beyond the struggle for this-worldly liberation (and, no doubt, Metz's political and more-than-political theology already gives us an example of this sort of relation). But then a further question becomes to what extent each thinker manages to provide a richly Christian description of the necessary features of such an analogical structure. The concreteness that Balthasar introduces by means of aesthetics and dramatics enters liberationist discourse mainly in the form of an empirical, phenomenological, and theological engagement with historical reality. The aesthetic and the dramatic are not negated in such an engagement, but they are historicized. Liberation theologians generally aver that the *doxa* and *logos* of Christian revelation, the crises of the contemporary situation, and any doxological spirituality that promises to address them must be interpreted precisely as they appear in history. This historical emphasis gives liberation theology determinate purpose in specific contexts and allows prayer to function as a critical hermeneutic of problematic historical situations. At the same time, the obvious danger is that certain transcendent aspects of the mystery of prayer will be deemphasized. In light of these considerations, the measure of success will be a form of liberation theology that manages to synthesize prayer, thought, and life in a theologically rigorous, richly textured, and practically engaged manner, without reductively distorting or discounting any of these elements in the process.

Using this standard, we shall analyze and assess the works of Enrique Dussel, Juan Luis Segundo, Gustavo Gutiérrez, Leonardo Boff, and Ignacio Ellacuría.[4] Among these thinkers, Dussel and Segundo come closest to reducing spirituality to some form of (not necessarily prayerful) ethical and political solidarity. The Levinasian character of Dussel's Marxism and the early anti-Pelagian and Ignatian leanings of Segundo's somewhat christologically inspired

Marxism enable them to offer some resistance against the problematically metaphysical and secularizing features of much post-Marxist critical theory. But more resistance is needed. In the end, neither thinker proposes a sufficiently prayerful response to the crises of modernity. On the whole, Dussel fares better than Segundo in this respect. Although Dussel does not say enough about the significance of prayer, he does leave certain openings for it. This is not the case with Segundo, who eventually characterizes prayer as a dehumanizing practice which would supposedly pose an obstacle to any genuinely human liberation.

By contrast, Gutiérrez, Boff, and Ellacuría think in a manner that is thoroughly shaped by a prayerful and profoundly Christian spirituality. There is little more that one could reasonably desire from their works in this respect. This is not to say that every detail is invulnerable to critique but rather that their general approach, far from being antithetical to prayer, is actually constituted by an elucidation of its theoretical and practical implications. In other words, they effectively show that doxology and liberation are one, and they do this without compromising either term. They uphold the integrity (that is, the particular respectability) of the one and the other precisely by demonstrating, in another sense, the integrity of the two (that is, their mutual inherence and inseparability). Doxology can be true in the fullest sense only if it is liberative, and liberation can be true in the fullest sense only if it is doxological. This complex, inclusive, and hopeful picture of God's involvement in reality can be called alternatively *integral liberation*, the more conventional term, or *integral doxology*—a term that will be used here to underscore the prayerfulness of this type of theological vision.

Gutiérrez, Boff, and Ellacuría perform the integration of prayer, thought, and life in different but complementary ways. Gutiérrez incorporates Carmelite and Dominican contemplative traditions; Boff revitalizes Franciscan spirituality; and Ellacuría draws out the significance of Ignatius's *Spiritual Exercises*. Hence, as a group, they carry forward four of the most prominent traditions of doxological spirituality that emerged from the apostolic flowering of the high Middle Ages. Moreover, of the three, Gutiérrez reflects most deeply on the subtle interconnections between doxology and lament (in the closest proximity to Metz's *Leiden an Gott*); Boff shows most clearly how prayer finds expression in the core doctrines of the Christian faith (hence, as doxological theory); and Ellacuría attests most powerfully to the relevance of prayer for the process of making concrete decisions in this violent world (that is, as an illuminative basis for Christian action). All three articulate a form of liberation spirituality that is explicitly counterviolent (even when it demands a real-world struggle). Moreover, each theologian also thinks in a manner that is at least potentially postmetaphysical, because analogically, aesthetically, and dramatically doxological. Without exception, prayer arises as a constitutive source of their various liberation-centered responses to the crises of modernity.

The chapter will come to a close with a consideration of Ellacuría, and for several reasons. First, his prayerful thought is especially noteworthy insofar as it finds expression in his martyrdom. The Christic witness of his life and death reveals the incredibly high stakes of his doxological spirituality, as well as its seriousness as a model for imitation. One cannot follow his example lightly. Second, his appropriation of the philosophy of Xavier Zubiri brings him, of the various liberation theologians considered here, most directly into the orbit of post-Heideggerian phenomenology, while providing something akin to the analogical structure that shapes Balthasarian and post-Balthasarian responses to Heidegger. Third, his reading of the poet Angel Martinez infuses his work with a doxological aesthetics, which rivals those that have appeared within and following Balthasar's trilogy, while exhibiting more explicitly counterviolent potential. Fourth, Ellacuría's interpretation of Ignatius opens up a dramatic soteriological perspective, which both avoids the pitfalls of Segundo's eventually nondoxological reading of Ignatius and preserves the major insights of Balthasar's more faithfully Ignatian and therefore thoroughly doxological theo-drama (despite Ellacuría's perhaps underdeveloped appreciation for the value of petitionary prayer). Finally, Ellacuría's interpretation of Ignatius offers a window into a very useful practice of spiritual discernment. In this respect, Ellacuría's work emerges not only as a specific case of liberation theology that is in *need* of discernment but also as a constitutively prayerful *example* of such discernment. In brief, he crystallizes the sort of hermeneutic that this chapter recommends.

It is on these many grounds that we shall conclude with Ellacuría. At the same time, all of the figures in this chapter contribute something positive to the chapter's execution, including even Dussel and Segundo, despite the limitations of their respective approaches. We shall begin with a critical discussion of their post-Marxist spiritualities and then proceed to examine, as a more adequate set of alternatives, the variety of approaches to integral doxology that appear in the works of Gutiérrez, Boff, and Ellacuría.

VARIETIES OF POST-MARXIST SPIRITUALITY

Against Idolatry: Enrique Dussel

First we shall consider two theorists of liberation whose works, to the extent that they are spiritual and doxological, are so in a generally post-Marxist sense, which involves significant retentions and departures from Marx, as well as some, though not finally enough, appropriation of the particular features of a Christian doxological spirituality. The Argentinian historian, philosopher, and theologian Enrique Dussel briefly discusses prayer in his early work, *El humanismo semita* (Semitic humanism, 1969). Although this is not a strictly theological text, Dussel cannot avoid speaking about God in the midst of it, insofar as his purpose is to provide a rigorous phenomenological account of "the Semitic spirit." The cultural phenomena of ancient Jewish life that he considers presuppose a prayerful theology, which he, at the same time, brackets in service of a phenomenological reduction. And yet, his description of this prayer-saturated culture is not entirely neutral. In comparison with the other two thought-forms that he studies in the companion volumes to this work—namely, Greek philosophy and its reconfiguration in Christendom—the Jewish (and very early Judeo-Christian) alternative that he discusses here receives significantly less criticism.

Thus with Metz, and against Heidegger, Dussel shows a clear preference for Hebraic, as opposed to Hellenistic, antiquity.

When Dussel introduces prayer in *El humanismo semita*, he does so by opposing it to the transcendental "I" of modern European philosophy. Against this "I," he embraces Martin Buber's theory of the "I-Thou" and argues that this dialogical structure has its roots in God's covenant with Abraham. He explains that, "in the origin of the Hebraic existential experience, there is a dialogue between a *you* (Abraham) and an *I* (Yahweh)." Dussel, therefore, crucially recognizes that, in Abraham's conversation with God—precisely in his prayer—Abraham is not the one who speaks first. Abraham is not the "I." Rather, Abraham is the addressee of divine speech, the one called to respond, the "you" (or, as Marion would say, the *interloqué*). Dussel clarifies, moreover, that Abraham is not merely an individual but rather "the father of the people" (*'aba* + *ham*). He is given as an inchoate corporate personality, as an entire eschatological community promised and blessed by God. What Dussel calls, somewhat curiously, the "essential *metaphysical structure* of Hebraic consciousness" is therefore constituted precisely as a dialogical relationship between a singular divine first person ("I," soon to be "I Am") and a plural human second person ("you all" [*vosotros*], soon to be Israel).[5] Dussel argues, finally, that this particular sort of vertical and horizontal experience of intersubjectivity undergirds the Jewish conception of the law as *torah*, which he contrasts with the Greek monistic, cosmological, and imperial *nomos*. Jewish prayer, accordingly, gives rise to a distinctive type of law-bound humanism, concerned especially with the needs of the poor (*'anavim*). This humanism is not specifically grounded in an account of the supposedly natural order of things (the status quo) but rather in "the transcendent and living consciousness of an originary *I*, the Creator of all and the Lord of history," who judges and in some sense condemns the regnant order.[6] Thus prayer arises in Dussel's text as a responsive, social, and prophetic phenomenon that is more or less synonymous with the Jewish covenant.

Dussel leaves this promising discussion of prayer largely undeveloped in his other works. For instance, in his *El dualismo en la antropología de la Cristiandad* (Dualism in the anthropology of Christendom; finished in 1968 and published in 1974), he ostensibly carries forward the line of analysis laid out in *El humanismo semita* but does so without offering any sustained consideration of prayer. By keeping silent on this issue, and by grounding his argument in certain contemporary philosophical sources, he almost gives the impression that a worldly, bodily, and ethically engaged phenomenology—supported by thinkers such as Heidegger, Merleau-Ponty, and Levinas—would suffice as an account of the human being, regardless of any sort of dialogical relationship with the God of Israel. To be sure, Dussel's prioritization of Levinas allows him to retain some sense of the biblical understanding of the person in relation to the *other*—for example, for Levinas, the poor, the widow, and the orphan; or, as Dussel tends to say, the one who cries out "I am hungry!"[7] However, as we have seen in chapter 3, there is reason to doubt whether Levinas does enough to preserve the biblical experience of a strictly prayerful and doxological openness to God. Thus the real question becomes whether Dussel's thought, insofar as it proves to be distinct from Levinas's, actually makes up the deficit.

The Levinasian dimensions of Dussel's work come to light very clearly in his *Philosophy of Liberation* (1976). Like Levinas, and like Marion as well, Dussel seeks to transcend ontology. However, unlike Marion, whose movement beyond being entails a movement beyond metaphysics, Dussel adopts the term "metaphysics," in line with Levinas's peculiar usage in *Totality and Infinity*, as a name precisely for that ethical transcendence that is constituted by a radical exposure to the other prior to ontology. When, in the same chapter, Dussel begins to define what he means by "liberation," Levinas's voice is unmistakable: in liberation, "ontology (phenomenology) gives way to metaphysics (apocalyptic epiphany of the other)." Later in the text he declares: "The one who takes responsibility for the oppressed, the one who is persecuted, imprisoned, tortured, and assassinated for taking responsibility for the poor, witnesses in the totality to the glory of the Infinite."[8] Hence, for Dussel, the praxis of liberation is constituted by metaphysics, doxology, and ethics in the precise Levinasian senses of these terms. The novelty of Dussel's approach has to do with his specification of Levinas's ethics in a Latin American context.[9] More precisely, it involves an effort to reconcile Levinas's ethics with certain elements of a Marxian critique of the prevailing political and economic order in Latin America. Dussel's philosophy of liberation, therefore, comes to light as a *Levinasian Marxism*.

It is important to recognize here that the way Dussel uses his Levinasian version of Marx is very similar to the way that Marion uses Dionysius, namely to critique idolatry and to provide a doxological alternative to it. If Levinas prepares both Marion and Dussel to protest the idolatry of being, it is Marx who enables Dussel to extend this analysis to the fetishization of the capitalist world system. Dussel defines "fetishization" in somewhat Levinasian terms as "the process by which a totality is made absolute, closed, divinized," but he applies this definition to the global "exploitation of labor by capital" in a way that makes clear its Marxian significance.[10] Likewise, just as in Marion's retrieval of Dionysius, so too in Dussel's appropriation of Marx, the *via negativa* does not culminate in mere negation but rather passes over into postontological doxology, that is, worship of the infinite beyond being. However, a difficulty arises insofar as Dussel permits a high degree of Levinasian ambiguity regarding the referent of this "infinite": is it reducible to *any* other (especially anyone in need), or is it actually and properly divine (the Lord of history)? Like Levinas, Dussel seems to leave this an open question.[11] He argues, for instance, that "a just economy, as the sum total of artifacts produced by human labor and distributed with equity among a people, is worship of the infinite: by giving food to the hungry and the poor, to the defenseless and the widowed, to the solitary and the orphaned, liturgy is rendered to the Absolute."[12] In this passage, Dussel does not assert that God is identical with the poor, but he does suggest that doxology coincides with solidarity and coincides virtually without remainder. At least, he does not indicate any remainder.[13]

Dussel is certainly right to insist that the struggle for a more just economy is a necessary and even largely constitutive element of any nonidolatrous doxology, and his clarity on this point distinguishes him in a very crucial way from Marion, whose account of the discourse of praise leaves this indispensable, materially economic aspect of true doxology largely unspecified. At the same time, however, if Dussel's argument is not merely about the necessity but ultimately the sufficiency of such solidaristic praxis (and his use of the word "is" in his statement that "a just economy . . . is worship of the infinite" allows this as a plausible interpretation), then his proposed doxological overcoming of idolatry becomes questionable in a way that Marion's does not. The risk of an ethical or political reduction cannot simply be denied in this instance, despite the acuity of Dussel's insight regarding the doxological status of active commitment to the poor and the idolatrous implications of the absence of such commitment.

The danger of this sort of reduction resurfaces in Dussel's *Las metáforas teológicas de Marx* (1993), particularly in relation to his analysis of Marx's use of the Psalms. Dussel quotes a line from the first edition of *Das Kapital*, in which Marx alludes to the opening verse of Psalm 42: "As the deer longs for clear water, so the soul of the bourgeois individual longs for money."[14] This satirical recasting of the verse forcefully protests the fact that the psalmist's desire for the living God has been replaced in capitalist society by an avaricious desire for wealth. However, it does not open up the question of the validity of the psalmist's own perspective, which resists idolatry not merely with an exclusively economic and ethical doxology but also, and above all, with a properly *theological* doxology. Tellingly, neither Marx nor Dussel reflects at this point on the meaning of the psalm's refrain, which is repeated three times: "Why are you downcast, my soul, why do you groan within me? Wait for God, whom I shall praise again, my savior and my God" (Ps. 42:6, 12; Ps. 43:5 NAB). A citation of this psalm that focuses exclusively on constructing a different sort of political economy in response to the suffering of the poor, however vital this task remains, misses the psalmist's point that the downcast soul desires above all the presence of God, the saving God, the God who is worthy of praise. To be sure, as Marion likewise recognizes, this presence depends in many cases (perhaps in all cases) on our solidaristic sharing of divine love (i.e., the redundancy of the gift); but this human, and to some extent materially economic, mediation does not exhaust the deep theological desire that is expressed by this ancient prayer.[15] Without this sort of desire, without in some way yearning for God *as such*, one is left in the position of attempting to fabricate a worldly solution to the problem of idolatry, in spite of the fact that the problem itself is fundamentally constituted by the very decision to rely on such fabrication.

In this respect, Dussel seems to remain too close to Marx. However, we must still consider whether Dussel's explicitly Christian theological writings challenge this assessment. He gives us a clue about where to look when he remarks, "My *Ethics and Community* has been an attempt at a Christian theological discourse that, while essentially biblical, is *at the same time* strictly Marxist."[16] Thus he seems to encourage us to treat this text in particular as a trustworthy account of his own theological vision in relation to his avowedly Marxist philosophy of liberation. In this work, he describes his ethics of liberation as a kind of "fundamental theology." He contends: "Community ethics is the *fundamental theology* of the theology of liberation, as it explains the premises, the conditions *sine qua non*, of theological discourse as a totality."[17] Dussel's claim that a radical commitment to the poor is an indispensable condition (*sine qua non*) of a nonidolatrous Christian theology is a legitimate and crucial proposition. It reiterates the teaching of the Law, the Prophets, and Jesus himself that we cannot approach God in the right way unless we devote ourselves to the concrete work of loving the neighbor. However, it does not follow that nothing else needs to be said about what establishes the possibility of theology as such. Whereas Metz's "practical fundamental theology" incorporates distinct political and prayerful dimensions, while integrating the two, Dussel's "fundamental theology" gives serious attention only to the former.

In the end, Dussel's theological proposal essentially follows the guidelines already laid down by his philosophy of liberation. Although prayer makes an appearance in several places throughout his works,[18] it does not have a consistently and explicitly determinative influence on them. And yet, perhaps what is most remarkable is that there are many points at which it *could*. The connections are always almost there. He simply tends not to develop them. As a result, his important critique of idolatry is not as strong as it could be. It is not as strong as that of the psalmist, or of other prayerful thinkers in the Jewish and Christian traditions who have recognized that seeking to orient ourselves toward the true and living God is the only credible way to begin to detach ourselves decisively from the many false ones.

Departures from Prayer: Juan Luis Segundo

Although the early works of the Uruguayan Jesuit theologian Juan Luis Segundo show some openness to prayer, his later works develop a spirituality that is explicitly opposed to it.[19] To see the early promise, it suffices to consider his *Grace and the Human Condition*, the second volume of his series *A Theology for Artisans of a New Humanity* (1968–72). This text develops, in part, as an argument against Pelagianism. Segundo contends that Pelagius's theology is problematic precisely insofar as it disregards "the absolute disproportion between all that is human, be it good or evil, and the divine that goes to make up eternal life." Thus Segundo effectively implies that Pelagius goes astray by neglecting the greater dissimilarity of the *analogia entis* and by locating salvation within the reach of human capabilities. Moreover, citing Péguy (an iconic figure of Balthasar's doxology), Segundo praises the night as a gift from God, which is meant to limit our anxious worldly activity and allow us to rest in "the calm hopefulness of a few quite hours." His comments here are redolent of Lacoste's meditations on the nocturnal character of liturgy. Finally, when we do take up the labors of the day and strive for greater freedom and justice in the world, we must do so, Segundo argues, with a voluntary submission to the will of God: "Only the person who surrenders himself to the Father's love can be free on earth." Likewise, he avers that only those who open themselves to the Spirit of God, which blows where it wills, can hope to experience the fullness of liberation.[20]

In the short section of the book that Segundo calls "Pelagianism in Christian History," he reveals that Ignatius of Loyola is the most crucial source for his own reflections on the possibility of an actively engaged spirituality that would nevertheless rely deeply on the grace of God and, thereby, avoid succumbing to Pelagian tendencies. Ignatius enables Segundo to contemplate God as wondrously hidden and revealed, as approachable in the audibility and the visibility of Christ, as the source of gifts that we receive and desire, as the origin of a call to which we must respond, and as the savior whom we are meant to adore "on our knees."[21] All in all, insofar as Segundo's theology remains closely tied at this stage of his thought to Ignatian spirituality, Segundo displays great respect for the prayerful essence of Christian spirituality and appears to think it on its own terms. He is not far from the doxological perspective elaborated by Balthasar and the post-Balthasarians.

However, already in the next volume, *Our Idea of God*, Segundo develops his understanding of prayer in a manner that foreshadows future difficulties. In a section called "Prayer, Providence, Commitment," he discusses prayer in relation to the classical problem of theodicy. In particular, he draws attention to "history's refutation of prayer," that is, the enormous litany of legitimate prayers that God seems to have left entirely unanswered.[22] Whereas Metz incorporates this historical reality of unalleviated suffering into an intensified experience of an apocalyptic cry, in which we await God's decisive culmination of history, Segundo takes it as a warrant to challenge the sort of divinely agentive theology that prayer typically presupposes. Dismissing any notion of divine intervention, he suggests that our prayers will be answered only to the extent that God's justice is made real through our own liberating actions. Prayer, for him, is merely the "interpretation" of our human efforts as signs of the Spirit; it is thus primarily self-reflective; it is about what we do in order to instantiate the action of God. Although Segundo, therefore, seeks to preserve some positive sense of prayer, he defines it in a way that appears to imply some kind of anthropological reduction of divine agency.

In effect, Segundo begins to situate spirituality within the realm of human technology. In a rather telling passage, he adopts the perspective of Jesus and has him instruct those who pray to him that their prayers will be answered only to the extent that human societies devise adequate solutions to their own problems. When, or if, this happens, it can be attributed to the grace of God, that is, to "my creative Spirit in you."[23] There is a somewhat Pelagian logic at work here insofar as this purported offer of grace seems wholly contingent on human achievement. Even though Segundo's appeal to a technological mastery of worldly elements is commendably oriented toward liberation, it still provokes a Heideggerian—and perhaps more deeply Christian—suspicion regarding the sort of will that is formed by associating the saving presence of God primarily with such human striving for power. Although Segundo's earlier Ignatian treatment of grace approximates the sort of doxology that promises to overcome metaphysics, here we see that his spirituality converges with the very technological attitude that Heidegger identifies with the essence of modern metaphysics—and this, it should be recalled, is an important aspect of Balthasar's critique of liberation theology.[24]

The lack of a clear distinction between spirituality and technology brings Segundo close to a Hegelian philosophy of history, according to which the absolute spirit of God would only come to fruition through its progressive development in the realm of human spirit. Divine freedom has concrete reality for Hegel, and largely for Segundo, only insofar as it is actualized in our own cultural and intellectual accomplishments. In keeping with Hegel, there is both a dialectical and evolutionary worldview in Segundo's thought that leaves it vulnerable to Metzian apocalyptic critique.[25] Moreover, Segundo's proximity to Hegel likewise implies some degree of proximity to Marx. However, at this stage of his writings, Segundo explicitly distances himself from the latter's strict atheism and materialism, arguing that history is not lacking in divinity but rather in some sense constitutive of its actualization.[26] In this respect, his thought remains more Hegelian than Marxian.

As the influence of Marx grows in Segundo's subsequent works, the status of prayer decreases. *The Liberation of Theology* sheds light on this process. In this text, Segundo proposes a hermeneutical circle that applies a roughly Marxian method of ideology critique to Christian thought. However, his strategy does not culminate with such critique but rather also requires a limited retrieval of theological sources. According to Segundo, Marx's refusal to do the latter is his most serious shortcoming. In contrast to Marx, Segundo avoids constructing his positive proposal in opposition to religion as such and instead seeks a "new way of interpreting the fountainhead of our faith (i.e., Scripture)." On the one hand, therefore, Segundo suggests that theology needs to be saved *from* Marx's blanket dismissal. On the other hand, however, he seems to believe that Marx's type of ideology critique is precisely that which promises *to save* theology. In his view, this sort of critique and the particular kind of "prior political commitment" that it entails establish the legitimating conditions for any interpretation of the Christian gospel today.[27] Prayer has very little, if any, explicit role in Segundo's account of what it would mean for theology to become liberated.

The increasing secularization that appears in *The Liberation of Theology* becomes definitive in Segundo's second major series, *Jesus of Nazareth: Yesterday and Today*. In the first volume, *Faith and Ideologies*, he offers an analogical treatment of these terms in which "faith" would transcend but also be embodied in "ideologies." Here we *seem* to have one of the formal requirements of a prayerful mode of liberation spirituality (i.e., an analogical structure). However, Segundo does not approach "faith" as a prayerful or theological term but rather as an "*anthropological* dimension, a dimension as universal as the human species itself, whether religion be involved or not."[28] "Faith," in this sense, does not necessarily have anything to do with theological doctrine or prayerful practice. Rather, it only implies a human worldview, a macrocosmic horizon of meaning and values. This category of "faith," therefore, pertains just as much to Marxist materialism as it does to Christianity. By contrast, Segundo identifies "ideologies" with the practical means that are employed to enact a particular worldview. In light of this somewhat helpful terminological clarification, he argues that the dialogue between Christian theology and Marxist theory should not be conceived merely as a debate between faith, on the one hand, and ideology, on the other, but should rather be approached as a much more complex interaction, in which different kinds of faith and ideology are present on both sides.

Segundo's argument proves problematic insofar as it renders traditional Christian faith—in the sense of a prayerful openness to the triune God—unthinkable except as merely one possible permutation of the universal human processes of evaluation and meaning-making (i.e., "metaphysics," in the sense that Heidegger employs in his *Nietzsche* lectures). Segundo's formal discussion is, therefore, not neutral. It is structured by a "faith," in his technical sense, and this "faith" is not Christian faith but rather a certain kind of post-Enlightenment critical humanism, which, without demanding strict allegiance to Marx's historical and dialectical materialism, also explicitly avoids contradicting it. Segundo shows great sympathy for the Marxist philosopher Milan Machoveč, who wonders whether or not the Bible, and particularly the figure of Jesus, could be understood in a way that would "enrich and deepen the Marxist heritage."[29] This is precisely the sort of hermeneutic that Segundo develops in the remaining volumes of this series.

Whereas Dussel's Marxism is innovative inasmuch as it is Levinasian, Segundo's is innovative inasmuch as it is christological—or, rather, as he prefers to say, "antichristological." He employs the latter term in order to indicate that, although he reflects directly on the liberative significance of Jesus, he does so in an anthropological mode that resists standard theological interpretations. Perhaps more than any other volume,[30] *The Christ of the Ignatian Exercises* puts Segundo's marginalization of prayer into sharp relief. Precisely there where he might have returned to his earlier Ignatian doxology, he makes his most decisive break with it. The rupture occurs emblematically in the middle of Ignatius's "First Principle and Foundation": whereas Ignatius instructs the retreatant to do whatever praises, reverences, and serves the Lord, Segundo concentrates almost exclusively on the element of service and contrasts it with the doxological acts of praising and reverencing. He argues that, "while the latter two terms remain ahistorical, the term 'service' comes to mean turning into reality." He goes on to assert that "the first two attitudes [praising and reverencing] hint at an obvious dehumanization of the human being." For Segundo, humanization happens when society learns to follow Jesus in a very particular way that entails a commitment to historical projects of liberation. He does not think that doxology has anything to contribute to these projects. In fact, he believes that it points in the opposite direction, away from historical reality and toward an illusory eternity. In short, he now maintains that prayer *dehumanizes*.[31]

At one level, the problem with Segundo's argument here is that it does not acknowledge the profound connections that Ignatius perceives between prayer and the imitation of Christ. Segundo's inattention to these connections is what allows him to misconstrue Ignatius's many references to petition, praise, and the prayerful disposition of *indiferencia* as signs of a "christological vacuum" at the very heart of the *Spiritual Exercises*. At another level, the problem is that Segundo no longer shows any interest in following Christ as such but rather only in appropriating what might prove useful for the construction of his own particular vision of a more humane world. This logic leads him to reject the same prayerful practices and dispositions insofar as they seem to belong to a problematic "test-christology," that is, a Christology that supposedly treats this life as a mere preparatory trial for another life. Segundo distinguishes this approach sharply from his own kingdom-building "project-christology." In short, he argues both that Ignatius's spirituality is not christological enough (insofar as it is prayerful and spiritually indifferent) and that it is not consistently christological in the right way (insofar it approaches history as a test instead of a project). Segundo thereby divorces *imitatio Christi* from doxological spirituality and inner-worldly from heavenly liberation—two separations that Ignatius himself does not condone.[32]

All in all, Segundo's final construal of prayer as a dehumanizing practice uncoupled from practical service situates his work in a typically modern tradition, inclusive of but not limited to Marx, which seeks to liberate humanity by freeing it from any sort of rigorously dialogical and doxological relationship with God. This sort of secularizing (albeit, in Segundo's case, perhaps not yet entirely secular) form of humanism seems to presuppose that the meaning of human existence is not only basically unrelated to prayer but also largely averse to it. Remarkably, Segundo endeavors to enlist Jesus and Ignatius in support of such a position. He is able to do so only by devaluing the prayerful manner in which they give themselves from themselves.

VARIETIES OF INTEGRAL DOXOLOGY

The Contemplation of Liberation: Gustavo Gutiérrez

Both Dussel and Segundo, therefore, revise Marxism in certain significant ways in relation to the sources of Jewish and Christian spirituality without, however, sufficiently resisting the stereotypically Marxist (and more broadly modern) tendency to marginalize prayer. This shared limitation provides an incentive to seek a different way of understanding a spirituality of liberation that would not sacrifice prayer for the sake of political solidarity but rather integrate the two into a single way of life that enhances and brings out the best of both. In such a spirituality, God would be glorified in all things: in praise and in service, in contemplation and in action, in the midst of this world's sorrows and absurdities and in an unimaginably beatific way for all eternity. This sort of integral doxology is constitutive of both the hopeful struggle for and the hoped-for advent of integral liberation, as Gutiérrez, Boff, and Ellacuría theorize it. They contend that we are called to receive, offer, desire—and, they would stress, *actively embody*—the liberating *doxa* and *logos* of Christ both historically and eschatologically. They develop this shared vision by drawing on distinct prayerful sources in the Christian tradition and by responding to the movements of the Spirit of Christ in their historical contexts. What we have, then, is a unified doxological spirituality of liberation disclosed through a variety of charisms.

The Peruvian Dominican Gustavo Gutiérrez is the author of the single most foundational work of Latin American liberation theology, *A Theology of Liberation* (1971).[33] It, therefore, seems fitting to begin with his particular attestation of integral doxology. Although he develops his understanding of prayer more deeply in subsequent writings, it is by no means lacking in this very early and definitive text.[34] To be sure, the Marxian undercurrent of *A Theology of Liberation* is unmistakable. Nevertheless, Gutiérrez keeps it from over-determining the meaning of the text as a whole by assigning it an inferior place within his account of the three levels of liberation. It supplies much of the content of the first two levels: namely, liberation from the socioeconomic oppression of the capitalist system and liberation of the human being who re-creates itself as the master of its own destiny. By contrast, the third level of liberation is not Marxist at all but rather profoundly Christian and theological. It is the liberation from sin and the definitive arrival of the kingdom, which is accomplished freely by God in Christ and offered to humanity as an unmerited gift that is irreducible to—and, in the best cases, foundational of—the other two levels.[35]

Gutiérrez's treatment of spirituality directly corresponds to this three-level account of liberation. He defines spirituality as an integrated way of life under the dominion of the Spirit, through which we both work for liberation (levels 1 and 2) and actively receive it as a divine gift (level 3). Political solidarity with the poor is crucial for this spirituality, but so too is a "contemplative life." He identifies this contemplative life with a prayerful "experience of gratuitousness," in which we freely recognize and encounter the freedom of the living God. In implicit harmony with Lacoste's account of liturgy, he explains that "this 'leisure' activity, this 'wasted' time [of prayer], reminds us that the Lord is beyond the categories of useful and useless" and, hence, that "God is not of this world." Thus, in Gutiérrez's judgment, prayer and contemplation transcend the necessary tasks of the political sphere and open us up to a transformative meeting with the unlimited graciousness of God. At the same time, as might be expected, Gutiérrez does not consider the contemplative life in isolation from the active life. On the contrary, like many other liberation theologians, he affirms the Ignatian principle (formulated explicitly by Nadal) of contemplation *in* action and connects it with the apocalyptic passage from Matthew 25 regarding the presence of Christ in the neighbor, especially the one in need.[36] In short, he situates prayer both beyond and within our necessary works of worldly service.

In addition to Ignatius and Matthew 25, Gutiérrez suggests several other promising sources for the contemplative dimension of his spirituality of liberation. He mentions, for instance, the collection of poems called *Psalms*, by the Catholic and Marxist Nicaraguan poet Ernesto Cardenal (who might be counted as another poetic alternative to Hölderlin). Nevertheless, like Balthasar, Gutiérrez prioritizes biblical experiences of prayer over contemporary aesthetic material. He looks to the biblical psalms themselves much more than he does to Cardenal's reinterpretations. He briefly alludes to Job as a figure of contemplation. He embraces Mary's *Magnificat* as a hymn of thanksgiving for the revolutionary actions of God, which express a clear preferential option for the poor. But, in the end, Gutiérrez offers Christ as the highest model for imitation. Christ perfectly unites the human striving for justice and the exorbitant self-generosity of divine love and thereby becomes an icon for everything that Gutiérrez wants to include in the spiritual life. In response to the paschal mystery in particular, Gutiérrez contends that the most appropriate attitude on our part is gratitude and joy. His crucial demand for a practically engaged protest against the world's unjust structures of impoverishment and death must be understood within the context of this Christic mode of doxological affirmation.[37]

Gutiérrez's simultaneously active and contemplative spirituality is formative of his proposed theological method, and in three distinct ways. First, it forms the historical Christian praxis *upon which* he argues theologians are meant to reflect critically in light of the Word of God. Thus spirituality becomes a focal point or privileged source of theological understanding. Second, although Gutiérrez argues that theology's reflection on spirituality should be *critical*—in a sense which, like Segundo's hermeneutic circle, allows Marxist social analysis to diagnose certain inadequacies in Christian praxis—Gutiérrez is adamant that the ultimate standard for this critique must be precisely the divine *logos* itself. One would, therefore, need to be receptive to this *logos* in order to formulate the right sorts of critical judgments. In this sense, a prayerful disposition is an essential part of Gutiérrez's theological hermeneutic and not merely a phenomenal element to be interpreted by it. Finally, spirituality is the telos of his theology. It is the synthetic form of prayerful thought and solidaristic life to which theology's critical reflection is finally oriented.[38]

Gutiérrez enriches this nuanced account of spirituality and theology in later works, such as *We Drink from Our Own Wells* (1983), *On Job* (1986), and *The God of Life* (1989). At the same time, he becomes increasingly reticent regarding any abiding ties to Marx. His trajectory proves to be the direct inverse of Segundo's: as the prayerfulness of Gutiérrez's thought increases, the explicit influence of Marxism declines. Gutiérrez begins to conceive the first two levels of liberation (socioeconomic and anthropological freedom) as more clearly *following from* the third (the contemplative experience of divine salvation), rather than as arising from their own extratheological sources (i.e., Marxist theory).[39] His commitment to the lives of the poor remains unchanged. It only receives a more clearly Christian and prayerful foundation.

Like Metz, Gutiérrez spends considerable time in these texts confronting the challenges that unjust suffering poses to the practice of prayer and, therefore, to theology.[40] The two most significant differences between their approaches are these. First, whereas Metz questions how we are supposed to speak of God after Auschwitz, Gutiérrez asks, "How are we to do theology *while Ayacucho lasts?*"—that is, while this impoverished and war-torn region of Peru, along with other similar places in Latin America, continues to be submerged in an overwhelming experience of violence? The tragedy in Ayacucho that Gutiérrez faced at the time of his writing could not yet have been classified merely as a memory of suffering, a *memoria passionis*. Rather, it had the status of an *ongoing* catastrophe. Gutiérrez's argument is that we need a prayerful spirituality capable of responding effectively to this (for him) contemporary reality and, by extension, to analogous situations of oppressive and terroristic violence occurring today.[41]

The second major difference has to do with the status of doxology. Whereas Metz proposes interrogative lament as a corrective to overaffirmative doxology and gives the bulk of his attention to this issue, Gutiérrez envisions a more dynamic interplay between lament and doxology and does not stress as greatly the need to avoid the excesses of the latter. Gutiérrez develops this sort of *composite*, as opposed to *corrective*, understanding of the tensions of prayer through his reflections on the contemplative experiences of John of the Cross and the biblical figure of Job, two traditional doxological sources that he reinterprets in connection with the collective spiritual journey of the Latin American people. These contemplative experiences give Gutiérrez's spirituality—which remains profoundly affected by the horrors of innocent suffering—a somewhat more positive quality than one finds in Metz's *Leiden an Gott*.

Quoting an important essay by J. Hernández Pico, and alluding to the classic spiritual text by John of the Cross, Gutiérrez characterizes the suffering of the poor in Latin America as a "dark night of injustice." He describes the difficulties, frustrations, and sense of profound loneliness that come with striving to be in solidarity with the poor in a world in which powerful interests are aligned against them. He argues that these struggles can give rise to a complex experience of prayerful contemplation, in which we come to realize that God is mysteriously working on us, purifying us, and relating intimately with us even in our trials. Gutiérrez ponders the almost paradoxical conditions of this experience: the painful fight against sin and injustice can seem to coincide with a new, delightful, and loving encounter with the presence of God. John of the Cross's Carmelite spirituality (of darkness and light, and of wounding yet loving flame) provides significant inspiration for Gutiérrez's perspective here. At the same time, Gutiérrez clarifies that his fellowship with the ecclesial communities of the poor is what primarily empowers him to continue singing God's praises even in the midst of great suffering.[42] This is the community that sustains his doxological confidence. Whereas Metz is understandably preoccupied with loss—the memory of those who are dead and gone, especially the millions of murdered Jews in the Shoah—Gutiérrez is filled with a sense of all those who are there with him, in the struggle, and this yields a practice of prayer with a noticeably different tenor.

A similar dynamic comes to light in Gutiérrez's reading of Job. Although his consideration of Job's innocent suffering encourages him to defend the practice of lament, it does not lead him to discount the importance of doxology. On the contrary, he argues that Job's lament is precisely that which ultimately brings Job to a doxological encounter with the living God. Gutiérrez shows that Job's protest of the injustice that presently afflicts him and the poor of the land is not silenced by any supposedly rational theodicy, such as that provided by his "friends" (or centuries later by Leibniz), but rather continues unabated until the very glory and word of God intervene "from the heart of the tempest."[43] To be clear, Gutiérrez insists that "those who suffer unjustly have a right to complain and protest."[44] He, there-fore, by no means asks them to restrict their theological discourse to the sort of praise and wonder that Job manages only at the very end and only by the unmerited grace of God. Rather, his point is that Job's type of honest and legitimate lamentation is not antithetical to doxological contemplation but rather, in many cases, the only viable avenue toward it. Throughout his analysis, Gutiérrez situates Job in the biblical tradition of agonic prayer that Chrétien approaches primarily through Jacob and that Metz approaches through the cries of the crucified Jesus and the victims of Auschwitz. In all of these cases, a certain kind of positive wrestling between divine and human freedom prepares the way (at least potentially) for an experience of greater intimacy and love, but Gutiérrez is somewhat closer to Chré-tien than he is to Metz in his treatment of this as a preeschatological possibility (a point of contrast that remains discernible even though Metz dares to characterize *Leiden an Gott* as a kind of mysticism).

Finally, one should note that the particularly Dominican char-acter of Gutiérrez's spirituality is evident in the manner in which he not only thinks doxologically but also seeks to *preach* that which he thinks. In the introduction to *The God of Life*, a book which takes as its epigraph the prayerful hymn of David that appears in 1 Chronicles 29:10–18, Gutiérrez explains his purpose as follows: "My desire is that this book may help readers to know more fully the God of biblical revelation and, as a result, to proclaim God as the God of life." In his readings of numerous scriptural texts he does not, like Segundo, deemphasize the prayerfulness of Christ nor, like Dussel, risk reducing worship to solidarity, but rather embraces all of these biblical data together as constitutive features of a life-giving interaction with the living God.[45] Gutiérrez's *Sharing the Word through the Liturgical Year* (1995) continues this trend. In these concise homilies on all of the Sunday readings of the Catholic lectionary, he not only speaks about prayer;[46] he also shares the fruits of his own contemplation in a manner that is accessible to the larger church and coordinated with its liturgical worship. All of the major themes of his liberation theology come together here, in his faithful exposition of God's liturgically celebrated and gloriously liberating word.

Thus in these two more recent works by Gutiérrez, the element of offering that is part of the general structure of doxology finds expression in explicit acts of proclamation, through which he communicates to a broad audience the historically and eschatologically transformative *logos* of God that he has received. In the end, therefore, Gutiérrez's approval of the Ignatian maxim *in actione contemplativus* and his constructive reinterpretation of the Carmelite tradition of the contemplative night ultimately complement, and do not replace, his performance of the properly Dominican principle: *contemplata aliis tradere* ("to transmit to others what has been contemplated"). The vast impact of his work on diverse communities around the world is a testament to the effectiveness of this approach.[47]

Glory Be: Leonardo Boff

Like Gutiérrez, the Brazilian Franciscan theologian Leonardo Boff thinks in a manner that is not only inclusive of prayer but also thoroughly shaped by it.[48] A few distinct points can be made about his approach. First, the particular sort of prayer that informs his thought is, for the most part, explicitly doxological but not in such a way that it would cease to be petitionary. Second, his theology is enriched by many concrete elements of Christian scripture and tradition, which not only prevent it from succumbing to any sort of secular distortion, but also give it a theoretical precision and aesthetic fullness rivaling other doxological proposals that we have encountered. Third, Boff's doxological contemplation must be seen as part of a synthetic and nonreductive spirituality, which is characterized not only by prayer but also, and integrally, by the life-affirming praxis of solidarity that prayer inspires. Finally, Boff develops his spirituality in response to the crises of the modern age, which he associates not only with a certain kind of metaphysics but also, and above all, with a certain kind of systemic violence perpetrated against the poor, against humanity, and against the earth itself. In all of these ways, Boff offers a clear example of the extraordinary promise of an integrally doxological spirituality of liberation.

It seems helpful to begin by considering what Boff means when, in a text devoted specifically to the Our Father, he refers to it as "the prayer of integral liberation." This phrase can be understood in three ways in light of Boff's account (which he notably situates in continuity with the patristic commentary tradition).[49] In one sense, Boff's point is simply that Jesus teaches us to pray for integral liberation. In this respect, one can rightly interpret the Our Father as a series of supplications which, taken together, express a desire for everything that the fullness of liberation entails. Thus the Lord's Prayer would not only be the point of access to a higher level of theological liberation, involving the redemption from sin and the gift of eternal life (Gutiérrez's third level). It would also offer an indispensable way of seeking even the concrete political aspects of liberation: the historical inchoation of the kingdom, the daily bread, the deliverance from real situations of evil (everything which might be associated with Gutiérrez's first level); these, too, are gifts that we request from God.[50]

The second way to understand Boff's description of the Lord's Prayer as a "prayer of integral liberation" has to do with his explicitly doxological reading of it. He argues that one can treat this prayer not only as a series of supplications but also as a clear affirmation of the already given presence of integral liberation in Christ. With reference to Tertullian, he avers that the Lord's Prayer provides a "summary of the whole gospel (*breviarium totius evangelii*)." In other words, this prayer acknowledges and honors all that God has already promised and accomplished in the Son. It not only asks that God's name be hallowed; it also hallows it and gives the reasons for this hallowing. In short, it is a prayer that gives praise for the liberating works of the Trinity disclosed in revelation. When at the end we

say "Amen," we do so, Boff contends, in order to express our confidence that Christ "has taken upon himself all the contradictions of
our dialectical existence and delivers us from them totally."[51] Hence,
there can be no doubt that, for Boff, the Lord's Prayer not only articulates a desire for a historical and eschatological transformation
that is yet to come but also glorifies the God who has already in
some sense achieved it.

Finally, Boff indicates that one can interpret the Lord's Prayer
as a "prayer of integral liberation" not only because this is what it
requests, not only because this is the source of its praise, but also
because this is what it effects when its hopes are actively incarnated
in the world. The task of the Lord's Prayer is not completed when it
is offered verbally to God. It also, at least implicitly, requires those
who pray it to do what they can "to establish a world that *objectively*
honors and venerates God."[52] In other words, we are supposed to
"objectify" the goods expressed by this prayer in the worldly structures and institutions that we create through our individual and
collective actions. Boff clarifies that, if this objectification is to be
authentic and avoid the dangers of idolatry, it needs to give glory to
the ontologically and ethically "holy" God, who, transcending every
form of worldly knowledge and politics (much like Marion's "Requisite"), also acts in history in defense of the poor and oppressed
(a point that is almost implied, but not quite specified, by Marion's
reflections on charity). Boff contends that the concrete realization
of the desires and the promises of the Our Father would be nothing
other than the advent of liberation itself. It would entail the overcoming of every false worship and every act of injustice: a perfect
love of God and love of neighbor.[53] In short, the Lord's Prayer provides the template for a liberating and liberated existence. It shows
us what to ask, what to sing, and what to do.

Boff's major theological treatises, particularly his books on
Christ, grace, and the Trinity, generally satisfy Balthasar's central
methodological criterion, namely that doxological *theoria* should
"control and give evidence of itself in every branch of theological
speculation."[54] In these works, Boff does not restrict his reflections

to the Lord's Prayer but rather expands them to include a variety of spiritual and theological sources.[55] His *Jesus Christ Liberator* (1972) offers a reliable summary of his views on Christ. A Chalcedonian principle runs throughout the entire text and allows him to present Christ as an exemplary model of the multiple dimensions of prayer. On the one hand, Boff stresses that Christ is thoroughly human. This means, for Boff, not merely that Jesus had a human nature but also that he "really participated in our human condition and took on our deepest longings," the very longings that constitute the passion of human prayer. On the other hand, Boff is very clear that Jesus is a thoroughly divine, and precisely Trinitarian, mystery. As much attention as Boff gives to the historical Jesus, this does not prevent him from contemplating Jesus as the divine Son and as the very glory and word of God. Therefore, just as Christ, qua human, longs with us for the coming of the kingdom, so too Christ, qua divine, participates in the infinite triune mutuality that Balthasar would call "absolute prayer." At the same time, Boff identifies Christ as the supreme model for liberative praxis in solidarity with the poor and oppressed. Jesus, therefore, comes to light as a perfect image not only of the right kinds of desire and worship but also of the necessary "objectification" of these aspects of prayer in corresponding actions.[56] The features of the Lord's Prayer are those of the Lord himself.

As in Boff's Christology, so too in his theology of grace, he manifests a clear commitment to a prayerful form of thought. At the beginning of his main text on the subject, *Liberating Grace* (1976), he defines grace in a way that makes it virtually indistinguishable from prayer: "Grace is relationship, exodus, communion, encounter, openness, and dialogue. It is the history of two freedoms, the meeting of two loves." He adds that "theology is reflection on this reality." Hence, for Boff, the life of grace is nothing other than the life of prayer, and theology is nothing other than the thought that thinks this life. It should, therefore, come as no surprise that Boff concludes this particular theological work with a quotation from a psalm, namely Psalm 139. To know grace is to acknowledge that we are utterly exposed to the loving presence of God and that we are constituted by this exposure in our inmost being.[57]

Boff employs his prayerful understanding of grace to diagnose the "dis-grace" of the modern world. He shows how the very crises that Heidegger identifies with ontotheological metaphysics and Balthasar associates with monistic metaphysics and its secularization intersect at many levels with the global structures of violence that contemporary critical theory—and liberation theology in particular—seeks to counteract. On the one hand, Heidegger, Balthasar, and Boff agree that modern technocracy is problematic to the extent that it pretends to establish the conditions for understanding being as such and as a whole. They both warn that the global dominance of technology threatens to reduce the human being to a mere utilitarian object, while simultaneously aggrandizing human subjectivity in an unstable way as a massive manipulating force. They identify one of the gravest consequences of this dominating subjectivity as a loss of meaning and flight of the gods: that is, nihilism. On the other hand, Boff supplements Heidegger's critique of metaphysics with a Latin American form of Marxian social analysis that closely associates the problems of techno-science with the deleterious worldwide operations of a "capitalist system." It follows that, for Boff, in contrast to Heidegger, there can be no merely aesthetic or poetic solution to the crises of modernity, drawn from a strictly European cultural canon. Rather, he believes with good reason that we also need significant socioeconomic and political transformations, which would do justice to the countless majority of human beings who have been consigned to the margins.[58]

And yet, as important as this political divergence from Heidegger is, it must be understood as part of a deeper doxological divergence. The drama of Boff's discussion is not found in the event of being and its destiny. Rather, the drama takes place as a conflict between grace and dis-grace. The question is not precisely about the meaning or truth of being but rather about how to discern rightly between a life that is open to the Spirit of God and one that is closed to it. In this respect, Boff would concur with Balthasar—and, by extension, de Lubac—that the crises of modernity are deeply connected with a certain kind of prayer-refusing atheism, a willful condition of being without God, which involves a dangerous reframing of human freedom as total self-sufficiency. In other words, Boff suggests that secularity, the loss of a "higher frame of reference," and precisely the disavowal of prayer are at the root of the social ills that we face.[59]

To be clear, Boff does not foreclose a possible redemption of modern science and technology. He argues that they can mediate the experience of grace, provided that certain conditions are met. Essentially, he suggests that science becomes graceful to the extent that it relinquishes its claims to ontic conceptual mastery and humbly accepts its role as an *aletheiological* practice of contemplation. In short, according to Boff, science mediates grace only if, and to the extent that, it sheds light on some aspects of the hidden *logos* and *doxa* of God that appear in the mysteries of creation. Boff's reasoning regarding technology is somewhat different. He maintains that, "despite the dangers it may contain, [technology] is a powerful tool for the creation of more justice. It can liberate human beings from the bonds of hunger, illness, and natural forces," and thereby "promote the love of God and human beings." In this respect, Boff's logic is closer to Segundo's than Heidegger's. He does not justify technology as poetic *techne* but rather as an aspect of liberative praxis. And yet, in contrast to Segundo, Boff ultimately preserves a clear distinction between spirituality and technology. The former appears within but also transcends the latter. Boff suggests that the Spirit of God works through our humanizing projects. But he is also very clear that this Spirit works in many other wondrous ways that we cannot fathom or comprehend.[60]

Boff's Trinitarian theology is no less prayerful than his Christology and his (pneumatological) theology of grace. His definitive treatise on the subject, *Trinity and Society* (1986), concludes with an 82-page-long reflection on the "Glory Be." He appropriates this quintessential expression of doxology as the basic structure and culminating gesture of his Trinitarian thought. Throughout this book, he glorifies the Trinity as a whole and each person distinctly, emphasizing their perichoretic relations. He contemplates the triune God in itself, as an eternal event of mutual love, and in its economic missions of creation, incarnation, and transformation. Although he prefers a traditionally Franciscan soteriology, in which the Word would become incarnate regardless of sin, he does not fail to present the paschal mystery as constitutive of the Son's glory. Moreover, in accord with de Lubac and against the modern philosophies of history that one finds in Lessing, Hegel, Marx, and Moltmann, Boff rejects any Joachimite succession of historical ages corresponding to each divine person, arguing instead that their operations are always thoroughly intertwined. Finally, he anticipates a final doxological "trinitization" of the whole of creation, in which all of the divine persons and all creatures will sing, dance, love, and be loved together. In all of these respects, Boff's Trinitarian doxology is not far from Balthasar's. The key difference is that Boff understands our historical and eschatological participation in this Trinitarian communion as requiring (which is not to say that it would be reducible to) a practical struggle for this-worldly liberation.[61]

We have seen that Boff's prayerful theology takes shape as a reflection on the Lord's Prayer and, moreover, that it finds expression in his major systematic works on Christ, grace, and the Trinity. It remains to consider its grounding in the Franciscan tradition. In his *Francis of Assisi: A Model for Human Liberation* (1981), Boff once again analyzes the crises of modernity in a somewhat Heideggerian, somewhat Marxian, and ultimately Christian doxological manner. That is, he locates the problem in terms of a reductively techno-scientific, capitalistic, and prayer-and-life-negating culture. He maintains that the most promising response to this problematic condition would involve not a refusal of the operations of *logos* but rather an effort to reorganize them under the guidance of a well-ordered *pathos* and *eros* (in which he also includes the self-giving practice of *agape*). He finds these affective qualities in Francis. And yet, Boff is adamant that Francis should not be classified as a "romantic," in the modern sense. Francis differs from the romantics insofar as he purifies the human experience of *pathos* and *eros* through acts of asceticism and praise. Far from becoming absorbed in the adventures of the affective self, Francis embodies a profound sense of detachment from it and a humble adoration before the divine mystery that infinitely transcends it.[62]

Boff observes that Francis approaches every creature as a member of God's cosmic family: everything is sister or brother. Nothing is merely an object to be used. Thus the whole of created reality, every little piece of it, offers an occasion for intimacy. In this respect, Boff's analysis converges harmoniously with Chrétien's. Moreover, both recognize that for Francis the cosmos is choral: it sings a hymn of praise. Because creation is, therefore, saturated with doxology, it deserves to be treated with reverence. What Boff adds to Chrétien's perspective is a detailed account of the ecological crisis itself, especially as it afflicts the Amazonian rainforest in his native Brazil. According to Boff, the earth does not merely sing God's praises; it also cries out in distress. Like the poor, and together with them, it needs to be liberated so that God might be more adequately glorified through it.[63]

Boff's Franciscan spirituality resonates with Chrétien's thought not only in its encouragement of intimacy with creatures and its emphasis on the doxological character of creation but also in relation to the desire for peace.[64] Like Chrétien, Boff argues that peace should not be understood as a mere cessation of violence but rather as a gift from God received in prayer. Boff likewise agrees with Chrétien that peace entails what Augustine calls the "tranquility of order." However, Boff is by comparison more insistent that we need to question precisely what kind of order is conducive to peace. In particular, he contends that the "medieval Christian order" (which violently excludes the Jewish, Muslim, pagan, and indigenous other) and the "new world economic order" (which sacrifices the world's poor to private interests) are incompatible with the sort of hospitality, humility, and gentleness that the "Prayer of Saint Francis" demands.[65] In short, for Boff, peace is something that God alone can grant us but not something that we can take for granted. The structures that have shaped our societies, both in the past and in the present, are not in his estimation sufficiently supportive of the sort of peace that God promises to give. Therefore, he concludes that we must struggle to refashion our institutions and ourselves as "instruments of peace" and, moreover, prayerfully seek and receive this instrumentality as a divine gift.

The basic dynamic of Boff's spirituality remains consistent throughout his many works. An urgent desire and longing for liberation is accompanied by unshakable joy and confidence in the liberating majesty of God. He understands our role in history as instrumental, sacramental, participatory with respect to this liberation. He exhorts us not only to glorify God—precisely the triune God of Christian revelation—but also to make this glorification effective and palpable, to channel it into concrete situations of injustice, and to recognize and affirm it in all of God's creatures. This is what it would mean to let *glory be*. In sum, Boff's writings point the way toward a novel mode of integrally doxological existence that would, if faithfully embodied, drastically challenge the violent course of modern civilization and usher in a new and unforeseen pattern of theological, anthropological, and cosmological sociality.

A MARTYR OF SPIRITUAL DISCERNMENT: IGNACIO ELLACURÍA

Boff's Franciscan project complements Gutiérrez's Carmelite and Dominican alternative, adding in certain cases a greater level of theological specificity, though perhaps without emphasizing quite as clearly the significance of lament. The integral affirmation of doxology and liberation is what most profoundly unites these two thinkers and, moreover, distinguishes their works from the less adequately doxological proposals of Dussel and Segundo. We turn now to the Spanish Jesuit Ignacio Ellacuría, as a third figure of integral doxology with his own unique and provocative approach. Ellacuría spent much of his adult life working in El Salvador. He was assassinated there, together with five other Jesuit priests and two women, on November 16, 1989.[66] Like the many other celebrated and uncelebrated martyrs of El Salvador, Latin America, and the entire global church, Ellacuría bears witness to the costly love of Christ in a violent world. This is one of the principal reasons to highlight him here. However, he is also noteworthy for his properly intellectual achievements, which, to be sure, are very much bound up with his practical life-and-death decisions. These achievements will be the main focus of the present discussion. We shall explore how Ellacuría treats prayer as a contemplative practice that is generative of liberative action and how he simultaneously situates prayer in the midst of such action, thereby producing a nonreductive synthesis of the two. In order to understand the structure and dynamism of Ellacuría's prayerful synthesis, it will be necessary to reflect on the Ignatian character of his thought and, particularly, on its status as a practice of spiritual discernment. In the end, our goal will be to grasp how the contemplative decision-making process and Christic way of life mapped out by the *Spiritual Exercises* (including the Principle and Foundation, all Four Weeks, and the Contemplation to Attain Love) shapes Ellacuría's theology and leads, within his historical context, more or less directly to his martyrdom.

First, however, two other crucial sources for Ellacuría's reflection and praxis need to be introduced, namely the philosopher Xavier Zubiri and the Jesuit poet Angel Martinez. Ellacuría's debts to Zubiri have been documented by many of the scholars who have studied his work.[67] By comparison, very little attention has been given to the influence of Martinez.[68] Moreover, neither figure has been sufficiently analyzed as a source for the prayerfulness of Ellacuría's thought. Here we shall consider both influences precisely in relation to the question of prayer. This will provide important background for a consideration of Ellacuría's engagement with Ignatius. Moreover, it will help to clarify some of the ways in which his work mirrors the analogical and aesthetic aspects of the Balthasarian and post-Balthasarian doxological tradition and thereby effectively addresses the metaphysical crises of modernity. Perhaps more than other liberation theologians, the philosophically inclined Ellacuría seems to invite this sort of dialogue.

The Philosophy and Poetry of Reality

From Zubiri, Ellacuría appropriates a *somewhat* metaphysical theory of reality that, like Przywara's analogical account of creaturely existence, is in some sense oriented toward prayer and certainly not simply antithetical to it. Some questions can be raised regarding the precise nature of Zubiri's philosophy, particularly, on the one hand, whether it sufficiently avoids the dangers of metaphysics as evaluated by Heidegger and, on the other hand, whether it does enough to move beyond the limits of Heidegger's phenomenological ontology. It will also be important to attend to some of the ways in which Ellacuría builds upon, and is therefore not merely predetermined by, Zubiri's project. Of particular note here is Ellacuría's emphasis on the historical character of reality. In the end, without arriving at the fullness of what might be desired from a postmetaphysical form of thought, Zubiri nevertheless gives Ellacuría something very much like the analogical structure that Balthasar treats as indispensable to doxology. Moreover, Zubiri situates this structure not within the question of being but rather within the question of *reality*—a difference that, however conceptually subtle, is potentially very far-reaching.

Zubiri's project takes place on the borders of what Heidegger would call metaphysics. It cannot be denied that something resembling an ontotheological constitution appears in Zubiri's thought. At the same time, however, Zubiri makes certain critical modifications to this constitution, some of which appear largely indebted to Heidegger (with whom he briefly studied),[69] others of which indicate an explicit attempt to transcend Heidegger. In "Introduction to the Problem of God," an essay added to the 1963 edition of his *Nature, History, God*, Zubiri distinguishes three stages of his intellectual journey to God. First, he points to a sense of "ultimateness" that grounds the human experience of being-in-the-world, and he gives it the somewhat technical name "deity" (which, like Marion's "saturated phenomenon *par excellence*," does not presuppose existence). In the second stage, he affirms the actual existence of this "deity" and begins to speak of it as "divine reality." Hence, in Zubiri's account, instead of the highest entity, which Heidegger's definition of the *causa sui* would strictly require, we have the ultimate grounding character of reality. But in either case its function is roughly isomorphic: that is, to be a necessary condition for the possibility of the whole gamut of things (whether this is called being or reality) and of the self (as a knowing subject), a condition which one can grasp with philosophical certainty as the first cause.[70] This is the "god of the philosophers" before whom Heidegger quickly asserts there can be no prayer.

And yet, in the third stage of the argument, Zubiri turns to prayer precisely in order to transcend this (merely) philosophical conception of divinity. He contends that the first cause can be the God of prayer only if that God is not merely a cause but an absolutely free, intelligent, and personal reality that belongs essentially to nothing and no one but itself: that is, the divine sovereign. He declares that it is only at this point that "we at last have God." Zubiri repeats and develops this ultimately prayerful intellectual itinerary in the book called *Man and God*, which Ellacuría edits and publishes posthumously for Zubiri in 1985. Drawing close to Marion's post-metaphysical thought, Zubiri now identifies God's grounding character not with "causation" but rather with the act of self-gift: "To ground, to be the foundation, is to outwardly self-express or self-give. What God outwardly self-gives (in the aspect we are studying) is reality. Therefore, reality is *donation*." Zubiri goes on to argue that the appropriate human response to such donation—that is, the only reliable mode of access to God as the supreme donor of reality—is to surrender oneself through acts of adoration, supplication, and peaceful repose.[71] Hence, if Zubiri is a metaphysician, he is not merely a metaphysician. He is also a thinker of prayer. Moreover, his thought would seem to be more explicitly and coherently prayerful than Heidegger's, insofar as it does not culminate in a prayer-*like* attitude toward the event of being but rather in a genuinely prayerful response to God as the giver of all things. In this respect, there is a decisive break between Zubiri and Heidegger.

The other major break that needs to be noted here has to do with the distinction between being and reality. Ellacuría sheds light on this distinction in his "La superacíon del reduccionismo idealista en Zubiri" (The overcoming of idealist reductionism in Zubiri, 1987).[72] He explains that, for Zubiri, the danger of idealist reductionism comes to light in two distinct ways, namely through the "logification of intelligence" and the "entification of reality." In the former, one reduces the act of thinking to the domain of a rational *logos* and thereby does not sufficiently acknowledge the sentient character of all human thought. In the latter, one reduces everything to an entity, composed of existence and essence, which has a fixed place in an intelligible and comprehensive system of being. As a result of these idealizing processes of logification and entification, Zubiri contends that a compelling sense of the ways in which we actually think and in which things actually appear has been lost (or perhaps not yet developed).

According to Ellacuría, Zubiri believes that Heidegger—unlike many other figures in the Western philosophical tradition from the pre-Socratics through Husserl—is not strictly engaged in either of these idealizing operations. And yet, Heidegger is not entirely exonerated either. In both instances, he comes in for a lesser charge. Heidegger's decision to situate philosophy in the context of the truth of being (*Sein*) that is available to human apprehension (*Dasein*) still gives, in Zubiri's judgment, too much weight to the reductive powers of the knowing subject. Even with Heidegger's remembering of being, a great deal remains forgotten. Zubiri, therefore, attempts to overcome the shortcomings of Heidegger's phenomenological ontology by developing his own account of the human being's sentient intelligence of reality. On the side of thinking and on the side of that which is given to be thought, Zubiri wants more openness to the actual characteristics of the things themselves than he finds in Heidegger. "Sentient intelligence" and "reality" are the formal categories that he uses to secure this openness.

Zubiri's project is, in some ways, very similar to Marion's. Both Zubiri and Marion, having taken Heidegger's work very seriously, seek to move beyond Heidegger's horizon of being in order to discover a manner of thinking that exhibits still greater respect for the never-fully-intelligible way in which real things give themselves. We have already seen that Zubiri identifies reality with donation. This apparent convergence between his thought and Marion's is not merely terminological: it indicates that there is some considerable agreement between the two regarding what is insufficiently disclosed in Heidegger's ontological thinking (i.e., the given as such). Moreover, in harmony with Marion and the rest of the apophatic tradition, Zubiri maintains that it is necessary to contemplate God as strictly "beyond being."[73] However, despite these similarities, it is safe to say that, in response to Marion's more technical phenomenological works, Zubiri would have to object that Marion's conception of givenness also remains insufficient, especially insofar as it becomes folded back into the Husserlian practice of suspending the question of reality. Thus Zubiri's effort to overcome idealist reductionism seems to place him in some sense not only beyond Heidegger and, therefore, with Marion but also beyond Marion. He wants not merely givenness but the reality of what is given. To the extent that Ellacuría carries forward Zubiri's critique of idealist reductionism, he likewise approximates a postmetaphysical position analogous to Marion's (and others').[74]

And yet, as much as Zubiri departs from Heidegger, both by turning very directly toward prayer and by drawing a distinction between being and reality, he continues to sound very Heideggerian when he takes up the task of describing humanity's existential rootedness in the world. Although his terminology is often different, the sense of being contingently embedded (Heidegger: "thrown"; Zubiri: "religated") in the dynamic structures of reality is very similar.[75] "Religation" (from *religare*, meaning "to bind") has certain interesting ties to the idea of "religion," as well as many other nuances that attest to the novelty of Zubiri's account. But what the two theories share is a profound sense of the inner-worldliness of humanity. This connection seems to become problematic only to the extent that, like Heidegger's *Ereignis*, Zubiri's existentially apprehended *realidad* would begin to constitute an overdetermining structure for the manifestation not merely of humanity but of God as well.[76] In other words, the danger is that certain immanent conditions of human experience would preestablish what it means for God to arrive, or perhaps even to live, as God—with the result that God's freedom, transcendence, and authentic divinity, on which prayer relies, would be somewhat conceptually compromised.

We have already seen that Zubiri explicitly affirms these features of God and does so precisely on the basis of prayer. But his texts do include a few passages that may not be entirely invulnerable to this sort of critique, and these need to be examined precisely because they have a direct bearing on Ellacuría's thought. In order to high-light the potential problem, it suffices to contrast Przywara's claim that the presence of God should be sought *in* and *beyond* creaturely existence with Zubiri's oft-repeated assertion that God is transcendent *in* things. This is what Zubiri calls the "theologal dimension" of reality. Zubiri unpacks this theory in the following passage from *Man and God*:

> To my way of thinking, to transcend does not mean to be "beyond" things, because on the contrary God is formally and intrinsically *in* them. The transcendence of God does not consist in being beyond things but the other way around. Transcendence is precisely a mode of being in them, that mode in accordance with which they could not be real in any sense, unless they formally included in their reality the reality of God, without this in any sense making God identical to the reality of things.[77]

Zubiri makes a similar point in another place when he says that, "if God were a reality beyond everything real, the great absent and alien, God would be a reality inaccessible in itself. That is not the case: God is constitutively accessible."[78]

These passages are problematic insofar as they posit an exclusive alternative between what one might call God's "immanent transcendence" (mysterious presence in things) and God's "transcendent transcendence" (independent divinity or aseity), whereas it seems preferable to contemplate the divine mystery by preserving a certain degree of tension between the two. There is nothing wrong with insisting, as Zubiri does, upon a constitutively accessible mode of God's transcendence, which would be given precisely through the power of reality as we both experience and experientially think it. But Zubiri's sometimes apparent denial of a meaningful sense in which God remains forever beyond this sort of access, utterly exceeding all preconditions, infinitely "distant" (in Marion's sense), can leave the impression that God is *merely* the evident ground of our reality and nothing more. It is as though God would be transcendent with respect to us but not exactly transcendent as such. Here we would have God qua foundation but not God qua God—that is, God in God's own absolutely hidden Godhead. In this respect, Przywara's strictly analogical doctrine (which is taken up by Balthasar and his followers) seems more adequately balanced, insofar as it does not locate the "beyond" (*über*) exclusively within the purview of the "in," but rather holds these two moments together as a dynamic polarity.[79]

The limitations of Zubiri's formulations are also somewhat evident in Ellacuría's appropriations of them. However, Ellacuría's focus on the biblical experience of God's free self-revelation both complicates and clarifies matters. In "The Historicity of Christian Salvation" (1984), Ellacuría argues against the claims that "transcendence must be outside or beyond what is immediately apprehended as real" and that "the transcendent must always be other, different, separated." In opposition to these "pernicious philosophical" positions (his words), he recommends a "radically different way of understanding transcendence, more in line with the way reality and God's action are presented in biblical thinking. This is to see transcendence as something that transcends *in* and not as something that transcends *away from*."[80]

Here Ellacuría is clearly borrowing from Zubiri's way of expressing things, although there are some important differences. First, like Zubiri, Ellacuría continues to oppose two different modes of divine transcendence that should rather be held in tension. His rejection of the dubious claim that God "must always," thus necessarily and, one might add, *exclusively*, lie beyond the sphere of inner-worldly reality is certainly reasonable. The scriptural revelation of God in history refutes this one-sided perspective. At the same time, Ellacuría's promotion of only a roughly Zubirian sense of God's transcendence *in* things does not enable him to express as well as he could the particular character of God's biblically attested transcendence, which appears to be located both *in* and *beyond* the world.[81]

Second, the most decisive distinction in this debate does not run between philosophy and scripture—at least not in the way that Ellacuría suggests—but rather between two different kinds of philosophically informed theology, one emphasizing transcendent transcendence and the other immanent transcendence. Ellacuría claims that the latter is "more in line with . . . biblical thinking." This may very well be the case, all things considered, but both views clearly depend upon certain identifiable philosophical and not merely scriptural positions, and neither seems to be able to exhaust what might be said about the mystery of God on the basis of scripture. Hence, the difference between a philosophical and a biblical theology does not appear to settle the question of which mode of divine transcendence, whether transcendent or immanent, should have priority, if any.

Nevertheless, the distinction between philosophical and biblical theology remains relevant insofar as it provides a way to differentiate between Zubiri's and Ellacuría's nonidentical accounts of an immanent mode of divine transcendence. Whereas Zubiri primarily associates this idea with the *theologal* character of reality, understood as such and as a whole, Ellacuría primarily associates it with the free, saving actions of God in history. Thus in Ellacuría's case, more clearly than in Zubiri's, that which ultimately justifies an emphasis on immanent transcendence is not the pursuit of a quasi-metaphysical account of the grounding structure of reality but rather the properly Christian task of prayerfully interacting with God precisely through the freedom of the economy of salvation. In this respect, Ellacuría's thought appears farther removed from metaphysics and its attendant dangers than Zubiri's manages to be.

At this point, we have begun to approach, without yet naming it, that aspect of Ellacuría's thought which several interpreters have recognized as his most significant departure from Zubiri, namely his radical *historicization* of the concept of reality.[82] Whereas Ellacuría shares Zubiri's desire to transcend the Heideggerian horizon of being, he does not stop with reality in general but rather moves toward a more focused consideration of reality precisely insofar as it gives itself historically. In the present context, we can see that this move is especially important, not merely because it lets Ellacuría develop a dimension of Zubiri's philosophy (a dimension that is already included within it), but also and more crucially because it opens the way for a different kind of thinking—a thinking that would not limit

itself to certain formal, transcendental, or eidetically phenomenological questions regarding the inescapable conditions for any possible manifestations of humanity or God, but which would rather
plunge into the more determinate questions that are posed by biblical and contemporary history.

It is at this point that one might consider Ellacuría's earlier
and arguably no less significant debt to the poet Angel Martinez.
Whereas Zubiri's account of reality is limited by his commitment
to the philosophical task of describing its most general structures,
this is not the case with Martinez, who, by contrast, approaches the
real precisely through a vivid depiction of its concrete historical appearances. Martinez has a very strong influence on Ellacuría during
the formative stages of his intellectual development in the 1950s (a
decade before he begins to work with Zubiri), acting not only as
a teacher but also as a spiritual and intellectual role model.[83] From
Martinez, Ellacuría acquires a rich doxological aesthetics which, like
many of the examples highlighted and inspired by Balthasar, blurs
the lines between poetic and prayerful perception and emerges from
a deep engagement with the core christological and Trinitarian mysteries of the Christian faith. At the same time, Martinez's poetic doxology is immersed in the crises of the contemporary world in a way
that anticipates the political trajectory of Ellacuría's later writings.
Martinez's effect on Ellacuría's thought is certainly not the same as
Hölderlin's effect on Heidegger's. Martinez's poetry does not lead
Ellacuría to dwell within the fourfold event of being but rather to
confront the injustice and inhumanity of a specific historical situation. As an aesthetic source, therefore, Martinez is much closer to
Charles Péguy, Nelly Sachs, and certainly Ernesto Cardenal than he
is to Hölderlin.

Ellacuría discovers in Martinez—as much in his person as in his
poetic work—a thoroughly integrated spirituality, in which poetry,
philosophy, theology, asceticism, and mysticism are closely woven
together into a single way of life.[84] This spirituality exhibits a clear
doxological structure. Ellacuría highlights this structure in one way
by quoting several lines from Martinez's collection, *Angel in el
país del águila* (Angel in the land of the eagle), in which Martinez,

speaking as a priest, gives creative expression to a very traditional eucharistic doxology: "—Through Him, with Him, and in Him / —I, like all things—, / all your joy in me, all honor / and glory to You, Omnipotent Father God, / in the unity of the Holy Spirit."[85] Unlike Heidegger, Ellacuría does not reduce the role of the priest to that of the poet but rather seeks to show how Martinez's poetic speech is taken up into his properly Christic (in his case, baptismal and ministerial) priesthood. In Christ and in the Holy Spirit, and together with all things, Martinez receives and offers the glory of God. This is a Trinitarian experience of *doxa* in the context of the liturgy.

Ellacuría draws out the doxological structure of Martinez's spirituality in another way by connecting his spirituality to the poetic existence of the saints. He explains that, in Martinez's understanding, the poet is "the realizer [*realizador*] of the word" and, therefore, "the saints are the supreme poets: they vivify and realize in their lives the word most high—that which Jesus transmits to us—, the Word that has likewise been realized in the flesh."[86] For Ellacuría and Martinez, then, just as for Balthasar, doxological aesthetics is not ultimately about taste, expression, sentiment, or anything merely "aesthetic"; it is about holiness. It is about receiving and offering the incarnate Word through one's linguistic and embodied actions in the world. Martinez's poetry is meant only as an artistic reflection of this more realistically, existentially, or corporeally poetic and thus adequately doxological sanctity.

In addition to the doxological moments of receiving and offering the glory and word of God, which we have just considered, Ellacuría also sheds light on the moment of desire. He quotes a stanza from Martinez: "We seek silence: / in order to listen to ourselves, / and in ourselves to the world, / and in it to God, we seek silence." As in Chrétien's thought, so too here, the receptive act of listening implies a search for that which has not yet been fully heard: the unheard-of. Martinez invites us to seek this mysterious excess in ourselves and in the world, but he does not strictly identify it with ourselves or with the world. As Ellacuría explains, in Martinez's poetry this life is not an end in itself but rather a "preparation for the ultimate journey." In the midst of the present world, "we prepare for an immortal world." Time is, therefore, transpierced by eternity, and this is the excess that we are longing to hear. The songs that we sing now with our words and our lives are ultimately meant to be taken up into that infinite music that Martinez calls the "eternal song of the source."[87] This is the final point of reference for the desire that is crystallized in the poetry and prayers of the world. Although at this point in his thought Ellacuría is already concerned with historical reality, his gaze is certainly not limited by it. Rather, his poetic doxology is open to a definitive, unknown, and undying future.

This openness to the transcendently transcendent beyond does not compel either Martinez or Ellacuría to avert his gaze from what is happening in the here and now. On the contrary, it enables them to see the present in a new and different light. The central metaphorical tension that runs throughout *Angel in el país del águila* has a clear historical referent. The "land of the eagle" is the United States. The irony, which Martinez intends to convey to his readers, is that this eagle is not a majestic bird of flight but rather a mechanically produced symbol—a lifeless image stamped on every dollar bill—which stands for a superficial, materialistic, and highly alienating socioeconomic system. The "angel" that arrives in this land refers, in part, to Padre Angel himself, who was in the United States when he began to develop the idea for this collection of poems. But it also refers more broadly, on the one hand, to the role of the prophetic or poetic messenger and, on the other hand, to the constitutively spiritual creature of traditional theology whose mysterious life is characterized by an unceasing contemplation of God. These three figurations of the angelic have a single message for the eagle: change your life![88] Recover a spiritual and contemplative sense of all things, relinquish your attachments to dehumanizing economic and political structures, remember who you are in God's eyes, and prepare to take flight: that is, to die and to be born anew, in this life and the next.[89]

Ellacuría already uses the term "liberation" (*liberación*) as a name for the sort of transformation or conversion that Martinez announces and desires. Ellacuría describes it as a liberation from our characteristically modern enslavement to material possessions. He and Martinez insist, however, that the solution to this materialistic problem does not involve becoming exclusively spiritual or angelic, that is, detached from the earth. On the contrary, they maintain that the blessed life that the angel represents needs to be incarnated within, and thereby transfigure, the lifeless condition of the eagle. In other words, a change is necessary within the limits of our own thoroughly human existence. Liberation, for us, lies somewhere in between these two provocative and, by themselves, incomplete images. Enslavement to materiality cannot be overcome by escaping from the material conditions of life but only by living in a new, interactively free way within them. Ellacuría is already very aware of the grave costs of this kind of liberated existence. He argues that it inevitably carries with it "some form of martyrdom and death." He continues, quoting Martinez: "Such is the mystery of life: to have life and to never lose it, / it is necessary to turn around to seek life in death."[90] The point here is definitely not to desire death. It is certainly to desire life, but precisely with the recognition that in the midst of this world's violence, which one will have to confront in order to seek the fullness of life both for oneself and for others, the likely and perhaps even inescapable result will be death. This is the logic that leads from Christ's incarnation to the mystery of the cross. As we shall see, it is also the logic of the *Spiritual Exercises* and of Ellacuría's own life.

The *Spiritual Exercises* as Principles of Discernment

Before discussing the decisive impact of Ignatius on Ellacuría's prayerful way of thinking and living, it should be noted that Zubiri and Martinez are not his only other significant sources. He also draws on the church's liturgy, on the Psalms, and on the witness of Monseñor Oscar Romero.[91] Moreover, in a short essay that he simply calls "Espiritualidad" (Spirituality, 1983), he gives a bibliography that includes prominent figures such as Karl Rahner (his teacher from 1958 to 1962),[92] Hans Urs von Balthasar, and Louis Bouyer, along with several fellow liberation theologians such as Jon Sobrino, Segundo Galilea, and J. Hernández Pico.[93] Finally, when he turns to Ignatius himself, he does not do so unaided. On the contrary, his own theological and practical interpretation is profoundly influenced by numerous teachers, mentors, and friends in the Jesuit order. In particular, he seems to have been especially inspired by Father Miguel Elizondo, S.J., who taught him both to internalize the *Spiritual Exercises* through careful study and to adapt them to meet the needs of new contexts.[94]

In his essay called "Spirituality," Ellacuría makes several points about this general subject that should be mentioned here before exploring his distinctively Ignatian approach. First, like Gutiérrez and Boff, he seeks to avoid what he calls both "spiritualist" and "materialist" reductions of the Christian life, arguing instead that these two dimensions depend on one another and are given together. He concludes, therefore, that they should be neither separated nor confused but rather held in tension. In this way, he demonstrates his commitment to something very much like an analogical thought-form. Second, he contends that this "differentiated unity" is not easy to maintain in the concrete. Rather, it requires "a permanent, alert, and committed discernment of the changing signs of the times and of the determinate historical practices that would actually be an adequate response [to them]."[95] According to Ellacuría, this sort of discernment is a central and necessary feature of Christian spirituality, understood precisely as a historically embedded reality.

Third, Ellacuría clarifies that, although Christian spirituality undoubtedly involves certain "spiritual practices (prayer, ascetical exercises, rules and norms of behavior, etc.)," it is constituted more fundamentally by "the operative presence of the Spirit, which is not merely an abstract Spirit, but the Spirit of Christ that carries us to the Spirit of God." To the extent that one understands prayer merely as a discrete action that we do, it can only be, for Ellacuría, a mere aspect of spirituality. However, to the extent that one thinks of prayer precisely as an interaction between divine and human freedoms, which God always already initiates and in which we participate through our whole linguistic and corporeal existence, then what Ellacuría calls "spirituality" becomes nothing other than prayer without ceasing. It is prayer disclosed as a dialogically theonomous—or, as he would say, theologal—way of life. Ellacuría's argument resonates with the Pauline idea (expressed in Romans 8) that spirituality is not primarily something that comes from us but rather something that the Spirit of God does *in* us.

Fourth, Ellacuría insists on a strict identification between the Holy Spirit and the Spirit of Christ, on the one hand, and between the Christ of faith and the historical Jesus, on the other. As he puts the point: "There are not two spirits, nor two Christs." These identifications protect the Christian character of his account of spirituality by situating it within the economic perichoresis of the second and third persons of the Trinity and by connecting it directly with the act of following Jesus in his historically given existence (as attested by the New Testament, which Ellacuría treats as normative). Finally, Ellacuría links Christian spirituality with a clear preferential option for the poor, which he discovers not only in Mary's *Magnificat* but also, and above all, in Christ's historical proclamation of the kingdom. He argues that both our contemplation and action should be oriented by this christologically mandated solidarity.[96]

All in all, Ellacuría offers a general account of Christian spirituality as an integrated, nonreductive, discerning, theologal, pneumatological, christological, solidaristic, and holistically prayerful way of life. His understanding of these characteristics is certainly compatible with—and probably to a large extent dependent on—his own practice and interpretation of Ignatius's *Spiritual Exercises*. However, in this context, he presents these characteristics as necessary for any authentically Christian life and not merely for one that would be shaped by specifically Ignatian principles. In short, he intends this account to be inclusive. Ellacuría provides a more focused discussion of Ignatian spirituality in his earlier text "Lectura latinoamericana de los *Ejercicios espirituales* de san Ignacio" (Latin American reading of the *Spiritual Exercises* of Saint Ignatius, 1974), which we possess only in the form of outlined lecture notes.[97] Here he shows how Ignatius gives these more general features of Christian spirituality a particular configuration. More precisely, he argues that the prayerful and practically oriented exercise of discernment that is necessary to avoid spiritualist and materialist forms of reductionism and to live in a manner that is faithful to the liberating Spirit of

Christ can be effectively enacted in accordance with the basic elements of the *Spiritual Exercises*: the Principle and Foundation, the Four Weeks, and the Contemplation to Attain Love.

Ellacuría is not especially interested in Ignatius's Rules for the Discernment of Spirits (to which he gives no sustained treatment), but rather in the overarching logic of the *Spiritual Exercises*, which he understands as a logic of discernment. In Ellacuría's view, Ignatius gives us a prayerful way of thinking (precisely meditating and contemplating) through which we are able to discern not only who God is for us but also how to live accordingly in the midst of our own historical reality. This way of reading Ignatius leads Ellacuría to grant a certain degree of priority to the Second Week, which focuses on the historical Jesus and culminates in the act of making a choice about how to follow him (i.e., the Election). But this particular interpretive approach also lets Ellacuría engage with other major components of the *Spiritual Exercises*.

In the remainder of this chapter, our task will be to take a closer look at Ellacuría's reading of Ignatius and consider how it informs his theology and praxis. In the process, we shall reflect on certain crucial similarities and differences between Ellacuría and Segundo, on the one hand, and Ellacuría and Balthasar, on the other—arguing that Ellacuría's Ignatian thought approaches a specific, promising, but not entirely unquestionable point in between the two, that is, in between an insufficiently doxological (Segundo) and perhaps not quite sufficiently historical (Balthasar) soteriological drama. Like Segundo, Ellacuría is mindful of certain potential liabilities in the *Spiritual Exercises*, or at least in some of the ways that they have been used, related especially to the supposedly ahistorical character of the Principle and Foundation. However, unlike Segundo, Ellacuría does not locate the danger in Ignatius's idea that human beings were created to praise, reverence, and serve God our Lord (which Segundo contrasts sharply with his own recommendation that we strive merely to serve humanity and, by extension, God through historical projects). On the contrary, Ellacuría affirms Ignatius's threefold doxological and practical Principle and Foundation and only insists that it raises an important question: "Who is this God our Lord for human beings[?]"[98] That is, who is the God whom we are called to praise, reverence, and serve and how, therefore, are we meant to do this? The Principle and Foundation becomes problematic, in Ellacuría's estimation, only to the extent that it is taken as a sufficient account of the relationship between humanity and God, instead of being treated as a prompt for further reflection and discernment.

Having clarified this issue, Ellacuría argues that the Four Weeks are what help us discern not only who God is for us but also how we are able to praise, reverence, and serve this God. These two aspects of his understanding of Ignatius directly correspond to the two soteriological foci of his larger theological work.[99] The former aspect concerns what Ellacuría tends to call the "history of salvation" or "salvation history," that is, the saving actions of the economic Trinity as disclosed especially in the Old and New Testaments. The latter aspect—how we are to praise, reverence, and serve this God— has to do with what Ellacuría tends to call "salvation *in* history," the "salvation *of* history," or sometimes simply "historical liberation." The saving actions of the Trinity remain foundational even here. That is, God is the prime mover not only in the definitive work of salvation that culminates in Christ's life, death, and resurrection, but also in the ongoing struggle to save or liberate historical reality itself. Although human beings have a significant role to play here, this struggle remains thoroughly theologal—that is, undergirded by divine freedom. Ellacuría contends that these two soteriological foci— salvation history and salvation *in* history—are precisely what need to be discerned according to Ignatius's method, that is, understood with clarity and appropriated as the basis for a concrete decision in light of the Four Weeks.[100]

While reflecting on the First Week, Ellacuría emphasizes that the revelation of God in Christ involves a direct confrontation with the personal, social, and structurally objectified sins of the world. He explains that the Son enters history in order to negate our concretely idolatrous and violent (i.e., sinful) negations of God and human beings, adding that these sinful negations, in turn, also concretely negate (which is to say kill) the divine-and-human Son. The cross manifests both sides of this conflict in a uniquely perspicuous way. As Ellacuría puts the point: "The revelation and the overcoming of sin are only given through the cross."[101] The crucifixion of Jesus is, therefore, pivotal for what Ellacuría calls "salvation history" or the "history of salvation." From the First Week, he thinks we should learn that the ordered relationship between creature and Creator that is envisioned by the Principle and Foundation has been drastically disrupted by our historical idolatry and violence and, moreover, that God has already responded through a radical, utterly incredible, and paradoxically victorious act of historical kenosis in the Son. This is the primary soteriological point—and it is one that he would share with Balthasar.

However, there is also a practically soteriological question regarding what we are supposed to do in response to this confrontation between Christ and sin in order to glorify God. Ellacuría contends that, in this respect, we need to discern the conditions of, and work tirelessly for, a real historical liberation. This liberation requires a "real undoing [*deshacer real*]":[102] that is, a holistically personal and structural conversion of the sort that Ellacuría already anticipates in his reading of Martinez. Here Ellacuría's emphasis is certainly different from Balthasar's. The difference has to do with Ellacuría's more insistent historicization of the conflict between Christ and sin, which he interprets as something that continues in our individual and collective praxis—continues precisely in such a way that the fate of historical reality is still at stake. There is a dramatic tension here that is similar to, but also more adamantly historical than, what one finds in Balthasar's *Theo-Drama*. Both Balthasar and Ellacuría agree that, because of the permanent validity of human freedom, everything is not already decided on the cross. But Ellacuría stresses, in a way that Balthasar does not, that this means that there is much more to say and to do with respect to realizing salvation in history.

Ellacuría's discussion of the First Week anticipates the basic structure and content of the rest of his remarks.[103] Nevertheless, the fact that the First Week foreshadows the rest does not mean that one can treat it as conclusive. On the contrary, like the Principle and Foundation, the First Week too must give way to a still more specific process of discernment, in which one reflects prayerfully on the life, death, and resurrection of Christ as interrelated but distinct historical moments of both God's historically definitive confrontation with sin and our contemporary theologal confrontations with it. In the context of the Second Week, Ellacuría argues that Christ, even in his public or "secular" life, must be understood as "the maximum presence of God to the human being and of the human being to God." This salvation-historical observation is perfectly congruent with Chalcedon and, moreover, indicative of the way in which Christ's entire existence (as Boff suggests) can be interpreted as a perfect icon of prayer. Ellacuría upholds these points while reflecting on a corresponding spiritual praxis of salvation in history, which he associates (very much like Metz) with the historical act of following Christ. Inspired by Ignatius's approach, he insists that one should follow Jesus not merely by treating him as "a pure external model to be imitated" but rather by cultivating "a personal adhesion to the person of Christ, in the presence of his humanity."[104] In other words, a certain degree of intimacy is necessary, an intimacy born of prayer and attentive meditation. To be a disciple and to carry forward Jesus's salvific mission, one must, according to both Ignatius and Ellacuría, converse and be with him, know him deeply, and immerse oneself in his way of life.

While discussing the Second Week, Ellacuría draws particular attention to the Meditation on the Two Standards, which is part of the Election. He argues that this meditation helps us to perceive more concretely who Jesus was in his life and who we should be in our own. In particular, he indicates that it specifies the nature of the conflict between Christ and the sins of the world. Whereas the demonic standard of sin is defined by worldly attachments to riches, honor, and pride, the holy standard of Christ is defined by the opposite characteristics of poverty, reproaches, and humility. He clarifies, moreover, that in order to follow Christ's standard most faithfully, it is necessary to commit oneself not only to the first or second of the Three Ways of Being Humble (which Ignatius also outlines as part of the Election) but also to the third, in which one passes beyond mere obedience and indifference and actually prefers to suffer poverty, reproaches, and real humiliation with Christ for the greater glory of God.[105]

In this way, Ellacuría avoids falling into the purported "christological vacuum" that Segundo perceives in the *Spiritual Exercises*. Moreover, he acquires the specific standard of holiness that allows him to discriminate between more and less adequate forms of Christian life in his own Latin American context. The task of spiritual discernment is, in this respect, somewhat straightforward: it requires one to look around at the reality of things and to consider which individuals, groups, and institutions are working primarily to accumulate greater riches, honor, and pride for themselves and which are, by contrast, emptying themselves of these attachments out of love for Christ and the poor. For Ellacuría, it is obvious that one should adhere to the latter standard. However, in particular situations, he acknowledges that the task of discerning exactly how to do this can become very complicated.[106] Although the "dominating civilizations, dominating social classes, and dominating individuals" certainly find themselves confronted by this criterion, it also by no means gives a free pass to Marxist or other kinds of revolutionary political organizations, which Ellacuría recognizes have likewise sought great riches, honor, and pride for themselves.[107] Instead this criterion favors a way of life that understands itself as oriented toward the cross—and, only through the cross, toward the resurrection.

Thus the Second Week (including the Election) leads directly to the Third and the Fourth. In the context of these weeks, Ellacuría once again not only reflects on salvation history, in this case crystallized by the paschal mystery. He also considers the ongoing struggle for salvation in history, which he argues involves a similar Christomorphic pattern of death and resurrection. He contends that, for Ignatius, "the Christian ought to *follow* the same way of death in order to arrive at the same glory of the resurrection." In Ellacuría's judgment, this christological mandate entails that there is no authenticity in discipleship without the real danger that is produced by the historical conflict with sin. At the same time, he affirms that "Christianity is also a celebration [*fiesta*], because the savior God is already among human beings."[108] He, therefore, recognizes (with Gutiérrez, Boff, Balthasar, and others) that the peril, anguish, and urgent longing implied by the cruciform character of Christian existence do not abolish the doxological and already revivified character of the very same existence; there is reason for joy even amid great sorrows.

Moreover, like Balthasar, Ellacuría avers that the self-giving love shown by Christ in the paschal mystery should become the model for our own filial kenosis. However, more clearly than Balthasar, he emphasizes that this radical identification with Christ has serious political implications in a world dominated by idolatrous and violent attachments to riches, honor, and pride. There needs to be, in his view, a real willingness to die in protest of these structures and, moreover, at least some real hope for a historical transformation of them. He even suggests that the *eschaton* depends, in some respects, on what we are willing to do in the here and now. He argues that "the eschatological death and resurrection are proclaimed and made possible in the historical death and in the historical resurrection" of those who authentically follow Christ.[109] It is important to recognize that Ellacuría does not reduce eschatology to history here. The two remain distinct. Rather, he presents certain christologically inspired events in history as preconditions for correlative events in the *eschaton*. He does so precisely in order to promote the sort of integral liberation that he already anticipates, together with Martinez, in 1958—a liberation that, though ultimately eschatological in the fullest sense (eternal life with God), would not leave history behind.[110] In this respect, he is closer to Gutiérrez, Boff, and other liberation theologians than he is to Balthasar, who nevertheless preserves some sense of the significance of historical Christian witness.

And yet, Ellacuría's final word is not mere action but rather *contemplation in action*. He discusses this theme in relation to Ignatius's Contemplation to Attain Love. He clarifies that the resurrected life of the Fourth Week is what allows Ignatius to recover a sense of the created world as a place of loving encounter with God. Ellacuría argues accordingly that it is only by following the Christic and historicized path of the Four Weeks, which includes the life and death struggle against real historical sin, that one can finally reach the glory of the resurrection and, thereby, arrive at the sort of well-ordered relationship between creature and Creator which, having already been formally anticipated by the Principle and Foundation, is given its required specificity only in this final act of contemplation. Thus this concluding exercise should not be abstracted from the rest of the *Spiritual Exercises* but should rather be understood as constantly referring us back to them as the necessary preparatory stages for an authentically prayerful communion with God in all things.[111]

In keeping with his usual pattern, Ellacuría considers in this context both who God is for us and how we are called to respond. In both cases, he develops a rich account of an active, self-giving, and utterly free communication of love. On the basis of Ignatius's prescribed meditations, Ellacuría observes that God's love works actively in creation and in history and is ecstatically present in all things, including especially in the sacred "temple" of the human being, and above all in the historical life, death, and resurrection of divine-human Jesus Christ. In response to this manifold and wondrously self-donating love, we are called to offer our entire selves— that is, the fullness of our freedom—in a return-gift of praise, reverence, and service. Ellacuría contends that this offering should take place in both prayer as a discrete meditative act and in other actions that channel its paradigmatic way of interrelating divine and human freedoms. He explains: "The dichotomy of prayer and action is an abstract or escapist dichotomy. Prayer is, in the concrete, one of the moments of action, the moment of reflective understanding [*captación refleja*] in the Christian modes of action, which does not imply that it should not have its adequate time." Thus Ellacuría clearly believes that time should be set apart for prayerful reflection. And yet, although this distinct moment is necessary, he argues that it is not sufficient without the larger context of action in which it takes place, that is, the Christic spirituality modeled on the whole of the *Spiritual Exercises.*[112] To imitate Christ, it is necessary to be contemplatives in action. This Christic unity of contemplation and action is the telos of the entire process of discernment that Ellacuría has been charting through his reading of Ignatius.

Ellacuría develops these points further in *Fe y justicia* (Faith and justice, 1977), particularly in the final chapter called "La contemplación en la acción de la justicia" (Contemplation in the action of justice).[113] It is instructive to contrast this text with Segundo's similarly titled *Faith and Ideologies*. Whereas Segundo reduces faith to an anthropological dimension of evaluation that is concretized in various practical ideologies, Ellacuría understands faith in connection with a Christian experience of contemplation that must be embodied in concrete actions of love and, therefore, justice. Ellacuría does not subordinate Ignatius's spirituality to a modern intellectual and political program, as Segundo eventually does most clearly in his *Christ and the Ignatian Exercises*, but rather preserves the integrity of Ignatian spirituality and merely seeks to draw out its contemporary implications. This is a crucial difference that leaves the prayerful and doxological character of Ellacuría's reading intact.

In relation to Balthasar, as we have already seen, Ellacuría puts significantly more emphasis on the need for a spirituality that is oriented toward the struggle for liberation and salvation *in* history. In this respect, he is heavily indebted to Ignatius (and not merely to Zubiri), but he also explicitly interprets Ignatius in a way that is conditioned by the contemporary situation in Latin America, and this results in an account that is necessarily more than exegetical. And yet, Ellacuría gives us reason to believe that this very sort of interpretive innovation is required by the historicizing momentum of Ignatius's own method of discernment. Thus, at a more formal level, he is able to defend the genuine Ignatian imprint of the nuances of his own particular reading by suggesting that they have emerged organically from actually doing the *Spiritual Exercises* in the here and now.

Nevertheless, from a Balthasarian perspective, there is room to question Ellacuría with respect to at least one issue, that is, Ellacuría's general inattention to the significance of petitionary prayer. Whereas Balthasar emphasizes that this sort of prayer is a crucial way in which human freedom (precisely as included in the Son) participates actively in the Trinitarian drama of salvation, Ellacuría tends to speak about prayer almost entirely as a moment of meditation, contemplation, or illumination which, though ideally conducive to our own historical action, does not generally seem to be oriented, in the mode of a request, toward making a direct impact upon God's own freedom or God's own heart. In his early text, "Liberación en los Salmos" (Liberation in the Psalms, 1967), Ellacuría does acknowledge that, in some of the Psalms, liberation is described as a "response of God to those who seek it," but this aspect of request does not continue to have a prominent place in his later discussions of spirituality.[114] In this respect, Ellacuría's work may remain somewhat too close to Segundo's, which after a certain point almost completely transforms prayer into an act of reflection.

For Balthasar, petitionary prayer constitutes one way of participating in the infinitely asymmetrical but still dramatic—and, therefore, real—interplay of divine and human freedoms, which occurs in Christ and in the Trinity. Ellacuría's account of spirituality has these basic elements. However, without a thorough discussion of petitionary prayer, his treatment of the free interaction of God and creation proves to be narrower than Balthasar's. This narrowness can be seen in two ways. On the one hand, as Balthasar understands it, the Christian tradition of making prayerful requests underscores the infinitely mysterious freedom of the triune God, who is able to act in ways that exceed our comprehension, both independently of our prayers and in response to them. In Balthasar's view, therefore, God's ongoing salvific action in history need not be exhausted by God's role as the theologal ground of our contemplatively illuminated praxis but rather could also continue in other wondrously unknown ways, for which it would perhaps be meaningful and necessary to pray. Moreover, Balthasar suggests that we are called to approach the apocalyptic end of history now, which Metz likewise anticipates as the full advent of God's freedom and glory, precisely through some sort of vigilantly expectant supplication, for example, "Come, Lord Jesus!" Hence, to the extent that Ellacuría neglects petitionary prayer, he perhaps does not accent certain aspects of God's freedom as strongly as he could. And this may be the case even though he clearly affirms God's freedom as foundational for his own doxologically Ignatian spirituality.

On the other hand, Balthasar's discussion of petitionary prayer actually gives greater weight to human freedom as well. It entails that our role in realizing the divine gift of salvation in history has multiple dimensions to it, including not only action that is inspired by prayerful meditation but also petitionary prayer as itself a powerful kind of action. In this regard, Ellacuría is perhaps a bit too quick in *Fe y justicia* to treat the "prayers for humanity" that are offered by "pure" contemplatives as though they were necessarily an insufficient way of intervening in history.[115] At one level, he certainly seems to have a point: it makes sense that even those who are contemplatives by vocation should, especially in certain dire circumstances which are present throughout much of Latin America and the wider world, do more than *merely* pray. At the same time, however, it also seems important to assert, more explicitly than he does, that when they (or we) pray genuinely for others, in hopes that God will hear and respond, this is *doing* something in God's eyes. This is a work that participates in salvation, not only by shedding light on what needs to be done in other spheres of human activity, but also by making an impression through Christ upon the Father's heart.

Although Ellacuría does not draw out the implications of petitionary prayer as clearly as Balthasar and others might hope he would, he does give a very clear expression to the doxological element of *offering*—and this is perhaps his greatest gift to us. In the final analysis, Ellacuría offers not only Christ but also himself, his very own corporeal life, in praise and in service of the divine majesty. It was this living and incarnate offering that resulted in his death. It is necessary to be clear that his murder was, like Christ's, a senseless and unholy act, utterly lacking in legitimate justification. Nevertheless, once again like Christ's, his death acquires some measure of meaning insofar as it occurs as the outcome of a rigorously doxological and visibly holy life. Whatever other factors were involved (and they are many and complicated), the fact remains that Ellacuría was assassinated because of a deliberate decision that he made through a structured process of prayerful reflection. The decision was this: to imitate Christ's confrontation with the sinful structures of the world. Ignatius's *Spiritual Exercises* were his guide in this regard. Although he certainly draws on Zubiri, Martinez, and other theoretical and poetic sources, Ignatius is the one who teaches him most about how to pray, think, and act in an integrated, liberative, and ultimately costly manner for the greater glory of God. Metz, Gutiérrez, and his close friend Jon Sobrino recognize that Ellacuría's Ignatian spirituality was absolutely decisive for him.[116] It is the key that unlocks the distinctive promise of his liberation theology. It is the defining characteristic of his simultaneously intellectual and historically embodied witness. And it is, therefore, what transforms his death—in itself, a sheer absurdity—into a paradoxical sign of divine love. Although our attention has been on Ellacuría's prayerful thought, we must also remember the stakes of this thought in the midst of concrete reality—and the once living, breathing, now murdered person who was not afraid to face them.

In this chapter, we have seen that liberation theology can take a variety of forms, some of which (e.g., Dussel and Segundo) are underdeveloped or problematic with respect to the task of thinking prayer, others of which (e.g., Gutiérrez, Boff, and Ellacuría) more adequately perform this task in continuity with the best of the Christian doxological tradition. Hence, there is a need for a process of spiritual discernment through which one can make distinctions between these kinds of divergent cases. The more promising formulations of liberation theology that we have considered follow a consistent pattern. They embrace the historical reality of prayer, understood as both a historical phenomenon and as a critical hermeneutic of history; they make connections between this prayerful way of thinking and a committed way of living in radical solidarity with the poor and oppressed; and they do so without significantly distorting or undermining the significance of prayer in the process. What results from this approach is a vision of integral liberation that is simultaneously a vision of integral doxology. For these theologians, to seek the liberating activity of God in all things is to glorify God in all things, and vice versa. These are two ways of describing the same holistic and nonreductive interaction between Trinitarian and creaturely freedoms. Gutiérrez, Boff, and Ellacuría recommend a synthetic practice of receiving, offering, desiring, and actively embodying the glory and word of God, as communicated by the Spirit of Christ in history. As they understand it, an authentic spirituality of liberation can be nothing other than an ever-greater participation in this spiritually given *doxa* and *logos*.

We have seen that Gutiérrez, Boff, and Ellacuría have different ways of specifying this possibility, which partly stem from distinct sources of inspiration: Carmelite and Dominican (Gutiérrez), Franciscan (Boff), and Ignatian (Ellacuría). This plurality is a sign of the beauty and the abundance of the Spirit's grace. Moreover, it demonstrates the deeply traditional character of these particular strands of liberation theology, which have a firm basis in the renewed sense of an apostolic vocation that swept over the church in the Middle Ages and propelled it into modernity, a vocation that called forth new ways of integrating doxological contemplation and action. For this reason, it would not be inaccurate to understand their integral doxology precisely as an *apostolic* doxology, a doxology that is not content with any form of eremitical or coenobitical withdrawal but is rather oriented toward a transformative engagement with the world. Theirs is a prayerful worldliness and a worldly prayerfulness. No simplistically dichotomous thinking can capture it.

Gutiérrez, Boff, and Ellacuría compel us to consider the power and cogency of this apostolic spirituality of liberation, which undoubtedly has implications for the whole church. At the same time, who can say even after reading these liberation theologians that there is not also ample room in the wondrously hospitable household of God for monastics, pure contemplatives, and cloistered persons leading extravagant lives of prayer, so long as they too remember and care for the poor in their midst? It seems illegitimate to impose an absolute choice between apostolic and monastic vocations on the whole church, insofar as some vocational differentiation appears inevitable. Nevertheless, what is concretely required of monastics in terms of their remembrance and care of the poor should, in the light of these integrally doxological forms of liberation theology, at least become a matter of serious, ongoing discernment. Chrétien's discussion of a Marian-and-Marthan double hospitality remains a helpful guide in this regard.

In continuity with Balthasar, Gutiérrez, Boff, and Ellacuría propose a form of spirituality that is explicitly doxological, but this does not prevent them from engaging more directly than he typically does with the depths of human suffering. Like Metz, Gutiérrez and Boff demonstrate that prayer is particularly relevant in this violent world insofar as it gives voice to the lamentations and urgent longings of humanity and does not drown them out with an overly positive discourse (whether this would be a strict theodicy or not). However, somewhat more explicitly than Metz, they hold this critical, agonistic perspective in tension with a doxological affirmation of the liberating activity of God that has in some sense already been revealed in Christ. In effect, they encourage us to honor God through questions, protests, and desperate cries for help, *as well as* through joyful forms of adoration, celebration, and contemplation. These are all features of their integral doxology.

In Ellacuría's case, the concerns of those who suffer are almost entirely transposed into the theologal struggle for justice in history. Whereas Gutiérrez and Boff highlight prayers of protest and request, Ellacuría makes a different kind of contribution by showing how prayerful *theoria* and liberative *praxis* can and should be connected through the medium of christological and spiritual discernment. The largely theoretical discernment that this chapter performs with respect to different versions of liberation theology helps to clarify the complexity of the field (a significant but preliminary task). By contrast, Ellacuría's more directly practical and embodied discernment helps him make a choice about how to think and live in a concrete situation, in dangerous fidelity to Christ, and for this reason his model of spiritual discernment is what ultimately merits the most serious imitation, by theologians and Christians in general.

Insofar as their works are constitutively prayerful and doxological, Gutiérrez, Boff, and Ellacuría find themselves in a fairly promising position with respect to the crises associated with modern metaphysics. In Boff the promise is somewhat more explicit than in Gutiérrez, and in Ellacuría it is more explicit still, as we have seen through his interpretations of Zubiri and Martinez. However, the degree of subtlety with respect to these issues is not as high as one finds in Marion, Lacoste, and Chrétien. Thus it seems that liberation theologians have something to gain from a more in-depth dialogue with their more avidly phenomenological peers, even though what they have to gain is already theirs *in potentia*. Henceforward, it seems that we should not seek to choose between phenomenology and liberation but rather find in the former an impulse to reflect ever more deeply on the richly textured phenomenalities of the latter.

However, liberation theologians are with good reason primarily interested in confronting certain contemporary structures of violence. In particular, they seek to resist whatever political, social, or cultural mechanisms tend to perpetuate the dehumanizing impoverishment of the majority of the human race. Selectively drawing on Marxian and other related forms of critical theory, they regularly associate this violence with the rise of modern capitalism. Whether this diagnosis is more nearly useful or misleading is a matter that needs to be discussed and decided elsewhere. Here it suffices to indicate that, whatever dynamics might sustain extreme poverty on a local and global scale, and whatever other conceptual tools might be necessary to provide a thorough assessment of this poverty, Gutiérrez, Boff, and Ellacuría make a compelling case that it needs to be combated with the full force of an actively embodied doxological and liberative spirituality. This is the point at which these theologians intervene most effectively in the contemporary conversation. Implicitly prepared to move beyond metaphysics (without losing the sense of doxological wonder that it both presupposes and threatens), they are also adamantly opposed to the continued exploitation and abjection of the most economically vulnerable. In both respects, they are powerfully supported by prayer.

In addressing the modern crises of metaphysics and violence, Gutiérrez, Boff, and Ellacuría therefore do not adopt the largely nondoxological and maximally apophatic strategy of Derrida or Caputo. They do not protest notions of divine presence; nor do they interpret such presence merely as a "weak" form of blessing and compassion within the event. Rather, they glorify and hope in the powerful and active presence of the triune liberator. In this way they seek to give encouragement to the forsaken and despairing. With Dussel, we see that a Levinasian current also runs through liberation theology. But Gutiérrez, Boff, and Ellacuría give to the ethical concern for the other that Levinas represents somewhat doxologically a fuller doxological formulation. More clearly than Metz, who for his part warns against certain excesses of Christian doxology without ever disregarding it, these three liberation theologians reveal Christian doxology's concrete, historical and political stakes.

In the next chapter, we shall see how a similar integrally doxological and apostolic spirituality associated with black liberation theology counteracts the interrelated metaphysics and violence of modern racism. This structure produces and organizes widespread conditions of impoverishment among darkly colored peoples. But it also does more than this: it *denigrates* these peoples by making their richly shaded flesh a sign of debasement (this is precisely what the word "denigrate" implies). Modern racism depends on a more or less metaphysical concept of the racial identity of these peoples. It assigns them a fixed place within a system of entities that can be disposed of at will by an ordering enframer (whether the consciousness of a master, the cultural imaginary of a society, or any uncritical discourse in which the word "black" or its cognates overtly or covertly function in a denigrating manner). This racial metaphysics is connected with horrific historical effects, which are, to this world's great shame, not yet confined to the past. Because Christian theology, even in its more prayerful and thus seemingly auspicious modes, has self-contradictorily been part of the genesis of this crisis and because Christian theology, precisely on the basis of prayer, still has much more that it can and must do to redress its wrongs (as well as those of modern thought and culture in general) and, thereby, to glorify God in a more credible and authentically liberative way, the present inquiry must continue. It should not stop while leaving the question of blackness, as it too frequently does, to the side.

The same Spirit of God that gives hope to the spiritually poor (in Metz's sense) and to the materially poor (in the sense espoused by various Latin American liberation theologians) also finds a voice in the songs of agony and praise that many black slaves and many of their descendants have never ceased to sing in (what perhaps still remains for them) a foreign land. These songs are the key not only to a theology that is black but also to a theology that is catholic—a term that means nothing if it does not entail a committed struggle against racism. They also arguably provide one of the most suitable loci of prayerful enunciation in which to gather together all the elements of the foregoing discussion and to bring them to some kind of provisional (which is to say, necessarily open-ended) synthesis.

CHAPTER 6

SONGS OF THE SPIRIT

James Cone

Let us turn then, finally, to the prayers of the slaves. Let us call to mind the fugitive wisdom of the hush harbor. Let us immerse ourselves in the doxological spirituality that has grown together with black diasporic existence for four long centuries of transatlantic terror and inhumane captivity and that contiues to live on amid the uncertain conditions of the present.[1] Here we shall seek to remember not only the prayerful songs whose sonorous refrains carry the sorrows and hopes of this black tradition through the undersides of American modernity but also the thoughts that these songs communicate. To do this, we shall study the works of one of their most thought-provokingly theological interpreters: James Cone. As in other cases, so too here, prayer becomes an indispensable source of intellectual and practical insight regarding the mysteries of God and the world. Moreover, it does so in ways that promise to open up a new future for humanity in which the major crises of the modern age will have been decisively addressed and many of the disastrous contradictions that have plagued the historical practice of Christian prayer will have been overcome. In the midst of modernity's ontologically abetted antiblack racism, any spirituality that hopes to be convincingly postmetaphysical and counterviolent must become a black spirituality. It must become a life of prayer haunted by the memory of the slaves and their divinely sustained and divinely oriented desires for freedom. This chapter clarifies the conditions of this urgently needed possibility.

Some theologians and scholars of spirituality unfortunately treat the tradition of black spirituals, if they do so at all, as no more than a marginal and inessential example. The unstated assumption is that the prayers of this tradition could only ever be meaningful for a minority population of black Christians and only then as a concession to this group's presupposed racial or cultural particularity, a concession that may be recognized as necessary in this instance but that still is not thought to have any real bearing on the meaning of Christian spirituality as such.[2] Even avid supporters of this tradition can perhaps inadvertently reinforce the impression that it is viable as a source only for a somewhat circumscribed, and to this extent not universally relevant, type of contextual theology.[3] This variously constituted practice of theological marginalization inhibits one from seriously considering the many ways in which the significance of *prayer itself*—that is, the meaning that it has throughout the ages and the particular promise that it carries in modernity—comes to a clear and approximately full expression precisely in this black tradition. Such theological marginalization not only jeopardizes the integrity of Christian prayer (that is, its moral character and coherence); it also undermines the integrally liberative impact that such prayer has the potential to make in this racially violent world. It thereby conspires with long-standing intellectual, cultural, and political processes of denigration, which both conceal and perpetuate the deadly consequences of modernity's antiblack idolatry.

In order to counteract these interconnected problems, this chapter will seek to demonstrate that and how the songs of the slaves condense the mystery of prayer in a sufficiently profound and integrative manner to warrant rigorous contemplation by the whole church and, moreover, how they do so in an especially important way in the midst of the crises of the modern age, including but not limited to antiblack violence.[4] James Cone, one of the founders of the movement of black liberation theology which first took shape in critical dialogue with the civil rights and Black Power struggles of the 1960s, will be our guide in this respect. He is a helpful interlocutor here insofar as he lays the groundwork for a contemporary retrieval of the spirituals as a constitutive source of Christian thought and life. Moreover, notwithstanding certain misconceptions to the contrary, he does so not only for a narrowly defined black community but also for others and potentially for all. He performs this task very clearly in the book that he specifically pens on the subject, *The Spirituals and the Blues* (1972), but he also devotes considerable energy to it in other major works. Indeed, the normative weight of the prayer tradition of the slaves is a central theme running throughout his entire corpus, and his black theology is unthinkable without it. The first section of this chapter will verify this claim.

However, the present argument is not only about the influence that this prayerful tradition has on Cone's thought. More importantly, it is about how Cone helps us to rediscover this tradition as a powerful icon of the meaning of prayer itself and of the postmetaphysical and counterviolent form of doxological spirituality that is desperately needed in modernity. To develop these crucial aspects of the discussion, it will be necessary to draw out the mostly implicit but nevertheless substantial points of contact that arise between Cone and the other key thinkers we have considered thus far. It will also be necessary to put Cone in dialogue with some critical interpreters of his theology. The second and third sections of this chapter, which treat the problems of metaphysics and violence, respectively, will provide this sort of comparative and synthetic discussion.

This way of reading Cone comes with certain perils. There are three, in particular, that deserve mentioning at the outset. Perhaps the most obvious of these is the danger of superficially "integrating" Cone's black theology into a predominantly nonblack theological discourse in a way that would compromise the critical convictions of the former and make very little meaningful impact on the latter. This sort of destructively assimilationist "integration" (which is not really an integration at all) needs to be resisted. Here we shall counteract it by affirming the black doxological tradition on its own terms and by highlighting its as-yet-unrealized potential to become the enabling context for, and not merely a dispensable element of, integral doxology in both church and society. The plan will be to understand this tradition as a crucial point of access to an authentic manifestation of the mystery of prayer that is shareable by all. This approach requires us to distinguish two ways in which this tradition comes to light as especially suitable for such a task.

In the first case, the prayer tradition of the slaves can be treated as normative for a general understanding of prayer insofar as it proves to be *more* rigorously doxological than any specifically "white"—by which one should understand racially oppressive or exclusionary—alternatives.[5] For the most part, with the possible exception of Heidegger (whose detrimental claims regarding Greco-German superiority must be held in tension with certain prayer-like thoughts of autochthony and hospitality that may be reworked counterviolently), the other sources we have explored in this project are not obviously antiblack in principle. One might plausibly conjecture that Balthasar, the post-Balthasarians, Metz, and the liberation theologians of Latin America have mainly devoted their attention elsewhere without thereby intending to indicate anything negative about blackness. All of these thinkers are, without exception, committed to Christian anthropological and soteriological doctrines that are formally inclusive of all people. Moreover, they not only uphold a radically self-giving form of Christian love; they also seek, in different ways, to combat those instances in which humanity fails in this amorous vocation, whether they construe these more generally as sin (Balthasar) and inhospitality (Chrétien and others) or more specifically as anti-Semitic violence (Metz) and worldwide impoverishment (Gutiérrez and others). The maximally apophatic spiritualities of Derrida and Caputo likewise underscore a desire and imperative to welcome the other.

Nevertheless, without disputing the individual and collective promise of the prayerful thinkers we have studied, one must still recognize that insofar as they pay very little, if any, attention to the harsh realities of racism and the prayers of black humanity, they effectively permit the antiblack ethos of the modern West to go unchallenged.[6] In short, therefore, they do not do as much as they could—or, more importantly, as much as *we should*—to overcome the profoundly damaging effects of "white" consciousness on contemporary theology, spirituality, politics, and culture, even though they have many of the tools to do so. The core argument here is that Christian doxology cannot presently do justice *to itself* unless it becomes *explicitly* informed by the prayerful songs of black people and, thereby, directly contravenes the idolatrous racism of modernity. This is one of the specific contributions of the prayer tradition of the slaves.

Second, this black spiritual tradition acquires normative status insofar as it proves to be *no less* rigorously doxological than other already evidently compelling options. We shall confirm this point by showing that the songs of the slaves concretize, in their own unique way, all of the essential aspects of the many reflections on prayer that we have examined in previous chapters. An incomplete list of these aspects would include the formal structure of prayer as a love-bound interaction of Trinitarian and creaturely freedoms; the formal structure of doxology as receiving, offering, and desiring the glory and word of God; an affirmation of humanity that is not merely secularizing; a radical unity of theology and spirituality; an analogical distinction between infinite and finite existence; a poetic openness to the mediation of divine excess in phenomena; an aesthetics of revelation, in which the senses, the imagination, and the whole body are brought into contact with the Trinitarian mystery of God as disclosed in the saving actions of Christ and the Holy Spirit; a deep apophasis, which expresses awe before the incomprehensibility of God; a sense of worldly responsibility rooted in responsiveness to a divine call; a sense of radical hospitality toward the neighbor that flows from hospitality toward the divine guest; a profound appreciation for the nonreductive unity of contemplation and action; the courage to offer not only praise but also urgent questions, supplications, and lamentations to God in hope that God will actually reply in dramatic and transformative ways; a critical historical consciousness, in which the fullness of divine glory is associated with the liberation of the poor and oppressed; a willingness to imitate Christ and potentially lose one's life in confrontation with the concrete crimes of the world; and, in all of these respects, a clear potential to address the contemporary crises of metaphysics and violence. Hence, the black doxological tradition should be treated as particularly normative not only because it is in certain crucial ways *more* but also because it is in none of these above-mentioned ways *less* adequate than other broadly promising (and, therefore, potentially catholic) sources of a Christian postmetaphysical and counterviolent spirituality.

For these two reasons, although the prayer tradition of the slaves constitutes only a limited part of the larger doxological whole that we have explored, it also manages to qualify as the singularly most conclusive part, which, having added what other parts lack, also aptly preserves the truth and coherence of this whole. Thus it emerges as the part that most clearly brings everything together (i.e., the logic of this treatise on prayer, the symbol that could express or stand for it, the sacred site of its most nearly adequate hypostatization). In this sense, it counts not merely as a piece but as a finale. Contemporary members of the church and society who have not yet internalized the significance of this tradition risk losing touch with the full promise of a prayerful way of thought and life. Therefore, far from being destructively assimilated, the spirituals will in this context show forth their capacity to heal, incorporate, and unify the mystery of prayer itself.

A second danger has to do with the deeply problematic practice of reducing blackness to a fixed essence or identity. This practice forecloses the possibility of liberation by inscribing black people within an illegitimately restrictive idea regarding what they must necessarily and universally be in order to be black (that is, in ordinary parlance, a stereotype). However, the naïve thought that we might abolish the term "blackness" altogether in order to escape this kind of metaphysical reductionism is also problematic. The image of blackness continues to direct our attention toward a highly complex and dynamic constellation of real human beings, generally of a darker hue and at least partly and relatively recently (i.e., within the last several millennia) descendant from Africa. There is immense diachronic, geographic, socioeconomic, phenotypic, genotypic, cultural, linguistic, personal, and theological diversity within this constellation, as well as various contingent patterns of solidarity and belonging that are not always very clear-cut. We need a discourse that is able to embrace this phenomenally excessive blackness and not simply bracket it for the sake of some allegedly color-blind universalism. This sort of positively black discourse is especially necessary as a means of resisting certain persistent forms of antiblack racism, which continue to have an especially devastating impact on the world's poorest and most ostracized black populations and which have the potential to be sustained and concealed precisely by the alleged abolition of color consciousness. At the same time, what it means to be black needs to remain a largely open question, located precariously between a past whose afflictions are known all too well by some (though disgracefully forgotten by others) and an unknown future in which the apparition of blackness will perhaps no longer function as a symbol of oppression.[7]

In view of these kinds of complexities, the goal must be to find a way to affirm blackness while refusing any sort of metaphysically reductive account of it and while supporting a preferential concern for the liberation of the poorest and most downtrodden black communities. The prayer tradition of the slaves is promising in all of these respects insofar as it brings blackness into the ambit of a doxological aesthetics and dramatics of liberation. This move empowers people of every color to contemplate blackness as integral to (which is not to say absolutely identical with) the glory and word of God that is historically revealed in Christ and is made present through the sanctifying actions of the Holy Spirit. Through this sort of integrally doxological contemplation, it becomes possible to welcome blackness as an eminently lovable divine gift, to insist on its irreducible excess beyond any racial or cultural essence, and to hope and struggle for forms of proximate and ultimate liberation that would concretely realize its already irrevocably given doxological status and thus bring freedom to those black persons (icons of the invisible God) who continue to be victimized by structures of economic and identity-based violence. In short, the spirituals open up a path beyond racial and cultural forms of black-identity-reductionism while preserving the most indispensable features of black liberation theology. To interpret Cone's work along these lines may require one to perceive greater indeterminacy and mutability in the meaning of blackness than he typically suggests, but there is another sense in which this perspective follows quite directly from his own prayerful reflections.

The third peril that needs to be mentioned here has to do with the danger of developing a positively black account of prayer that proves to be insufficiently hospitable to nonblack others, including both other people of color (who are not merely black or who may, whatever their complexion, not identify with this signifier) and phenotypically white people (many of whom remain uncritically implicated in the structural dynamics of "whiteness"). What needs to be avoided in both of these respects is a violent form of problack assimilationist "integration" that would disregard or reductively dehumanize anyone who is not recognizably black. We shall address this concern by considering the extent to which Cone's interpretation of the doxological spirituality of the slaves enables him not only to develop relationships of solidarity with an international and multicolor network of the poor and oppressed (including many of the political and liberation theologians who speak on their behalf), but also to formulate certain reasonable conditions of a loving whiteblack communion that have yet to be fully satisfied. These two facets of Cone's work point in the direction of a truly unlimited, prayerful hospitability.

In the end, the prayerful songs of the slaves teach us at least two extraordinary and inseparable lessons: first, that Christian doxological spirituality has the potential to become more, and not less, authentically universal by allowing itself to become black and, second, that blackness has the potential to become more, and not less, fully liberated by recognizing itself as doxological. Among the many scholars who have studied these songs, Cone is the one who does the most to clarify these two points, and this is the main reason for prioritizing him here. While engaging with his account, we shall attempt to hear what is unheard-of in his words, to let the theological thought-forms of the spirituals shed light on the contemporary crises that we have considered throughout, and ultimately to recognize the slaves themselves as our hitherto vastly underappreciated intellectual and spiritual "masters" (in the ancient sense of experienced teachers). Their mastery is not disclosed as a kind of domination but rather as a humble expression of the wisdom of Christ, who would not hesitate to become black if this meant (as it does) entering into the communities and lives of an unjustly denigrated people in order to give them a reason to persevere, to hope, and to pray.

THE PRAYERFUL ROOTS OF BLACK LIBERATION THEOLOGY

The first task is to acquire a fresh interpretation of Cone that does not neglect the prayerful roots of his thought. His earliest works, such as *Black Theology and Black Power* (1969) and *A Black Theology of Liberation* (1970), certainly reflect the historical circumstances from which they arose. In particular, they draw upon various movements of "black radicalism" (to adopt Gayraud Wilmore's term), which were led by black intellectuals and activists such as Malcolm X, Stokely Carmichael, Amiri Baraka, and many others. These radical movements tended to be motivated above all by an uncompromising stance against various prevalent forms of local and global antiblack racism, which remained stubbornly unmoved by Martin Luther King Jr.'s moral suasion strategy and which were not sufficiently undone by certain nevertheless momentous civil rights victories.[8] The volatile context of black revolutionary struggle that these movements represent can be sensed on nearly every page of Cone's first writings. Other factors in the composition of these works include the kerygmatic perspective of Barth's *Church Dogmatics*, which Cone appropriates in his doctoral dissertation, and the almost inescapable atmosphere of existential philosophy and theology, signified by figures such as Sartre, Camus, and the early Heidegger, on the one hand, and Bultmann, Tillich, and other Christian inheritors of this general approach, on the other, which Cone certainly does not ignore. Finally, there was the emergence of the political theology of hope, especially as articulated by Moltmann and influenced by the Frankfurt School.

Cone learns something from all of these sources, but the highest criterion that enables him to discern how to use them critically and selectively within his own distinctive version of black liberation theology is provided by the prayerful tradition of the antebellum black church, which he accesses significantly, though not exclusively, through the spirituals. The hermeneutical priority of this pre–Civil War black spirituality can be seen clearly in *Black Theology and Black Power*. Here Cone maintains that both the nonviolent resistance of King and the subsequent call for black power have their roots in this spirituality.[9] Similarly, he suggests that the faithful obedience to revelation (accented by Barth), the profound need for self-affirmation amid absurdity (emphasized by existential thought), and the politico-theological relation between eschatological and historical hope (stressed by Moltmann) are all anticipated by it.[10] He finds prefigurations of these contemporary theoretical and practical commitments in spirituals such as "Oh, Freedom!," "Go Down, Moses," and "Joshua Fit de Battle of Jericho." He also discovers them in the prayerfully inspired sermons and actions of pre–Civil War black preachers, such as Richard Allen, Absalom Jones, Highland Garnet, Nathaniel Paul, and Nat Turner.[11]

To be precise, one should acknowledge that the collective witness of these early black preachers plays a somewhat more prominent role in *Black Theology and Black Power* than do the spirituals themselves. Cone draws particular attention to an iconic incident in which, while at prayer in St. George's Methodist Episcopal Church of Philadelphia in 1787, Allen, Jones, and several other black members of the congregation were interrupted by several "white" members who, forcefully pulling Jones up from his knees, told the group: "You must get up—you must not kneel here."[12] In Cone's narrative, this event symbolizes the origin of an independent black church that was forced to become independent precisely in order to find the freedom to pray and to pray rightly—that is, to pray apart from the racist distortions of Christianity that were overwhelmingly present in the wider church. According to Cone, therefore, it was for the sake of prayer itself, and for the sake of the concrete realization of divine love and righteousness which the authenticity of prayer implied, that a new black tradition had to be developed. This tradition—and, in a sense, this tradition *alone*, so long as the choice continued to be between black and "white" options—would preserve the integrally liberative promise of prayer in the midst of such pervasive antiblack oppression. Only this tradition maintained the conditions for the possibility of actually glorifying the God of biblical revelation, radically affirming black humanity in the midst of their absurd social situation, and concretely liberating all people of whatever color from the evils of a slaveholding society.

One can, therefore, begin to see how virtually every claim that Cone advances in *Black Theology and Black Power* has its roots, in one way or another, in this integrally doxological black spirituality, as represented by Allen, Jones, and others. This point finds further confirmation insofar as this spiritual tradition not only grounds Cone's positive assertions and appropriations but also his most decisive critiques. It is precisely on the basis of this tradition that he significantly parts ways with certain non-Christian or anti-Christian forms of black radicalism[13] and speaks out against the dangers not only of the "white" church but also of the post–Civil War black church.[14] Furthermore, although he refers frequently to Barth, Tillich, Moltmann, and others, there is a reason why his work does not seem to be strictly *about* them and, in fact, might easily be used to identify the limitations of their respective approaches. The reason is that his work's main objective is to recover the power of a specifically black spiritual tradition that these thinkers do not adequately articulate. Cone's basic principle of judgment might, therefore, be summarized as follows: To what extent do these various intellectual, social, and ecclesial possibilities do justice to the prayerful forms of thought and existence that are disclosed in the spirituals of the slaves and the spiritually motivated struggles of antebellum black preachers—and, conversely, to what extent do they conceal the integrally liberative promise that is inherent in this tradition? This is the principle that shapes his most foundational elaboration of the meaning of black theology and distinguishes it from various black and nonblack alternatives.

Cone expresses the hermeneutical priority of antebellum black spirituality once again in *A Black Theology of Liberation*, arguing that it is the inspiration for his "passionate" theological language and the primary "tradition" upon which his theology depends.[15] However, the influence of this tradition does appear to stay largely beneath the surface of the text, giving way to a more overt engagement with primarily nonblack interlocutors. In fact, a similar claim could even be made, though somewhat less convincingly, about *Black Theology and Black Power*. One has to read this text carefully in order to discern just how vital the spirituality of the pre–Civil War black church is for the overall logic. The general point would be that, in both of these early books, although Cone relies deeply on this prayerful tradition, he does not always specify as clearly as possible when and where it becomes decisive for his arguments. To some extent, this understated approach may account for the complaint voiced by some of his early critics that he does not seem to ground his theology firmly enough in identifiably black sources.[16]

Cone writes *The Spirituals and the Blues* at least partly in order to address this concern.[17] However, this text does not only enable him to defend the blackness of his theology. It also allows him to clarify the theological and, indeed, doxological character of his account of blackness—which he, therefore, avoids treating merely as a racial or cultural category. In short, the central argument of *The Spirituals and the Blues* is that neither the historically revealed actuality of God, nor the meaning of black existence, nor the promise of integral liberation that unites the two can be approached adequately today—that is, in the midst of the ongoing aftermath of slavery—without remembering the prayer tradition of the slaves and reorienting the church's contemporary theology and praxis around it. At this point, the spirituals become explicitly definitive for his entire project of black liberation theology.

Although the blues and other more nearly secular forms of black music inform Cone's thought, they do not occupy the gravitational center of it in the way that the prayerful songs of the slaves do. Whereas the blues powerfully communicate the harsh realities of black existence in a racist society, the spirituals secure the possibility of a doxological mode of black existence in such a society, and this is the possibility that Cone most directly seeks to realize. Moreover, although he is interested in studying both the spirituals and the blues as "cultural expressions of black people," this does not imply that his theology is merely an exercise in interpreting cultural expressions. On the contrary, he incorporates elements of black art and culture only while holding them accountable to a theologically significant tradition of prayer and prayerful reflection that emerges from the songs of the slaves. He defines his task in this way: "There is a complex world of *thought* underlying the slave songs that has so far escaped analysis. Further theological interpretation is needed to uncover this thought and the fundamental worldview that it implies."[18] Retrieving the slaves' prayerful—and, he insists, intellectually rigorous—vision of reality and rearticulating it for today is his primary concern. This is what makes his work theological in a not merely "cultural-expressivist" sense.[19]

It is somewhat interesting to note that Cone now narrates the antebellum black church's primordial break with the aberrant structure of "white" Christianity not in terms of Allen's and Jones's decisive departure from St. George's, but rather in terms of the slaves' rejection of the slaveholders' idolatrous—because constitutively racist—style of worship. In this text, Cone treats the slaves themselves as the primary progenitors of the black spiritual tradition. He holds that they certainly remembered some theological insights from the West African traditions of their ancestors but were also greatly inspired by their primarily oral exposure to the foundational stories and doctrines of the Christian faith.[20] He argues that the confluence of these elements enabled the slaves to inaugurate a distinctive form of spirituality and theology rooted in a new and liberating experience of God. As he puts it: "They shouted and they prayed; they preached and they sang, because *they had found something*. They encountered a new reality; a new God not enshrined in white churches and religious gatherings." Cone shows that, in opposition to all "white" slavery-justifying idols, the slaves discovered a *solidaristically black* God who loved and sided with them. Moreover, in his judgment, they rightly recognized that this was the only God who was actually worthy of worship in such a racially oppressive society.[21]

Cone distinguishes several features of the slaves' particular way of contemplating and glorifying this God.[22] He argues that, in their prayers and hymns, they bore witness to a God who created them as beloved and beautiful children, who promised to liberate them like the Hebrews of old, who entered into the most radical solidarity with them through Jesus's suffering and death, who gave them hope through the glorious event of the resurrection, who freed them from the bonds of sin and despair, and who presently empowered them in their historical acts of resistance against the demonic powers of the slave system.[23] Cone reconstructs this rich theological tapestry from the mere fragments that we have of the slaves' largely forbidden, often forcibly illiterate, and yet unmistakably profound spiritual practice. Without referring extensively in this text to secular proponents of black radicalism; neoorthodox, existential, or political theologians; or any other likely theorists, Cone articulates the major features of his black liberation theology nearly on the basis of the spirituals alone. The point is not that these other sources are no longer relevant; rather, it is that their relevance is determined by their degree of conformity to the integrally doxological spirituality of the slaves.

Ultimately, it is not enough to say that Cone's thought is partly informed by the spirituals. One must recognize that the spirituals are foundational to his overarching perspective and inseparable from his sense of his own personal identity. He internalizes them through his childhood experience of worship in the Macedonia A.M.E. Church in Bearden, Arkansas. Mediated by this experience, they become for him not merely texts of the past but rather a form of living memory and hope that will be forever deeply ingrained in his own doxologically black existence—that is, in Augustinian terms, in his own *confession*. Having alluded to this autobiographical aspect of his work on the first page of *The Spirituals and the Blues*, Cone emphasizes it again throughout the entire introduction to *God of the Oppressed* (1975) and weaves it into a more richly textured personal narrative in the first few chapters of *My Soul Looks Back* (1982).[24] Thus when he discusses the songs of the slaves, he does not do so as an outside observer but rather as an internal participant in their ongoing vitality. In short, they are formative of his Christian and black subjectivity. They are the inner compass that enables him to navigate the complex terrains of a racially divided academy, church, and society.

The constitutive presence of this spiritual tradition continues to be evident in Cone's *For My People* (1984), in his essay collections *Speaking the Truth* (1986) and *The Risks of Faith* (1999), and even in his primarily historical study *Martin & Malcolm & America* (1991).[25] Most recently, it emerges as one of the major focal points of *The Cross and the Lynching Tree* (2011). In this text, he shows how, despite his early critiques of the post–Civil War black church, at least *some* members of this ecclesial institution managed to preserve the theological promise of the spirituals throughout the lynching era (from roughly 1880 to 1940) and thereby prepared for the rise of the civil rights movement. Once again, whereas the blues, along with other forms of black art and culture, give Cone access to the often bitter and contradictory realities of black life during this period, the songs of the slaves, as they are passed on from generation to generation, more fully capture his specifically prayerful orientation. Having appreciated the concerns of some of his womanist critics, he draws particular attention to many black women, such as Ida B. Wells, Nellie Burrows, Fannie Lou Hammer, and several others, who relied upon and carried forward this integrally doxological spirituality in their world-changing struggles against racial and patriarchal oppression. In the end, this same spirituality continues to undergird his kerygmatic affirmation of the paradoxically salvific power of the cross, his distinctively black account of existential courage amid the terror of lynching, and his holistic sense of the historical and eschatological hope of taking black bodies down from the cross.[26] In short, although it has been refined and adapted over the years, Cone's black liberation theology remains today, as it was in the beginning, deeply rooted in the prayers and hymns of his enslaved ancestors.

FROM METAPHYSICAL TO DOXOLOGICAL BLACKNESS

Having established that Cone's thought is shaped by his remembrance of the spirituals, we must now consider in what respects it both enhances and preserves the promise of doxology. On the one hand, part of what needs to be shown is that his theology has the potential to overcome the metaphysical and violent treatments of blackness that are constitutive of antiblack racism in the modern age. This is the crucial element that he contributes to the cumulative sense of doxological spirituality that has emerged from previous chapters. On the other hand, it will be necessary to demonstrate that the most important insights of the other thinkers of prayer that we have studied can be incorporated into the particular theological vision that Cone formulates on the basis of the spirituals. In this way, he will help us to recognize not only the particularity but also the remarkable catholicity and far-reaching significance of these songs.

In the present section, we shall focus on the crises associated with modern metaphysics by examining Cone's work in relation to Heidegger's critique and proposal (chapter 1), Balthasar's complex appropriation and refusal of Heidegger (chapter 2), and the variety of options that represent some form of mediation between Heideggerian and Balthasarian approaches (chapter 3). We shall likewise consider to what extent Cone's doxology effectively resists the racist violence that is maintained through the enforcement of a metaphysically reductive account of black identity. Cone's engagements with Barth and the somewhat Heideggerian Tillich—which one should remember are subservient to his efforts to translate antebellum black spirituality into a contemporary theological context—bring his work very close to Balthasar's analogical, aesthetic, and dramatic doxological theory. However, there are also ways in which Cone, like the phenomenological post-Balthasarians, manages to avoid some of the questionable ties to metaphysics that Balthasar retains. While sustaining the sort of doxological contemplation that this tradition affirms as a positive alternative to metaphysics, Cone importantly adds a reflection on the beauty of blackness to this contemplation. He thereby corrects the tendency of even the most critically aware members of this postmetaphysical tradition to ignore the negative effects that racist "whiteness" has had, and continues to have, both on black human beings and on the very integrity of prayer itself. In the course of clarifying these points, we shall also see how they challenge both J. Kameron Carter's and Victor Anderson's critical accounts of Cone as a problematically metaphysical thinker.

First, one should note that, although Cone follows Barth and Bonhoeffer in rejecting the *analogia entis* in favor of a more clearly Christocentric account of the *analogia relationis*, he certainly does not thereby dismiss the idea of an analogical structure. On the contrary, he explicitly affirms this structure as "a given relationship in which humans are free to be for God because God is free for them in Christ." What we have, then, at the most formal level—which, for Cone, remains much closer to Christology than ontology—is precisely an asymmetrical but reciprocal meeting of divine and human freedom. This is the basic conceptual scaffolding of prayer, which we have seen Balthasar recognize in both Przywara's Thomistic doctrine of being and Barth's *Church Dogmatics*. The point here is that Cone undeniably preserves this sense of analogy in his black liberation theology. After praising God as the infinitely transcendent Creator of all things, Cone expresses his conviction that "the transcendence of God prevents us from deifying our own experiences, which results in pantheism." He continues: "God is neither nature nor our highest aspirations. God is always more than our experience of God." In short, for Cone, God is ever greater and freely so. God is not reducible to the world, to being, or to human consciousness. Moreover, we are able to communicate with God through a relationship that God freely inaugurates with us in creation and in Christ. He contrasts this view with certain metaphysical conceptions of God (without, however, developing this point at great length).[27]

J. Kameron Carter argues that Cone embraces certain key aspects of Barth's theology (specifically its christological concreteness and divine transcendence). However, Carter also interestingly notes that Cone implicitly affirms Balthasar's concerns regarding the dangers of the more nearly dialectical, as opposed to analogical, formulations that appear in some of Barth's texts. According to Carter, Cone seems to agree with Balthasar that Barth's dialecticism could compromise a genuinely *creaturely* participation in the christologically given glory and word of God. Carter endorses Cone's somewhat Balthasarian assessment of this Barthian problem but not Cone's ostensibly Tillichian solution, which Carter contends dangerously implicates Cone's project in a Heideggerian existential ontology that reduces divine transcendence to the horizon of worldly *Dasein*. In sum, Carter's worry is that, while reasonably seeking to validate the creaturely conditions of theology in a manner that is more adequate than Barth's dialecticism, Cone makes an overcorrection and ultimately collapses the mystery of God into a creaturely struggle for being and authenticity along Heideggerian-Tillichian lines. Carter suggests that this shortcoming occurs as a "shift" in Cone's thought, beginning after *Black Theology and Black Power* and reaching its full proportions in various texts of the 1970s and 1980s.[28]

Carter's analysis is helpful insofar as it uncovers the proximity between Cone and Balthasar precisely on the question of analogy, insofar as it clarifies that Cone employs Tillich at least partly in order to make up for a perceived deficit in Barth's account of the creaturely side of the God-human relationship, and insofar as it shows what would be especially problematic about too strong a reliance on Tillich. However, Carter's argument can be contested on at least one point: he does not establish that Cone ever appropriates Tillich in a way that actually violates an analogical principle or (which amounts to the same thing) reorients black theology in a lamentably immanentist or monistic direction. The grounds for Carter's critical evaluation of the "later" Cone are destabilized by the highly selective and limited manner in which Cone draws upon Tillich's thought—and, more precisely, by the fact that he does so mainly in order to articulate only one dimension of the particular sort of divine-human relation that is disclosed by the prayer tradition of the slaves.

A close reading reveals that Cone does not endorse Tillich's ontology as a whole, a move which would be problematic for the reasons that Carter highlights.[29] On the contrary, Cone focuses almost exclusively on the somewhat circumscribed doctrine of courage. Already in *Black Theology and Black Power*, he borrows Tillich's vocabulary of courageous self-affirmation in the midst of absurdity only as one way of expressing the point that black human beings— precisely as a beautiful part of creation and contrary to the prevailing logic of "white" society—are adamantly *not nothing* and should, therefore, act and live accordingly.[30] For Cone, the existential empowerment that Tillich discusses has something in common with the Black Power movement: both encourage the creature to assert itself against what threatens or contradicts it. But there is another commonality as well: in Cone's account, neither of these modes of self-determination (and especially not Tillich's) is sufficient apart from a more nearly Barthian sense of the christological advent of the "wholly other" God in glory and word. Cone promotes the specific courage to be black precisely as an entailment of the creaturely side of an analogical—and, indeed, doxological—relationship that has its source in the sovereign actions of the biblically revealed and solidaristically black God who was discovered and faithfully worshiped by the slaves. For Cone, the ultimate warrant for the subjective and resistive power of black human beings does not lie merely within the realm of human concerns, however existential or ultimate they may be, but rather has its origin in a concrete colloquy with the liberating God of Moses, of the Prophets, and of Jesus himself. All in all, if there is a shift in Cone's thought toward a more situational or anthropologically inflected theology, the change is very slight: early and late, he affirms particular *aspects* of Barth's and Tillich's projects, while insisting that neither offers a framework that is entirely adequate to the normative spirituality of the antebellum black church.[31]

Nevertheless, Carter is right to suggest that, through the combination of these two figures (Barth and Tillich), Cone's theology begins to approximate the formal structure of Balthasar's. However, the affinity between Cone and Balthasar does not only have to do with the doctrine of analogy but also with the elaboration of a doxological aesthetics. We have already encountered certain elements of this aesthetics above, but additional detail is warranted here. Cone shows that the divine *doxa* and *logos* that appear in the songs of the slaves are not simply manifestations of the event of being (as they would be in Heidegger's onto-doxology) but rather constitutive features of the biblically disclosed promise of integral liberation.[32] Throughout his discussion, he clarifies that the slaves tended to approach the glory and word of God as inseparable dimensions of God's active presence in the whole Trinitarian economy of salvation, including not only the wonders of the Old and New Testaments, but also the slaves' own contemporary experiences and hopes, in which they were convinced that God was still at work.

The slaves displayed their receptivity to this manifold presence of the triune liberator in lines such as: "I did know my Jesus heard me, / 'Cause de spirit spoke to me, / And said, 'Rise my child, your chillun, / And you shall be free.'" Moreover, in response to God's mighty deeds in the past and the present, they would offer joyful praise, singing: "Glorious morning, / Glorious morning, / My savior rise from de dead" and, after their own emancipation, "Slavery chain done broke at last, / Going to praise God till I die." Finally, without ever ceasing to receive and offer praise for what God had already done, they would also desire a more complete realization of God's victory over sin and death, expressing this longing in verses such as: "I'm going back with Jesus when he comes, when he comes" and "I'm boun' for de promised land." Although they knew the Lord was with them, and in this sense always already given, they would also cry out: "Be with me Lord! Be with me!," indicating thereby that the presence of God remained to a significant extent experientially withheld.[33] In these respects, the spirituals that form the basis of Cone's thought exhibit the essential features of a genuinely Christian doxological aesthetics, which has the potential to serve as an alternative not only to metaphysics but also to Heidegger's quasi-metaphysical onto-doxology and certain mostly nondoxological models of post-Heideggerian prayer.

For Cone, and for the enslaved Christians whose songs he interprets, there can be no question of siding with the post-Heideggerian tradition of Derrida and Caputo, which maximizes the apophatic potential of prayer at the expense of its doxological characteristics. Cone would likely respond to this tradition in much the same way that he responds to secular existentialists such as Sartre and Camus and to "death of God" theologians such as Thomas Altizer and Richard Rubenstein. On the one hand, Cone believes that, at their best, these thinkers are sincerely grappling with the question of unjust suffering and the grave challenge that it poses to the very idea of God. We have seen that Caputo, following Levinas and Derrida, is likewise motivated by these very legitimate sorts of concerns (which, moreover, we shall consider again in relation to Metz below). However, on the other hand, Cone is also somewhat skeptical regarding what he perceives to be the generally "white" post-Nietzschean preoccupation with the absence of God. Speaking in the name of black Christians, he asserts: "We do not want to know how we can get along without God, but how we can survive in a world permeated with white racism." In his judgment, this sort of survival depends on more than a nominalistic deconstruction of metaphysics' conceptual idolatry. It requires a more determinate mode of resistance. Not convinced that the most egregiously false "god" has actually died even in postmodernity, and seeking to preserve a positively doxological basis for hope, Cone declares that we must "kill the white God, so that the presence of the black God can become known in the black-white encounter."[34] Thus he targets a particular idol, associated with "white" racist violence, and does not seek to negate it through merely apophatic tactics but rather by holding it up against the more brilliant light of the God of integral liberation who is adored by the slaves.

Although Cone's implicit argument against the excesses of a generalized postmodern apophasis has clear merits to it, there is perhaps still some room to examine whether he does enough to incorporate a distinctively Christian form of apophasis into his own doxological thought. In other words, it seems important to consider whether he employs negation merely as a weapon against "whiteness" or also in some other more intriguingly positive way that is consistent with the Christian tradition of prayer. From the perspectives of Marion and Lacoste in particular, his work could appear somewhat vulnerable in this regard. First, although Cone employs Tillich only in a very limited fashion, the few debts that he does retain could nevertheless seem to render his project too explicitly ontological to satisfy Marion's Dionysian standard of postontological praise. Similarly, although Lacoste, like Cone, maintains certain ties to a somewhat Heideggerian existential anthropology, he might still reasonably question whether Cone demands a sufficiently strict eschatological reserve. Insofar as Lacoste opposes the nocturnal character of liturgy to the Schleiermacherian tradition of religious experience, he would perhaps be especially wary of Cone's frequent inclusions of God within the category of "black experience" (notwithstanding the fact that Cone distinguishes his use of this category significantly from Schleiermacher's).[35] However, Cone has the potential to reply compellingly on both of these counts. First, in response to Marion and in line with Lacoste, he could argue that being remains appropriate as an anthropological category, even if it proves to be inadequate to the divine mystery itself (which, as we have seen, he certainly does not reduce to any sort of worldly being). Second, in response to Lacoste, he could clarify that black experience, precisely insofar as it is disclosed by the spirituals, actually occupies the preeschatological site that Lacoste associates with liturgy, as is made evident by those songs that Cone argues emphasize "the inability of the present to contain the reality of the divine future."[36]

And yet, the most significant point of rebuttal may have to do with the fact that Cone does not put the accent on either postontological or preeschatological modes of apophasis but rather on a specifically kerygmatic and cruciform mode of it. He contends: "God's word is *paradoxical*, or, as the old untutored black preacher used to say, 'inscrutable,' a mystery that one can neither control nor fully understand. . . . Nowhere is that paradox, that 'inscrutability,' more evident than in the cross. A symbol of death and defeat, God turned it into a sign of liberation and new life."[37] Cone's orientation toward the simultaneously liberating and horrifying enigma of the cross situates his thought closer to those aspects of Marion's and Lacoste's work that depend less on their antagonism toward Heidegger and more on their specifically post-Balthasarian engagements with the paschal mystery. In other words, Cone's preferred *via negativa* is located firmly within the christological event of salvation and, therefore, shows less evidence of the abstractive or formal strategies of negation that are characteristic of those Neoplatonic and post-Cartesian philosophical traditions that continue not only to undergird contemporary phenomenology but also to direct its attention primarily toward the problem of the finitude of human consciousness in general. One finds an extreme form of this approach in Derrida's deconstruction and a more moderated form in Marion's and Lacoste's phenomenologically justified negations of ontological idolatry and immanentized eschatology, respectively. Each of these thinkers has a reasonable desire to counteract Heidegger's absolutization of *Dasein*'s (or his *own*) experience of being. However, whereas Marion and Lacoste do so somewhere in between a formally constituted phenomenology and Christian doxology, Cone does so more thoroughly within the logic provided by the latter. What he perhaps loses in philosophical complexity (he does not claim to write philosophy), he gains in christological concreteness.

On the whole, therefore, one might argue that Cone's partly apophatic—but still in some sense predominantly kataphatic—form of doxology has more in common with Balthasar's approach than it does with Marion's or Lacoste's. And yet, Cone does not engage in the kinds of metaphysical speculation that Balthasar still allows himself. He does not develop the sorts of general (part Thomistic, part Heideggerian) reflections regarding being itself or more daring (anti-Hegelian or post-Hegelian) theories regarding the Trinitarian grounding of inner-worldly negation, which together render Balthasar's trilogy somewhat—though, as we have seen, by no means devastatingly—questionable on certain defensible postmetaphysical grounds. Thus there may be reason to associate Cone more closely with Chrétien, who keeps his distance from those methodologically abstractive aspects of the phenomenological works of Marion and Lacoste that Cone likewise disregards and who develops a doxological aesthetics with far fewer questionable metaphysical entailments than one finds in Balthasar's nevertheless impressive corpus.

To be sure, Cone's retrieval of doxological sources cannot be said to rival the immense scope of Balthasar's or Chrétien's *ressourcement*, and this may be a real limitation. At the very least, it justifies an attempt to bring Cone into dialogue with a larger tradition of prayerful thought. Nevertheless, Cone makes up for Balthasar's and Chrétien's problematic neglect of black sources and, moreover, does not deviate in any detrimental way from the central melody of their doxological chorus. Once again, poets—whether blues musicians, figures of the Harlem Renaissance, or the authors of the spirituals themselves—have a prominent place.[38] In this regard, Cone upholds the sense shared by Balthasar and Chrétien that prayerful thought depends significantly on a poetic apprehension of reality. At the same time, Cone likewise agrees with Balthasar and Chrétien (against Heidegger) that the normative status of poetry remains relative to God's own glorious self-verbalization in Christ and in the rest of scripture.[39] Moreover, in harmony with Balthasar and Chrétien, he includes the beauty of nature in his doxology. In particular, he quotes a poignant line from Harriet Tubman, which she voiced after arriving in the North: "I looked at my hands to see if I was de same person now I was free. Dere was such glory ober everything, de sun came like gold trou de trees, and ober de fields, and I felt like I was in heaven."[40] This experience of wonder at her own body and at the surrounding world mediated a sense of intimacy with God—that is, not merely a connection with the sacredness of the fourfold (as in Heidegger) but precisely with the liberating God who freed her from bondage. Thus, as Cone interprets it, Tubman's experience of glory in nature still belongs within the purview of the historically given mystery of salvation.

Furthermore, as in Chrétien's thought, so too in Cone's, the body comes to light as a locus of beauty, of language, and of contact with the divine. Cone draws particular attention to the "rhythm, the passion, and the motion" of the ring shout and finds a similar manifestation of black corporeality in contemporary worship.[41] He observes that "the Spirit sometimes makes you run and clap your hands; at other times you just want to sit still and perhaps tap your feet, wave your hands, and hum the melody of a song."[42] Whereas Chrétien highlights all of the senses and parts of the body as channels of grace, Cone concentrates on the diversity of the body's *movements*. He thereby shows that, in order to respond to the call of God (and the black spiritual tradition certainly knows a great deal about the structure of call and response), it is perhaps not always sufficient to sing. At times, one must also dance and let one's entire body catch the rhythm of the song. At other times, there is a stronger need for bodily repose and recollection. Contemplative stillness is not foreign to the black church's experience of prayer. Finally, Cone draws attention to the fact that many black people came to understand their bodily struggles in light of Jacob's wrestling match with the angel, an episode which we have seen is also dear to Chrétien. Spirituals such as "Wrestling Jacob," "We Are Climbing Jacob's Ladder," and "Wake Up, Jacob" attest to the wounds of speech and body through which black slaves were nevertheless compelled to seek some form of proximity with God.[43]

According to Cone, the black body traverses but by no means exhausts the mystery of God's excessive givenness to humanity. In Marion's sense, therefore, it qualifies precisely as an icon. It receives a brilliantly dark light from God and also offers this light to others, who may catch a glimpse of God's counterintentionality in it. This is the hidden meaning behind the hymn that Cone tells us was his mother's favorite: "This little light of mine, / I'm goin' to let it shine."[44] When she sings this song, it is a question precisely of *letting* the radiance of God's self-giving love show forth through the visibility of her black flesh. Because God has created and redeemed this very flesh in Christ, Cone contends that it is "beautiful"; something about which to be "glad" and to "shout"; indeed, "a manifestation of God's presence on earth." He insists, moreover, that it therefore demands not only attention but also "obedience"—that is, acts of listening, welcoming, and reverence—from others. In his judgment, this is the central failure of even the most evidently devout forms of "white" doxology.[45] At the same time, one can sense here his closeness to the attitudes of Christian love that Balthasar and the post-Balthasarians have discovered throughout the Christian doxological tradition.

In the end, Cone's doxological aesthetics differs from those elaborated by other representatives of Christian doxology mainly—and yet crucially—insofar as it includes a clear perception of *doxological blackness*. This term can be understood in two ways. On the one hand, it refers to an irrevocable fact of existence, which is not only rooted in the creative and redemptive actions of the triune God but which is also phenomenologically evident: namely that black is beautiful.[46] This is simply—but also diversely and complexly—a *given*. To be black is ipso facto to reflect something of the glory and word of God. On the other hand, doxological blackness can refer to those aspects of black culture, thought, or praxis that *intentionally* affirm this beloved relation to God in a doxologically rigorous manner. The spirituals and Cone's theology belong to this latter category. We are dealing here with a spirituality in which blackness has become self-consciously doxological and doxology has become self-consciously black. In other words, blackness and doxology have become semantically inseparable, which is not to say strictly indistinguishable.[47]

It remains to consider how doxological blackness, in these two senses, relates to the problematic structure of thought that Victor Anderson calls "ontological blackness." His critical account of this structure has various aspects, which need to be distinguished in order to make an adequate assessment. There is a rhetorical aspect, namely a form of "racial apologetics" in which black intellectuals seek to defend the legitimacy of blackness by refashioning the doctrine of heroic genius that was central to the "white" racial ideology of post-Enlightenment romanticism and idealism. Anderson's worry is that, insofar as the black rhetoric of racial apologetics mimics this "white" racial ideology, it seems to involve a problematic struggle to acquire mastery over the self, over nature, over society, and over the other—a struggle that he associates with Western imperial domination and its perhaps most salient metaphysical representative, Hegel.[48]

Another aspect of Anderson's critique has to do with his elaboration of the specifically metaphysical features of ontological blackness. The main feature in question here is a stipulated "essence" of blackness that would be universally and necessarily constitutive of black existence or experience inasmuch as it is black. Anderson contends that this supposed essence is too often construed in terms of a dialectical negation: the meaning of blackness as such and as a whole is to suffer from and struggle against "whiteness." According to Anderson, this particular type of essentialism is problematic not only insofar as it illegitimately reduces the pluriform excess of blackness to a fixed identity, but also insofar as it confines this identity to the posture of a reactive underside. The latter move effectively forces a choice between blackness and liberation (or what Anderson prefers to call "cultural fulfillment," that is, "the reflexive integration of basic human needs and subjective goods").[49] It does so by presenting blackness as so thoroughly inseparable from the conditions of oppression and struggle that it comes to seem strictly incompatible with the actual achievement of liberation.

Finally, there is a genealogical aspect to Anderson's account. He maintains that, in order to give a sense of narrative coherence and legitimacy to their racial apologetics and metaphysical definition of blackness, many black theorists and theologians attempt a "hermeneutics of return" in which they ground their claims in supposedly originary sources, such as slave narratives and spirituals. He appreciates the motivation of this interpretive practice, suggesting that those who engage in it seem to be concerned with finding sources of inspiration that can uplift the black urban underclass in the midst of its ongoing struggles with poverty, violence, and nihilism. However, he continues to find this approach objectionable, insofar as it conceals African sources, seems to violate the texts by using them ideologically, and supports a totalizing vision of blackness as constituted by "black faith."[50]

Anderson's proposed path toward overcoming this manifold structure of ontological blackness begins with the early Nietzschean distinction between heroic (Apollonian) and grotesque (Dionysian) aesthetics. Anderson suggests that the ambiguity, irresolution, and even potential tragedy of the latter mode of aesthetics correspond more adequately to the complex realities of contemporary black life. Without leaving Nietzsche behind, Anderson turns to bell hooks in order to promote a "postmodern blackness" and to Cornel West in order to advocate "a race-transcending prophetic criticism."[51] In these ways, although he does not deny the need for political protest in solidarity with the disenfranchised (including many black communities), he nevertheless calls for a rather high degree of deconstructive play with respect to the various rhetorical, metaphysical, and genealogical determinations of blackness that he contends are characteristic of much contemporary black discourse, including Cone's black liberation theology and its descendants.

Several—but not all—of Anderson's points can be granted while carrying forward Cone's doxological spirituality of liberation. First, in order to retrieve Cone's project for today, one might admit the necessity of clarifying more strongly than he does that oppression is not an essential predicate of blackness. The confusion surrounding this issue seems to be exacerbated by Cone's claim that, in addition to being a physiological trait, blackness is also "an *ontological* symbol for all those who participate in liberation from oppression."[52] Cone's point here might be expressed somewhat less ambiguously as follows: *insofar as* blacks have been oppressed historically, their existence has the potential not only to signify but also to show concretely what it means for anyone to be suffer from oppression and to be liberated through the gracious actions of God. Anderson's critique demonstrates that one cannot afford any longer to omit this "insofar as," which removes the (otherwise supposedly implicit) universality and necessity from the connection that Cone draws between blackness and oppression. At the same time, once Cone's assertion is qualified in this manner, it retains its relevance, both as a way to remember the violence that has been perpetrated against many black people precisely because they are black and as a way to bring out the far-reaching theological significance of a nevertheless historically rooted tradition of black prayer and struggle. In short, Anderson's legitimate desire to avoid restricting blackness to an essential condition of oppression does not compel one to reject Cone's (now necessarily more explicitly delimited) reflections regarding the many black people who have been victimized and their symbolic or representational power. Moreover, it seems important to note that Cone associates blackness with an entire process of liberation, which includes not only the state of oppression but also its actual overcoming.

If the question is about the meaning of blackness in general, then Anderson's account of the groteseque could disclose certain important features of this reality that are neglected by Cone's admittedly more heroic mode of liberationist aesthetics (though Cone's analysis of the blues arguably provides at least one significant point of access to the sort of experiential ambiguity that Anderson seeks to prioritize). In any case, however, Nietzsche's early Dionysianism is not without its own questionable ideological motivations. One must ask: would the slaves who first composed the spirituals or the contemporary inheritors of this prayerful tradition be able to find their voices within such a non-Christian, vitalistic aesthetics?

Anderson's more recent constructive work, *Creative Exchange*, reveals that his positive account of religious pragmatism likewise proves to be only marginally hospitable to the mystery of prayer as manifested in the songs of the slaves. In typically modern fashion, he reduces this mystery to a feature of worldly experience. He argues that "adoration, praise, and prayer are our ways of expressing our valuation and appreciation for the World that meets us all with its limits and possibilities, its actualities and potentialities, its capacity to enchant and disenchant."[53] Here prayer becomes nothing more than a Zarathustran—and in this sense, according to Heidegger and Marion, hypermetaphysical—act of assigning values to an otherwise strictly ambiguous universe. God has no appearance in this definition of prayer, not even as a Feuerbachian projection, but has instead been entirely replaced by the "World." The neutrality of this term makes it nearly indistinguishable from Heidegger's *Ereignis* and the other post-Heideggerian horizons that come to take its place. In this regard, Anderson's work remains much more closely tethered to the problematic features of modern metaphysics than does Cone's doxology.

To be sure, as Anderson would insist, the active participation in a black doxological spirituality, of the sort that is mapped out by the spirituals and theorized by Cone, cannot be considered a necessary criterion for participating in blackness in general. In other words, it is important to acknowledge that black life can still be meaningfully black even when it is not characterized by what Anderson calls "black faith." Nevertheless, the first sense of doxological blackness, which one also finds in Cone's work, opens up a way for Christians to honor the beauty and dignity of all black people, regardless of their various theological or spiritual commitments. Cone certainly does not exclude blues artists and other nontheological figures of black thought and culture from his account of beautiful blackness. At the same time, he sees them as partially reflecting a deeper grandeur, which is not contingent on acts of self-creation and self-definition, nor ever potentially compromised by the ambiguities of black existence, but rather permanently guaranteed by the almighty love and liberating activity of God. Whatever may be involved in anyone's unique embodiment of blackness, the most significant feature will, according to Cone's spirituality, not be a worldly experience of the grotesque but rather an inestimable (if hidden) promise of divine freedom. The merit of Cone's project, in contrast to Anderson's, is that it allows and encourages one to affirm this promise unreservedly.

Although Cone's theology may exhibit certain characteristics of the modern heroic genius that Anderson analyzes, Anderson's account of this rhetorical form is more directly applicable to the explicitly romantic discourse of W. E. B. DuBois (on whom Anderson's discussion greatly depends) than it is to Cone's prayerful and, as such, decisively *theo*-dramatic approach. For Cone, in contrast to DuBois, human beings can be heroic only in a derivative sense, that is, as sanctified witnesses of the liberating actions of Christ and the Spirit. The triune God alone is the true hero, the one deserving all glory, honor, and praise.[54] Moreover, that there is an apologetic aspect to Cone's work is probably also undeniable; and yet, it would be reductive to insist that apology is its only function. As Cone sees it, there is something positively dignified about the creaturely gift of blackness that would need to be affirmed regardless of any opposition to "white" racial ideology. In other words, he is not fundamentally interested in defending the "blackness that whiteness created," as Anderson suggests,[55] but rather in embracing the blackness that God creates and frees. Finally, although virtually all of the obstacles that Anderson associates with the "hermeneutics of return" must be admitted,[56] they cannot take away Cone's or anyone else's right to listen to the spirituals and think and live from them. The crucial point would be that these songs are not only traces of a largely irretrievable past but also dynamic wellsprings of a living spirituality in the present. In all of these ways, therefore, Cone's articulation of doxological blackness manages to transcend the problematic structure of a metaphysical or ontological blackness, to which Anderson's post-Nietzschean blackness ironically remains somewhat more closely related.

THE HOSPITALITY OF BLACK SPIRITUALITY

If Cone's retrieval of the spirituals enables him to navigate the crises of modern metaphysics rather successfully, it also puts him in a position to respond powerfully to the crises of modern violence. As we have seen throughout, although these two sets of crises are interrelated, the one is not entirely reducible to the other. In what follows, we shall examine the significance of Cone's spirituality in relation to the analogous approaches of Metz (chapter 4) and the liberation theologians of Latin America (chapter 5). This section will also give us an opportunity to revisit certain questions regarding the themes of responsibility and especially hospitality, which emerged in the first three chapters and then intersected in various complex ways with the more explicitly political discussions of the last two chapters. At issue is precisely how to specify the inner-creaturely relations that are entailed by an authentic embodiment of the life of prayer in a violent world.

As in the previous section, so too here, our goal will be to understand how Cone's approach both enhances and preserves the rigor of Christian spirituality. On the one hand, he makes a distinctive contribution by employing doxological blackness against the horrors of modern racism, which other thinkers have largely neglected. On the other hand, he combats these horrors while maintaining a serious commitment to the practice of loving and welcoming the other, a practice that in his work, as in the Christian spiritual tradition as a whole, finds its ultimate source of support in the human being's prayerful receptivity to the self-giving love of God. In short, therefore, Cone supports a genuinely Christian form of universal hospitality. However, in order to make sense of these two aspects of Cone's thought (doxological blackness and universal hospitality), it is necessary to make a further distinction in the latter. If such hospitality is believable in this violent age, it must find expression in active solidarity with the poor and oppressed, both locally and globally, regardless of their complexion, confession, or any other determinate characteristic. At the same time, its complete realization as a social ideal also entails a confrontational struggle against those who consistently manifest a failure of hospitality, a struggle in which the ultimate goal must not be mere negation but rather conversion and communion. Cone's black doxological spirituality includes both of these determinations, which, for the sake of clarity, one might distinguish as the *solidaristic* and *agonistic* dimensions of hospitality. Moreover, contrary to the general suspicion voiced by J. Deotis Roberts and others, Cone's thought achieves its highest degree of universality precisely through the latter. Thus that which he contributes to the Christian spiritual tradition, namely the fight against racism, is also the very feature of his thought that most definitively respects this tradition as a tradition of self-giving, unbounded love.

One might question whether Cone, like Heidegger, ultimately compromises hospitality through autochthony. We have already seen how Cone's prayerful affirmation of God's transcendence beyond worldly being and beyond the historical limits of black experience allows him to evade this charge precisely to the extent that this charge concerns the vertical relation between God and creation. Nevertheless, one might still object that, as an apparent defender of black nationalism, Cone seems to remain dangerously close to the sort of excessively autochthonous thinking that leads Heidegger to champion the German homeland and a particular sort of Greco-German artistic and intellectual culture as containing superior manifestations of being itself, to the exclusion and degradation of other places, communities, and traditions (whether specifically Jewish or, in his judgment, forgettably foreign).

Levinas starts a decisive turn against this inhospitality, a turn that is explicitly carried forward in innovative ways by Derrida and Caputo; by Marion, Lacoste, and Chrétien; and, as we have seen in the last chapter, also by Dussel. Among these critical interpreters of Levinas, Dussel is the one who takes the greatest risks in terms of treating his own people as the other. His intention is not so much to say that "I" should be hospitable to the "other" (whoever this other might be) but rather that "they" (the Western imperial powers) should be hospitable to "*their* other" (i.e., the poor communities of Latin America that "I" represent). The potential for this sort of apparent reversal is, in some sense, already implied by the political and rhetorical circumstances of Levinas's initial formulation. As a member of an excluded Jewish minority, he addresses a predominantly non-Jewish European intellectual community in order to demand that the "other" (read: I, my people) be treated with respect. Both Levinas and Dussel suggest that the rhetorically prioritized direction of the obligatory asymmetrical relation of hospitality needs to shift in order to counteract specific asymmetries of power. The primary one who is allowed to claim the status of the "other" in any given situation is the subaltern one: that is, the one already inhabiting a structural position of vulnerability. And yet, Levinas's ethics—along with the many modified versions that come after it—also necessarily retains a strictly universal characteristic, according to which even those with less power would be responsible for welcoming the more powerful (and perhaps even vicious) other, in which case the question becomes what exactly must be involved in such welcoming.

When considering Cone, it is necessary to recognize that he avoids the sort of dominating (anti-Semitic and imperialistic) nationalism that persists even in Heidegger's post-Rectoral period of superficially innocuous poetic thinking. In short, Cone's thought is not in the service of oppression. His particular appeal to black power does not authorize an unrestricted use of force in accord with any kind of crude doctrine of "blood and earth" (a National Socialist position against which Heidegger would eventually offer some, but not enough, resistance). Nor does Cone seek to give black people lordship over others, in any kind of simplistic inversion of the master-slave dialectic (which he acknowledges has been a danger in certain forms of black nationalism that have given way to hatred and resentment).[57] Furthermore, although he maintains that some sort of black separatism has been necessary, he clarifies that it should not be understood as an ideal but rather as a provisional survival strategy to be used only so long as the violently separative structures of antiblack racism (which were implemented first) remain intact.[58] His reasons for giving measured support to this more nearly autochthonous possibility do not have to do with any sense of intrinsic black superiority (which he adamantly rejects in opposition to the ontologically antiwhite racial ideology that he perceives in some of the rhetoric of the Nation of Islam). Rather, his recommendation depends strictly on the exigencies of an asymmetrically weighted historical situation.[59]

On the whole, Cone's affirmation of blackness has much more in common with Dussel's use of Levinas than it does with Heidegger's appropriation of Hölderlin. The goal of Cone's work is not to restrict the essential truth of being to a narrow region but rather to insist that genuine hospitality be extended to black people in defiance of a modern epoch that has consistently maligned them. He asks only that they be respected, without reserve, as beautiful members of the all-inclusive household of God. He exhorts us to remember their centuries-deep wounds and to embrace their still unfulfilled desires for freedom. Although these requests are extraordinarily modest in principle, their actual significance is revolutionary. The entire trajectory of modern Western civilization, insofar as it has been built upon an ideology of "white" racial superiority, would need to be set on a completely new course. Massive changes would be required in the areas of political, economic, and intellectual investment. Relations between communities and nations would need to be substantially reenvisioned. An almost certainly costly (i.e., real, believable) commitment would need to be made by both church and society to overcome the vast statistical disparities and entrenched patterns of segregation, marginalization, and denigration that persist today.

Cone expresses the contemporary situation of racial perception rather poignantly when, in a recent essay published in 2005, he argues that "It is not easy for whites to listen to a radical analysis of race because blackness is truly *Other* to them—creating a horrible, unspeakable fear. When whites think of evil, they think of black. . . . We are the most potent symbols of crime, welfare dependency, sexual harassment, domestic violence, and bad government."[60] One only needs to recall the many lamentable references to the demonic Ethiopian figure in monastic literature or the misguided identifications of blackness with sin that are characteristic of the *Song of Songs* commentary tradition to see just how deeply embedded this sort of antiblack xenophobia has become even in some of the most otherwise promising sources of Christian doxology.[61] Cone's argument is that the communities of the United States and of the world at large need to move from a priori dispositions of fear and rejection toward more open and more genuine forms of self-emptying love. What is needed is real hospitality in the face of this supposed "other," that is, Cone and his people.[62]

While Cone's somewhat self-referential treatment of hospitality situates him much closer to Dussel than to Heidegger, the prayerful character of his thought distinguishes him rather sharply from both of these still-too-modern philosophers and brings him more in line not only with Balthasar and the post-Balthasarians (as we have seen above) but also, and more profoundly, with the more concretely counterviolent representatives of Christian spirituality that we have considered in the last two chapters: Metz, Gutiérrez, Boff, and El-lacuría. Like the latter group, Cone promotes an integrated but non-reductive relation between prayer and solidarity. In other words, he seeks to articulate the prayerful "fellowship with God" upon which "the true struggle of liberation in history is based,"[63] and he does so without conflating the two. In addition to exhibiting this formal similarity, his simultaneously political and more-than-political theology also reflects many specific features of these related theological approaches.

In accord with Metz, Cone draws out the anamnestic and apocalyptic dimensions of his prayerful theology, asking in the words of the black spiritual and poetic tradition, "Oh, how can we forget?" and, in anticipation of the second coming of Christ, "Where shall I be when the first trumpet soun'; soun' so loud till it woke up de dead?" Moreover, like Metz, he believes that the memory of suffering and the apocalyptic hope in a definitive future in which even death will be overcome do not negate our responsibility for history but rather intensify it, giving it its true focus and orientation. Although in this respect his work might also be likened to Moltmann's political theology, it in fact proves to be closer to Metz's insofar as it remains strongly committed to the sovereignty of God.[64] For this reason, too, it must be recognized as distinct from the secularized political "theologies" of the Frankfurt School and of Carl Schmitt (from whom Cone's project differs quite profoundly).[65]

Cone likewise situates his theology "after Auschwitz." To be sure, he does not devote as much energy to addressing this singular horror as Metz does. Nevertheless, he by no means forgets it. His typical approach is to argue that, just as many theologians, such as Barth, Bultmann, and Bonhoeffer—and one might add Metz to this list—have acknowledged the need for Christians to confront the anti-Semitic violence in which their own tradition and church have been deeply implicated, so too theologians today need to recognize that a very similar demand applies to the situation of antiblack racism.[66] For Cone, it is not ultimately a question of preferring to resist one sort of oppression more than or instead of another but rather of correcting the blatant neglect of antiblack racism, which has characterized much Eurocentric theological reflection especially, and perhaps most condemnably, in the United States. In the end, Cone positions black humanity not in competition with but rather in solidarity with the Jewish people, whom he recognizes as the chosen people of God.[67]

Furthermore, once again in concert with Metz, Cone treats the prayer tradition of Israel as a privileged source of his nevertheless specifically Christian thought—a source whose spirit he rediscovers in the songs of the slaves.[68] These interlocking traditions are the key to his way of approaching the question of theodicy, which is pressed upon him not only by Camus, Sartre, and Rubenstein (the Jewish author of the classic text *After Auschwitz*) but also by various black intellectuals, including especially William R. Jones, who asks provocatively whether God is a white racist.[69] Cone's reflections on this issue ultimately resonate somewhat more with Gutiérrez and Boff than with Metz, insofar as he more explicitly promotes a doxological view of the paschal mystery as a viable response to the nevertheless inexplicable realities of innocent suffering. Advancing a version of the *Leiden-in-Gott* argument that Metz resists, Cone contends that Christ "took the humiliation and suffering of the oppressed into God's own history." In his judgment, this event of infinite divine compassion on the cross was a crucial source of the slaves' resilient hope and joy. At the same time, he insists that it did not prevent them from crying out in anguish and questioning God in unison with Job, the psalmists, and the Markan Jesus, as is made evident by the prayers of Daniel Payne and Nathaniel Paul and by various sorrowful songs such as "Sometimes I feel like a motherless chile." This black experience of *Leiden an Gott* lies at the heart of Cone's doxological spirituality and keeps it from supporting any excessively positive and, therefore, experientially disconnected discourse of pure consolation.[70]

As a self-proclaimed theologian of liberation (indeed, as arguably the first one), Cone can also be paired somewhat naturally with Gutiérrez, Boff, and Ellacuría. In fact, his work is not only similar to but also explicitly *conversant* with theirs. He embraces concepts drawn from their writings and refers to each of these theologians by name.[71] Although tensions have surfaced between some Latin American and black theologians regarding the relative prioritization of economic and racial forms of analysis and the ambiguous status of a subjugated black community that finds itself located in a globally dominant nation (the United States), Cone has not treated these controversies as warranting any sort of withdrawal from the conversation but rather as opportunities for mutual critique and enrichment. Like his mentor, Martin Luther King Jr., Cone gradually begins to reflect more directly on the conditions of extreme poverty that affect not only many blacks in the United States but also many diversely colored communities throughout the world, arguing ultimately that in order to make the spiritual "Oh Freedom! Oh Freedom!" a reality, we need to side with "the poor in all colors."[72]

In Cone's work, the preferential option for the poor is not a replacement for the doxological affirmation of blackness. The two are related but distinct.[73] On the one hand, especially after Anderson's critique, it is necessary to acknowledge that not all black people are poor and, even more strongly, that blackness is not defined *essentially* by the condition of oppression, whether this oppression happens to be in any precise instance more nearly racial or socioeconomic. Those black persons who have, by whatever course of events, become largely freed from such historically prevalent scourges on the black community do not cease to participate in the beauty of blackness and, thereby, in the abundance of God's generosity; hence, their potential iconicity must not be discounted. At the same time, they are called and obligated to remain in active solidarity with the victims of history and must not allow themselves to become content with their own individual freedoms (a danger which Cone perceives in some contemporary black churches).[74] On the other hand, there are innumerable impoverished black people throughout the world who have been made to suffer, not only from a maldistribution of wealth, but also from the added effects of racially motivated hatred and indifference. In this respect, one rightly speaks of intersecting— and, therefore, double—oppressions.[75]

Thus Cone helps us to see that the preferential option for the poor continues to be binding on black populations, including those that are oppressed, but especially including those that have begun to experience some degree of liberation. In this respect, he recognizes that the Christian commitment to the poor exceeds the doxological affirmation of blackness. At the same time, he also shows that this commitment does not exhaust the sort of solidarity that is required as a simultaneously prayerful and political response to our racially violent age, a solidarity which exceeds the preferential option for the poor precisely insofar as it specifically includes the doxological affirmation of blackness as an additional imperative. In Cone's judgment, therefore, it is necessary to resist both classism and racism and not only the latter by means of the former. In these ways, his work manages both to retain and supplement the core practical insights of the Latin American tradition of liberation spirituality.

As we have seen, Cone's integration of doxology with urgent petition and lament, precisely on the basis of the prayerful complexity of the spirituals, brings him very close to the inclusive accounts of prayer that are supplied by Gutiérrez and Boff.[76] However, in some other respects his thought more closely resembles Ellacuría's. Although he does not directly appropriate Ignatius's *Spiritual Exercises*, he nevertheless arrives at very similar conclusions regarding the continuity between salvation history and salvation *in* history; the conflict between Christ and sin, which takes place in Jesus's life, death, and resurrection and in the worldly struggles of the church; the identification of the Holy Spirit with the Spirit of Christ; the need to "discern" the actions of this Spirit, since there can be no complete system of a priori ethics; the reality of the "crucified peoples" (whom Cone finds on the lynching tree); the necessity of a spirit of "indifference," which he understands precisely as the freedom to act in potentially costly ways in order to follow the christologically disclosed will of God; and, finally, the expectation that this course of action will not necessarily result in historical victory but may instead actually lead to one's own personal suffering and death.[77] Moreover, Ellacuría's martyrdom finds an analogue in the self-sacrificial witness of Martin and Malcolm: two black theological prophets (Christian and Black Muslim, respectively) who crystallize different aspects of Cone's own distinctive way of retrieving the spirituality of the slaves. In the end, although Segundo offers a brief discussion of Cone's theology,[78] it seems that Gutiérrez, Boff, and perhaps especially Ellacuría more deeply resonate with it as an embodied practice of thinking prayer.

Cone's hospitality to the voices of the "Third World" is not limited to Latin American liberation theologians. He also seeks to cultivate a solidaristic relationship with African theologians, characterized above all by a practice of mutual listening. In harmony with Desmond Tutu, he identifies several points of common ground between black Christians in Africa and in the United States: the endurance of an interconnected history of modern antiblack racism, which has been expressed through European imperialism and colonialism, South African apartheid, and the slavery and subjugation of blacks throughout the Americas; a concomitant struggle to be freed from these various forms of domination; and a shared faith in Christ as the savior of the world.[79] And yet, while acknowledging this common ground, Cone affirms John Mbiti's point that there are many contextually specific experiences and concerns that might lead African and black American theologians to develop their projects in very distinctive directions.[80] As Cone sees it, both the similarities and the differences give purpose to their continued dialogue—which, therefore, exhibits the sort of analogical structure that Balthasar understands as essential to both prayerful and innercreaturely love.

Cone reasonably protests Mbiti's reluctance to embrace the theme of liberation. For this reason, Cone seems likely to find more agreement with other formulations of African theology, such as Jean-Marc Ela's explicitly liberative and biblically prayerful *African Cry*.[81] Nevertheless, Cone's disagreement with Mbiti's stance on liberation does not prevent him from affirming Mbiti's focus on the task of Africanizing or indigenizing the gospel.[82] In the course of their dialogue, Cone introduces a principle of autochthony (i.e., cultural and geographical rootedness), not so much in order to promote the specific characteristics of his own people, but rather as a way of welcoming the distinctive traditions of another. He argues, in effect, that the "other," namely, Mbiti and the African people, deserve the freedom to dwell and to think in their own ways, on their own soil, and beneath their own skies. But what we have here is, therefore, a form of hospitality that respects precisely the other's autochthony. On the one hand, this is something altogether different from a Heideggerian perspective in which hospitality is more often than not restricted by the autochthonous conditions of his own intellectual-cultural region. On the other hand, it reflects positive insights regarding prayerful or prayer-like dwelling in a particular place that Heidegger's Hölderlinian thought helps one perceive.[83]

Cone demonstrates the hospitality of his work in another way through his encounter with certain localized expressions of Christianity in Asia. Reflecting, for example, on a series of theological workshops that he led for a group of Korean Christians in Japan, he recalls that, in order to reach out to this community and help them make sense of their own struggles against discrimination and injustice, he "recited such spirituals as 'Go Down Moses,' 'Oh, Freedom,' and 'Oh Mary, Don't You Weep.'"[84] He goes on to describe how these songs mediated an experience of deepening solidarity and mutual learning between the participants and himself. Although firmly rooted in the history of black people in the United States, these prayerful texts were able to speak across cultures and languages and open up a shareable perspective on the liberating love of God. They let Cone both communicate with and receive new insight from the other. Such is the nature of his "black ecumenism," a category in which he includes not only the effort to repair rifts between Christian denominations but also the struggle to participate in the integral liberation of every human being, especially insofar as they are subject to analogous conditions of poverty and oppression in various contexts.[85]

If the spirituals, then, undergird Cone's solidarity with the world's poor and oppressed, and with the global community of political and liberation theologians who speak on their behalf, they also establish the conditions under which he seeks to bring about the conversion of those who participate in oppression. No doubt, it is one thing to welcome the fellow victim and quite another to embrace the victimizer. In the latter case, this embrace clearly calls for a powerful form of resistance against the causes of the violence, and yet it must truly be an embrace—that is, a self-giving act of love—if there is to be any hope in a truly universal exercise of hospitality capable of ultimately overcoming Schmitt's fateful friend-enemy distinction. The question then becomes whether Cone's agonistic discourse, which is directed especially against "whiteness," remains sufficiently recognizable as a form of prayerfully inspired hospitality.

This question compels us to reexamine Cone's debate with Roberts, which has been too frequently misconstrued as a struggle between an essentially separatist doctrine of liberation and a thoroughly accommodationist account of integration. The actual point of disagreement is much more subtle. Although neither theologian disputes the idea that both liberation and reconciliation are necessary, they have significantly different ways of parsing this conjunction. Whereas Roberts presents it as a polarity in need of balance—and, therefore, as a delicate task of holding together two competing elements[86]—Cone treats it as a single soteriological event, which he argues must be affirmed in its entirety. He can, therefore, insist, in a way that Roberts cannot, that "God's reconciliation is God's liberating work."[87] This identification entails two conceptually distinct claims, which Cone contends must be appreciated in the right order: first, that there can be no real reconciliation without the precondition of liberation and, second, that the fullness of liberation is possible only as reconciliation. He suggests that Roberts and many of

SONGS OF THE SPIRIT

the evidently "white" theologians who quickly gravitate toward his ostensibly more balanced sort of black theology have not grasped the seriousness of the first, and necessarily prior, implication.[88] In other words, they have not recognized the need for white people to die to their antiblack "whiteness" and "*become black with God!*"[89] Roberts's metaphor of balance creates the false impression that the interests of liberation (for blacks) and reconciliation (with whites) have to be negotiated, as though an obligatory increase in the latter would have to be paid for with a supposedly acceptable diminishment in the former, and as though the desired result would be some kind of mid-level parity of the two. Cone rightly resists this idea.

Of course, the fact that there are limitations to Roberts's proposal does not automatically imply that Cone's is wholly adequate. It remains possible to ask whether Cone's demand that others "become black" is actually compatible with a vision of integral liberation that is supposed to culminate in universal hospitality. And yet, he would object that this is not the right way to pose the question. He would suggest that we first consider whether there is any conceivable way that the persistent refusal to "become black" could be compatible with the very same vision. Here to "become black" means nothing other than to enter into the spirituality of oppressed black people, to pray and struggle with them for their freedom, to welcome their beauty as an indispensable element of Christian doxology, and—as a matter of sheer consistency—to abolish every form of "white" domination, including overt acts of violence and the more hidden dimensions of privilege and harm that are expressed "through marriage, schools, neighborhood, power, etc."[90]

Cone contends that this conversion to a practically embodied black spirituality is not only necessary but also nearly sufficient to bring about genuine fellowship among white and black people. He justifies this (for some counterintuitive) claim by arguing that such a conversion would be liberative not only for blacks but also for whites, who would find themselves freed from their destructive attachments to racist "whiteness" and welcomed into a newness of life shareable by all. Thus even *whiteness itself*—the lightly colored flesh, not the historically oppressive structure—would have the potential to be recovered as a beautiful and peaceful aspect of God's beloved community. Cone does not disqualify this possibility. He explicitly hopes for it. Indeed, he even treats it, to some extent, as an "awesome responsibility" that God places upon *black* people, who Cone provocatively asserts are called to "serve" white people by courageously confronting them with their history of sinfulness and by offering them the gift of a more adequately doxological perspective, even if this means, as it sometimes does, risking their own lives in the process.[91] Although there is, then, a call to Christian love on both sides, there is also a difference, according to which participants in "whiteness" would be obligated to *empty* themselves in order to receive the divine gift of blackness and, conversely, black human beings would be required to *give* themselves (i.e., assertively manifest themselves) as witnesses to a gloriously liberated, radically inclusive, and thus authentically Christian life.

In short, once this differentiated requirement of self-emptying and self-giving love is satisfied, Cone perceives no other major impediment to a reconciled mode of multicolor existence in the church and society. Liberation and reconciliation are not "balanced" in his account; rather, they are disclosed as one uncompromisingly apocalyptic reality breaking into world history. He presents liberation and reconciliation as virtually indistinguishable aspects of the same ethically obligating divine promise, which we receive in prayer and are meant to embody through prayerfully inspired actions. Moreover, it is precisely in this way that he takes hospitality seriously as a universal vocation—more seriously, in fact, than if he had left the historical violence of "whiteness" unchallenged.

Cone's idea of "becoming black" is perhaps best understood as a demand that the black doxological tradition be respected not merely as a guest but also as a host: that is, as a determinate context in which others are capable of finding spiritual strength and renewal. The refusal to enter into another's home when persistently invited—indeed, as is often the case, an obvious flight from the very neighborhood—indicates a substantial failure in the structure of a mutually exercised asymmetrical hospitality, which is supposed to be constitutive of Christian love. To refuse to enter into the "wounded words" (Chrétien) of the black community is to restrict the sphere of divine-and-human welcoming in a way that impoverishes and does harm to all parties involved. The multiracial intimacy that Cone envisions requires measured conflicts and costly antiracist conversions, but in this way it actually calls for a higher level of intimacy: a closeness in which white persons would be able to share deeply in the passions, sorrows, and resilient hopes of their black brothers and sisters. For Cone, the "courage to pray" (Metz) is a courage to let go of death-dealing idols, to face the pain of centuries of racialized harm, and to risk receiving from the divine liberator a new experience of humanity and communion shareable by all. Cone's challenging words are counterviolent. They express an unfailing hope, nourished by the songs of the slaves, that God's freedom and love will eventually prevail.

Through the spirituals, therefore, Cone develops a doxological perspective that not only avoids what is most problematic about metaphysics but also combats various intersecting aspects of violence, in hopes of more closely approximating a genuinely peaceful communion between God and all of God's creatures. He thereby sheds light on the contemporary promise of prayer *as such*. As we have seen, his powerful contemplation of doxological blackness constitutes an advance over other analogous doxological approaches, which have, to their discredit, largely ignored the tremendous threat that modern structures of "whiteness" have posed to the very integrity of Christian theory and praxis. At the same time, we have seen that Cone manages to preserve and incorporate the most indispensable features of a rigorously Christian doxological spirituality that is poised to address the many crises of modernity.

To be sure, there is certainly room for further theological development after Cone. The twofold claim that his work not only contributes something crucial to but also retains what is essential to the Christian understanding of prayer should be distinguished from the much less plausible assertion (not endorsed here) that it exhausts everything that could be beneficially considered in relation to this topic. The nearly incomparable depth and richness of Balthasar's and Chrétien's retrievals of the Christian doxological tradition; the extraordinary subtlety of Marion's, Lacoste's, and Chrétien's forays with phenomenology; the variously problematic but by no means unfruitful efforts of Heidegger and the post-Heideggerians; the critical self-awareness displayed in Metz's response to the dialectics of Enlightenment and the horrors of the Shoah; the ardent love for the poor manifested in Gutiérrez, Boff, and Ellacuría, as well as in Dussel and Segundo; and the overwhelming torrent of theological possibilities not even considered here all point to an excess beyond Cone's thought, which greatly limits its potential to stand as any sort of absolute consummation of the unity of prayer and reflection. The dream of this kind of total synthesis is, in any case, much more likely to provoke suspicion than eager anticipation among scholars today. Thus there can really be no hope of transforming Cone's thought into a comprehensive system of theological knowledge, and this is not even something that one can any longer reasonably desire. Cone himself confesses that his theology is "to be expected to have certain weaknesses, because no one can know the whole truth."[92] To say that Cone's project is limited is, therefore, not to critique it but to recognize it for what it is.

Nevertheless, the burden of this chapter has been to show that this sort of limitation, which all intellectual endeavors share in one way or another, is not somehow especially characteristic of and debilitating for any theology that arises out of the black spiritual tradition. There is a need to resist defining this tradition too quickly, as David Tracy and others have done, in terms of its apparently "fragmentary" nature.[93] It would be better to approach it through Tracy's analysis of the "classic," a term which implies not merely particularity but rather an intensely particular disclosure of the universal.[94] The spirituals are classics of Christian prayer. They open up a world of thought in which the ever ancient and ever new mystery of prayer can be received as it gives itself from itself. In Cone's judgment, the Catholic Church's refusal to perceive the potential universality of blackness is precisely that which prevents it from responding adequately to its true calling as a catholic (i.e., universal) church.[95] He even sees this refusal reflected in the works of some black Catholic theologians, who he suggests have focused too much on the historical fact of a black Catholic tradition and not enough on the broader theological significance of this fact.[96] These concerns now have the potential to be somewhat alleviated—that is, if Catholic theologians learn to welcome and be welcomed by the black doxological tradition in all its divinely given power and complexity.

In the end, black theology seems destined to be not only one subset of theology among others but also one of the possible names that can be given to any practice of theology which, striving to be all that it can and must be as a reflection on the traditional and contemporary significance of prayer, also knows *why* it cannot neglect in this regard the doxological spirituality of darkly colored peoples. If Cone does not always emphasize this catholic meaning of black theology as much as he could (and there are some who think he does not),[97] then at least this chapter demonstrates one way to read Cone faithfully with this possibility in mind. At this moment of world history, there may be no better locus in which to rediscover what is most crucial about the mystery of prayer itself than in the strong and sanctified and Spirit-filled songs of the slaves. It is, therefore, with these songs that we bring the present discussion to a close and seek only a few final words to offer by way of conclusion.

CONCLUSION

The last chapter clarifies how the many apparently disparate elements that make up this argument are in fact capable of coming together to form a unified perspective, one consistent with the prayer tradition of the slaves. In this sense, the last chapter already serves as a more or less adequate synopsis of the argument as a whole. Nevertheless, a few closing remarks that rearticulate certain central themes will bring the unity of this entire work into clearer focus. In the preceding discussions, we have pursued two lines of prayerful thought and observed their interweaving: one seeking to overcome the dangers of metaphysics through postmetaphysical doxology, the other resisting certain structures of violence through counterviolent spirituality. Although part one emphasized the first of these lines of prayerful thought and part two the second, both lines have been present throughout. These are the two basic tacks that we have taken in order to think about the implications of prayer amid the crises of modernity.

By elucidating the significance of prayer in these two ways, this text has also protested the prayer-denying secularity of the modern age. It has done so not by disputing the goodness of modern aspirations to critical freedom of various intellectual, cultural, and political kinds. On the contrary, through its prayerful confrontations with metaphysics and violence this book has delineated many specific manners in which such critical freedom can be preserved and deepened in interaction with the infinite freedom of God. Post-metaphysical doxology and counterviolent spirituality are two ways to name such a prayerful interaction, which in each case leaves the critical freedom of the human subject both intact and transformed. Furthermore, the thought that arises from prayer (theology) and the life that embodies it (spirituality) have never been divorced in this text but rather approached as one radically united contemplative-and-active mystery.

In short, prayer has appeared in this work not only as a form of thought and life that is imperiled by certain crises of modernity (associated with secularity, metaphysics, violence, and the separation of theology and spirituality) but also as a powerful respondent to such crises. Prayer does not merely ask for greater freedom and love in the midst of modernity's fraught circumstances; it makes these resplendent gifts more accessible. To rescue prayer from the neglect and antipathy it has endured in much modern culture is thus not merely to preserve one religious practice among others. More importantly, it is to rediscover the wonder of thought beyond conceptual idolatry, to reaffirm the transcendent dignity of life amid a viciously destructive world, and to prepare our crisis-ridden epoch for a more divine, human, and amorous future. In all of these ways, prayer clears a path for integral liberation.

To be sure, prayer is not magic. It does not grant its practitioners direct, efficient control over the elements of the cosmos. Nor can we therefore expect it to act as an omnipotent incantation that, when pronounced amid the crises of modernity, would immediately set everything aright. Even in its ideal forms, prayer's transformative power would not be automatic, since its operations are not strictly "causal" but rather contingent on the freedoms of a relationship. But to make matters worse, history does not give us ideal forms. Like other historical realities, prayer has often been vitiated by idolatrous and violent misuse. Its promise has been falsified in many of its appearances, including many nominally Christian appearances. And even if, for instance, the prayer of Christ is thought to be pure from every defect, our perception of it is likely not. Indeed, in history we perhaps only ever experience concrete manifestations of thought and life that have been marred by multiple levels of crisis-sustaining corruption. Prayer is by no means exempt from this perilous situation.

However, corruptibility cannot make a decisive argument against prayer mainly because it also makes a very powerful argument against prayerlessness. Both options are caught up in the maladies of history. Moreover, there are some good reasons, given the ubiquity of the danger, to prefer prayer over prayerlessness. The love-bound interaction of infinite and finite freedoms that constitutes the most adequate historical expressions of prayer and that becomes particularly illuminated in Christ and in the whole field of free relations between the triune God and creation which he brings into play remains an unparalleled sign of hope in this badly aggrieved world. The integrated goods of theory and practice that such genuinely Christian prayer both seeks and supplies are reflected in various ways in many non-Christian traditions of prayer. More work could be done to clarify these connections. This would constitute a comparative or dialogical extension of thinking prayer beyond the scope of the present project. But the point that this book has developed more directly is that the goods that arise within the Christian tradition of prayer are unmatched in their *comprehensiveness* by any benefits that seem to accrue to adamantly prayer-denying or only ambiguously prayer-like alternatives. Although such alternatives may promote laudable humanistic and ecological goals within the limited reach of finite freedom (which prayer for its part can easily share), they also implicitly acquiesce to whatever final deprivations or permanent corruptions are entailed by this self-imposed limitation. By contrast, prayer lets desire speak to the full extent that it can and thereby enables us to envision maximally desirable possibilities for thought and life that both include and transcend what we have the capacity to achieve on our own.

This extraordinary promise of prayer remains largely unrecognized in the modern academy. Granted, if prayer has a place in a scholar's private religious practices, his or her colleagues will not necessarily object (though some such personal scrutiny may occur). Moreover, if a researcher in whatever discipline takes prayer as an object of study, this may be accepted so long as he or she keeps the methods of this investigation purified of prayer's influence (though some suspicion is likely to persist even in such cases). But the idea that educated thinkers could be legitimately and beneficially prayerful precisely in their thinking is nearly unheard-of today. The exceptional case here would be certain theologians (not necessarily all) who remain mindful of this ancient vocation. But even these theologians may sometimes begin to doubt whether prayer is an activity one can realistically pursue *as* an intellectual. Or, if they do not doubt it, they may still want to reflect more on this possibility in order to understand it better themselves and to communicate their role as prayerful theologians more effectively to others. I hope that this book has been helpful in this regard. The thought that prayer generates is among the kinds of thought that call for serious intellectual pursuit, and the significance of this kind of thought is momentous. Thinking prayer is neither a "square circle" nor an obsolete relic of an immature and irresponsible past. It is a rigorous contemplative practice of great theoretical and practical relevance amid the crises of modernity.

Throughout this book, we have interpreted prayer in close relation with another term that both specifies it and contrasts with it: doxology. To a large extent, prayerful thought coincides with doxological thought. Doxology proceeds by receiving, offering, and desiring the glory and word of God. Receiving means being actively open to, embracing, and internalizing gifts that come from a divine anteriority that outstrips all possible finite recollection. Offering means joining in the circuit of Trinitarian giving by presenting to God and to others that which one has received and doing so with joy and gratitude. The moment of offering is that which gives doxology its most recognizable identity as a sacrifice of praise. Although this oblation is no less meaningful if performed in silence, it also finds beautiful expression in poetry and music, above all in the hymn. Finally, there is always more to be desired in the infinite divine mystery than such doxological acts of receiving and offering make accessible. Hence, *eros*, unfulfilled expectation, and eschatological hiddenness, which one might want to associate more closely with prayer as a desirous act of request, are likewise constitutive features of doxology.

To concentrate on the gifts of *doxa* and *logos* is to suggest that the sensoriality and linguisticality of human existence, so dear to phenomenological and poetic traditions, have a vital role to play in prayer. God comes to meet us through these inescapable existentials, which are therefore not merely givens of worldly being but channels of divine excess that simultaneously disclose and hide a truly divine gift and divine giver. Christian doxology locates the fullness of this glory and word of God in Christ. For Christians, therefore, it is not only aesthetics and discourse in general that sustain doxology but also in a very special way the aesthetically and discursively textured revelation that takes place in Jesus's life, death, and resurrection. The salvation that he brings, not merely through his coming-to-presence (incarnation) but more concretely through his particular teachings, actions, and final redemptive hour is that which most powerfully inspires Christians to raise their voices in songs of thanksgiving and praise.

Nevertheless, Christ by no means authorizes a mode of doxological thought that would forget the uncertainties, longings, and needs that continue to beset the fragile lives of this world. In his humanity, he shares in our unknowing and our plaintive cries. And if Christ does not justify such forgetting, neither can any phenomenological or poetic thinking that exhibits doxological characteristics. Thus although it is important to interpret prayer in light of doxology, it is also necessary to let prayer appear in ways that are not overdetermined by doxology's predominantly affirmative, epistemically confident, and highly consoling manners of thinking. A practice of prayerful thought that can credibly claim to preserve the full force of humanity's critical freedom emerges only in that space where the passions, questions, doubts, accusations, and negations of worldly existence are allowed to trouble doxology and to test it—which does not mean to abolish it.

On one level, doxological thought must let itself be unsettled by the nescience of prayer. Insofar as the term "knowledge" suggests transparently accessible presence, indubitable objectivity, and verifiable judgment (as it does within much modern rationalist and empiricist epistemology), it seems less appropriate to the many searching and enigmatic conditions of prayer than is the term "thinking," which refers to a more open-endedly inquisitive practice. To be sure, thought and knowledge have been very closely associated in the Christian doxological tradition. To think is perhaps inevitably to desire to know more about mysteries that one already inchoately knows. In light of this close semantic connection, it makes little sense to separate these two notions absolutely. Nevertheless, it is important to recognize that any sort of knowledge that prayer may grant would be, in its permanent mysteriousness, perpetually worth continuing to think about and perhaps even largely impenetrable. Moreover, one must admit that prayer is often better described as an experience of not knowing. At the opposite extreme, there are agnostically oriented thinkers who are inclined to deny the possibility of knowledge altogether because they persist in defining knowledge exclusively in ways that make it incompatible with divine and creaturely mystery. Although this uncompromisingly apophatic approach may helpfully accent the insatiable longings of prayer and its hospitality toward incomprehensible otherness, its generalized practice of negation often occurs at the expense of the determinate doxological content that also makes prayer particularly promising amid the crises of modernity.

On another level, doxological thought must let itself be disturbed by the suffering of prayer. This book has argued that we need a kind of doxology that is shot through with a piercing cry from the depths, a thunderous roar that bears the weight of the world's anguish and raises it up to God, as Jesus's psalmic voice does on the cross and as countless other sufferers have done throughout the ages. Amid the gruesome history of this world, there can be no authentic prayer without the trembling silence, the terrifying scream, or the uncanny blending of the two which tears at the very fabric of covenantal trust but also perhaps proves its immeasurable endurance. In other words, the pain of concrete existence, together with the many tragedies and oppressions that produce it, must be allowed to take hold of prayer, even if this means, as it often does, turning to God in protest or anger. Here doxology comes into unnerving contact with the too-often-marginalized practice of lament.

In some cases a prayer that arises from suffering will not enter into a fight against God (as legitimate as this antagonism is within the interplay of divine and human freedoms) but instead place a final, perhaps desperate hope in God as the only one who may yet respond decisively to this world's lamentable situation. In such cases, prayer recalls the original meaning of life's "precarity": *precari* is to pray, to request. A precarious life would be one that not only needs help in the midst of crisis but also dares to ask for it—perhaps because there seems to be nothing left to do except beg for deliverance. Christian supplication in particular is emboldened by the conviction that the Father's merciful heart cannot possibly withstand the onslaught of petitionary voices that are brought to it through the tireless pleas of the crucified Son. In this light, petition remains a kind of Christocentric and Trinitarian doxology, albeit it in the future tense. It anticipates praising the triune God, who one trusts will not fail to save.

Prayer is, therefore, thinkable not only as doxological but also as apophatic, lamentatious, and petitionary. These aspects, which one should avoid hypostasizing, merge and intermingle in various ways and give shape to innumerable free interactions between the Trinity and creation. Thinking prayer respects and inhabits these internal tensions of prayer. Moreover, it can respond most effectively to the crises of modernity only if it remains attentive to this complex range of prayer's possibilities. In these ways, theology becomes an intellectual practice that aspires to glorify and contemplate the divine wellspring of eternal freedom and love without becoming too satisfied with its own conceptual formulations or impervious to the horrors of reality.

Having said this, one must immediately add that such contemplation becomes lifeless without action. A theology that does not find its motivations and greatest significance in spirituality—that is, in a life formed through the dramatic inter-*action* of divine and creaturely freedoms—is a dead theology complicit in the "death of God," the "death of man," and innumerable other deaths in the modern age. It is a "theology" in name only. Christ did not leave the world with only the distant memory of his incarnate glory and word, which might be endlessly theorized, but rather offered us his Spirit as a lasting source of vitality, holiness, and liberative action in every age. As a pneumatological and corporeal practice, thinking prayer demands much more than mere thinking. It requires holistic affirmations of life in all its variegated forms. It is thus not simply a cognitive exercise but a spirit-filled way of living, in which the Spirit of Christ takes hold of the incessant movements of our breathing bodies: in welcoming others and in giving to them, in laboring for daily needs and in fighting for peace and justice, and in all other manners of life-giving, life-sustaining, and life-restoring activity. Even in dying, and in preparing to follow Jesus to the cross, prayer finds a way to affirm life by enkindling hope for a resurrected life to come. Ideally one would not cease praying (that is, conspiring with the Spirit) in any of these activities, however practical or mundane they may become. Nor would one cease thinking critically, in the midst of such spiritual dialogues and material struggles, about what we all can and must do in specific situations to give greater glory to the living God. Spirituality is therefore what thinking prayer becomes when it strives to be energetically enamored with the full array of life's possibilities and thus credibly doxological in every deed and word.

What is left to say at this point except, perhaps, a concluding prayer? To end the book in this manner may appear too insistent. To pray in order to prove that one prays is not really to pray. A closing prayer that would ostensibly verify the prayerfulness of the entire text could thus inadvertently call the authenticity of this very prayerfulness into question. Nevertheless, the recognition that this is not merely a book about prayer but in some significant sense a book of prayer is crucial to its proper understanding. For this reason, I shall accept the risk of articulating a single prayer to stand precariously for all the others that echo in the preceding pages and let the argument come to a close on this note. The following prayerful verse, which I have selected as one of the epigraphs of this work (pairing it with the famous line from Evagrius that establishes true prayer as the supreme criterion of the theologian), offers a prayer for prayer. More precisely, it asks for a "little time" in which prayer might be able to occur amid a seemingly interminable "storm" and perhaps especially anticipates a joyous time of prayer that would take place

once this storm is done. This humble petition expresses a largely forgotten desire of a barely remembered and badly afflicted people, a
desire that calls persistently for further thought. In the midst of crisis, these words ask for a modicum of freedom and suggest its definition. Freedom is the prayer that takes place both within the storm
and after it. "I've been in the storm so long; / O give me little time to
pray"—that is, grant me in and after this period of distress more of
that interactively divine and human freedom which, by asking for it,
I have already begun to receive.

NOTES

Introduction

1. That the Christian tradition includes other senses of prayer in addition to that of request is amply displayed by the historical survey, "Prière," in Marcel Viller, ed., *Dictionnaire de spiritualité*, cols. 2196–2347. See also the rich array of possibilities that Steven Chase discusses in *The Tree of Life*. John of Damascus's classic definition of prayer as "the raising of one's mind and heart to God or the requesting of good things from God" (*De fide orthodoxa*, 3, 24) likewise conveys both a broader and a specifically petitionary meaning.

2. See Ps. 148 and Dan. 3:57–90. One might also recall Francis of Assisi's "Canticle of Brother Sun."

3. Thomas Aquinas, *Summa Theologiae*, II-II, 83, 1, ad. 1. The prayerfulness of Aquinas's broader opus has been demonstrated by Jean-Pierre Torrell, O.P., in *St. Thomas Aquinas*, vol. 2, *Spiritual Master*, and in *Christ and Spirituality*.

4. As Teresa says in her *Interior Castle*: "For in reflecting upon it carefully, Sisters, we realize that the soul of the just person is nothing else but a paradise where the Lord says He finds his delight" (bk. 1, ch. 1).

5. One finds this wider sense at work in Geoffrey Wainwright's *Doxology*. Though very attentive to concrete acts of praise, Wainwright also sees them as providing a structure for the whole of Christian thought and existence.

6. Already in prebiblical Greek, *doxa* has the sense of seeming or appearing. It can mean the way some*thing* appears to someone, hence, an

opinion or belief; but it can also mean the way that some*one* appears, hence, reputation or public stature. Within the Hebrew Bible, the word *kabod* is used as a term for God's wondrous manifestations in creation and history but also for God's intrinsic greatness, with little effort to isolate the one meaning from the other. The Septuagint and the New Testament adopt the Greek *doxa* for the same purpose, and in the latter the revelation of God in Christ takes on both senses (i.e., brilliant disclosure and inner majesty). By contrast, the ancient meaning of *logos* tends to be associated less with appearance and more with language, reason, and order. Plato, notably, contrasts *doxa*, as the realm of mere opinion, with *logos*, as the realm of true, philosophical knowledge. In ordinary Greek, *logos* could indicate simply a word or an utterance. The biblical tradition implicitly unites these two senses by teaching that God's speech is that which gives order to the created world and, through the gift of the law, gives order to the life of Israel. In the Gospel of John, of course, we read that the *logos* becomes flesh. Jesus's body is thus identified with the macrocosmic and covenantal principle of order through which God speaks. For further detail, see the entries on *doxa* and *logos* in Kittel and Friedrich, eds., *Theological Dictionary of the New Testament*.

7. This might be considered the central thesis of Augustine's *Expositions of the Psalms*, insofar as this text tends to present each psalm as a template for the transformed desires and ardent praise of the *totus Christus*. See Jason Byassee, *Praise Seeking Understanding*.

8. If one were to object that the phenomena and hermeneutical criteria proper to theology are not so much provided by prayer as by doctrine, a question would then need to be raised concerning the precise nature of doctrine. Without attempting to settle this question here, it may suffice to suggest that the teachings of the church are best understood as a historically emergent set of intentionally clarificatory statements, having various degrees and kinds of authoritative status, regarding all that which has been disclosed within, or in close relation to, the mystery of prayer, including all of the determining conditions that are proper to the whole spectrum of interactions between divine and creaturely freedom that prayer brings to light. It would follow, moreover, that prayer is not in itself devoid of the determinations that are truthfully articulated as doctrine but rather always already conditioned by them, even if this means, as it sometimes does, that prayer is conditioned in this way *before* the teachings themselves have come to be explicitly formulated. In such cases, *prayer precedes doctrine* and may provide the basis for its development. Nevertheless, it is also important to

recognize that those who pray have begun and will continue to do so only because they have at some point learned about its significance. This education, however informal, may involve a range of doctrines, including not only those that are specifically about prayer but also those that are more directly about other topics that remain inseparable from prayer (e.g., Christ, grace, the Trinity, etc.). In such cases, *doctrine precedes prayer*, even while often referring back to it.

It is also worth noting that perhaps the most foundational doctrinal text—i.e., the Creed, whether the Apostles' or the Nicene—tends to be recited precisely as a prayer, occurring, among other places, at the heart of the church's liturgy. At the very least, this traditional locus of recitation should be taken as a sign that the two (doctrine and prayer) are not *absolutely* distinct. Moreover, it is certainly conceivable that a theologian would choose not to focus on prayer per se but on some other topic in the Christian tradition (such as those mentioned above). These choices are certainly legitimate. Nevertheless, if one asks what theology is about in general, prayer may very well offer one of the most comprehensive answers, inasmuch as it has the potential to incorporate the great panoply of free relations that occur between God and all that which is other than God, particularly human beings. Other mysteries could certainly rival its comprehensiveness (e.g., salvation or love), but even in these cases prayer would provide an indispensable access point. That being said, in order to preserve and appreciate prayer as a distinct act it seems important to focus on it specifically in some instances, instead of merely letting it become dispersed throughout all of the other theological loci. This means that we actually need to think about concrete manifestations of prayer, in the form of *prayers*, as we shall do throughout the following argument (albeit usually as already interpreted by this or that theologian).

9. This definition of spirituality applies just as much to the Christian monastic traditions of East and West as it does to the medieval apostolic movements that have given rise to various contemporary forms of religious and lay spirituality that are oriented toward active service in the world. Without restricting this vast range of possibilities, one may be legitimately struck by the particular elegance of the Benedictine teaching regarding the harmonious connection between *orare* and *laborare*. In a sense, this motto says it all: the two are distinct, but the one (*orare*) is found in the other (*lab-orare*). Prayer takes place even in what we do. For an introduction to the key figures and themes of Benedictine spirituality, see Laura Swan, ed., *The Benedictine Tradition*.

10. On the interplay of the missions of Son and Spirit, see Kathryn Tanner, *Christ the Key*, 140–206.

11. Mark McIntosh is among the scholars who rightly call for this sort of integration, arguing that it should be rooted in "the believing community's encounter with God." However, his definition of theology as the "*expression*" of this encounter and spirituality as the "*impression*" of it generates certain unnecessary ambiguities. The prayerful thought that is constitutive of theology might be understood not only as expressing the encounter but also as more deeply internalizing it, through a process of thorough analysis and reflection. Similarly, the prayerful way of life that is constitutive of spirituality seems not only to involve a reception of the encounter but also an active (externalizing) embodiment of it in particular contexts. In short, the prefixes "ex-" and "in-," which indicate outward and inward movements, do not capture the relevant distinction, which really has to do with the dynamic relationship between thought and life, both of which have exteriorizing and interiorizing aspects that are "pressed" upon them by the prayerful encounter with God. See McIntosh, *Mystical Theology*, 11.

12. Taylor, *A Secular Age*, 3, 25–41, and 303–4.

13. In this regard, it is worth supplementing Taylor's analysis with the words of Alexander Schmemann: "Secularism, I submit, is above all a *negation of worship*. I stress:—not of God's existence, not of some kind of transcendence and therefore of some kind of religion. If secularism in theological terms is a heresy, it is primarily a heresy about man. It is the negation of man as a worshiping being, as *homo adorans*: the one for whom worship is the essential act which both 'posits' his humanity and fulfills it." See Schmemann, "Worship in a Secular Age," 118.

14. In the fourth "General Observation" of his *Religion within the Limits of Reason Alone*, Kant includes what he calls "the *spirit of prayer*," by which he means "a heartfelt wish to be well-pleasing to God in our every act and abstention," within the limits of his supposedly purely rational and ethical religion. He even suggests that it should be "present in us 'without ceasing'" (183). And yet, aside from the intention to do the will of God, Kant argues that there is nothing about the tradition of prayer—as disclosed in private and public worship, in acts of petition, in mystical ecstasies, etc.— that is worthy of retrieval by reasonable adults. He grants that children may find some benefit in it (186). But for the rest he contends that it must necessarily be a sign of hypocrisy and a distraction from real virtue. His position depends on a rather restricted sense of the good, which he treats as something that we must have the ability to know adequately through the

mere exercise of reason and as something that does not involve any sort of dialogical and mutually loving encounter between humanity and God. These points are certainly disputable.

15. Beyond locating prayer somewhat condescendingly within the "religion of magic," Hegel also more approvingly discusses what he calls the "cultus." Here he illuminates subjective and objective aspects of the experience of prayer and mystical union, but also problematically subordinates them to the rationalism of his philosophical dialectic. See Hegel, *Lectures on the Philosophy of Religion*, 189–97 and 228. For his part, Nietzsche aggressively opines, "Prayer has been invented for those people who really never have thoughts of their own and who do not know any elevation of the soul or at least do not notice it when it occurs" (*Gay Science*, par. 128, p. 184).

16. Socrates's apparent "deconstruction" of Euthyphro's account of religious devotion foreshadows the sort of questioning that has become more prevalent today. Similarly, his apology for his divinely appointed role as a "gadfly" on public institutions seems to anticipate certain forms of modern critical theory. And yet, at least as Plato portrays him, Socrates asserts himself in service of a higher good, which he does not hesitate to praise as universal and divine. In this respect, the figure of Socrates—and its later offshoots—may admit of some degree of prayerful and prophetic re-inscription.

17. Taylor, *A Catholic Modernity*, 16 and 25.

18. In his *Genealogy of Nihilism*, Connor Cunningham highlights both sides of this aporia, discussing the first as the nihilism of "ontotheology" and the second as the nihilism of "meontotheology" (xiii).

19. Aristotle, *Metaphysics* 1.2, 4.1, 6.1, and 12.7. Note that, whereas Aristotle understands the highest task of the philosopher to be a kind of contemplation in which one participates in the unmoved mover's eternal "thinking on thinking," the present work encourages a kind of contemplation that would seek greater participation in the life of God through a perpetual thinking on—or, better, *through*—prayer.

20. Ibid., 1.2.

21. The introduction to Cunningham and Candler's *Belief and Metaphysics* is indicative of this strategy, as is the essay that William Desmond contributes to the same collection, "Confidence of Thought," 11–40. While making a strong case for the ideas of creation and wonder, these texts do not manage to legitimate the traditional understanding of metaphysics as a universal, necessary, demonstrable, ontological system of certain knowledge. Instead, they seem to point to a different style of thinking, less apodictic,

less absolutist, which Desmond in particular describes as "thinking love" (38) and as a kind of "intimacy" with "otherness" (26). Is "metaphysics" the most appropriate name for this sort of approximately prayerful thought? If there have been certain historical connections between the two, does this remain the optimal arrangement for the future? These are questions that we shall consider throughout.

22. David Bentley Hart offers a very sharp (perhaps too sharp) example of this sort of critique in *Beauty of the Infinite*, 35–152.

23. Denys Turner provides a characteristically nuanced defense of this teaching in his *Faith, Reason, and the Existence of God*, arguing that it in no way contravenes his earlier explorations of the mystical paths of knowing-as-unknowing in *The Darkness of God*.

24. This point does not contradict Henri de Lubac's or Karl Rahner's distinct ways of distancing themselves from the concept of "pure nature" by recovering a more classical sense of the pervasively gracious presence of God. "Natural" prayer and theology, in the precise sense employed here, may very well depend on a divine self-gift that exceeds the mere act of creation, even though they are, qua "natural," not explicitly guided by the positive revelation that is communicated through Christian scripture and tradition.

25. See Karl Barth, "No! Answer to Emil Brunner."

26. Theodor Adorno and Max Horkheimer give a classic formulation of this claim in their *Dialectic of Enlightenment*. Enrique Dussel critically appropriates their thesis in the second appendix of *Invention of the Americas*, in which he connects the negative (irrationally or mythically violent) side of modernity with its *Eurocentrism*, i.e., with the systematic marginalization and domination of the non-European other that has characterized European theory and politics at least since the fifteenth-century origins of its colonial expansion. He proposes "transmodernity" as a vision of the future that would incorporate the achievements of modern critical freedom while overcoming its many life-negating contradictions through a genuine performance of global solidarity (136–40). The hope of the present project is that prayer will open up a viable path toward a fuller form of the radically inclusive liberation that Dussel anticipates in his account of transmodernity.

27. J. Kameron Carter's *Race* and Willie James Jennings's *The Christian Imagination* draw connections between the modern negations of Jewishness and blackness, arguing that these negations stem from a common "white" and "supersessionistic" distortion of the Christian imagination. Although there are clear connections here, it seems important to emphasize,

somewhat more strongly than Carter and Jennings do, that the need to affirm both Jewish and black existence from a Christian perspective requires two significantly distinct lines of analysis, which can attend to the complexities of each case. Hence, we shall primarily treat these as different questions.

28. This point harmonizes with Kathryn Tanner's discussion of the socially critical potential of doctrines of divine transcendence in *Politics of God*, 68.

29. This turn, which begins with Walter Benjamin's idea of a "weak messianic force" and takes on a different set of meanings in Jacques Derrida's "messianicity without messianism," initially emerges as a legitimate reaction against the destructive excesses of twentieth-century utopianism. For a concise overview, see Simon Choat, *Marx through Post-Structuralism*, 88–90. The contention of the present work is that, like the apophatic deconstruction of metaphysics, this counteractive weakening of the messianic is directed against a genuine threat but also needs the guidance of doxology in order to avoid falling into a host of other difficulties associated with the opposite extreme.

30. These perspectives are largely excluded from the critical account of doxology that Giorgio Agamben develops in *The Kingdom and the Glory*. In this text, Agamben displays a characteristically modern desire to think prayer only while presupposing its vacuity. Here we shall obviously make no such presupposition but instead seek to think prayer on its own terms. This more open and positive approach will allow us to see that Heidegger's apparently doxological response to the "governmentality" of technology is problematic not only because it lacks sufficient political consciousness but also because it distorts the promise of doxology (253); that Balthasar's doxological theory is not only aesthetic but also dramatic, and in this sense far from inoperative (197–98); and that the liberative, and thus not merely empty, possibilities of doxological spirituality have been powerfully attested by many communities on the undersides of history.

31. Some Catholic moral theologians have argued that prayer opens up a renewed potential for understanding the meaning of conscience. See, for example, Dennis Billy and James Keating's *Conscience and Prayer*.

32. As we shall see, a spirituality that authentically bears witness to this divine peace in the midst of a violent world will have to do so, precisely in conformity with Christ, through some sort of explicit confrontation with the persons or institutions that presently sustain the conditions of harm or injustice. In certain horrific circumstances, this *may* even require a momentary use of coercive force. In such cases, the counterviolent potential

of prayer may not be limited to strictly nonviolent acts of resistance, even though it seems clear that these should be employed as a rule whenever the situation does not absolutely demand otherwise. Moreover, whether any situation, however grave, actually justifies a particular strategy of provisionally violent resistance will always be a matter that calls for serious prayerfully ethical discernment in view of the double commandment of love and all other relevant considerations. For a powerful testimony to prayerful nonviolence, see Dorothy Day, *The Long Loneliness*.

33. See, for example, Isa. 1:15–20, Jer. 2:28–29, Mic. 2:1–2, and Amos 5:21–24. One might also consider the "prophetic" reading of the Psalms that Walter Brueggemann develops in *Israel's Praise*. Brueggemann analyzes and resists the falsification of prayer that was already a crisis for biblical Israel and, he suggests, continues to be a crisis in the contemporary church.

34. See the introduction to John Milbank, Catherine Pickstock, and Graham Ward, eds., *Radical Orthodoxy*, 1–20. Catherine Pickstock's *After Writing* is one of the most explicitly doxological works in this contemporary theological tradition. Pickstock is certainly right to insist, against Derrida's reading of the *Phaedrus*, that the figure of Socrates has the potential to disclose a doxological—and thus not merely metaphysical—alternative to sophistry. But this point does not eliminate the grounds for questioning whether Plato's version of Socratic doxology sufficiently differentiates Plato's larger philosophical project from those problematic aspects of metaphysics that concern Derrida and others. Pickstock's discussion of the Roman Rite is less susceptible to this sort of questioning, insofar as the christological, Trinitarian, and eucharistic features that she considers, in impressive phenomenological detail, open up an unmistakably different horizon of thought and existence.

35. Kevin Irwin analyzes the context and reception of this principle in his "*Lex Orandi, Lex Credendi*."

36. For an overview of the literature, see Dwight Vogel, "Liturgical Theology." See also David Fagerberg, *Theologia Prima*, 108–28.

37. Louis-Marie Chauvet confirms this point in his *Symbol and Sacrament*. His discussion of the sacramental structure of gift, reception, and return-gift (278) is largely congruent with the doxological structure of receiving, offering, and desiring elaborated above, especially insofar as this becomes embodied in an ethically significant spirituality. Moreover, his argument in favor of a sacramental "overcoming of onto-theology" (46–83) resonates deeply with the present attempt to draw out the promise of a post-metaphysical form of doxological contemplation.

38. McGinn, "Letter and the Spirit," 28.

39. Schneiders, "Hermeneutical Approach," 56–57.

40. Schneiders, "Discipline of Christian Spirituality," 204–5.

41. Schneiders, "Study of Christian Spirituality," 16. McIntosh voices similar concerns about Schneiders's methodological proposal in *Mystical Theology*, 19–22.

42. Of course, some works might legitimately tend in one of these directions or the other, without being required to do so by a preestablished methodological separation. At the same time, it seems important to encourage some sustained interaction between these emphases across the board for the sake of a richer and more adequate understanding. Whatever need we might have for abstract theological treatises and experientially oriented accounts of spirituality, this need does not seem to surpass the somewhat competing need for synthetic accounts of the Christian mystery of prayer that bring out its intellectual rigor, aesthetic depth, and practical significance all at the same time, albeit always through a particular set of focused explorations. At the very least, this latter approach should be recognized as an important target for the Christian intellectual community as a whole.

43. Philip Sheldrake demonstrates the fruitfulness of this sort of combined study of spirituality and theology throughout his many works. One might consider, for example, his *Spirituality and Theology*, which includes insightful reflections on the Trinity in light of the distinctive spiritualities of Julian of Norwich, Ignatius of Loyola, and George Herbert (99–164).

44. Exemplary in this regard, at least in terms of intention, would be the dialogical efforts of Thomas Merton, as attested, for instance, by *Zen and the Birds of Appetite*. In his *Thomas Merton and the Monastic Vision*, Lawrence Cunningham adeptly describes how Merton manages, at the very same time, both to open himself deeply to the wisdom of the Zen tradition through his personal relationship with D. T. Suzuki and to understand the fruits of this encounter in an explicitly doxological and christological manner (60–63).

45. At this point, however, it may be useful to note certain affinities between the present work and the still-emergent body of spiritual, theological, and philosophical writings by the Anglican feminist theologian Sarah Coakley. In particular, her turn toward contemplative prayer; her sense that this tradition may open up a path beyond metaphysical "foundationalism" without succumbing to the aporias of postmodernity; her recognition that our "vulnerability" to the Spirit of God and indeed to the entire Trinity (especially as revealed in Rom. 8) does not contradict but actually strengthens

our critical freedom; her exploration of the deep connections between prayer and desire; and even her growing awareness of the doxological significance of blackness all cohere, in large measure, with the postmetaphysically and counterviolently doxological interpretation of prayer, theology, and spirituality that is advanced here. At the same time, she also engages in many important debates concerning gender and sexuality, which, though lying beyond the scope of the present project, are by no means antithetical to it. For a concise overview of her intellectual trajectory, see her retrospective "Prayer as Crucible." One might also recognize some proximity between the present argument and the doxological approach to Trinitarian theology that Catherine Mowry LaCugna articulates in *God for Us*, 319–75.

Chapter 1. Doxological Impurity

1. Here one might object to the apparent implication that any historical doxology could be pure, in the sense of conforming absolutely to its ideal. Similarly, one might contend that what is needed today is a practice of hospitality that transgresses the deadly constructs of purity wherever they appear and openly receives all manner of this world's immeasurable complexity. These concerns can be addressed in the following ways. First, there is no implication here that doxological purity is perfectly realizable in this life. There is only the recognition that, in order to seek it, one needs to make discernments between more and less adequate approaches. Second, the present work advocates a Christian doxological spirituality that can begin to approach a condition of genuine purity only if it is realized as hospitality, which is to say welcoming love. The claim here is that Heidegger's doxology becomes most distorted and dangerous precisely to the extent that he subordinates it to certain typically modern codes of (doxologically impure) "purity" that negate the deepest promise of Christian doxology as a genuinely hospitable form of thought and existence.

2. There are important distinctions between Heidegger's terms for being. *Seiendheit* is Heidegger's name for the beingness of beings, i.e., the general concept of what it means for a being to be, as thought within the tradition of metaphysical ontology. *Das Seiende* is Heidegger's word for a particular being or entity. *Sein* and *Seyn* both refer to the being of beings, thought in "destruction" of traditional ontology, i.e., in a mode of questioning concerning that which is most original and essential to being as such. *Seyn* hearkens to an older German way of letting being appear in language,

which emphasizes its historical-destining character, and for this reason Heidegger sometimes shows a preference for this term in his later works. I have avoided the somewhat common practice of translating *Sein* and *Seyn* with a capitalized "Being" or "Beyng," which may give the false impression that these are proper names for a divinity. I have also refrained from altering the lowercase spelling, whether as "be-ing" or "beyng." For these are not ancient English words but technical neologisms or inventions. The simple translation as "being" preserves the sense that when Heidegger speaks of *Sein* or *Seyn*, what he says should potentially affect our understanding of what we call, in ordinary English speech, "being." In what follows, Heidegger's distinctions should be clear from context.

3. *Ereignis* can be translated most simply as "event," but some interpreters have decided upon the English neologism "enowning" in order to bring out the idea of "own-ness" or appropriation which is integral to Heidegger's use of this term. See the translators' foreword to Heidegger's *Contributions to Philosophy*, xx–xxi. Nevertheless, the approach taken here will be, alternatively, to leave the word untranslated or to paraphrase it with a variety of different expressions, which bring out different facets of its meaning at relevant points in the conversation.

4. This positive dimension of Heidegger's critique is already somewhat evident in his 1929 essay "What Is Metaphysics?," 89–110. In this text, he retains "metaphysics" as a name for the alternative mode of thinking that he will later situate beyond metaphysics. The positive dimension of Heidegger's critique also appears in *Being and Time*, in connection with his proposed destructuring (*Destruktion*) of the tradition of ontology from the Greeks through Hegel, which, he insists, is not merely a work of negation but a positive recovery of the question of being (17–23).

5. Marion argues that Heidegger's "destruction" of the Cartesian *ego* in *Being and Time* does not prevent a recuperation of it (different but nevertheless significant) in the form of *Dasein*; he also contends, however, that Heidegger's distance from Descartes increases in the period after *Being and Time*. See Marion, "Heidegger and Descartes," 67–96.

6. Heidegger, "Question concerning Technology," 26–27.

7. Ibid., 26.

8. In his "God in Heidegger's Thought," the Catholic theologian Bernhard Welte offers a rather positive assessment of Heidegger's search for the truly divine God. At the beginning of the essay, Welte quotes a personal letter that he received from Heidegger, in which Heidegger warmly approves of Welte's interpretation of his work but nevertheless suggests that it "could

be enriched by a discussion of the nature of modern technology" (85). From the present analysis, we can see why this may be no minor quibble. Heidegger's critical account of modern technology is central to his sense of what is problematic and even nihilistic about theology's typical manner of proceeding. Nonetheless, Heidegger's largely positive reception of Welte's reading of him as a religious seeker is also a clear indication that Heidegger's thought is not reducible to a merely secular or atheistic philosophy.

9. Heidegger, "Word of Nietzsche," 59–62. This essay expresses in condensed form many of the arguments that Heidegger develops in his earlier multivolume series of lectures on Nietzsche.

10. Ibid., 110.

11. Ibid., 67.

12. Ibid., 103.

13. Heidegger makes the connection between Nietzsche's supposedly nihilistic thought and technology explicit when he argues that, in becoming the *Übermensch*, "man . . . rises up into the subjectivity of his essence," while "nature appears everywhere . . . as the object of technology" (ibid., 100). Michael E. Zimmerman helpfully clarifies that Heidegger's interweaving of these two themes depends to a significant extent on his early appropriation of Ernst Jünger's view of modern technology as the concrete realization of the metaphysics of the will-to-power. See Zimmerman, *Heidegger's Confrontation with Modernity*, 46–93. For an account of the various ways that Heidegger seems to misread Nietzsche and to overlook his postmetaphysical and antinihilistic potential, see Michael Allen Gillespie, *Nihilism before Nietzsche*, 175–77.

14. Heidegger, "Word of Nietzsche," 111.

15. Laurence Paul Hemming is correct to identify in Heidegger's thought a certain kind of "atheism" (at least with respect to the metaphysical "God" and the Christian God) which, nevertheless, clears the way for a different sort of "lively piety," which seems to appear here in the Nietzschean exclamation "I seek God! I seek God!" See Hemming, *Heidegger's Atheism*, 269. But serious questions remain regarding exactly what sort of piety this can be and whether Heidegger's apparent refusal of Christian theology is actually necessary in order to overcome the dangers of metaphysics.

16. Heidegger, "Onto-Theo-Logical Constitution," 42 and 127.

17. Ibid., 57–60. See also Heidegger's discussions of the ground in *The Essence of Reasons* [*Vom Wesen des Grundes*] and *The Principle of Reason* [*Satz vom Grund*].

18. Heidegger, "Onto-Theo-Logical Constitution," 60, 69, 70, and 72.

19. See, inter alia, Merold Westphal, *Overcoming Onto-theology*, 285; Westphal, *Transcendence and Self-Transcendence*, 35; Marion, *God without Being*, 35; and Caputo, *Heidegger and Aquinas*, 153.

20. Heidegger, "Onto-Theo-Logical Constitution," 72.

21. Ibid., 69. Translation slightly amended.

22. Ibid., 67.

23. Adriaan Perpezak and Kevin Hughes illustrate this point by suggesting that Heidegger's opposition between ontotheology and prayer cannot account for the sort of thought that occurs in Bonaventure's *Itinerarium*. See Peperzak, "Religion after Onto-Theology?," 108, and Hughes, "Remember Bonaventure?," 529–45.

24. The fact that, after leaving the Catholic Church, Heidegger becomes increasingly interested in Luther's theology is certainly a relevant consideration here. However, as Sean McGrath demonstrates, this interest does not lead Heidegger to propose a form of antimetaphysical but still determinately Christian faith along Lutheran lines but rather to develop a phenomenological sense of existential godforsakenness that seems to imitate Lutheran faith only while simultaneously rejecting it. See McGrath, *Early Heidegger and Medieval Philosophy*, 151–84.

25. Heidegger, "Phenomenology and Theology," 52.

26. As Caputo notes, Heidegger's existential analysis in *Being and Time* emerges from his early commentaries on Paul and Augustine. See Caputo, "People of God, People of Being," 87.

27. On the not merely ontic significance of Thomistic *esse*, see McGrath, "Heidegger's Approach to Aquinas," 286, and Marion, "Thomas Aquinas and Onto-Theology," 38–74.

28. Heidegger, appendix to "Phenomenology and Theology," 61.

29. One might consider looking back to Heidegger's 1920–21 lecture course, which has been translated as *The Phenomenology of Religious Life*, in order to reflect on Heidegger's positive significance for the question of prayer. This is the approach taken by Benjamin Crowe in his "Heidegger and the Prospect for a Phenomenology of Prayer." Although this very early period of Heidegger's thought is somewhat illuminating—not least because it demonstrates his familiarity with Christianity—it is nevertheless problematic for the present conversation for several reasons. First, as Crowe points out, Heidegger's discussion of religious experience omits a consideration of prayer (ibid., 126). Second, Heidegger moves decisively away from this sort of research in the later and definitive stages of his career. Finally, that which approximates prayer in this lecture course (i.e., religious experience)

only has the status of a *noema* and does not significantly shape Heidegger's *noesis*, whereas that which approximates prayer in later works (namely, the poetry of Hölderlin and others) deeply affects his entire manner of thinking and bears upon the question of what it means to think.

30. Throughout this period, Heidegger gives three lecture courses and composes several essays on Hölderlin's poetry. He also produces many other writings which, even though they are not explicitly about Hölderlin, nevertheless invoke him at decisive moments, develop themes that emerged originally from Heidegger's readings of his poems, or discuss other poetic figures belonging to a Greco-German canon who play much the same role: e.g., Homer, Sophocles, Meister Eckhart, Angelus Silesius, Rilke, Goethe, Trakl, though Heidegger clearly distinguishes Hölderlin as the purest of the poets.

31. Heidegger, "Thing" (1950), 161–80. Heidegger recalls "the Old High German meaning of the word 'thing' [*Ding*]," which he opposes to the metaphysically inscribed *causa, ens, res,* and object (175).

32. Ibid., 176.

33. Heidegger, *Contributions to Philosophy*, 288.

34. Heidegger, "Building Dwelling Thinking" (1951), 147.

35. Heidegger grounds his account of poetic dwelling in a line from the poem which begins "In lovely blue" (*In lieblicher Bläue*): "Full of merit, yet poetically, man / Dwells on this earth." Although this poem is now considered to be of uncertain origin, Heidegger attributes it to Hölderlin and reveres this line as one of the poet's most important sayings. See "Poetically Man Dwells," 214, 222, and 226.

36. Heidegger, "Question concerning Technology," 13.

37. Heidegger, "What Are Poets For?" (1950), 89–92.

38. Heidegger, *Contributions to Philosophy*, 291. Tellingly, the short section "VII. The Last God" (pp. 285–93) is not the last section; rather, it is followed and surpassed by "VIII. Be-ing" (pp. 298–359).

39. Heidegger, *Mindfulness*, 225.

40. Heidegger, "What Are Poets For?," 92.

41. In this regard, Jean Greisch raises a crucial question: "Is the 'last God' a God to whom humans can pray or to whom they can offer sacrifices? Can we kneel without renouncing ourselves or can we celebrate the 'last God' in any sense of the term?" His detailed textual analysis leads him to a negative conclusion. See Greisch, "Poverty of Heidegger's 'Last God,'" 260. And yet, there is a meditative and even prayer-like quality to the *Contributions*, which allows Rüdiger Safranski to describe them somewhat aptly as "Heidegger's rosary." See Safranski, *Martin Heidegger*, 309. But Greisch

is certainly right to suggest that the "last God" does not invite a traditional practice of prayer, in which one might genuinely hope for a response.

42. Consider the title of section 253, "Last," in *Contributions to Philosophy*, 285.

43. Heidegger, "Hölderlin and the Essence of Poetry," 58.

44. Ibid., 61. Heidegger comments here on Hölderlin's "As when on a holiday" ("Wie wenn am Feiertage").

45. Ibid., 64.

46. For an introduction to this grim aspect of Heidegger's legacy, consult Richard Wolin, ed., *The Heidegger Controversy*; Zimmerman, *Heidegger's Confrontation with Modernity*, 3–133; Emmanuel Faye, *Heidegger: The Introduction of Nazism*; and Safranski, *Martin Heidegger*, 202–352.

47. Robert Savage, *Hölderlin after the Catastrophe*, 8–15.

48. Heidegger, "Hölderlin and the Essence of Poetry," 51.

49. Heidegger, "Remembrance," 126–34.

50. Ibid., 136.

51. Caputo reminds us, however, that Heidegger's Greco-German concepts here continue to depend on their explicitly excluded biblical counterparts. See his "People of God, People of Being," 90.

52. Heidegger, "Remembrance," 115.

53. Ibid., 173n2.

54. Derrida, *Of Spirit*, 75.

55. Heidegger, "Remembrance," 112.

56. The tradition of commentaries on the Song of Songs may be recalled in this context as a more orthodox theological analogue.

57. Heidegger, "Remembrance," 112, 117, 160, and 161. Edward Said's diagnosis of orientalist modes of thinking in *Orientalism* should be kept in mind here.

58. Heidegger, "Remembrance," 171. To be clear, Heidegger identifies the homeland with Germany, not as it exists factually in the present, but rather as the mythical-historical site in which the German people can receive its divinely intimated destiny from the poets and thereby prepare for a more complete appropriation of their proper being in the future.

59. Ibid., 164.

60. Heidegger, "What Are Poets For?," 112.

61. Heidegger, *Introduction to Metaphysics*, 108.

62. Heidegger, "Letter on Humanism," 217.

63. Heidegger, "Remembrance," 156; Heidegger, "What Are Poets For?," 135; and Heidegger, "Poetically Man Dwells," 214.

64. Heidegger, *Contributions to Philosophy*, 289.

65. Heidegger, *On Time and Being*, 5, 17, 19, and 22.

66. Heidegger, "Conversation on a Country Path," 85.

67. Heidegger, "Memorial Address," 55.

68. For an insightful discussion of Heidegger's relation to Meister Eckhart, see Bret W. Davis, *Heidegger and the Will*, 122–45. Caputo brings out the significance of Angelus Silesius, as a representative of the Eckhartian tradition, in *Mystical Element in Heidegger's Thought*, 60–66 and 97.

69. Heidegger, "Conversation on a Country Path," 62, 86, and 90. In his thinking of being in this text, Heidegger does not prioritize the term *Ereignis* but rather *Gegnet*, which the translator renders as "that-which-regions." Although it would be imprecise to equate these two notions, they are nevertheless clearly interrelated.

70. Heidegger, "Memorial Address," 48 (emphasis original).

71. Heidegger, "Building Dwelling Thinking," 147 and 158.

72. Heidegger, "What Are Poets For?," 135. Here Heidegger interprets the famous line from Rilke's *Sonnets to Orpheus*: "Song is existence . . ."

73. Heidegger, "Conversation on a Country Path," 62.

74. Heidegger, "Thinker as Poet" (1947), 9.

75. Heidegger, "Building Dwelling Thinking," 147.

76. Heidegger, "What Are Poets For?," 122–23.

77. Heidegger, "Building Dwelling Thinking," 148.

78. It must be admitted that Christian doxology does not enable us to disregard our ultimately deadly exposure to the forces of history and nature in favor of a purely life-giving exposure before God but rather requires us to dwell mindfully at the intersection of the two. A certain degree of acceptance of the given conditions of existence upon the earth, including our mortality, therefore has a significant place in prayer. However, Heidegger's account of death as an unsurpassable definition of humanity puts excessive constraints on prayer and the hope out of which it grows. It dissuades one from living actively in the prayerful expectation that God finally has power over the world.

Chapter 2. Doxological Theory

1. Cyril O'Regan examines the complexities of this relationship in "Von Balthasar's Valorization and Critique," 123–58, and in "Hans Urs von Balthasar and the Unwelcoming of Heidegger," 264–98. The central thesis

of both texts, which is likewise supported here, is that Balthasar endorses various aspects of Heideggerian thought only while subjecting this thought to a serious, multifaceted critique. D. C. Schindler develops a similar discussion, with primarily epistemological concerns, in his *Hans Urs von Balthasar and the Dramatic Structure of Truth*. In this chapter, we shall examine this Balthasarian-Heideggerian connection in relation to the question of prayer.

2. Balthasar, *Theo-Logic*, 1:37, 38, 43, and 51.

3. This is a common move among many post-Heideggerian Catholic thinkers. One might especially consider Rahner's similar arguments in *Spirit in the World*, 179–83, and *Hearer of the Word*, 49–51.

4. Przywara's *Analogia Entis* preserves a sense of the inner-worldly tension with which Heidegger is particularly concerned, though not exactly in the same terms. Whereas Przywara emphasizes the similarity-in-difference between creaturely essence (*Sosein*) and existence (*Dasein*), Heidegger's account of the *Austrag* focuses on the interplay between being (*Sein*) and beings (*Seienden*). This terminological distinction is not insignificant. However, the fact remains that both thinkers have ways of expressing the distance and nearness of the inner-worldly form of ontological mystery, and Balthasar works to integrate their respective insights. The most important departure from Heidegger, however, is that both Balthasar and Przywara situate the dynamisms of the world within a divine horizon. See Przywara, *Analogia Entis*, 28, and Balthasar, *Theo-Logic*, 1:227–48.

5. Balthasar, *Theo-Logic*, 1:126.

6. Ibid., 79–130.

7. Ibid., 231–38 and 268.

8. Ibid., 126.

9. Ibid., 272.

10. Przywara, *Analogia Entis*, 23. This usage is evident throughout the two volumes on metaphysics in Balthasar's trilogy: *Glory of the Lord*, vol. 4, and *Glory of the Lord*, vol. 5.

11. Przywara, *Analogia Entis*, 86, my translation. All subsequent English translations of foreign works are mine unless otherwise indicated.

12. Ibid., 86–94.

13. Ibid., 104–41.

14. Ibid., 43–119.

15 Ibid., 240.

16. Heidegger, *Aristotle's "Metaphysics"* Θ 1–3, 38. See Hemming, *Heidegger's Atheism*, 204.

17. Balthasar, *Glory of the Lord*, 5:446. Both Caputo and Hemming reflect on the difficulties entailed in any attempt to identify Aquinas's sense of divine subsistent being with Heidegger's use of *Sein*. See Caputo's *Heidegger and Aquinas* and Hemming's *Heidegger's Atheism*, 190–99. In *Glory of the Lord*, vol. 5, Balthasar avoids the central difficulty by interpreting Heidegger's *Sein* in terms of another concept of Thomas's, namely the "*actus essendi* as non-subsisting abundance" (*Glory of the Lord*, 5:446). Balthasar thereby translates *Sein* as a creaturely reality that is grounded in, and does not ground, the absolute freedom of God.

18. Balthasar, *Theo-Logic*, 1:50, 75, and 207.

19. Balthasar, *Glory of the Lord*, 5:643–44.

20. Balthasar had discussed Heidegger and Hölderlin, along with many other pivotal figures of modern German art and philosophy, in his much earlier three-volume work, originally published from 1937 to 1939: *Apokalypse der Deutschen Seele*. The account of Hölderlin occurs in *Band I: Der deutsche Idealismus*, 293–346, and the treatment of Heidegger, together with Rilke, appears in *Band III: Die Vergöttlichung des Todes*, 193–315. Balthasar's assessment in *Apokalypse* is not altogether different from the one that he makes in *The Glory of the Lord*. In both texts, the central problem is that God is subsumed within the finite human spirit's experience of being or nature. For a summary of Balthasar's early arguments, see Aidan Nichols, *Scattering the Seed*, 82–90 and 203–19, and Alois M. Haas, "Hans Urs von Balthasar's 'Apocalypse of the German Soul,'" 45–57.

21. Balthasar, *Glory of the Lord*, 5:315, 318, 320, and 331.

22. Ibid., 310.

23. Ibid., 446–50.

24. Although the questions of analogy and aesthetics can be distinguished in this manner, John R. Betz clarifies that they must not be separated. In his two-part essay, "Beyond the Sublime: The Aesthetics of the Analogy of Being," Betz shows that various excessive and immanentist tendencies of modern and postmodern aesthetics are resisted effectively only by retrieving an analogical balance between the beautiful (splendor-in-form) and the sublime (splendor-beyond-form).

25. Early examples of this effort include Balthasar's *Presence and Thought: An Essay on the Religious Philosophy of Gregory of Nyssa*; *Cosmic Liturgy: The Universe according to Maximus the Confessor*; *Origen, Spirit and Fire*; and *Two Sisters in the Spirit: Thérèse of Lisieux and Elizabeth of the Trinity*.

26. Balthasar, *Prayer*, 14, 26, 39, and 46. The shorter account of prayer which Balthasar provides in his later (1985) book *Christian Meditation* is more condensed but generally consistent with the earlier treatment. One may, therefore, conclude that, whatever distinctions have been proposed between "contemplation" and "meditation," Balthasar understands these dimensions of prayer in very similar ways.

27. Balthasar, *Prayer*, 45.

28. See, for instance, Balthasar's discussion in *Theo-Drama*, 3:263–82.

29. Balthasar, *Prayer*, 108–11.

30. Ibid., 142 and 148.

31. Balthasar, *Theo-Logic*, 3:369–76.

32. Balthasar, *Glory of the Lord*, 1:137–40 and 163. Balthasar appropriates this sense of Christian "gnosis" from various passages in Paul, John, and the Alexandrian tradition represented by Clement and Origen.

33. Ibid., 164 and 186.

34. For a concise treatment of the history of *theoria* in both its metaphysical and distinctively Christian appearances, see Kevin Hart, "Contemplation: Beyond and Behind."

35. Balthasar's engagements with Dionysius and John of the Cross reveal his inclination to prioritize the kataphatic dimensions of their works, even to the point of questioning certain apophatic excesses (which Balthasar associates, however, with a Neoplatonic mystical tradition that is closer to metaphysics than to the Christian forms of revelation that metaphysics seems to threaten). At the same time, he demonstrates that the prayers and thoughts of Dionysius and John of the Cross are by no means merely apophatic and, moreover, that when they are there is a way to treat this apophasis as an internal element of a Christian doxological aesthetics. The question one might ask in response to Balthasar's discussions is whether more needs to be said regarding the epistemological disruptions that such more nearly apophatic experiences of prayer could produce within such an aesthetics. See Balthasar, *Glory of the Lord*, 2:144–210, and *Glory of the Lord*, 3:105–71.

36. Karen Kilby voices a similar concern in *Balthasar: A (Very) Critical Introduction*. She objects to Balthasar's adoption of a "God's eye view," arguing that this theological style performatively contradicts his various statements regarding the need for epistemic humility (13–14). Kilby's critique may be too strong. Balthasar perhaps does not so much fall into contradiction as he takes a risk (questionable, to be sure, but perhaps not

devastatingly so) which keeps his prayerful thought somewhat close to the dangers of metaphysics. Exactly how close is not easy to determine; there is some proximity and some differentiation here. On a sympathetic reading, he does not negate the attitude of prayer (as Kilby suggests, 160) but rather relies on a "pleromatically" apocalyptic mode of it, in the sense that O'Regan employs in *Theology and the Spaces of Apocalyptic.*

37. Balthasar, *Glory of the Lord*, 4:37. For Balthasar, this forgetting was not limited to, nor even primarily represented by, Przywara as an individual theologian. Rather, it was a pervasive feature of the larger neoscholastic framework of Catholic theology that held sway in the first half of the twentieth century. See Kerr, "Foreword,'" and Henrici, "Hans Urs von Balthasar," 12.

38. Balthasar, *Theology of Karl Barth* (1951), 157.

39. Ibid., 83 and 163.

40. Balthasar, *Theo-Drama*, 3:220–22 and 257–58. See also Peter Casarella, "Hans Urs von Balthasar, Erich Przywara," 192–206.

41. The question regarding whether the metaphysical theory of the *analogia entis* is a valuable marker of Catholic identity is less relevant for the present discussion than the ecumenically shared vocation to think doxologically in accord with the glory and word of God that are disclosed in Christ. This shared calling implies an infinitely greater potential for unity than has been realized. For a closer look at the relationship between Przywara, Barth, and Balthasar, see Stephen Wigley, *Karl Barth and Hans Urs von Balthasar*, 1–44.

42. Balthasar, *Glory of the Lord*, 1:53.

43. Balthasar, *Glory of the Lord*, 4:155.

44. Balthasar, *Glory of the Lord*, 6:14 and 19, and 7:24.

45. For a genealogy of the idea of the "West," together with other related terms, see Dussel, *Invention of the Americas*, 132–35. For a theologically informed discussion of the origins and meaning of "whiteness," see George Yancy, ed., *Christology and Whiteness.*

46. Balthasar, *Dare We Hope.*

47. See Mignolo, *Local Histories/Global Designs.* Roberto Goizueta's *Christ Our Companion* demonstrates the possibility of a Christian aesthetics that hopes to reach beyond the limits of a European cultural canon in order to engage with lives and experiences of those on the borders of modernity.

48. Balthasar, *Glory of the Lord*, 7:213, 216, and 233.

49. Ibid., 354 and 367.

50. An additional danger arises in Balthasar's case insofar as he tends to interpret the disposition of *Gelassenheit* as an essentially *feminine* way of receiving and responding to an initiatory *masculine* principle. Although he contends that the entire church, which is constitutively Marian, is called to exhibit a feminine receptivity to the will of God, this sort of broader application does not prevent his gendered mode of expression from determining the concrete social relations between women and men in problematic ways. For a subtle and critical assessment of Balthasar's treatment of gender (which lies beyond the scope of the present study), see Lucy Gardner and David Moss, "Something like Time; Something like the Sexes," 69–137. In Balthasar's corpus, one may consider especially *Theo-Drama*, 3:283–360.

51. Balthasar, *Glory of the Lord*, 5:33, 37, 39, and 45.

52. Balthasar clarifies this point in his discussion of Ignatius's "application of the senses" in *Glory of the Lord*, 1:373–77.

53. Balthasar, *Glory of the Lord*, 5:102–4.

54. For a broader discussion of Balthasar's theological appropriation of Ignatius's *Spiritual Exercises*, see McIntosh, *Christology from Within*, 55–57; Werner Löser, S.J., "Ignatian Exercises in the Work of Hans Urs von Balthasar," 103–20; and Ben Quash, *Theology and the Drama of History*, 76–79.

55. Balthasar, *Prayer*, 167.

56. Balthasar, "Beyond Contemplation and Action?," 302.

57. Balthasar, "Theology and Sanctity," 181, 183, 192, and 207.

58. Balthasar, *Theo-Drama*, 1:125.

59. Balthasar, *Theo-Drama*, 2:57.

60. Ibid., 296.

61. Balthasar, *Theo-Drama*, 5:96. Here Balthasar takes the words of Adrienne von Speyr as his own. He reveals the proximity of his and von Speyr's understandings of prayer in *First Glance*, 62–64.

62. Balthasar, *Theo-Drama*, 5:95.

63. Balthasar, *Theo-Drama*, 2:302.

64. Christopher Steck's *Ethical Thought of Hans Urs von Balthasar* demonstrates that, although Balthasar's aesthetic and dramatic reflections "do not immediately translate into material norms, . . . they do offer a normative model of neighbor love that, while general, is instructive" (112).

65. Balthasar, *Theo-Drama*, 1:69.

66. Balthasar, *Theo-Drama*, 4:116.

67. Balthasar, *Theo-Drama*, 1:321.

68. Balthasar, *Theo-Drama*, 4:325.

69. Ibid., 320–22.

70. Ibid., 328.

71. Here "metaphysical" must be taken in the critical sense, used by Heidegger and partly appropriated by Balthasar (under other names), which has its clearest attestations in the modern metaphysics of Hegel and others. Balthasar does not think the Catholic tradition's analogical metaphysics is to blame here but rather the sort of destructive technological attitude that Heidegger, but not Balthasar, would identify with the destiny of metaphysics as such.

72. Balthasar, *Theo-Drama*, 4:91–92.

73. Balthasar, "Liberation Theology," 140 and 142.

74. Balthasar, *Theo-Drama*, 4:446 and 458; Henri de Lubac, *Drama of Atheist Humanism* and *La postérité spirituelle de Joachim de Flore*.

75. Balthasar, *Theo-Drama*, 4:482–83.

76. Balthasar, "Liberation Theology," 141.

77. Balthasar, *Theo-Drama*, 4:486, and "Liberation Theology," 144.

78. Balthasar, *Theo-Drama*, 4:192.

79. Ibid., 241–42, 320, and 386.

80. Balthasar, *Glory of the Lord*, 3:400–517. Péguy is one of Charles Taylor's preferred examples of modern Christian consciousness in the final chapter of *Secular Age*, 745–52. Taylor recognizes the "important place" that Péguy has in Balthasar's thought but does not develop this point (ibid., 847n37). Kevin Mongrain makes a compelling case for Péguy's significance in "Poetics and Doxology: Von Balthasar on Poetic Resistance."

81. Balthasar, *Glory of the Lord*, 3:422.

82. Ibid., 427, 450, 475, and 488–89.

83. Ibid., 423, 429, and 435.

84. Ibid., 490.

85. Ibid., 424, 466, 471, and 508.

86. Ibid., 476 and 488.

87. Ibid., 434, 457, 459, and 508.

88. Ibid., 498 and 503–7. See also Péguy, *Mystery of the Holy Innocents*, 86–97.

89. Balthasar, *Glory of the Lord*, 3:447, and *Dare We Hope*, 213.

90. Balthasar, *Glory of the Lord*, 3:415, 441, and 445.

91. Ibid., 418–21, 452, and 484.

92. Ibid., 460 and 494–95.

Chapter 3. Doxological Subtlety

1. Dominique Janicaud coins this expression in his "Theological Turn
of French Phenomenology," trans. Bernard G. Prusak, which originally
appeared as *La tournant théologique de la phénoménologie français*, and
has been published as the first part of the volume *Phenomenology and the
"Theological Turn": The French Debate*. This volume also includes, as its
second part, four shorter contributions by Michel Henry, Paul Ricoeur,
Jean-Luc Marion, and Jean-Louis Chrétien, which were initially collected
in Jean-Francois Courtine, ed., *Phénoménologie et théologie*. In his widely
cited argument, Janicaud highlights various theological violations of strictly
Husserlian phenomenological method that he analyzes mainly in the works
of Levinas, Marion, and Henry, though he does not fail to mention Chrétien. By contrast, he gives Merleau-Ponty, Ricoeur, and the early Heidegger
a more positive appraisal, insofar as they push beyond Husserl while nevertheless showing more methodological restraint. He identifies the later
Hölderlinian Heidegger as the root of the problem: "Without Heidegger's
Kehre, there would be no theological turn. Assuredly. But this affirmation
is not a legitimation" (Janicaud, "Theological Turn," 31). Lacoste does not
appear in Janicaud's study, but an essay of his is included in the more recent
collection, edited by Bruce Ellis Benson and Norman Wirzba, *Words of Life:
New Theological Turns in French Phenomenology*, 42–67. Levinas offers a
Jewish form of the theological turn, and Henry's interpretation of Christianity in terms of auto-affection departs in certain crucial respects from the
Catholic and catholically ecumenical theological tradition. Hence, one is left
mainly with Marion, Lacoste, and Chrétien as Catholic figures. To be sure,
Emmanuel Falque could be added to this list. However, we shall focus on
the other three here because they have thus far approached the question of
prayer more directly. But one might consider, for instance, Falque's *Metamorphosis of Finitude*.

2. As anecdotal evidence of this connection, all three have made multiple contributions to *Communio: Revue Catholique Internationale*, the
French branch of the theological journal which Balthasar helped to found
and which continues to celebrate his work. See, for instance, Marion's "Le
présent et le don," "Le phénoménalité du sacrement," and "Le saint invisible"; Lacoste's "L'altération" and "De la technique à la liturgie"; and
Chrétien's "L'humilité selon saint Bernard" and "La beauté comme inchoation de la gloire."

3. Balthasar advances this kind of argument against Marion in *Theo-Logic*, 2:134n5 and 177n9.

4. There have been numerous studies of Marion's work, for instance: Kevin Hart, ed., *Counter-Experiences*; Ian Leask and Eoin Cassidy, eds., *Givenness and God*; Christina Gschwandtner, *Reading Jean-Luc Marion*; Shane Mackinlay, *Interpreting Excess*; Robyn Horner, *Rethinking God as Gift*; and Tamsin Jones, *Genealogy of Marion's Philosophy of Religion*. There is no comparably extensive body of literature on Lacoste and Chrétien, though Gschwandtner's recent *Postmodern Apologetics?* does give a clear presentation of all three.

5. Caputo, *Mystical Element*, 236 and 249.

6. Caputo, *Heidegger and Aquinas*, 9, 278, and 283.

7. Caputo, *Radical Hermeneutics*, 268–88.

8. Caputo, *Demythologizing Heidegger*, 186, 199, and 214.

9. Caputo, *Against Ethics*, 15; Levinas, *Totality and Infinity*, 199, and Levinas, *Otherwise Than Being*, 140–49. In the latter text, Levinas argues that one bears witness to this glory through the sincerity of an approach to the neighbor which says above all "here I am," exposed and open for you, responsible for you, hospitable to you, even hostage to you. This act of *saying*, in which nothing need be *said*, no ontology or theology articulated, nothing disclosed about the essential truth of being or of God, constitutes, in the words of Levinas, "kerygma and prayer, glorification and recognition." Without rejecting doxology entirely, he proposes an ethically reduced mode of doxology that occurs strictly and exclusively in the gesture whereby one shows oneself to be radically available for one's neighbor. *Doxa* has been uncoupled from manifestation; *logos* has been reduced to the vulnerable act of speaking prior to all spoken content; but together they form the basis for a style of thought which is not altogether estranged from doxology, even though it also represents, in some sense, an ethical alternative to doxology.

10. Caputo, *Prayers and Tears*, 35–41; Derrida, "How to Avoid Speaking," 20, 41–42, 46, and 59; and Derrida, "*Sauf le nom*," 68.

11. Caputo, *Prayers and Tears*, 38 and 69–116; Derrida, "How to Avoid Speaking," 41; and Derrida, "On a Newly Arisen Apocalyptic Tone," 117–73.

12. Caputo, *Prayers and Tears*, 286 and 291; Caputo, "Shedding Tears beyond Being," 99; and Derrida, "Circumfession," 122.

13. Caputo, *Weakness of God*, 283 and 286.

14. Ibid., 84, 180, and 258.

15. Marion, *Idol and Distance*, xxxvi, xxxviii, 22, 126, 245, and 249. Marion draws explicitly on Balthasar, *Glory of the Lord*, 2:144–210.

16. Marion, *Idol and Distance*, 25 and 180.

17. Ibid., 160 and 166.

18. Ibid., 174–75. When Marion says that "the death of Christ on the cross, like ours also, offers only a particular—that is, irreducible—case of the finally trinitarian distance" (ibid., 176), he risks making the very idea of distance, like Hegel's negation, too explanatory. Thus, although Marion greatly surpasses Hegel (in a Balthasarian manner) by situating this quasi-explanation within a strictly doxological or donatological discussion, the mere fact that he supplies a divine ground for death leaves room for concern. For an analysis of the extensive, though often merely implicit, and perhaps not finally sufficient resistance that Marion provides against Hegel throughout his theological and phenomenological texts, see O'Regan, "Crossing Hegel," 95–133.

19. Marion, *Idol and Distance*, 156.

20. For example, Marion argues that "Denys employs . . . the most concrete logic of a double solidarity, in charity as in its refusal. Here, each person relies rigorously on the other, since the gift of grace arrives only through redundancy. . . . Each [person] becomes, for the other, a sacrament of the Christ or of his absence. Each person becomes ineluctably responsible for his neighbor and offers on his face the sole vision of God which the neighbor will perhaps ever see" (ibid., 169).

21. Balthasar, *Glory of the Lord*, 2:151–52, 202, and 208.

22. Marion, *Idol and Distance*, 151–53 and 160.

23. Ibid., 165. Marion, unfortunately, does not call into question Dionysius's ranking of various orders in the church in terms of their "proper capacity" to receive the gift (164). Like Balthasar (see "Theology and Sanctity," 183–84), Marion appears insufficiently concerned with the problems that stem from this banally hierarchical aspect of the Areopagite's admittedly complex, and by no means thoroughly banal, hierarchical theory.

24. With reference to Ricoeur's hermeneutical theory, one could understand Marion as attending here to the world "in front of" the text without, however, compromising what is most deeply at stake in the world "of" the text. See Ricoeur, *From Text to Action*, 88.

25. Marion, *Idol and Distance*, 9–13. Unlike Caputo, Marion appropriates Aquinas not merely on the basis of a "mysticism" that would hide within the silences of his *sacra doctrina*, but rather in view of certain doxological features of his actual discourse. In other words, for Marion,

the decisive point has to do with Thomas's Dionysian, and thus doxologically mystical, theology more than with his supposed "mysticism"—a term which Michel de Certeau will show to be anachronistic in any case. See de Certeau, *Mystic Fable*, 76.

26. Marion, *Idol and Distance*, 244.

27. Ibid., 184–91. These are not exact quotes from Marion; the quotation marks are used here to designate two distinct formulae, which represent, respectively, predicative and hymnic discourse.

28. Ibid., 211–33.

29. Ibid., 251.

30. Ibid., 220. This can be said of many of Derrida's later essays as well, which were not yet available at the time of Marion's writing.

31. Ibid., 36–55, 113, and 131.

32. Marion, *God without Being*, 25–107.

33. Ibid., 7–8, 83–102, and 139–82.

34. Caputo makes a similar claim in "The Hyperbolization of Phenomenology." He writes: "I do not find what Janicaud finds [in Marion's work], that phenomenology has been hijacked by theology, but almost the contrary: that theology has been invaded by phenomenology and that it is theology that suffers a distortion" (82). On this point, Caputo's analysis is sound. The difficulty arises when he endeavors to reduce theology absolutely, in Derridean fashion, to a matter of "faith, not glory" (88), to "the order of intention not of givenness" (89): that is, to a style of prayer that admits of very little or no doxology, at least if this is understood as a reciprocal act starting from the self-donation of God.

35. Marion, *Prolegomena to Charity*, 138.

36. See Marion's *Reduction and Givenness*, 197; *Being Given*, 7–19; *In Excess*, 1–29; and *Erotic Phenomenon*, 9–40.

37. Benson and Wirzba have given currency to this term in their edited volume, *The Phenomenology of Prayer*. In the introduction, they stress that "prayer is a phenomenon that complicates the neat boundaries of phenomenology and thus requires that we think more carefully about phenomenology itself" (9). Hence, they use the phrase "phenomenology of prayer" only while inviting readers to interrogate its meaning, its limits, and its possibility. In her essay on Marion in the same volume, "Praise—Pure and Personal?," Gschwandtner critiques certain individualistic aspects of Marion's phenomenological treatment of prayer (which she locates in texts after *Idol and Distance*) but does not call into question the suitability of Marion's post-Husserlian phenomenology to the task of thinking prayer. As elements

of a "phenomenology of prayer" in Marion's work, one might consider, for instance, the description of the *interloqué* in *Reduction and Givenness*, 200–202; the analysis of *l'adonné* in *Being Given*, 248–319; and the chapters on the icon and on revelation in *In Excess*, 104–62.

38. This chapter presents a revised version of an essay entitled, "In the Name: How to Avoid Speaking of 'Negative Theology,'" which Marion delivered and discussed with Derrida at a conference organized by Caputo. The proceedings of this conference appear in Caputo and Michael Scanlon, eds., *God, the Gift, and Postmodernism.*

39. Marion, *In Excess*, 151–52. Many years after *God without Being*, Marion offers a thorough reassessment of Aquinas in his "Thomas Aquinas and Onto-theology," 38–74. Marion argues that Heidegger's account of the ontotheological structure of metaphysics does not pertain to Aquinas's theology because the latter avoids, through the ever greater apophasis of analogy, any univocal concept of being or entity which would apply to God. Marion's final judgment is that the divine *esse* contemplated by Thomas lies beyond "being" in the metaphysical sense (66).

40. Marion, *In Excess*, 158–62.

41. Ibid., 25.

42. Ibid., 23–24, 158, and 161–62, and Marion, *Being Given*, 94–102.

43. Kathryn Tanner makes a similar argument in rather strong terms in "Theology at the Limits of Phenomenology," in which she contends: "Like any idolatrous mirror, the saturated phenomenon of revelation returns back to givenness the gaze givenness fixes upon it; givenness receives back from revelation what it all along wants to see in it—its own universality, its equivalence with phenomenality. The saturated phenomenon par excellence becomes in this way the idol par excellence (in the negative sense of 'idol' that Marion employs in his theological writings)" (209). In short, phenomenology, even the new sort that Marion develops, cannot on its own provide an antidote to idolatry. One might also argue that the supreme actuality of God, which Marion seems to suspend here, is precisely what is affirmed and praised by Aquinas's theological doctrine of *esse*. Thus Marion's apparent decision to do "without being" may be, to the extent that is motivated by the desire for certainty, closer to metaphysics than to its prayerful overcoming. As Marion himself already shows in *The Idol and Distance*, such an overcoming does not rule out the possibility of glorifying God with help from the still vastly imperfect name of being (253). This clarification makes Marion's eventual defense of Thomistic *esse* all the more significant. Despite the problematically apodictic strategies of his phenomenology, Marion is

perhaps best understood as ultimately rejecting any ontology that negates prayer, not any prayer which might include its own version of ontology. The divine actuality that he brackets in some works is reinstated by the prayerfulness of other works.

44. Marion, *Erotic Phenomenon*, 23, 24, and 215, and *God without Being*, 131 and 137.

45. Joeri Schrijvers offers an opposite evaluation in his "In (the) Place of the Self." Citing Derrida, he warns against a return of ontotheology in Marion's interpretation of Augustine (681). Moreover, he suggests that "a philosopher, who, as a rule, does not love God very much (or at least too little)" would not be able to read or appreciate this work (679). These two "concluding critical remarks" (ibid.) work against each other. The observation that a philosopher who has decided as a rule not to love God will perhaps not be able to understand this text confirms its distance from metaphysics, whereas, by contrast, the tendency to restrict rigorous thought to the stipulated rules of this sort of philosopher proves only a deep fidelity to the basic impulse of metaphysics, despite whatever appeals may be made to the necessity of its overcoming.

46. Marion, *Au lieu de soi*, 10, 31–36, 261–68, and 324.

47. Ibid., 43–45, 87, and 196,

48. The richness of Marion's doxological reading of Augustine puts the poverty of Derrida's and Caputo's deconstructive interpretations into sharp relief. For Marion, Augustine is a source of much more than a question and a passion. Moreover, although Marion seems to imitate Balthasar less here than he did in *The Idol and Distance*, he once again cites Balthasar as an authority (ibid., 196 and 297). The phenomenological studies of the intervening years, which Marion re-appropriates throughout, give his analysis a theological style that is, even more apparently than before, uniquely his own.

49. Ibid., 100–105, 213–17, 235–41, 272–73, 304–13, and 342–52.

50. Ibid., 57.

51. Ibid., 31, 57, and 261.

52. Lacoste, *Note sur le temps*, 122.

53. In addition to Heidegger, other important sources for Lacoste's phenomenology include Levinas, whose influence we shall consider below; Husserl, from whom he retains an attraction to the analysis of consciousness; and Merleau-Ponty, to whom he is somewhat indebted for his account of the fleshly character of human existence. See Lacoste's *Note sur le temps*, 24–25; *La phénoménalité de Dieu*, 33–39; and *Présence et parousie*, 64.

54. Lacoste, *Note sur le temps*, 78–87 and 183–85. Lacoste affirms Balthasar's account of the *"analogia entis concreta,"* which includes the qualifier "concrete" because it resituates Przywara's ontological doctrine in Christology. Lacoste also pairs this Balthasarian expression with a similar formula of his own, *"analogia temporis et aeternitatis,"* which transposes the analogy of being into the discourse of time. One should note, too, that Lacoste embraces Barth's analysis of the covenantal character of creation.

55. Lacoste, *Note sur le temps*, 41, 53, 129–31, and 152.

56. Ibid., 198 and 215.

57. Lacoste, *Experience and the Absolute*, 14–22.

58. Ibid., 2.

59. Ibid., 20–53, 77–79, 91, and 145–49. The problem with what Caputo calls the "mystical element" in Heidegger's thought would be, by implication, that it occurs outside the structure of liturgical patience. More generally, Lacoste works against the grain of much recent philosophical and theological reflection in order to contend that what matters most is not that thought can sometimes become mystical (i.e., quasi-parousiacal) but rather that it is meant to remain liturgical (i.e., vigilantly preparousiacal).

60. Lacoste, admittedly, makes very little use of the term "metaphysics" and also insists parenthetically: "Our intention is not, of course, to represent a 'postmodern' position, the concept of which, if it exists, remains enigmatic to us" (ibid., 162). This discursive caution does not alter the fact that his argument is relevant to the task of overcoming the dangers of metaphysics in modernity.

61. Ibid., 2 and 101.

62. Ibid., 131 (italics added). In Lacoste's judgment, although Hegel positions his philosophical account of religion against Schleiermacherian feeling—in order to construct a theology with more objective eschatological content—Hegel remains inscribed in Schleiermacher's project precisely because he likewise fails to respect the distance of the *eschaton*. In contrast to Schleiermacher and Heidegger, Hegel must be credited with more clearly distinguishing initial and final modes of existence and with insisting upon the definitiveness of the latter. And yet, Hegel paradoxically shares with these thinkers the tendency to collapse the parousia into temporal consciousness.

63. Lacoste, *Note sur le temps*, 52–55, and *Experience and the Absolute*, 73–75.

64. Lacoste, *Experience and the Absolute*, 161.

65. Lacoste, *Note sur le temps*, 9.

66. Ibid., 116, 156–57, 174, and 215. In a later essay called "L'apparaître du révélé," in *Présence et parousie*, Lacoste argues that the "form" of revelation which Balthasar theorizes theologically in volume 1 of *Glory of the Lord* has the precise phenomenological status of a textually transmitted and faithfully received memory. This designation does not exclude it from the realm of appearance but rather specifies the proper mode of its appearance (332–33).

67. Lacoste, *Experience and the Absolute*, 43, 141, and 193–94.

68. In *Sources of the Self*, Charles Taylor describes modernity and postmodernity partly in terms of an aesthetic shift toward the "subtler languages" (391) of poetry and the arts, which no longer directly represent "the great chain of being and the publicly established order of references" proper to premodern "metaphysics or theology" (491) but instead offer an "epiphany . . . of something only indirectly available, something the visible object [or poem] can't say itself but only nudges us towards" (469). In the extreme case of "auto-telic" art, there is only an epiphany of the art itself (420). The language of Chrétien's poetry is, in Taylor's terminology, subtle but not auto-telic. It exemplifies what Taylor terms "the invocative uses of language" (490), precisely insofar as it occurs *in* and *as* a voice that calls.

69. Chrétien, "Retrospection," 125.

70. Chrétien, *Lueur du secret*, 139 and 180–82.

71. Chrétien, *L'effroi du beau*, 53, 58–64, 70–71, and 82.

72. Chrétien, *Unforgettable and the Unhoped For*, 1–20, 28, and 30–33.

73. Janicaud, "Theological Turn of French Phenomenology," 66–68; Chrétien, *La voix nue*; and Chrétien, "Wounded Word." Benoît Thirion's *L'appel dans la pensée de Jean-Louis Chrétien* likewise situates Chrétien's work largely within a phenomenological genealogy.

74. Chrétien grants in "The Wounded Word" that phenomenology does not strictly posit the existence of the addressee of prayer. However, he adds immediately that "the manner in which one addresses him, names him, speaks to him, the nature of what one asks and can ask of him, the fear or the confidence with which praying turns toward him—all this depends on the *being of this addressee* as it *appears* to the faithful one" (ibid., 149, italics added). In other words, the decision to suspend the existence of the addressee would seem to violate the manner of appearance of the phenomenon itself, insofar as this phenomenon presupposes such an existence. Therefore, in relation to prayer, phenomenology seems inevitably to deny itself in one way or another: either it brackets transcendence and thereby distances itself from the phenomenon in question, or it welcomes transcendence and

thereby tests its own methodological requirements. Chrétien's thought occurs in the midst of these tensions and refuses, precisely for the sake of *thinking prayer*, to resolve them prematurely in one direction or another.

75. Chrétien, *Sous le regard de la Bible*, 19.

76. Chrétien, *Reconnaissances philosophiques*, 303. One might observe here a difference of emphasis between Lacoste's and Chrétien's interpretations of Balthasarian inchoation: whereas Lacoste insists that any experience of God in history is *only* inchoative, Chrétien accents the idea, which he attributes not only to Balthasar but also to Aquinas, that "that which commences with the life of grace is truly the life eternal" (299).

77. Chrétien, *Call and the Response*, 6–9, 16, and 40.

78. Ibid., 130. Chrétien articulates a similar idea in "Penser la chair avec Péguy" (To think the flesh with Péguy), 126. He also does not fail to mention Merleau-Ponty in this context.

79. Chrétien, *Symbolique du corps*.

80. Chrétien, *Ark of Speech*, 77–110.

81. Chrétien, *Unforgettable and the Unhoped For*, 69, 70, 74–75, 87–89, and 117.

82. Ibid., 105 and 116. In many respects, Chrétien's argument here is redolent of the one that Lacoste advances in *Note sur le temps*, though Chrétien seems to be, by comparison, less concerned with analyzing the conditions of our finitude and more focused on contemplating that which exceeds them.

83. Chrétien, *Call and the Response*, 35.

84. Chrétien, *Ark of Speech*, 35–36.

85. Chrétien, "Ce que la parole ne cesse de promettre," 29 and 40.

86. Chrétien, *Ark of Speech*, 1–2.

87. Chrétien, *Sous le regard de la Bible*, 8, 18–20, 22, and 26–27.

88. Chrétien, "Ce que la parole ne cesse de promettre," 51–60.

89. In "L'humanité des larmes," 61–86, Chrétien clarifies that our cries, and even our tears themselves, are a significant mode of speech given and received by God. Whether in joy or in distress, tears manifest both the excess of life and the authenticity of our human response to it. Chrétien's argument in this essay can be read as a Christian doxological alternative to Derrida's discussion of tears at the end of his *Memoirs of the Blind*, 126–29.

90. Chrétien, *L'antiphonaire de la nuit*, 10. See also the discussion of this text in Glenn Williams Fetzer, *Palimpsests of the Real*, 33–38.

91. Chrétien, *L'intelligence du feu*, and *L'antiphonaire de la nuit*, 24 and 40.

92. Chrétien, "Hospitality of Silence," in *Ark of Speech*, 65.

93. Chrétien, *Ark of Speech*, 65 and 72.

94. Chrétien, *Lueur du secret*, 17–34.

95. Chrétien, *Call and the Response*, 35 and 130.

96. Chrétien, *Ark of Speech*, 10–11.

97. Chrétien, *Saint Augustin et les actes de parole*.

98. Chrétien, "La double hospitalité," 50–51.

99. Chrétien, *Hand to Hand*, 3–4. Cf. Genesis 32:25–29. Benson analyzes the agonic aspect of Chrétien's thought in some detail in "Chrétien on the Call That Wounds," 208–21.

100. Chrétien, "La prière selon Kierkegaard," 110–17.

101. Chrétien, *L'effroi du beau*, 77 and 80, and *Ark of Speech*, 144.

102. Chrétien, *Saint Augustin et les actes de parole*, 263–64.

103. Chrétien, "La joie d'être," 275–81 and 287–94.

104. Chrétien, *La joie spacieuse*.

105. Chrétien, *L'effroi du beau*, 76.

106. Chrétien, *Ark of Speech*, 37, 122, 139, and 148.

107. Ibid., 129 and 132–33. In "Witness of Humility," Wirzba proposes a form of Christian humility, inspired largely by the writings of Chrétien, as a promising response to a modern age in which "technology has . . . become for us the new sacred and the new sublime," an age in which "we bring more and more of the world, even the rudiments of life itself, under the stamp of our control." He continues: "The results of this control—wasted communities, blown up mountains, poisoned and eroded soils, oceanic 'dead zones,' biological and viral 'super-pests,' war upon war, and workers' anxiety—are getting harder to ignore" (236). Wirzba here implicitly echoes and amplifies Heidegger's complaints about the technological fate of metaphysics and modernity but turns to Chrétien in order to address this crisis. Chrétien offers his own critique of modern technology in "Lucidité de l'usage," 89–115.

108. Chrétien, *Ark of Speech*, 143.

109. Chrétien, *Répondre*, 170, 177, 183–89, and 200–202.

110. Ibid., 180–88, and Derrida, *Gift of Death*, 86.

111. Chrétien, *Répondre*, 194–95.

112. Chrétien, *Répondre*, 209, 213, 221, 225, and 235–37. Chrétien argues explicitly against Kant's modernist hope, expressed in *Religion within the Limits of Reason Alone*, regarding a radical and salvific revolution of the will which would be brought about by our own freedom (214–19).

113. Chrétien, "Trouver et chercher," 178–79 and 195.

114. Ibid., 149–50, 169, and 172.

115. Chrétien, *Pour reprendre et perdre haleine*, 11–27, and Chrétien, "La respiration cosmique de Paul Claudel," 227–55.

116. Chrétien, *Pour reprendre et perdre haleine*, 127–47.

Chapter 4. Poverty of Spirit

1. See Rahner, "Current Problems in Christology." Mongrain shows that this Irenaean tradition is no less foundational to Balthasar's doxological theory, which seeks to glorify God and humanity together in Christ. See Mongrain, *Systematic Thought*, 30.

2. Metz, "Heidegger und das Problem der Metaphysik," 1–22. This article summarizes the argument of the dissertation. See Ashley, *Interruptions*, 27 and 60.

3. Metz, "Theologische und Metaphysische Ordnung," 1–14. Ashley offers a detailed account of Metz's collaboration with Rahner during this period, arguing in particular that Metz, in his editing of Rahner's *Hörer des Wortes*, tends to emphasize the historical dimension of Rahner's transcendental Thomism and, departing somewhat from Rahner, prioritizes the knowing subject's openness to the "personal other" (*der Andere*) instead of the "thingly other" (*das Andere*). See Ashley, *Interruptions*, 78–79.

4. Metz, *Christliche Anthropozentrik*, 47–49 and 120n5.

5. Ibid., 109–10. See also Metz, "Freiheit als philosophisch-theologisches Grenzproblem," 287–311.

6. Whether Aquinas should be singled out for this achievement among other great Christian theologians is certainly debatable, as is for that matter the question of whether Aquinas actually provides a very clear form of resistance against Greek cosmocentrism. Louis Dupré's *Passage to Modernity* could lead one to locate the shift more firmly in the Franciscan tradition (38). For these reasons, it seems easy enough to agree with Ashley's judgment that, "while suggestive, Metz's book [*Christliche Anthropozentrik*] is too sketchy to succeed" (*Interruptions*, 92). However, Metz's decision to focus on Aquinas can be appreciated as a rhetorical strategy, given the context of mid-twentieth-century Catholic Thomism in which he worked. Moreover, that he finds this shift hidden in Aquinas is remarkable.

7. Metz, *Christliche Anthropozentrik*, 120 and 128.

8. Metz, *Advent of God*, 4, 7, 19–20, and 25.

9. Ibid., 9 and 14.

10. Ibid., 35.

11. Ibid., 32–35.

12. Metz, *Poverty of Spirit*, 4, 6, 12, 13, 19, and 21.

13. Ibid., 4, 13, and 32.

14. Ibid., 23, 26, and 40–46.

15. Ibid., 51–52.

16. For a detailed comparison, see Son-Tae Kim, *Christliche Denkform*.

17. Even in *Theology of the World*, when Metz gives qualified support to the rise of modern secularity, he does so on the basis of an explicitly Christian theological understanding of the incarnation and defines the term "secularity" not as atheism but rather as a divinely instituted worldliness or finite creatureliness, which must be distinguished from sinful worldliness and embraced as a sanctifiable reality which, though different from God, remains open to the workings of God's Spirit (13–50).

18. Consider, for instance, Gaspar Martinez, *Confronting the Mystery of God*, 38–46; Titus Guenther, *Rahner and Metz*, 17–107; and Ashley, *Interruptions*, 93–134.

19. Metz, *Faith in History and Society*, 39. For a thorough treatment of the relationship between Metz and Kant, see Rudolf Langthaler, *Gottvermissen*.

20. Tom Bottomore, *Frankfurt School and Its Critics*, 12.

21. This sort of classification has value as a rough heuristic, and in this respect one can understand what Metz means when he uses it, but it should not be taken in the direction of a deterministic essentialism, in which one would supposedly be able to deduce from the mere fact of a particular socio-economic status an entire range of other necessarily correlated characteristics.

22. Metz, *Faith in History and Society*, 46–51, 64, 109, and 156–57. Horkheimer critiques Kantian epistemology on similar grounds in "Traditional and Critical Theory," 188–243.

23. Metz, *Faith in History and Society*, 77, 79, 97, and 263n43.

24. Ibid., 261n35. Adorno, *Negative Dialectics*, 87–89 and 361–65.

25. Metz, *Faith in History and Society*, 104 and 265n6. Metz's target here is not Heidegger's thought per se but rather "any positive theory reconciling humankind and nature," which inevitably results in a "crude ontologization of humanity's passion" (104). However, a strong case can be made that Heidegger's reflections on *Ereignis* fit under this category.

26. Ibid., 23, 70–72, and 81.

27. Ibid., 71.

28. Ibid., 78 and 92–93. It is certainly plausible that Rahner's interpretations of Ignatian *indiferencia* lie in the background of Metz's spirituality.

See Ashley, *Interruptions*, 95, and Philip Endean, *Karl Rahner and Ignatian Spirituality*, 66–67.

29. Metz, *Faith in History and Society*, 93 and 210.

30. Ibid., 26. Even if one were to accept Horkheimer's claim that "any treatment of materialism is misguided . . . which is interested primarily in metaphysical questions" and, accordingly, recognize the possibility of a nonmetaphysical materialism, this concession would not fundamentally alter Metz's concerns regarding how a materialistic outlook threatens subjectivity; see Horkheimer, "Materialism and Metaphysics," 21.

31. Bouretz, *Witnesses for the Future*, 165–223 and 425–76.

32. Taubes, *Political Theology of Paul*, 70–76. Taubes senses a strong resonance between Benjamin's messianism and Romans 8:19–29, in which Paul speaks about the divine Spirit's intercession in prayer (73). He does not find the same resonance in Bloch's still somewhat spiritual works, such as, for instance, *Spirit of Utopia*.

33. Derrida, *Specters of Marx*, 59. For a brief summary of Marx's relation to Judaism, see Julius Carlebach, "Judaism," 273–75.

34. Judith Butler's critical analysis of the "hierarchy of grief" according to which some deaths seem more "grievable" than others—precisely, more "grievable" than those interpreted *as* other—exposes the violence that is involved in failing to mourn as a society for all those who have died and not merely for those whose lives are treated as normal or nonthreatening. See her *Precarious Life*, 32. However, it is telling that this text offers no discussion of prayer to the divine subject of history, nor of hope in the resurrection of the dead.

35. Metz, *Faith in History and Society*, 80, 82, 109, and 112.

36. Ibid., 163, 172, 179, 182, and 185.

37. Morrill, *Anamnesis as Dangerous Memory*, 67–72.

38. Metz, *Faith in History and Society*, 118–24 and 267n30.

39. Ibid., 81, 83, and 159.

40. Ibid., 186.

41. Ibid., 116.

42. For an account of this renewed attention, see Michael Hollerich, "Carl Schmitt," 110. In particular, the present assessment of Schmitt stands in opposition to Taubes's more irenic reading, in which he interprets Schmitt as a Catholic counterpart to Karl Barth (*Political Theology of Paul*, 64). Taubes has a point, insofar as both Barth and Schmitt promote *some* form of decisive action as a remedy to the largely noncommittal liberalism that prevailed in religion and politics in the early twentieth century and proved

largely ineffectual in Weimar Germany. However, Barth—like Balthasar, like Metz—importantly identifies the sovereign subject of this needed action as God, precisely the God of Abraham, Isaac, and Jacob, and of the love of enemies.

43. See Tracy Strong's foreword in Carl Schmitt, *Political Theology*, vii and xxix–xxxi; see also Raphael Gross, *Carl Schmitt and the Jews*.

44. Schmitt, *Political Theology*, 36.

45. Metz, *Faith in History and Society*, 36, and Schmitt, *Political Theology II*.

46. Schmitt makes his debts to Hobbes most explicit in his 1938 text, *The Leviathan in the State Theory of Thomas Hobbes*.

47. In their *Politische Theologie*, Michaela Rissing and Thilo Rissing locate the most significant distinction between Schmitt and Metz in the latter's orientation toward the future, i.e., apocalyptic thought (142–49).

48. Schmitt, *Political Theology II*, 54. See also Steven Ostovich, "Carl Schmitt, Political Theology, and Eschatology."

49. Erik Peterson, *Monotheism as a Political Problem*, 68–105.

50. Peterson argues that Christianity's Trinitarian doctrine effectively replaces "political theology" (which he understands to be an exclusively Jewish and pagan monarchical phenomenon) with the supposedly apolitical anticipation of an eschatological peace that can be "won by no emperor, but is solely a gift of him who 'is higher than all understanding'" (ibid., 105). By contrast, Moltmann seeks to move beyond both monarchical political theology and Peterson's apolitical alternative by offering a political interpretation of the Trinity. Moltmann does this largely by appropriating Joachim of Fiore's doctrine regarding the three kingdoms of world history, a doctrine which informs much modern philosophy of history after Lessing. See Moltmann, *Trinity and the Kingdom*, 191–222. We have seen already, in the discussion of Balthasar's *Theo-Drama*, that he and de Lubac are eager to avoid the dangerous effects of this Joachimite tradition, which seems not only to jeopardize the economic *perichoresis* between Son and Spirit, which is crucial for Christian spirituality as *imitatio Christi*, but also to diminish the sense of God's sovereignty over history, which is indispensable not only to Balthasar's apocalyptic doxology but also to Metz's. Nevertheless, Moltmann reserves an important place for prayer, redefined without sovereignty, as a conversation between friends. He says that "the prayer of the friend is neither the servility of the servant nor the importunity of the child; it is a conversation in the freedom of love, that shares and allows the other to share" (221). This friendship with God is a vital aspect of the mystery

of prayer, but this aspect remains most mysterious and meaningful only if God—that is, the triune God of salvation—remains sovereign and is not subsumed into the passion of the world.

51. Schmitt, *Political Theology II*, 91.

52. Ibid., 35, 96, and 113; Peterson, 68.

53. Metz, "Monotheism and Democracy," 146.

54. Maritain, *Man and the State*, 24–27. Metz would, incidentally, agree with Maritain's conviction that neither the state nor the people but only God is properly called "sovereign" (53) and, moreover, at a basic level, with Maritain's hope for a "Christianly inspired" but still democratic and pluralistic society (167).

55. Metz, *Followers of Christ*, 12, 35–39, and 41. Metz refers in this context to Bonhoeffer's *Cost of Discipleship*.

56. Metz, *Followers of Christ*, 47–52, 55, and 57–58.

57. Ibid., 60–61.

58. Ibid., 64–65.

59. Ibid., 64–67. Metz is not alone in his desire to retrieve the tradition of lament for contemporary theology. See especially the essays collected in Eva Harasta and Brian Brock, eds., *Evoking Lament*. Of particular interest is Matthias Wüthrich's contribution, "Lament for Naught?," 60–76. Analyzing Barth, Wüthrich draws attention to a danger that could also be diagnosed in Balthasar, namely that the theological emphasis on Christ's victory over nothingness could seem to compromise the theological relevance of the historical actuality of nothingness (71). Metz's *Leiden an Gott* preserves a place for the latter.

60. Metz, *Followers of Christ*, 66.

61. Ibid., 79–83.

62. Metz, "Courage to Pray," 5–8, 11, 17, 19, and 24–28.

63. Ibid., 9.

64. Emil Fackenheim describes the Shoah as a "*whole* of horror": "it was not random, piecemeal, accidental, but rather integrated into a *world*" (*To Mend the World*, 238).

65. Fackenheim insists on this point but also sees it as thoroughly aporetic. He argues that prayer is necessary now, more than ever, "because the prayed-for Messiah is necessary"; however, the very same prayer is "inaccessible because a Messiah that can come yet at Auschwitz did not come, is himself inaccessible" (ibid., 328).

66. In addition to several distinct essays, the key text is *Memoria Passionis: Ein provizierendes Gedächtnis in pluralistischer Gesellschaft* (The

remembrance of suffering: A provocative memory in pluralistic society). A more recent work, *Mystik der offenen Augen: Wenn Spiritualität aufbricht* (Mysticism of open eyes: When spirituality breaks open) develops similar themes but with less direct attention given to Auschwitz.

67. Metz, "Facing the Jews," 44.

68. Metz, "Christians and Jews," 40–41. Elie Wiesel makes a similar point: "I think that Christians have to try to understand what has happened to the Christian tradition. After all, Christianity is a religion of love. What happened to love? . . . Why were the Jews abandoned by so many Christians?" See Ekkehard Schuster and Reinhold Boschert-Kimmig, eds., *Hope against Hope*, 100.

69. Metz, "Facing the Jews," 41, translation slightly amended.

70. Metz, "Christians and Jews," 39 and 47–48, and "Church after Auschwitz," 123. See also *Nostra Aetate* 4, which states: "God holds the Jews most dear for the sake of their Fathers; He does not repent of the gifts He makes or of the calls He issues—such is the witness of the Apostle [Paul]."

71. Metz, "Christians and Jews," 42, and "Facing the Jews," 39 and 41.

72. In *To Mend the World*, Fackenheim tells the story of a Catholic priest named Bernhard Lichtenberg who, on November 10, 1938 (the day of *Kristallnacht*), witnessed violence and vandalism being perpetrated with impunity against the Jews in Berlin, and having seen this injustice—precisely with *open eyes*—"went back to his church and prayed publicly 'on behalf of the Jews and the poor concentration camp prisoners.' And he continued to recite his public prayer every day until, on October 23, 1941, he was at length arrested" (289). Lichtenberg was eventually killed for this public sign of prayerful solidarity. Fackenheim concludes that, in contrast to the many Christians who kept silent or closed their eyes to the violence, Lichtenberg courageously pointed the way toward a possible healing: hence, "Lichtenberg's prayer is *itself* a *Tikkun* [mending]" (292).

73. Metz, "Facing the Jews," 39.

74. Metz, "Theology as Theodicy?," 65–67 and *Memoria Passionis*, 52.

75. Metz, "Theology as Theodicy?," 55. Mary Boys, for instance, offers a richer historical—and consequently less eidetic—portrayal of first-century Judaism and the Jewishness of Jesus in *Has God Only One Blessing?*, 91–137.

76. R. Kendall Soulen's account of the standard way of typologically relating the Old and New Testaments reveals what would seem to be the

inevitability and the danger of this general approach (though, to be sure, the details can vary, and they matter a great deal). By contrast, Soulen's discussion of ancient and modern Gnostic anti-Judaism demonstrates the evidently greater danger involved in seeking to separate Christianity sharply from Judaism. See his *God of Israel and Christian Theology*; cf. Boys, *Has God Only One Blessing?*, 209–10.

77. During a dialogue at Münster in 1967, Metz was moved to declare that "we can pray *after* Auschwitz because people prayed *in* Auschwitz" only because he was pressed to do so by the Marxist philosopher Milan Machoveč, who, having cited Adorno's (alleged) claim that "after Auschwitz, there are no more poems," asked Metz whether, correlatively, there could be any prayers. The infamous saying of Adorno is in fact somewhat more nuanced: "To write poetry after Auschwitz is barbaric." Here "barbaric" has a technical meaning: it indicates the negative side of the dialectic of modern culture. Adorno's point is that, although the beauty of poetry would appear to be the very antithesis of the horror of Auschwitz, it is in fact, as a historical product, almost inevitably implicated in the very social and economic mechanisms that allowed Auschwitz to happen (consider the effective history of Hölderlin). Adorno's statement does not entail a straightforward prohibition, "no more poems," but rather only a critical awareness of modern culture's negative dialectics. His message is very similar to Benjamin's: "There is no document of civilization which is not at the same time a document of barbarism." See Metz, "Christians and Jews," 40; Adorno, "Cultural Criticism and Society," 330; and Benjamin, "Theses on the Philosophy of History," 257.

78. Metz, "Christians and Jews," 40, and *Memoria Passionis*, 9, 68, and 101. See also Celan and Sachs's *Correspondence*.

79. For a detailed study of the ambivalent relationship that Celan maintained with Heidegger throughout his life, including a few brief, mysterious encounters, see James Lyon's *Paul Celan and Martin Heidegger*.

80. This excerpt from Celan's "Psalm" is quoted in Derrida, "Shibboleth," 42. For the German original of the poem and a different, full English translation, see Celan, *Selected Poems and Prose*, 156–57.

81. Derrida, "Shibboleth," 42.

82. Lacoue-Labarthe, *Poetry as Experience*, 71 and 73.

83. Celan, *Selected Poems and Prose*, 260–61; Derrida, "Poetics and Politics of Witnessing," 70.

84. Celan, *Selected Poems and Prose*, 166–67.

85. Metz, *Memoria Passionis*, 98.

86. Celan, *Selected Poems and Prose*, 140–41, and Lacoue-Labarthe, *Poetry as Experience*, 83.

87. Sachs, *Seeker, and Other Poems*, 50–51, translation slightly modified.

88. Metz, *Memoria Passionis*, 101.

89. Ibid., 34, 67–68, and 100–101.

90. Despite his rather strong claims in *Memoria Passionis* regarding a "present eschatology" in the cry, Metz still does not believe that everything is already given. On the contrary, he continues to pray, *Maranatha!* He also adds an explicitly pneumatological element to this apocalyptic prayer, arguing that we should plead specifically for the gift of the Holy Spirit, who, according to the teachings of Jesus in Luke 11, will be given by the Father to those who ask. Thus, with both a christological and pneumatological accent, Metz insists that we must never cease to "ask God for God." However, this sense of apocalyptic longing and deferral, which we have encountered before, does not prevent Metz from acknowledging, in a rather bold way, that we are always already affected by the intimate presence of God, even in our anguish. See *Memoria Passionis*, 59, 95–96, and 149.

91. Metz, "Christians and Jews," 41.

92. Metz, "Theology as Theodicy?," 69–70, and *Memoria Passionis*, 3 and 7.

93. Metz, *Mystik der offenen Augen*, 63–65.

94. Ibid., 57 and 75–77.

95. Derrida demonstrates the teleological—and, therefore, not merely neutral or descriptive—character of Schmitt's concept of the political in *Politics of Friendship*, 132–33. In place of this teleology, Metz proposes a prayerfully sustained, practically engaged, and apocalyptically sharpened universal solidarity.

Chapter 5. Discernment of Spirits

1. Recent proponents of liberation theology have made significant advancements. In their works, the theory of dependency has given way to new analyses regarding the power dynamics of a neoliberal, neocolonial, and neoimperial age. The polarities of the Cold War era have been replaced and reconfigured by a growing awareness of the tragedies and ambiguities of globalization. Structures of economic domination have been shown to

intersect with other kinds of oppression related to cultural, racial, and sexual identities. These analytical advancements have been crucial. The main problem with the younger generation is that they have not yet given sufficient attention to the prayerful and doxological characteristics of an adequately Christian spirituality of liberation. For this reason, the present chapter focuses mainly on an earlier generation of liberation theologians to retrieve its spirit for today. For a sense of the current state of the conversation, see Marcella Maria Althaus-Reid, Ivan Petrella, and Luiz Carlos Susin, eds., *Another Possible World*; Petrella, ed., *Latin American Liberation Theology*; and Catherine Keller, Michael Nausner, and Mayra Rivera, eds., *Postcolonial Theologies*.

2. This point is by no means incompatible with Petrella's timely call for a more practically oriented renewal of liberation theology through dialogue with the social sciences. In his *Beyond Liberation Theology*, Petrella suggests that "whether people live or die is most directly related, not to theology, but to disciplines such as economics, political science, medical anthropology, sociology, development studies" (135). There is certainly some truth to this perspective. The preferential option for the poor needs to become concrete, in part, by being mediated through these disciplines. And yet, Petrella's hypothesis that "perhaps the future of liberation theology lies beyond theology" (148) and may require its "dissolution" as theology (150) is incompatible with the present argument. Instead of opting for one or the other, it seems that liberation theology should strive to become at once both more practically liberative and more theological (i.e., prayerful).

3. To be sure, other critics could be mentioned aside from Balthasar. However, to do justice to their particular arguments would require more discussion than is possible here. Nevertheless, it seems that if certain Balthasarian concerns could be alleviated, this would indicate a great deal about many other lines of critique (including those by some of the representatives of "radical orthodoxy") which either depend on or share many significant points in common with Balthasar's theological perspective.

4. This sampling of Latin American liberation theologians is meant to be representative, not exhaustive. Moreover, "representative" here does not mean that they disclose every aspect of this tradition that is worthy of attention but rather only that they help us appreciate some of the central issues. Here it would have been very possible to consider other prayerful works such as José Comblin, *Cry of the Oppressed*; Pedro Casaldáliga and José María Vigil, *Political Holiness*; Jon Sobrino, *Spirituality of Liberation*;

and Segundo Galilea, *Way of Living Faith*—to name just a few. Space does not permit anything like a comprehensive account.

5. Dussel, *El humanismo semita*, 49–50.

6. Ibid., 57–58.

7. Dussel, *El dualismo*, 263–70 and 282–8.

8. Dussel, *Philosophy of Liberation*, 48, 58, and 99. See also Levinas, *Totality and Infinity*, 33–52.

9. Nelson Maldonado-Torres questions the validity of this way of appropriating Levinas, arguing that Dussel "gives himself authority by portraying the role of the Other himself" (*Against War*, 183). The tension here is not unique to Dussel but is rather already evident in Levinas, insofar as the *implied* concrete other lying behind the purported abstractness of his discourse is precisely the Jewish people, those not comprehended and, therefore, violently rejected by the ontological and political totality of Europe. Dussel recognizes that the Jews and the people of Latin America find themselves in analogous situations of violence. In the case of these victimized communities, the almost paradoxical assertion of their *own alterity* must be understood as a historical act of resistance. And yet, the virtual inevitably of this practice of othered self-enunciation (or self-referential other-enunciation) does not take away the danger that Maldonado-Torres perceives. There will always be the need to attend to other others—with a hospitality that transgresses the limits of identity. We shall return to this tension in the next chapter.

10. Dussel, *Philosophy of Liberation*, 73, 95, and 97. Dussel's particular way of critiquing capitalist fetishism anticipates Denys Turner's recommendation that liberation theologians not merely deny any affiliation with Marx's atheism but rather take more seriously its connections with the apophatic traditions of Christian mystical theology stemming from Dionysius. Dussel maintains that, for Marx, "to deny the divinity of a fetishized system is . . . the negation of a negation." In this way, he highlights the doubly negative (i.e., formally Dionysian) character of Marx's atheism—which, by negating a negation of God, does not strictly predicate anything positive or negative of God. See Turner, "Marxism, Liberation Theology," 242.

11. Maldonado-Torres makes a similar point when he argues that Dussel seems to blend "the trans-ontological and the sub-ontological," i.e., the hyperousiological source of being, on the one hand, and the poor who have been expelled from the ontology of the system, on the other (*Against War*, 182). It is perhaps telling that Dussel more recently resolves this ambiguity

in favor of an "*exclusively* . . . anthropological" meaning of the other in his *Ethics of Liberation*, xxi.

12. Dussel, *Philosophy of Liberation*, 104.

13. Roberto Goizueta confirms this reading of Dussel in his *Liberation, Method and Dialogue*, arguing that, for Dussel, "the worship that God desires is service" (98). At the same time, Goizeuta maintains that "more systematically than other liberation theologians Dussel explicitly challenges and disavows any reductionism, including that of the closed negative dialectic" (148). To be sure, Dussel disavows *this* sort of reductionism: his Levinasian approach to transcendence suffices to break out of any kind of post-Hegelian dialectical totality, even the negative sort proposed by Adorno. But the specific reduction of doxology to solidaristic praxis seems to be, on the contrary, precisely secured by Dussel's appropriation of Levinas. For a more extensive account of the relationship between Dussel and Levinas, see Michael Barber, *Ethical Hermeneutics*, 1–81.

14. Dussel, *Las metáforas teológicas*, 208.

15. A similar sort of discussion can be developed around Marx's use of Ps. 115. Dussel notes that Marx pays particular attention to verse 4: "Their idols are silver and gold, the work of human hands" (NAB). It is not difficult to see how he might use this verse to critique the fetishism of capitalist society (ibid., 210–11). But, once again, neither he nor Dussel takes the opportunity to meditate on the meaning of the psalm as a whole, which is disclosed in lines such as: "Not to us, LORD, not to us, but to your name give glory" and "the house of Israel trusts in the LORD, who is their help and shield" (Ps. 115:1, 9 NAB).

16. Dussel, "Theology of Liberation and Marxism," 98.

17. Dussel, *Ethics and Community*, 222.

18. One last example that should be mentioned is the poem "Psalm 5— A Paraphrase," by Ernesto Cardenal (in his collection *Psalms*), which Dussel includes as an epigraph in his *History of the Church*.

19. Alfred Hennelly helpfully identifies some of the elements of a latent spirituality in Segundo's works; nevertheless, he does not bring out the potentially negative significance of Segundo's gradual departure from a constitutively prayerful spirituality. See Hennelly's *Theologies in Conflict*, 140–56. The present reading seeks to fill this lacuna.

20. Segundo, *Theology for Artisans*, vol. 2, *Grace and the Human Condition*, 63, 73, 139, and 158. The original title of this series is *Teologia abierta para el laico adulto* [Open theology for the adult laity].

21. Ibid., 48–49.

22. Segundo, *Our Idea of God*, 42.

23. Segundo asserts: "It is as if Jesus had said something like this: 'Through my resurrection and sending of the Spirit, I have replaced proclamation with reality. Henceforth I shall never calm the storm again as I once did. But my Spirit will calm the storm when you have mastered the technique of constructing ships strong enough to ride out its waves. I shall never again return to feed a multitude in the desert, but I shall do it when my creative Spirit in you has led them to improve the earth's soil and distribute its fruit better'" (ibid., 44).

24. It is conceivable that one would want to side in this debate with Segundo and against Heidegger precisely insofar as the latter's doxology involves a dangerous form of ontological fatalism, which discourages the very sort of responsible and solidaristic action that Segundo rightly demands. Thus, instead of simply succumbing to Heidegger's critique of modern technology, Segundo's liberation theology could expose its limits and perils. To the extent that the increasing control of nature that human beings have sought in modernity allows them, for instance, to "improve the earth's soil and distribute its fruit better," Segundo seems right to suggest that this technology should be affirmed as a grace, i.e., a divine gift, which is no less gracious for having been mediated by the work of human hands. Nevertheless, the problem with Segundo's approach is that it seems to limit God's action to the domain of human action.

25. Segundo appropriates this Hegelian logic at least partly through his reading of Nikolai Berdyaev in his *Berdiaeff: Une réflexion chrétienne sur la personne*, 299–313. He develops his evolutionary perspective in dialogue with Teilhard de Chardin in the fifth volumes of both of his major series.

26. Segundo, *Our Idea of God*, 8, 10n6, and 178.

27. Segundo, *Liberation of Theology*, 9, 17, and 90–94.

28. Segundo, *Faith and Ideologies*, 15. The original title of this series is *El hombre de hoy ante Jesús de Nazaret* [The human being of today after Jesus of Nazareth].

29. Ibid., 319.

30. A few points can be made about the second and third volumes. In *The Historical Jesus of the Synoptics*, Segundo largely neglects Jesus's practice of prayer and his teachings regarding prayer and, of course, omits the Johannine doxological perspective (which, by contrast, Balthasar prioritizes). He does make a few points about the Our Father, emphasizing that

it is a prayer for the coming of the kingdom, for the realization of the will of God on earth, and that its effectiveness is guaranteed by the work of the Spirit, which he continues to understand in a somewhat Hegelian, i.e., anthropologically reductive, manner (143–44, 208n20, 212n13). Likewise, in *The Humanist Christology of Paul*, which is essentially a commentary on the first eight chapters of Romans, Segundo quotes the famous passage in Romans 8:26–27 regarding the intercessions of the Spirit without the slightest mention of its significance for the life of prayer. Moreover, he transfers Paul's eschatological anticipation of divine glory onto a predominantly historical and human plane (126–44). In both works, Segundo gives the distinct impression that prayer has very little to do with the meaning of the New Testament for his own time—that is, the critically reconstructed meaning that he thinks alone has relevance now in a more mature and enlightened age (i.e., modernity).

31. Segundo, *Christ of the Ignatian Exercises*, 111, 116, and 124.

32. Ibid., 41, 49, 61, and 71. We shall see, in light of Ellacuría's engagement with Ignatius, that Segundo's theologically costly dichotomies are not necessary. Liberation theology can be developed in concert with Ignatian spirituality without subjecting the latter to this sort of distortion.

33. Although he had been inspired by Dominican theologians for much of his life—including Marie-Dominique Chenu, Yves Congar, Edward Schillebeeckx, and perhaps especially Bartolomé de Las Casas—Gutiérrez did not become a member of the Order of Preachers until 1999. Nevertheless, the influence of this tradition can be discerned in works that precede this date.

34. Gutiérrez, *Theology of Liberation*. The revised edition cited here contains a new introduction (from 1988) that adds greater emphasis to the importance of prayer (xxxi). Many interpreters of Gutiérrez's works have drawn attention to the prayerful spirituality that runs throughout them. See, for instance, the foreword by J. Matthew Ashley and the introduction by Daniel Groody in *Gustavo Gutiérrez: Spiritual Writings*, 11–15 and 21–43; Carlos Luy Montejo, *Armut und Spiritualität*, 57–74; Alexander Nava, *Mystical and Prophetic Thought*, 79–105; and Robert McAfee Brown, *Gustavo Gutiérrez*, 61–62. However, this aspect of his thought is not always emphasized. Curt Cadorette's nevertheless very rewarding book, *From the Heart of the People*, does not directly address it.

35. Gutiérrez, *Theology of Liberation*, 19–24, 86, 89–91, and 132. Although Gutiérrez seeks to move beyond the scholastic "distinction of

planes model," in which the natural and the supernatural are treated as two independent orders, and although he therefore rejects any straightforward division between profane and salvation history, he nevertheless does not subscribe to a *strictly* monistic theory of reality. On the contrary, he maintains a clear analogical distinction between the modern utopian project of building a new society and the essentially gratuitous and Christic manifestation of the kingdom of God: the latter begins to appear within the former but also decisively transcends it (39–46 and 86).

36. Ibid., 6, 74, 112–16, and 119.

37. Ibid., 108, 119–20, 169, and 231n48. See Ernesto Cardenal, *Psalms*.

38. Ibid., 3–12 and 117.

39. McAfee Brown's defense of Gutiérrez in response to certain critics who accuse his work of being overdetermined by Marxism is compelling. McAfee Brown is not wrong to suggest that such a defense could be constructed on the basis of *A Theology of Liberation* alone. However, his decision to prioritize *We Drink from Our Own Wells* is significant. There is a shift between these two texts toward a less ambiguous and more thoroughly prayerful hermeneutic. See McAfee Brown, "Spirituality and Liberation," 395–404.

40. Gutiérrez already discusses Metz's thought in *Theology of Liberation*, arguing that Metz's critique of privatized religion does not sufficiently address the particular crises of the Latin American context (126–30). However, the more significant encounter that he has with Metz in this earlier work occurs in the form of a positive but unstated agreement regarding the theological and practical implications of the poverty of spirit, which both he and Metz understand as a radical Christic availability to the will of God and as a call to solidarity with the materially poor (162–74). One should not overlook the fact that *Theology of Liberation* ends precisely on this solidaristically *kenotic* note.

41. Gutiérrez, *On Job*, 102, and *God of Life*, 117. We have seen that Metz does not neglect this contemporary reality altogether. In fact, his mysticism of "open eyes" is very much concerned with it. But Gutiérrez's focus on the present is nevertheless more pronounced.

42. Gutiérrez, *We Drink from Our Own Wells*, 22, 129–35, and 170n2. See also J. Hernández Pico, "La oración."

43. Gutiérrez, *On Job*, 39–49 and 68.

44. Ibid., 101.

45. Gutiérrez, *God of Life*, xviii and 45–47.

46. Gutiérrez, *Sharing the Word*, 54, 122, 193, and 251.

47. For a sense of Gutiérrez's worldwide impact, see Marc Ellis and Otto Maduro, eds., *Future of Liberation Theology*.

48. Brief discussions of Boff's spirituality can be found in Horst Goldstein, *Leonardo Boff*, 75–81 and 96–100, and in Mathai Kadavil, *World as Sacrament*, 154–59. However, more remains to be said regarding the significance of the distinctively prayerful and doxological nature of this spirituality.

49. For a fuller treatment of this tradition, see Karlfried Froehlich, "Lord's Prayer."

50. Boff, *Lord's Prayer*, 7, 59, 82, and 115.

51. Ibid., 11, 51, and 122.

52. Ibid., italics added.

53. Ibid., 44–45 and 95.

54. Balthasar, *Glory of the Lord*, 1:165.

55. We shall briefly consider each of these three theological topics here, leaving aside the question of Boff's ecclesiology, which would require a much lengthier discussion. See Kjell Nordstokke, *Council and Context*.

56. Boff, *Jesus Christ Liberator*, 61, 159, 253, and 291–92. In another work called *Way of the Cross—Way of Justice*, Boff offers a reflection on the traditional Catholic devotion known as "The Stations of the Cross." Describing his motivations, he states: "Theology is true insofar as it is translated into meditation, prayer, conversion, the following of Christ, and commitment to our fellow human beings" (vii). These diverse aspects of his spirituality are inseparable and mutually enriching. Having formulated the fruits of prayer into a Christology, he now seeks to "transmute" (viii) them back into prayer and life. His goal is to produce a "prayerful theology or theological prayer" (x), precisely the sort of synthesis that we are seeking in this work.

57. Boff, *Liberating Grace*, 3, 6, and 216. These are the prayerful words that Boff believes most powerfully evoke the experience of grace: "O Lord, you have probed me and you know me; / . . . / Truly you have formed my inmost being; / You knit me in my mother's womb. / I give you thanks that I am fearfully, wonderfully made; / Wonderful are your works" (Drury's translation of Boff's translation of Ps. 139).

58. Ibid., 60–69. To be clear, Boff believes that "communist state capitalism" must be critiqued as well as its privatized Western forms; moreover, he contends that this critique needs to take place on similar grounds: i.e., in view of the consequences for the poor and modernity's disgraceful negations of prayer and life (114).

59. Ibid., 61.

60. Ibid., 63. As an example, Boff reflects on Teresa of Ávila's contemplative experience of the indwelling of the Trinity, as recounted in the *Interior Castle* (ibid., 211–12).

61. Boff, *Trinity and Society*, 134–47, 152, 174, 185, 188, 207, and 228–31.

62. Boff, *Francis of Assisi*, 4–15 and 34. Boff's engagement with Francis enables him to recover a solidaristic form of spiritual poverty, which he deploys in response to the crises of modernity. In this respect, he comes very close to Metz and Gutiérrez. Boff explains that, for Francis, the virtue of poverty involves "a way of being by which the individual lets things be what they are; one refuses to dominate them, subjugate them, and make them the objects of the will to power" (35). This disposition frees Francis to enter into loving communion with God; with other human beings, especially the poorest and most outcast members of society; and with all the celestial and earthly creatures of the universe. Francis's practice of poverty, therefore, combines elements of Heideggerian *Gelassenheit*, Balthasarian kenosis, and liberationist solidarity into a single way of life.

63. Boff, *Cry of the Earth*, xi, 1–4, 86–103, and 211.

64. Boff takes up this topic in a short text called *The Prayer of Saint Francis*. The focus of this book is the prayer, commonly but inaccurately attributed to Francis, that begins "Lord, make me an instrument of your peace," which Boff explains first appeared in 1913 in Normandy in connection with the Catholic devotion to the Sacred Heart of Jesus. He contends that, although Francis did not actually compose this prayer, it faithfully expresses his spirit and offers great hope for contemporary society (5–9).

65. Ibid., 22 and 36–39.

66. The other victims of this crime were Celina Ramos; Elba Ramos; Ignacio Martín-Baró, S.J.; Segundo Montes, S.J.; Amando López, S.J.; Juan Ramón Moreno, S.J.; and Joacquin López y López, S.J. For an account of the facts and context of these murders, along with personal and theological remembrances of those who were killed, see Jon Sobrino, Ignacio Ellacuría, et al., *Companions of Jesus*.

67. See, for instance, Kevin Burke, *Ground beneath the Cross*, 26–33 and 43–120; Antonio González, "Assessing the Philosophical Achievement," 73–87; Robert Lassalle-Klein, "Ignacio Ellacuría's Debt to Xavier Zubiri," 88–127; and Michael Lee, *Bearing the Weight*, 40–72.

68. Lassalle-Klein offers a brief but helpful discussion in his introduction to *Love That Produces Hope*, xviii–xx, drawing on Rudolfo Cardenal's biographical essay, "De Portugalete a San Salvador." But more needs to be said about the theological significance of this connection.

69. Burke, *Ground beneath the Cross*, 28.

70. Zubiri, *Nature, History, God*, 311–13.

71. Zubiri, *Man and God*, 101, 144, and 148–49.

72. Ellacuría, "La superación del reduccionismo idealista," 403–30.

73. Zubiri, *Nature, History, God*, 338.

74. To be sure, Marion is not the only contemporary figure with whom Zubiri's thought resonates. One might also recognize a certain affinity with Merleau-Ponty and Levinas—and, consequently, with Dussel, who, incidentally, studied for a time with Zubiri and who identifies some overlap between Zubiri's discussion of reality and Levinas's account of alterity. See Linda Martín Alcoff and Eduardo Mendieta, eds., *Thinking from the Underside*, 17, and Dussel, "Domination—Liberation," 36n10. Dussel's ethically obligating other, approached precisely through the flesh, would perhaps be one of the most crucial figures of that very richness of reality that escapes the Heideggerian comprehension of being, which Zubiri seeks to recover. These are connections that deserve greater attention, especially insofar as they indicate Zubiri's—and, therefore, Ellacuría's—potential to contribute to a postmetaphysical doxology.

75. Zubiri, *Man and God*, 17–88.

76. Ellacuría highlights this connection between Heidegger and Zubiri explicitly in relation to the manifestation of God in "Existencialismo ateo" (Atheistic existentialism, 1968), particularly in the section entitled "El humanismo onto-teo-lógico de Heidegger" (The onto-theo-logical humanism of Heidegger"), 625–44. Here Ellacuría is perhaps somewhat too sympathetic to Heidegger's idea that the dimension of the sacred (*Heil*) mediates any possible arrival of the truly divine God. Ellacuría closely aligns Heidegger's notion of the sacred with Zubiri's formal account of "deity," which appears in the first stage of his intellectual progression toward God (642–44).

77. Zubiri, *Man and God*, 131.

78. Ibid., 140.

79. Przywara's expression appears to have the advantage over Zubiri's, even though, in another respect, Przywara's larger project (*Analogia Entis*) is arguably somewhat vulnerable to Zubiri's post-Heideggerian critique of the entification of reality.

80. Ellacuría, "Historicity of Christian Salvation," 254.

81. Ellacuría qualifies his position when he argues that "God is transcendent among other reasons, not by being absent, but by being freely present—sometimes in one way and sometimes in another, choosing the

ways freely as the Lord, with different levels of intensity, in God's own self-giving will" (ibid., 255). With the brief phrase "among other reasons," Ellacuría leaves open the possibility of speaking of different kinds of transcendence, contingent on divine freedom, which would not all necessarily be immanent to our perception of inner-worldly reality. He, therefore, does not strictly foreclose the sort of properly analogical logic that seems most helpful here, even though he tends to underscore only the immanent side of it. In *The Touch of Transcendence*, Mayra Rivera appropriates the Zubirian-Ellacurían idea of God's immanent ("intracosmic") transcendence and contrasts it with the supposed position of radical orthodoxy that God is only transcendent beyond things (41–54). The in-built tensions of Przywara's thought-form allow one to avoid making any undesirably dichotomous choices in this debate.

82. See Burke, *Ground beneath the Cross*, 53 and 58–60; González, "Assessing the Philosophical Achievement," 79–80; and Lasalle-Klein, "Ignacio Ellacuría's Debt to Xavier Zubiri,"104–9.

83. Lasalle-Klein and Rudolfo Cardenal emphasize the intensity of the connection between these two figures, as attested by Ellacuría's personal letters to Martinez, in which he writes such intimate lines as: "Your life echoes in mine, in its deepest and most spiritual dimensions." See Lasalle-Klein, introduction to *Love That Produces Hope*, xix, and Ellacuría, "Correspondencia con Angel Martinez," 197–213.

84. Ellacuría, "[Angel Martinez Baigorri, S.J.]," 118.

85. Angel Martinez, *Angel in el país del águila*, quoted in Ellacuría, "Angel Martinez, poeta esencial," 162.

86. Ellacuría, "[Angel Martinez Baigorri, S.J.]," 119.

87. Ellacuría, "Angel Martinez, poeta esencial," 146, 192, and 194.

88. The demanded conversion here is arguably more specific than that which is communicated to Rilke, and subsequently to Balthasar, by the archaic torso of Apollo.

89. Ellacuría, "Angel Martinez, poeta esencial," 129–34, 145, and 183.

90. Ibid., 149 and 157.

91. Ellacuría's *Freedom Made Flesh* (originally *Teología política*, 1973), 233–46; "Liberación en los Salmos" (1967), 107–21; and his essays collected under the heading "Sobre Monseñor Romero," 75–116.

92. For an account of Ellacuría's debts to Rahner, see Martin Maier, "Karl Rahner," 128–43.

93. Ellacuría, "Espiritualidad," 47.

94. Lasalle-Klein, introduction to *Love That Produces Hope*, xv–xvi.

95. Ellacuría, "Espiritualidad," 47–49.

96. Ibid., 51–56.

97. Ellacuría, "Lectura," 59–106. The following argument presupposes and builds upon Ashley's analysis of this text (along with some of Ellacuría's other explicitly Ignatian texts) in his "Ignacio Ellacuría and the *Spiritual Exercises*" and "Contemplation in the Action of Justice." The present discussion makes an additional contribution mainly by highlighting the theme of discernment and by situating Ellacuría's reading of Ignatius within a larger assessment of the significance of prayerful thought in the context of the crises of modernity.

98. Ellacuría, "Lectura," 69.

99. The two soteriological foci discussed here appear, among other places, in Ellacuría, *Freedom Made Flesh*, 3–19, and "Historicity of Christian Salvation." For a more complete account of Ellacuría's soteriology and its significance, consult Lee, *Bearing the Weight*.

100. It does not seem possible to establish with certainty whether Ellacuría's distinction between salvation history and salvation in history *emerges* from or is only subsequently *applied* to his experience of the *Spiritual Exercises*. One reason is simply that his practice of the Exercises (beginning in 1947) predates his first explicit elaboration of this distinction (in *Teología política* in 1973, translated as *Freedom Made Flesh*), which in turn predates his most comprehensive commentary on the Exercises, in which this distinction appears (1974). But it is fair to conclude that, for Ellacuría, the *Spiritual Exercises* cannot be understood on their own terms without *some* such distinction: that is, they compel one to meditate and contemplate not only what God has done for us in the past but also what we are called to do in our own contemporary contexts and, therefore, what God continues to do salvifically through us. And this is the crucial point: his twofold soteriology is entailed by his Ignatian spirituality.

101. Ellacuría, "Lectura," 69–73.

102. Ibid., 74–75.

103. In fact, Ellacuría uses the First Week as the basis for one of his talks for the decisive meeting of Central American Jesuits in 1969, entitled "Nuestra situation," 177–96. In this text, he expresses many of the ideas outlined in his later, 1974 reading of the whole *Spiritual Exercises*.

104. Ellacuría, "Lectura," 77–79.

105. Ibid., 83–86.

106. In order to counteract what he considers the "specifically evil" forms of violence that he sees everywhere around him—the violence that

is produced by our many sinful attachments to riches, honor, and pride—Ellacuría argues that there are a range of Christian options, represented by Charles de Foucauld (nonviolent nonresistance), Martin Luther King Jr. (nonviolent resistance), and Camilo Torrez (provisionally violent resistance). He distinguishes these options without absolutely affirming or rejecting any of them. His point is that we need to discern what is the most appropriate form of counterviolent Christian discipleship in specific circumstances. See his *Freedom Made Flesh*, 217–26.

107. Ellacuría, "Lectura," 87. For Ellacuría's many nuanced responses to Marxism, see the collection of essays "Marxismo y teología de la liberación," 461–517.

108. Ellacuría, "Lectura," 94, 97, and 99.

109. Ibid., 93, 94, and 98.

110. For further confirmation of this point, see Ellacuría, "Escatología e historia," 95–124.

111. Ellacuría, "Lectura," 100–101.

112. Ibid., 102–5.

113. Ellacuría, *Fe y justicia*.

114. Ellacuría, "Liberación en los Salmos," 114.

115. Ellacuría, *Fe y justicia*, 214. In the same context, and for similar reasons, Ellacuría critiques the Dominican maxim *contemplata aliis tradere*. In his estimation, it allows prayer to remain too separable from worldly engagement. With Gutiérrez, however, we have seen that this need not be the case.

116. See the following essays in *Love That Produces Hope*: Metz, "Toward a Christianity of Political Compassion," 250–53; Gutiérrez, "No One Takes My Life from Me," 68–72; and Sobrino, "Ignacio Ellacuría, the Human Being, and the Christian," especially 42–60.

Chapter 6. Songs of the Spirit

1. For a fuller account of the development, the diversity, and the meaning of this spirituality during the period of slavery, see Albert Raboteau, *Slave Religion*.

2. Commenting on this marginalizing tendency, Bryan Massingale argues that the Catholic Church in particular will not be able to break its historical ties to antiblack racism until it rids itself of the "pervasive belief that European aesthetics, music, theology, and persons—and only

these—are standard, normative, universal, and truly 'Catholic.'" The present chapter has been written with this insight in mind. See Massingale, *Racial Justice*, 80.

3. See, for example, Angie Pears, *Doing Contextual Theology*, 111–17, and Sigurd Bergmann, *God in Context*, 3 and 13. Certainly there is some value in theological projects that are self-consciously produced in and for a particular context; and certainly every work of theology, whether one recognizes it or not, is conditioned by the contexts from which it arose; and certainly, therefore, one cannot expect the merits of any work of theology to be preserved perfectly and unambiguously as it is translated into contexts that are significantly different from those in which it first took shape. None of this is in dispute here. The problem is that the label "contextual" tends to confer upon black theology, and other marginalized theological traditions, an explicitly distinct and unequal status. It discourages one from considering whether these sorts of theology could be relevant to the entire body of Christ and in this sense become genuinely catholic—potentially in the same category as the theology of Augustine (an African) or any other theology that might be studied simply *as theology*, while also, of course, having significant contextual features.

4. This elevated status is certainly not the *exclusive* property of the spirituals. Nevertheless, the positive argument here is that it does in fact pertain to them. This leaves open the possibility for analogous claims to be defended with respect to other extraordinary traditions of prayer within the globally diverse church.

5. Cone draws a distinction between the structurally racist form of "whiteness" that is constituted as an oppressive force against blackness and the mere phenomenon of lighter-skinned or so-called white people. He acknowledges that the latter phenomenon does not necessarily entail the former structure of power. At the same time, he contends (and he has good reasons to do so) that the two have largely coincided in modern history. See Cone, *Black Theology of Liberation*, 7–8 and 204n4. To be clear, the problem here is not with any theology that happens to be developed by phenotypically white people but rather with any theology that has certain characteristics of racist "whiteness." In this chapter, we shall use the terms "white" and "whiteness" in quotation marks when referring specifically to racist distortions of given—and thus in themselves inoffensive and even beautiful—modes of lightly colored embodiment.

6. Gutiérrez, for his part, does add an explicit condemnation of racism to his revised edition of *Theology of Liberation*, xxii.

7. David Theo Goldberg makes the point about the dangers of "color-blind" racism in *Threat of Race*, 17–30. By contrast, Paul Gilroy stresses the dangers of a reified conception of race in *Against Race*, 11–53. Between these two positions on the question of race and, more particularly, of blackness, we find an aporia: there seems to be a need to employ this term and to deconstruct it at the same time. The suggestion made here is that the historical concreteness and transcendent hope that one finds in the spirituals may give them an unmatched ability to disclose new theoretical and practical pathways through this aporia, at least among those who have some attraction to a Christian experience of prayer and are interested in its contemporary implications.

8. Gayraud Wilmore, *Black Religion and Black Radicalism*.

9. Cone, *Black Theology and Black Power*, 108–9 and 137.

10. Ibid., 97, 102, and 114.

11. Ibid., 94–103.

12. Ibid., 95.

13. Ibid., 33 and 48–50. See also Cone, *My Soul Looks Back*, 54–57.

14. Cone, *Black Theology and Black Power*, 71–90 and 103–15.

15. Cone, *A Black Theology of Liberation*, 20, 26, 34, and 58.

16. Cone, *My Soul Looks Back*, 59–60, and "Interpretation of the Debate," 430–36. Cone mentions the critical remarks of Charles Long, Carleton Lee, Gayraud Wilmore, and his brother Cecil Cone.

17. Cone, *My Soul Looks Back*, 61.

18. Cone, *Spirituals and the Blues*, 3, 19, 102–3, and 125.

19. The allusion here is to George Lindbeck's category of "experiential-expressivism," as formulated in *Nature of Doctrine*, 16, albeit with one significant modification: "cultural expressivism" does not seek to ground theology in universal human experience but rather in the experience of a particular culture. Moreover, the relevant distinction in the present argument is not between an experiential and grammatical account of doctrine but rather between a more adequately and less adequately prayerful form of theology. It is important to clarify that Cone is not simply a "cultural-expressivist" in order to show that the Christian prayer of black people, and not merely black culture as such, supplies the decisive hermeneutical principle for his theology. By contrast, one might consider the approach of Dwight N. Hopkins. Although he likewise reflects deeply on the spirituals—in works such as *Shoes That Fit Our Feet*, 13–48, and *Down, Up, and Over*—he tends to treat these songs as normative primarily insofar as they are expressive of black culture. He gives them essentially the same theological status as the

folk stories of Brer Rabbit, the novels of Toni Morrison, and the political reflections of W. E. B. DuBois. He presents all of these disparate elements together as one set of *nonprioritized* sources. Like Hopkins, Cone incorporates many elements of black culture, even of a more nearly secular nature; however, unlike Hopkins, he gives a much clearer interpretative priority to prayerful sources.

20. Raboteau gives a fuller picture of the debate regarding African "retentions," while discussing important differences between the levels of adaptation and destruction that took place in Latin and British American slave contexts. He suggests that the large plantations, greater influx of African slaves, and certain aspects of the Catholic milieu (especially sacramentality and devotion to saints) allowed for a higher degree of religious mixture in South America and the Caribbean. At the same time, he believes that some stylistic features of African worship (related especially to movement, song, and the call-and-response structure) survived in the more predominantly Protestant, North American tradition of slave spirituals. See Raboteau, *Slave Religion*, 44–92.

21. Cone, *Spirituals and the Blues*, 29 and 33. See also Cone, *Black Theology of Liberation*, 63–66.

22. That "contemplation" is an appropriate term to describe certain dimensions of the black spiritual tradition has been demonstrated in an unparalleled way by Barbara Holmes in *Joy Unspeakable*.

23. Cone, *Spirituals and the Blues*, 33–34, 41, 44–52, 71–77, and 83–87.

24. Ibid., 1; Cone, *God of the Oppressed*, 1–14; and Cone, *My Soul Looks Back*, 17–40, 42, 48, 57, and 80–81. For another example of the individually transformative power of the spirituals, see Raboteau's moving testimony in *Sorrowful Joy*, 35. Raboteau interestingly connects the themes of this black tradition of prayer with his experiences of Roman Catholic and Eastern Orthodox liturgies and with the witness of other holy men and women, such as Thomas Merton, Dorothy Day, St. Cuthbert, and St. Francis.

25. Cone, *For My People*, 63–64; *Speaking the Truth*, 17–34 and 129–41; *Risks of Faith*, 13–27; and *Martin & Malcolm & America*, 227.

26. Cone, *Cross and the Lynching Tree*, 1–29, 126–45, and 152–60.

27. Cone, *Black Theology of Liberation*, 8, 77, and 92.

28. Carter, *Race*, 161, 171, 175, 182, and 425n55.

29. In his "Tillich and the Postmodern," John Thatamanil seeks to defend Tillich against the sort of "postmodern" theological critique that Carter's work seems to represent. Thatamanil points to the apophatic aspects of

Tillich's theory of symbolic language, the understanding of God not only as ground but also as abyss, the refusal to represent God as an existent entity, the classification of causality and substance merely as symbolic terms, and even Marion's contention that the mere decision to refer to God as being is not sufficient to qualify one as a strictly metaphysical (i.e., ontotheological) thinker (291–93). And yet, if there are therefore certain respects in which Tillich resists Heidegger's precise definition of metaphysics, it does not follow that all of the problems have been sufficiently alleviated. Tillich's considerable dependence on the speculative tradition uniting Scotus, Boehme, and Schelling (298) and his elaboration of a somewhat idealist ontological framework for theology leave room for suspicion, not merely on general "postmodern" grounds (which vary in adequacy), but more exactly on the grounds of a rigorous thinking of prayer—a possibility which Carter develops, in his own way, through his interpretation of Jarena Lee (*Race*, 333–37).

30. Cone, *Black Theology and Black Power*, 7.

31. Cone, *Black Theology of Liberation*, 60. One should not conclude, therefore, that Cone recommends equal doses of both Barth and Tillich or believes that any sort of conjunction between the two would suffice. Rather, for him, Barth's doxological approach appears to correspond more closely to the theology of the slaves, whereas Tillich's focus on the conditions of human existence provides an important—albeit somewhat secondary—addendum, which helps to fill out the finite side of the analogical relation.

32. Cone, *Spirituals and the Blues*, 32 and 50.

33. Ibid., 41–42, 46, 50–51, and 80.

34. Cone, *Black Theology of Liberation*, 59, 63, and 79.

35. Ibid., 24.

36. Cone, *Spirituals and the Blues*, 90.

37. Cone, *Cross and the Lynching Tree*, 156.

38. Cone, *Spirituals and the Blues* and *Cross and the Lynching Tree*, 93–119. For an analysis of the underappreciated poetic significance of the spirituals, see Lauri Ramey, *Slave Songs*.

39. As an example, see the wealth of biblical references in Cone, *God of the Oppressed*, 57–76. His other texts attest to this perspective as well.

40. Cone, *Spirituals and the Blues*, 81.

41. Ibid., 44.

42. Cone, *Speaking the Truth*, 21.

43. Cone, *Cross and the Lynching Tree*, 23–25.

44. Ibid., 25; Cone, *God of the Oppressed*, 12.

45. Cone, *Black Theology and Black Power*, 149–51.

46. Ibid., 18.

47. One might prefer to call this phenomenon *black doxology*, in order to stress the fact that it makes the practice of doxology explicit. However, the term "doxological blackness" still applies insofar as the substantive proves to be somewhat interchangeable.

48. Anderson, *Beyond Ontological Blackness*, 61–76 and 120–21.

49. Ibid., 15, 30, 49, 91, and 93.

50. Ibid., 93 and 99.

51. Ibid., 118–58.

52. Cone, *Black Theology of Liberation*, 204n5.

53. Anderson, *Creative Exchange*, 140.

54. Anderson, *Beyond Ontological Blackness*, 64–76.

55. Ibid., 13.

56. Anderson develops his critique of this procedure at greater length in *Creative Exchange*, 53–79.

57. Cone, *God of the Oppressed*, 139. He explicitly hopes for a day in which "the *status* of master no longer exists" (218).

58. Ibid., 221.

59. Cone, *Black Theology and Black Power*, 15–17.

60. Cone, "Martin, Malcolm, and Black Theology," 61.

61. See David Brakke, "Ethiopian Demons," 501–35, and Mark Scott, "Shades of Grace," 65–83.

62. To be clear, neither Cone nor the authors of the spirituals would have anyone believe that black people are uniquely holy simply by virtue of being black. On the contrary, he argues that black people, like all people, are susceptible to sin and can, therefore, act in ways that are contrary to the will of God. He observes that many of the slaves, while confessing their need for prayer and forgiveness in song, emphasized "the ethical responsibilities of members within the black community" (*Spirituals and the Blues*, 74–76). His point, therefore, is certainly not that black people should be embraced only on the condition that they would be perfectly blameless in the Lord's eyes. This would be an impossible requirement. Rather, his position is that black people deserve to be welcomed as normal, fallible human beings who, having been created and redeemed in Christ, are inestimably worthy of love.

63. Cone, *God of the Oppressed*, 132.

64. Ibid., 145–49 and 208.

65. In a sense, this entire section is dedicated to the task of showing that Cone's political theology is not absolutely determined by the friend-enemy distinction that Schmitt argues is definitive of the political. Beyond

this distinction, which admittedly is somewhat operative (see *Black Theology and Black Power*, 26 and 145), there is a more thoroughgoing logic of hospitality stemming from the life of prayer.

66. Cone, *Black Theology and Black Power*, 13, and *Black Theology of Liberation*, 42–43 and 78–79.

67. Cone, *God of the Oppressed*, 58.

68. Ibid., 151–63.

69. William Jones, *Is God a White Racist?*, 98–120. These pages summarize Jones's critical reflections on Cone. The central limitation of Jones's argument is that he demands that God's liberating will for black people be historically "demonstrated," "substantiated," and "established" (these are some of his terms), as though the validity of Cone's theological hope in the midst of unjust suffering would necessarily depend on his ability to supply a verifiable (indeed, already verified) defense of God's justice concerning black humanity—i.e., a rational theodicy in the strict sense, albeit of a more empirical nature than Leibniz's deductive alternative. This sort of verification is something that Cone cannot be asked to provide, except in the mode of a promise, which is precisely what he offers through his recollection of the exodus and the Christ-event. Cone's belief in God as the liberator of the oppressed—including blacks in the United States—is nothing other than a prayerful and practically embodied hope grounded in this biblical promise.

70. Cone, *God of the Oppressed*, 161 and 173–74, and *Cross and the Lynching Tree*, 19 and 27. Cone not only refuses to endorse any particular theodicy. He also avoids the related Hegelian danger of positing a negative principle in the Godhead as a kind of explanatory ground for inner-worldly suffering. We have seen that Balthasar and Marion adopt a modest version of this strategy, through their reflections on the distance between the Trinitarian persons as a quasi-foundational origin of inner-worldly differences and negations. Carter expresses a similar idea and even critiques Cone for omitting this sort of speculation (*Race*, 168). However, the fact that Cone does not develop a Trinitarian explanation of the insubstantiality of evil does not, as Carter suggests, imply that Cone treats evil as an ontological substance in some sort of Hegelian—and ultimately nihilistic—fashion. On the contrary, it means that he refuses to participate in this entire conversation. Cone responds to evil not with elaborate theory (whether Neoplatonic or modern dialectical) but rather with salvation-historical doxology, anguished prayer, and serious struggle. In this respect, he is much closer to Metz.

71. Cone, "From Geneva to São Paulo," 376; "Black American Perspective on the Future of African Theology," 396; and *Cross and the Lynching Tree*, xiv.

72. Cone, *Martin & Malcolm & America*, 234–43; *Risks of Faith*, 82–95; and *My Soul Looks Back*, 136.

73. Cone, *Speaking the Truth*, 154.

74. Cone, *My Soul Looks Back*, 92.

75. Cone learns from his womanist colleagues that poor black women have historically suffered from the additional burden of sexism, and he increasingly attends to this problem (ibid., 117–23). For fuller accounts of such intersectionality, see Delores Williams, *Sisters in the Wilderness*, 60–83, and Shawn Copeland, *Enfleshing Freedom*, 23–46. Emilie Townes develops a distinctive form of womanist doxological spirituality in response to this complex reality in her *In a Blaze of Glory*. A thorough engagement with this important body of literature lies beyond the scope of the present project.

76. One might draw another parallel between Gutiérrez and Cone insofar as they both explicitly connect doxological spirituality with the liturgical act of preaching. Cone reflects on the tradition of black preaching in *God of the Oppressed*, 17.

77. Cone, *Black Theology and Black Power*, 38, 40, 51, and 56–57; *Black Theology of Liberation*, 7; *God of the Oppressed*, 139–44; and *Cross and the Lynching Tree*, xiv.

78. Segundo, *Liberation of Theology*, 25–34.

79. Cone, "Black American Perspective on the Future of African Theology," 395–97, and Tutu, "Black Theology/African Theology," 385–92.

80. Cone, "Black American Perspective on the Future of African Theology," 393–95, and Mbiti, "African Views American Black Theology," 379–84.

81. Ela, *African Cry*, vi, 94–95, and 113.

82. Cone, "Black American Perspective on the Future of African Theology," 399–400.

83. See Jennings, *Christian Imagination*, 64.

84. Cone, "Black American Perspective on the Asian Search for a Full Humanity," 361.

85. Cone, *Speaking the Truth*, 147. Specifically within the context of the United States, Cone is somewhat mindful not only of black but also of Hispanic, Native American, Asian American, and other marginalized communities that have suffered from the history of "white" racism. Once again,

he calls for a dialogue that affirms similarities and differences, as well as shared experiences of worship. See his *For My People*, 157–74.

86. Roberts, *Liberation and Reconciliation*, 8 and 18.

87. Cone, *God of the Oppressed*, 216–17.

88. Ibid., 219.

89. Cone, *Black Theology of Liberation*, 65.

90. Cone, *Black Theology and Black Power*, 148.

91. Cone, *God of the Oppressed*, 137–38.

92. Cone, *My Soul Looks Back*, 61.

93. Tracy, "African American Thought," 29–38, and Jon Nilson, *Hearing Past the Pain*, 43.

94. Tracy, *Analogical Imagination*, 99–153.

95. Cone, *Speaking the Truth*, 57.

96. Cone, "Black Liberation Theology and Black Catholics," 731–47.

97. See, for example, Michael Battle, *Black Church in America*, 112–13.

BIBLIOGRAPHY

Adorno, Theodor. "Cultural Criticism and Society." In *Classical Sociological Theory*, edited by Craig Calhoun, Joseph Gerteis, James Moody, Steven Pfaff, Kathryn Schmidt, and Indermohan Virk, 319–30. 1st ed. Malden, MA: Blackwell, 2002.

———. *Negative Dialectics*. Translated by E. B. Ashton. New York: Seabury, 1973.

Adorno, Theodor, and Max Horkheimer. *Dialectic of Enlightenment: Philosophical Fragments.* Edited by Gunzelin Schmid Noerr. Translated by Edmund Jephcott. Stanford, CA: Stanford University Press, 2001.

Agamben, Giorgio. *The Kingdom and the Glory: For a Theological Genealogy of Economy and Government*. Translated by Lorenzo Chiesa. Stanford, CA: Stanford University Press, 2011.

Alcoff, Linda Martín, and Eduardo Mendieta, eds. *Thinking from the Underside of History: Enrique Dussel's Philosophy of Liberation*. Lanham, MD: Rowman and Littlefield, 2000.

Althaus-Reid, Marcella Maria, Ivan Petrella, and Luiz Carlos Susin, eds. *Another Possible World*. London: SCM, 2007.

Anderson, Victor. *Beyond Ontological Blackness: An Essay on African American Religious and Cultural Criticism*. New York: Continuum, 1995.

———. *Creative Exchange: A Constructive Theology of African American Religious Experience*. Minneapolis: Fortress, 2008.

Aquinas, Thomas. *Summa Theologica [Summa Theologiae]*. Translated by the Fathers of the English Dominican Province. Notre Dame, IN: Christian Classics, 1981.

Aristotle. *Metaphysics*. Vol. 2 of *The Complete Works of Aristotle*. Princeton, NJ: Princeton University Press, 1995.

Ashley, J. Matthew. "Contemplation in the Action of Justice: Ignacio Ellacuría and Ignatian Spirituality." In Burke and Lassalle-Klein, *Love That Produces Hope*, 144–67.

———. "Ignacio Ellacuría and the *Spiritual Exercises* of Ignatius of Loyola." *Theological Studies* 61 (2000): 16–39.

———. *Interruptions: Mysticism, Politics, and Theology in the Work of Johann Baptist Metz*. Notre Dame, IN: University of Notre Dame Press, 1998.

Augustine. *Exposition of the Psalms*. Edited by John E. Rotelle, O.S.A. Translated by Maria Boulding, O.S.B. Hyde Park, NY: New City Press, 2000–2004.

Balthasar, Hans Urs von. *Apokalypse der Deutschen Seele: Studien zu einer Lehre von Letzten Haltungen*. Einsiedeln: Johannes Verlag, 1998.

———. "Beyond Contemplation and Action?" In *Explorations in Theology*, vol. 4, *Spirit and Institution*, translated by Edward T. Oakes, S.J., 299–308. San Francisco: Ignatius Press, 1995.

———. *Christian Meditation*. Translated by Sister Mary Theresilde Skerry. San Francisco: Ignatius Press, 1989.

———. *Cosmic Liturgy: The Universe according to Maximus the Confessor*. Translated by Brian Daley, S.J. San Francisco: Ignatius Press, 2003.

———. *Dare We Hope "That All Men Be Saved"?* Translated by David Kipp and Lothar Krauth. San Francisco: Ignatius Press, 1988.

———. *A First Glance at Adrienne von Speyr*. Translated by Antje Lawry and Sergia Englund, O.C.D. San Francisco: Ignatius Press, 1981.

———. *The Glory of the Lord: A Theological Aesthetics*. Vol. 1, *Seeing the Form*. Edited by Joseph Fessio, S.J., and John Riches. Translated by Erasmo Leiva-Merikakis. San Francisco: Ignatius Press, 1982.

———. *The Glory of the Lord: A Theological Aesthetics*. Vol. 2, *Studies in Theological Style: Clerical Styles*. Edited by John Riches. Translated by Andrew Louth, Francis McDonagh, and Brian McNeil, C.R.V. San Francisco: Ignatius Press, 1998.

———. *The Glory of the Lord: A Theological Aesthetics*. Vol. 3, *Studies in Theological Style: Lay Styles*. Edited by John Riches. Translated by

Andrew Louth, John Saward, Martin Simon, and Rowan Williams. San Francisco: Ignatius Press, 1986.

———. *The Glory of the Lord: A Theological Aesthetics*. Vol. 4, *The Realm of Metaphysics in Antiquity*. Edited by John Riches. Translated by Brian McNeil, C.R.V., Andrew Louth, John Saward, Rowan Williams, and Oliver Davies. San Francisco: Ignatius Press, 1989.

———. *The Glory of the Lord: A Theological Aesthetics*. Vol. 5, *The Realm of Metaphysics in the Modern Age*. Translated by Oliver Davies, Andrew Louth, Brian McNeil, C.R.V., John Saward, and Rowan Williams. San Francisco: Ignatius Press, 1991.

———. *The Glory of the Lord: A Theological Aesthetics*. Vol. 6, *Theology of the Old Covenant*. Edited by John Riches. Translated by Brian McNeil, C.R.V., and Erasmo Leiva-Merikakis. San Francisco: Ignatius Press, 1991.

———. *The Glory of the Lord: A Theological Aesthetics*. Vol. 7, *Theology of the New Covenant*. Edited by John Riches. Translated by Brian McNeil, C.R.V. San Francisco: Ignatius Press, 1989.

———. "Liberation Theology in the Light of Salvation History." Translated by Erasmo Leiva. In *Liberation Theology in Latin America*, edited by James V. Schall, S.J., 131–46. San Francisco: Ignatius Press, 1982.

———. *Origen, Spirit and Fire: A Thematic Anthology of His Writings*. Translated by Robert Daly, S.J. Washington, DC: Catholic University of America Press, 2001.

———. *Prayer*. Translated by Graham Harrison. San Francisco: Ignatius Press, 1986.

———. *Presence and Thought: An Essay on the Religious Philosophy of Gregory of Nyssa*. Translated by Mark Sebanc. San Francisco: Ignatius Press, 1995.

———. *Theo-Drama: Theological Dramatic Theory*. Vol. 1, *Prolegomena*. Translated by Graham Harrison. San Francisco: Ignatius Press, 1988.

———. *Theo-Drama: Theological Dramatic Theory*. Vol. 2, *Dramatis Personae: Man in God*. Translated by Graham Harrison. San Francisco: Ignatius Press, 1990.

———. *Theo-Drama: Theological Dramatic Theory*. Vol. 3, *Dramatis Personae: Persons in Christ*. Translated by Graham Harrison. San Francisco: Ignatius Press, 1992.

———. *Theo-Drama: Theological Dramatic Theory*. Vol. 4, *The Action*. Translated by Graham Harrison. San Francisco: Ignatius Press, 1994.

————. *Theo-Drama: Theological Dramatic Theory.* Vol. 5, *The Last Act.* Translated by Graham Harrison. San Francisco: Ignatius Press, 1998.

————. *Theo-Logic: Theological Logical Theory.* Vol. 1, *Truth of the World.* Translated by Adrian J. Walker. San Francisco: Ignatius Press, 2000.

————. *Theo-Logic: Theological Logical Theory.* Vol. 2, *The Truth of God.* Translated by Adrian J. Walker. San Francisco: Ignatius Press, 2004.

————. *Theo-Logic: Theological Logical Theory.* Vol. 3, *The Spirit of Truth.* Translated by Graham Harrison. San Francisco: Ignatius Press, 2005.

————. "Theology and Sanctity." In *Explorations in Theology,* vol. 1, *The Word Made Flesh,* translated by A.V. Littledale with Alexander Dru, 181–209. San Francisco: Ignatius Press, 1989.

————. *The Theology of Henri de Lubac: An Overview.* Translated by Joseph Fessio, S.J., and Michael M. Waldstein. San Francisco: Ignatius Press, 1991.

————. *The Theology of Karl Barth: Exposition and Interpretation.* Translated by Edward T. Oakes, S.J. San Francisco: Ignatius Press, 1992.

————. *Two Sisters in the Spirit: Thérèse of Lisieux and Elizabeth of the Trinity.* San Francisco: Ignatius Press, 1992.

Barber, Michael. *Ethical Hermeneutics: Rationality in Enrique Dussel's Philosophy of Liberation.* New York: Fordham University Press, 1998.

Barth, Karl. "No! Answer to Emil Brunner." In *Karl Barth: Theologian of Freedom,* edited by Clifford Green, 151–67. Minneapolis: Fortress, 1991.

Battle, Michael. *The Black Church in America: African American Christian Spirituality.* Malden, MA: Blackwell, 2006.

Benjamin, Walter. "Theses on the Philosophy of History." In *Critical Theory and Society: A Reader,* edited by Stephen Bronner and Douglass Kellner, 255–63. New York: Routledge, 1989.

Benson, Bruce Ellis. "Chrétien on the Call That Wounds." In Benson and Wirzba, *Words of Life,* 208–21.

Benson, Bruce Ellis, and Norman Wirzba, eds. *The Phenomenology of Prayer.* New York: Fordham University Press, 2005.

————. *Words of Life: New Theological Turns in French Phenomenology.* New York: Fordham University Press, 2010.

Bergmann, Sigurd. *God in Context: A Survey of Contextual Theology.* Burlington, VT: Ashgate, 2003.

Betz, John. "Beyond the Sublime: The Aesthetics of the Analogy of Being." *Modern Theology* 21, no. 3 (July 2005): 367–411; 22, no. 1 (Jan. 2006): 1–50.

Billy, Dennis J., C.Ss.R., and James Keating. *Conscience and Prayer: The Spirit of Catholic Moral Theology*. Collegeville, MN: Liturgical Press, 2001.

Bloch, Ernst. *The Spirit of Utopia*. Translated by Anthony A. Nassar. Stanford, CA: Stanford University Press, 2000.

Boff, Leonardo. *Cry of the Earth, Cry of the Poor*. Translated by Phillip Berryman. Maryknoll, NY: Orbis, 1997.

———. *Francis of Assisi: A Model for Human Liberation*. Translated by John W. Diercksmeier. Maryknoll, NY: Orbis, 2006.

———. *Jesus Christ Liberator: A Critical Christology for Our Time*. Translated by Patrick Hughes. Maryknoll, NY: Orbis, 1978.

———. *Liberating Grace*. Translated by John Drury. Maryknoll, NY: Orbis, 1981.

———. *The Lord's Prayer: The Prayer of Integral Liberation*. Translated by Theodore Morrow. Maryknoll, NY: Orbis, 1983.

———. *The Prayer of Saint Francis: A Message of Peace for the World Today*. Translated by Phillip Berryman. Maryknoll, NY: Orbis, 2001.

———. *Trinity and Society*. Translated by Paul Burns. Maryknoll, NY: Orbis, 1988.

———. *Way of the Cross—Way of Justice*. Translated by John Drury. Maryknoll, NY: Orbis, 1980.

Bonhoeffer, Dietrich. *The Cost of Discipleship*. Translated by R. H. Fuller. Revised by Irmgard Booth. New York: Touchstone, 1995.

Bottomore, Tom. *The Frankfurt School and Its Critics*. New York: Routledge, 1984.

Bouretz, Pierre. *Witnesses for the Future: Philosophy and Messianism*. Translated by Michael B. Smith. Baltimore: Johns Hopkins University Press, 2010.

Boys, Mary C. *Has God Only One Blessing? Judaism as a Source of Christian Self-Understanding*. Mahwah, NJ: Paulist, 2000.

Brakke, David. "Ethiopian Demons: Male Sexuality, the Black-Skinned Other, and the Monastic Self." *Journal of the History of Sexuality* 10, no. 3/4 (July/Oct. 2001): 501–35.

Brueggemann, Walter. *Israel's Praise: Doxology against Idolatry and Ideology*. Philadelphia: Fortress, 1988.

Burke, Kevin F. *The Ground beneath the Cross: The Theology of Ignacio Ellacuría*. Washington, DC: Georgetown University Press, 2000.

Burke, Kevin F., and Robert Lassalle-Klein. *Love That Produces Hope: The Thought of Ignacio Ellacuría*. Collegeville, MN: Liturgical Press, 2006.

Butler, Judith. *Precarious Life: The Powers of Mourning and Violence*. New York: Verso, 2006.

Byassee, Jason. *Praise Seeking Understanding: Reading the Psalms with Augustine*. Grand Rapids, MI: Eerdmans, 2007.

Cadorette, Curt. *From the Heart of the People: The Theology of Gustavo Gutiérrez*. Oak Park, IL: Meyer-Stone Books, 1988.

Caputo, John D. *Against Ethics: Contributions to a Poetics of Obligation with Constant Reference to Deconstruction*. Bloomington: Indiana University Press, 1993.

———. *Demythologizing Heidegger*. Bloomington: Indiana University Press, 1993.

———. *Heidegger and Aquinas: An Essay on Overcoming Metaphysics*. New York: Fordham University Press, 1982.

———. "The Hyperbolization of Phenomenology: Two Possibilities for Religion in Recent Continental Philosophy." In *Counter-Experiences: Reading Jean-Luc Marion*, edited by Kevin Hart, 67–94. Notre Dame, IN: University of Notre Dame Press, 2007.

———. *The Mystical Element in Heidegger's Thought*. New York: Fordham University Press, 1986.

———. "People of God, People of Being: The Theological Presuppositions of Heidegger's Path of Thought." In *Appropriating Heidegger*, edited by James E. Faulconer and Mark A. Wrathall, 85–100. New York: Cambridge University Press, 2000.

———. *The Prayers and Tears of Jacques Derrida: Religion without Religion*. Bloomington: Indiana University Press, 1997.

———. *Radical Hermeneutics: Repetition, Deconstruction, and the Hermeneutic Project*. Bloomington: Indiana University Press, 1987.

———. "Shedding Tears beyond Being: Derrida's Confession of Prayer." In *Augustine and Postmodernism: Confessions and Circumfession*, edited by John D. Caputo and Michael J. Scanlon, 95–114. Bloomington: Indiana University Press, 2005.

———. *The Weakness of God: A Theology of the Event*. Bloomington: Indiana University Press, 2006.

Caputo, John, and Michael Scanlon, eds. *God, the Gift, and Postmodernism*. Bloomington: Indiana University Press, 1999.

Cardenal, Ernesto. *Psalms*. New York: Crossroad, 1981.

Cardenal, Rudolfo. "De Portugalete a San Salvador: De la mano de cinco maestros." In *Ignacio Ellacuría: "Aquella libertad esclarecida,"* edited by Jon Sobrino and R. Alvarado, 42–58. San Salvador: UCA Editores, 1999.

Carlebach, Julius. "Judaism." In *A Dictionary of Marxist Thought*, edited by Tom Bottomore, Laurence Harris, V. G. Kiernan, and Ralph Miliband, 273–75. Malden, MA: Blackwell, 1991.

Carter, J. Kameron. *Race: A Theological Account*. New York: Oxford University Press, 2008.

Casaldáliga, Pedro, and José María Vigil. *Political Holiness*. Translated by Paul Burns and Francis McDonagh. Maryknoll, NY: Orbis, 1994.

Casarella, Peter. "Hans Urs von Balthasar, Erich Przywara's *Analogia Entis*, and the Problem of a Catholic *Denkform*." In *The Analogy of Being: Invention of the Anti-Christ or Wisdom of God?*, edited by Thomas Joseph White, 192–206. Grand Rapids, MI: Eerdmans, 2010.

Celan, Paul. *Selected Poems and Prose of Paul Celan*. Translated by John Felstiner. New York: W. W. Norton, 2001.

Celan, Paul, and Nelly Sachs. *Paul Celan and Nelly Sachs: Correspondence*. Edited by Barbara Wiedemann. Translated by Christopher Clark. River-on-Hudson, NY: Sheep Meadow Press, 1995.

Chase, Steven. *The Tree of Life: Models of Christian Prayer*. Grand Rapids, MI: Baker, 2005.

Chauvet, Louis-Marie. *Symbol and Sacrament: A Sacramental Reinterpretation of Christian Existence*. Translated by Patrick Madigan, S.J., and Madeleine Beaumont. Collegeville, MN: Liturgical Press, 1995.

Choat, Simon. *Marx through Post-Structuralism: Lyotard, Derrida, Foucault, Deleuze*. New York: Continuum, 2010.

Chrétien, Jean-Louis. *L'antiphonaire de la nuit*. Paris: Édition de l'Herne, 1989.

———. *The Ark of Speech*. Translated by Andrew Brown. New York: Routledge, 2004.

———. "La beauté comme inchoation de la gloire." *Communio* 30.2, no. 178 (Mar.–Apr. 2005): 65–76.

———. *The Call and the Response*. Translated by Anne A. Davenport. New York: Fordham University Press, 2004.

———. "Ce que la parole ne cesse de promettre." In *Promesses furtives*, 25–60. Paris: Les Éditions de Minuit, 2004.

———. "The Hospitality of Silence." In *The Ark of Speech*, 39–75. New York: Routledge, 2004.

———. "La double hospitalité." In *Marthe et Marie*, 9–53. Paris: Desclée de Brouwer, 2002.

———. *L'effroi du beau*. Paris: Éditions du Cerf, 1987.

———. *Hand to Hand: Listening to the Work of Art*. Translated by Stephen E. Lewis. New York: Fordham University Press, 2003.

———. "L'humanité des larmes." In *Promesses furtives*, 61–86.

———. "L'humilité selon saint Bernard." *Communio* 10.4, no. 60 (July–Aug. 1985): 112–27.

———. *L'intelligence du feu: Résponses humaines à une parole de Jésus*. Paris: Bayard Éditions, 2003.

———. "La joie d'être." In *La voix nue*, 275–94.

———. *La joie spacieuse: Essai sur la dilatation*. Paris: Les Éditions de Minuit, 2007.

———. "Lucidité de l'usage." In *Promesses furtives*, 87–115. Paris: Les Éditions de Minuit, 2004.

———. *Lueur du secret*. Paris: Éditions de l'Herne, 1985.

———. "Penser la chair avec Péguy." In *Promesses furtives*, 117–29.

———. *Pour reprendre et perdre haleine: Dix brèves méditations*. Montrouge Cedex: Bayard Éditions, 2009.

———. "La prière selon Kierkegaard." In *Le regard de l'amour*, 107–24. Paris: Desclée de Brouwer, 2000.

———. *Promesses furtives*. Paris: Les Éditions de Minuit, 2004.

———. *Reconnaissances philosophiques*. Paris: Éditions du Cerf, 2010.

———. *Répondre: Figures de la résponse et de la responsabilité*. Paris: Presses Universitaires de France, 2007.

———. "La respiration cosmique de Paul Claudel." In *La joie spacieuse*, 227–55.

———. "Retrospection." In *Unforgettable and the Unhoped For*, 119–29.

———. *Saint Augustin et les actes de parole*. Paris: Presses Universitaires de France, 2002.

———. *Sous le regard de la Bible*. Paris: Bayard Éditions, 2008.

———. *Symbolique du corps: La tradition chrétienne du "Cantique des Cantiques."* Paris: Presses Universitaires de France, 2005.

———. "Trouver et chercher." In *Promesses furtives*, 139–95.

———. *The Unforgettable and the Unhoped For*. Translated by Jeffrey Bloechl. New York: Fordham University Press, 2002.

———. *La voix nue: Phénoménologie de la promesse*. Paris: Les Éditions de Minuit, 1990.

———. "The Wounded Word: The Phenomenology of Prayer." Translated by Jeffrey L. Kosky. In *Phenomenology and the "Theological Turn": The French Debate*. New York: Fordham University Press, 2000.

Coakley, Sarah. "Prayer as Crucible: How My Mind Has Changed." *Christian Century*, March 22, 2011, 32–40.

Comblin, José. *Cry of the Oppressed, Cry of Jesus: Meditations on Scripture and Contemporary Struggle*. Translated by Robert Barr. Maryknoll, NY: Orbis, 1988.

Cone, James. "A Black American Perspective on the Asian Search for a Full Humanity." In *Black Theology: A Documentary History*, vol. 2, *1980–1992*, edited by James Cone and Gayraud Wilmore, 358–70. Maryknoll, NY: Orbis, 1993.

———. "A Black American Perspective on the Future of African Theology." In Cone and Wilmore, *Black Theology: A Documentary History*, vol. 1, 393–403.

———. "Black Liberation Theology and Black Catholics: A Critical Conversation." *Theological Studies* 61 (2000): 731–47.

———. *Black Theology: A Documentary History*. Vol. 1, *1966–1979*. Maryknoll, NY: Orbis, 1993.

———. *Black Theology and Black Power*. Maryknoll, NY: Orbis, 2008.

———. *A Black Theology of Liberation*. Twentieth Anniversary Edition. Maryknoll, NY: Orbis, 2005.

———. *The Cross and the Lynching Tree*. Maryknoll, NY: Orbis, 2011.

———. *For My People: Black Theology and the Black Church*. Maryknoll, NY: Orbis, 1984.

———. "From Geneva to São Paulo: A Dialogue between Black Theology and Latin American Liberation Theology." In *Black Theology: A Documentary History*, vol. 2, 371–87. Maryknoll, NY: Orbis, 1993.

———. *God of the Oppressed*. Maryknoll, NY: Orbis, 2010.

———. "An Interpretation of the Debate among Black Theologians." In Cone and Wilmore, *Black Theology: A Documentary History*, vol. 1, 425–40.

———. *Martin & Malcolm & America: A Dream or a Nightmare*. Maryknoll, NY: Orbis, 1991.

———. "Martin, Malcolm, and Black Theology." In *The Quest for Liberation and Reconciliation: Essays in Honor of J. Deotis Roberts*, edited by Michael Battle, 53–62. Louisville, KY: Westminster John Knox, 2005.

———. *My Soul Looks Back*. Maryknoll, NY: Orbis, 1986.

———. *Risks of Faith: The Emergence of a Black Theology of Liberation, 1968–1998*. Boston: Beacon, 1999.

———. *Speaking the Truth: Ecumenism, Liberation, and Black Theology*. Grand Rapids, MI: Eerdmans, 1986.

———. *The Spirituals and the Blues: An Interpretation*. Maryknoll, NY: Orbis, 2008.

Copeland, M. Shawn. *Enfleshing Freedom: Body, Race, and Being*. Minneapolis: Fortress, 2010.

Courtine, Jean-Francois, ed. *Phénoménologie et théologie*. Paris: Criterion, 1992.

Crowe, Benjamin. "Heidegger and the Prospect for a Phenomenology of Prayer." In *The Phenomenology of Prayer*, edited by Bruce Ellison Benson and Norman Wirzba, 119–33. New York: Fordham University Press, 2005.

Cunningham, Connor. *Genealogy of Nihilism: Philosophies of Nothing and the Difference of Theology*. New York: Routledge, 2002.

Cunningham, Connor, and Peter M. Candler Jr., eds. *Belief and Metaphysics*. London: SCM, 2007.

Cunningham, Lawrence. *Thomas Merton and the Monastic Vision*. Grand Rapids, MI: Eerdmans, 1999.

Davis, Bret W. *Heidegger and the Will: On the Way to* Gelassenheit. Evanston, IL: Northwestern University Press, 2007.

Day, Dorothy. *The Long Loneliness. The Autobiography of the Legendary Catholic Social Activist*. New York: HarperCollins, 1997.

de Certeau, Michel. *The Mystic Fable*. Vol. 1, *The Sixteenth and Seventeenth Centuries*. Translated by Michael B. Smith. Chicago: University of Chicago Press, 1992.

de Lubac, Henri. *The Drama of Atheist Humanism*. Translated by Edith M. Riley. New York: Sheed and Ward, 1950.

———. *La postérité spirituelle de Joachim de Flore*. 2 vols. Paris: Éditions Lethielleux, 1979 and 1981.

Derrida, Jacques. "Circumfession." In the lower margins of Geoffrey Bennington's *Jacques Derrida*. Chicago: University of Chicago Press, 1999.

———. *The Gift of Death*. Translated by David Wills. Chicago: University of Chicago Press, 1995.

———. "How to Avoid Speaking: Denials." Translated by Ken Frieden. In *Languages of the Unsayable: The Play of Negativity in Literature and Literary Theory*, edited by Sanford Budick and Wolfgang Iser, 3–70. New York: Columbia University Press, 1989.

———. *Memoirs of the Blind: The Self-Portrait and Other Ruins*. Translated by Pascale-Anne Brault and Michael Naas. Chicago: University of Chicago Press, 1995.

―――. *Of Spirit: Heidegger and the Question*. Translated by Geoffrey Bennington and Rachel Bowlby. Chicago: University of Chicago Press, 1989.

―――. "On a Newly Arisen Apocalyptic Tone in Philosophy." In *Raising the Tone of Philosophy: Late Essays by Immanuel Kant, Transformative Critique by Jacques Derrida*, edited by Peter Fenves, 117–73. Baltimore: Johns Hopkins University Press, 1993.

―――. "Poetics and Politics of Witnessing." In *Sovereignties in Question: The Poetics of Paul Celan*, edited by Thomas Dutoit and Outi Pasanen, 65–96. New York: Fordham University Press, 2005.

―――. *Politics of Friendship*. Translated by George Collins. New York: Verso, 1997.

―――. "*Sauf le nom*." In *On the Name*, edited by Thomas Dutoit, translated by David Wood, John P. Leavy, and Ian McLeod, 35–88. Stanford, CA: Stanford University Press, 1995.

―――. "Shibboleth: For Paul Celan." In *Sovereignties in Question: The Poetics of Paul Celan*, edited by Thomas Dutoit and Outi Pasanen, 1–64. New York: Fordham University Press, 2005.

―――. *Specters of Marx: The State of the Debt, the Work of Mourning, and the New International*. Translated by Peggy Kamuf. New York: Routledge, 1994.

Desmond, William. "The Confidence of Thought: Between Belief and Metaphysics." In *Belief and Metaphysics*, edited by Connor Cunningham and Peter M. Candler Jr., 11–40. London: SCM, 2007.

Dreyer, Elizabeth A., and Mark S. Burrows, eds. *Minding the Spirit: The Study of Christian Spirituality*. Baltimore: Johns Hopkins University Press, 2005.

Dupré, Louis. *Passage to Modernity: An Essay in the Hermeneutics of Nature and Culture*. New Haven: Yale University Press, 1994.

Dussel, Enrique. "Domination—Liberation: A New Approach?" In *Beyond Philosophy: Ethics, History, Marxism, and Liberation Theology*, edited by Eduardo Mendieta, 21–39. Lanham, MD: Rowman and Littlefield, 2003.

―――. *El dualismo en la antropología de la Cristiandad: Desde el origen del cristianismo hasta antes de la conquista de América*. Buenos Aires: Editorial Guadalupe, 1974.

―――. *Ethics and Community*. Translated by Robert R. Barr. Maryknoll, NY: Orbis, 1988.

————. *Ethics of Liberation: In the Age of Globalization and Exclusion.* Translated by Eduardo Mendieta, Camilo Pérez Bustillo, Yolanda Angulo, Nelson Maldonado-Torres, and Alejandro A. Vallega. Durham, NC: Duke University Press, 2013.

————. *A History of the Church in Latin America: Colonialism to Liberation (1492–1979).* Translated by Alan Neely. Grand Rapids, MI: Eerdmans, 1981.

————. *El humanismo semita: Estructuras intencionales radicales del pueblo de Israel y otro semitas.* Buenos Aires: Editorial Universitaria de Buenos Aires, 1969.

————. *Invention of the Americas: Eclipse of the "Other" and the Myth of Modernity.* Translated by Michael D. Barber. New York: Continuum, 1995.

————. *Las metáforas teológicas de Marx.* Estella, Spain: Editorial Verbo Divino, 1993.

————. *Philosophy of Liberation.* Translated by Aquilina Martinez and Christine Morkovsky. Eugene, OR: Wipf and Stock, 2003.

————. "Theology of Liberation and Marxism." In *Mysterium Liberationis: Fundamental Concepts of Liberation Theology,* edited by Ignacio Ellacuría and Jon Sobrino, 85–102. Maryknoll, NY: Orbis, 1993.

Ela, Jean-Marc. *African Cry.* Translated by Robert R. Barr. Eugene, OR: Wipf and Stock, 1986.

Ellacuría, Ignacio. "[Angel Martinez Baigorri, S.J.]." In *Escritos filosóficos,* vol. 1, 117–25.

————. "Angel Martinez, poeta esencial." In *Escritos filosóficos,* vol. 1, 127–95.

————. "Correspondencia con Angel Martinez." In *Escritos filosóficos,* vol. 1, 197–213.

————. "Escatología e historia." In *Escritos teológicos,* vol. 2, 95–124. San Salvador: UCA Editores, 2000.

————. *Escritos filosóficos.* Vol. 1. San Salvador: UCA Editores, 1996.

————. *Escritos teológicos.* Vol. 4. San Salvador: UCA Editores, 2002.

————. "Espiritualidad." In *Escritos teológicos,* vol. 4, 47–57.

————. "Existencialismo ateo." In *Escritos filosóficos,* vol. 1, 625–44.

————. *Fe y justicia.* Bilbao, Spain: Editorial Desclée de Brouwer, 1999.

————. *Freedom Made Flesh: The Mission of Christ and His Church.* Translated by John Drury. Maryknoll, NY: Orbis, 1976.

————. "The Historicity of Christian Salvation." In *Mysterium Liberationis: Fundamental Concepts of Liberation Theology,* edited by Ignacio Ellacuría and Jon Sobrino, 251–89. Maryknoll, NY: Orbis, 1993.

———. "Lectura latinoamericana de los *Ejercicios espirituales* de san Ignacio." In *Escritos teológicos*, vol. 4, XX59–106.

———. "Liberación en los Salmos." In *Escritos teológicos*, vol. 4, 107–21.

———. "Marxismo y teología de la liberación." In *Escritos teológicos*, vol. 1,
461–516. San Salvador: UCA Editores, 2000.

———. "Nuestra situación colectiva vista desde la primera semana." In *Escritos teológicos*, vol. 4, 177–96.

———. "Sobre Monseñor Romero." In *Escritos teológicos*, vol. 3, 75–116.
San Salvador: UCA Editores, 2002.

———. "La superación del reduccionismo idealista en Zubiri." In *Escritos
filosóficos*, vol. 3, 403–30. San Salvador: UCA Editores, 2001.

Ellis, Marc H., and Otto Maduro, eds. *The Future of Liberation Theology:
Essays in Honor of Gustavo Gutiérrez*. Maryknoll, NY: Orbis, 1989.

Endean, Philip. *Karl Rahner and Ignatian Spirituality*. New York: Oxford
University Press, 2001.

Fackenheim, Emil. *To Mend the World: Foundations of Post-Holocaust Jewish Thought*. New York: Schocken Books, 1989.

Fagerberg, David W. *Theologia Prima: What Is Liturgical Theology?* 2nd ed.
Chicago: Hildebrand, 2004.

Falque, Emmanuel. *The Metamorphosis of Finitude: An Essay on Birth and
Resurrection*. Translated by George Hughes. New York: Fordham University Press, 2012.

Faye, Emmanuel. *Heidegger: The Introduction of Nazism into Philosophy
in Light of the Unpublished Seminars of 1933–1935*. Translated by Michael B. Smith. New Haven: Yale University Press, 2009.

Fetzer, Glenn Williams. *Palimpsests of the Real in Recent French Poetry*.
Amsterdam: Editions Rodopi, 2004.

Francis of Assisi. "The Canticle of Brother Sun." In *Francis and Clare: The
Complete Works*, translated by Regis J. Armstrong, O.F.M. Cap., and
Ignatius C. Brady, O.F.M., 37–39. Mahwah, NJ: Paulist, 1982.

Froehlich, Karlfried. "The Lord's Prayer in Patristic Literature." In *A History of Prayer: The First to the Fifteenth Century*, edited by Roy Ham-
merling, 59–78. Leiden: Brill Academic, 2008.

Galilea, Segundo. *The Way of Living Faith: A Spirituality of Liberation*.
New York: Harper & Row, 1988.

Gardner, Lucy, and David Moss. "Something like Time; Something like the
Sexes—An Essay in Reception." In *Balthasar at the End of Modernity*,
69–138. Edinburgh: T&T Clark, 1999.

Gillespie, Michael Allen. *Nihilism before Nietzsche*. Chicago: University of Chicago Press, 1996.

Gilroy, Paul. *Against Race: Imagining Political Culture beyond the Color Line*. Cambridge, MA: Harvard University Press, 2000.

Goizueta, Roberto S. *Christ Our Companion: Toward a Theological Aesthetics of Liberation*. Maryknoll, NY: Orbis, 2009.

———. *Liberation, Method and Dialogue: Enrique Dussel and North American Theological Discourse*. Atlanta: Scholars Press, 1988.

Goldberg, David Theo. *The Threat of Race: Reflections on Racial Neoliberalism*. Malden, MA: Wiley-Blackwell, 2009.

Goldstein, Horst. *Leonardo Boff: Zwischen Poesie und Politik*. Mainz: Matthias-Grünewald-Verlag, 1994.

González, Antonio. "Assessing the Philosophical Achievement of Ignacio Ellacuría." In Burke and Lassalle-Klein, *Love That Produces Hope*, 73–87.

Greisch, Jean. "The Poverty of Heidegger's 'Last God.'" In *French Interpretations of Heidegger: An Exceptional Reception*, edited by David Pettigrew and François Rafoul, 245–64. Albany: SUNY Press, 2008.

Gross, Raphael. *Carl Schmitt and the Jews: The "Jewish Question," the Holocaust, and German Legal Theory*. Translated by Joel Golb. Madison, WI: University of Wisconsin Press, 2007.

Gschwandtner, Christina M. *Postmodern Apologetics? Arguments for God in Contemporary Philosophy*. New York: Fordham University Press, 2013.

———. "Praise—Pure and Personal? Jean-Luc Marion's Phenomenology of Prayer." In *The Phenomenology of Prayer*, edited by Bruce Ellis Benson and Norman Wirzba, 168–81. New York: Fordham University Press, 2005.

———. *Reading Jean-Luc Marion: Exceeding Metaphysics*. Bloomington: Indiana University Press, 2007.

Guenther, Titus F. *Rahner and Metz: Transcendental Theology as Political Theology*. Lanham, MD: University Press of America, 1994.

Gutiérrez, Gustavo. *The God of Life*. Translated by Matthew J. O'Connell. Maryknoll, NY: Orbis, 1991.

———. *Gustavo Gutiérrez: Spiritual Writings*. Edited by Daniel G. Groody. Maryknoll, NY: Orbis, 2011.

———. "No One Takes My Life from Me; I Give It Freely." In Burke and Lassalle-Klein, *Love That Produces Hope*, 68–72.

———. *On Job: God-Talk and the Suffering of the Innocent*. Translated by Matthew J. O'Connell. Maryknoll, NY: Orbis, 1987.

———. *Sharing the Word through the Liturgical Year*. Maryknoll, NY: Orbis, 1997.

———. *A Theology of Liberation: History, Politics, and Salvation*. Translated by Sister Caridad Inda and John Eagleson. Maryknoll, NY: Orbis, 2005.

———. *We Drink from Our Own Wells: The Spiritual Journey of a People*. Translated by Matthew J. O'Connell. Maryknoll, NY: Orbis, 1984.

Haas, Alois M. "Hans Urs von Balthasar's *Apocalypse of the German Soul*." In *Hans Urs von Balthasar: His Life and Work*, edited by David L. Schindler, 45–57. San Francisco: Ignatius Press, 1991.

Harasta, Eva, and Brian Brock, eds. *Evoking Lament*. New York: T&T Clark, 2009.

Hart, David Bentley. *The Beauty of the Infinite: The Aesthetics of Christian Truth*. Grand Rapids, MI: Eerdmans, 2003.

Hart, Kevin. "Contemplation: Beyond and Behind." *Sophia* 48 (2009): 435–59.

———, ed. *Counter-Experiences: Reading Jean-Luc Marion*. Notre Dame, IN: University of Notre Dame Press, 2007.

Hegel, G. W. F. *Lectures on the Philosophy of Religion: The Lectures of 1827*. Edited by Peter C. Hodgson. Translated by R. F. Brown, P. C. Hodgson, and J. M. Stewart, with H. S. Harris. One-Volume Edition. Oxford: Oxford University Press, 2012.

Heidegger, Martin. *Aristotle's "Metaphysics" Θ 1–3: On the Essence and Actuality of Force*. Translated by Walter Brogan and Peter Warnek. Bloomington: Indiana University Press, 1995.

———. *Being and Time*. Translated by Joan Stambaugh. Albany: SUNY Press, 1996.

———. "Building Dwelling Thinking." In *Poetry, Language, Thought*, 141–60.

———. *Contributions to Philosophy (From Enowning)*. Translated by Parvis Emad and Kenneth Maly. Bloomington: Indiana University Press, 1999.

———. "Conversation on a Country Path." In *Discourse on Thinking: A Translation of "Gelassenheit,"* translated by John M. Anderson and E. Hans Freund, 58–90. New York: Harper & Row, 1966.

———. *The Essence of Reasons*. Translated by Terrence Malik. Evanston, IL: Northwestern University Press, 1969.

———. "Hölderlin and the Essence of Poetry." In *Elucidations of Hölderlin's Poetry*, translated by Keith Hoeller, 51–65. Amherst, NY: Prometheus, 2000.

———. *Introduction to Metaphysics*. Translated by Gregory Fried and Richard Polt. New Haven: Yale University Press, 2000.

———. "Letter on Humanism." In *Basic Writings: From "Being and Time" (1927) to "The Task of Thinking" (1964)*, edited by David Farrell Krell, 213–65. New York: HarperCollins, 2008.

———. "Memorial Address." In *Discourse on Thinking: A Translation of "Gelassenheit,"* translated by John M. Anderson and E. Hans Freund, 43–57. New York: Harper & Row, 1966.

———. *Mindfulness*. Translated by Parvis Emad and Thomas Kalary. New York: Continuum, 2006.

———. *On Time and Being*. Translated by Joan Stambaugh. New York: Harper & Row, 1972.

———. "The Onto-Theo-Logical Constitution of Metaphysics." In *Identity and Difference*, translated by Joan Stambaugh, 42–74. Chicago: University of Chicago Press, 2002.

———. "Phenomenology and Theology." Translated by James G. Hart and John C. Maraldo. In *Pathmarks*, edited by William McNeill, 39–62. New York: Cambridge University Press, 1998.

———. *The Phenomenology of Religious Life*. Translated by Matthias Fritsch and Jennifer Anna Gosetti-Ferencei. Bloomington: Indiana University Press, 2004.

———. ". . . Poetically Man Dwells . . ." In *Poetry, Language, Thought*, 209–27.

———. *Poetry, Language, Thought*. Translated by Albert Hofstadter. New York: HarperCollins, 2001.

———. *The Principle of Reason*. Translated by Reginald Lilly. Bloomington: Indiana University Press, 1991.

———. "The Question concerning Technology." In *The Question concerning Technology, and Other Essays*, translated by William Lovitt, 3–35. New York: Harper & Row, 1977.

———. "Remembrance." In *Elucidations of Hölderlin's Poetry*, translated by Keith Hoeller, 101–73. Amherst, NY: Prometheus Books, 2000.

———. "The Thing." In *Poetry, Language, Thought*, 161–80.

———. "The Thinker as Poet." In *Poetry, Language, Thought*, 1–14.

———. "What Are Poets For?" In *Poetry, Language, Thought*, 87–139.

———. "What Is Metaphysics?" In *Basic Writings: From "Being and Time" (1927) to "The Task of Thinking" (1964)*, edited by David Farrell Krell, 93–110. New York: HarperCollins, 2008.

———. "The Word of Nietzsche: 'God Is Dead.'" In *The Question concerning Technology and Other Essays*, translated by William Lovitt, 53–112. New York: Harper & Row, 1977.

Hemming, Laurence Paul. *Heidegger's Atheism: The Refusal of a Theological Voice*. Notre Dame, IN: University of Notre Dame Press, 2002.

Hennelly, Alfred. *Theologies in Conflict: The Challenge of Juan Luis Segundo*. Maryknoll, NY: Orbis, 1979.

Henrici, Peter, S.J. "Hans Urs von Balthasar: A Sketch of His Life." In *Hans Urs von Balthasar: His Life and Work*, edited by David L. Schindler, 7–44. San Francisco: Ignatius Press, 1991.

Hollerich, Michael. "Carl Schmitt." In *The Blackwell Companion to Political Theology*, edited by Peter Schall and William Cavanaugh, 107–22. Malden, MA: Blackwell, 2004.

Holmes, Barbara A. *Joy Unspeakable: Contemplative Practices of the Black Church*. Minneapolis: Fortress, 2004.

Hopkins, Dwight N. *Down, Up, and Over: Slave Religion and Black Theology*. Minneapolis: Fortress, 2000.

———. *Shoes That Fit Our Feet: Sources for a Constructive Black Theology*. Maryknoll, NY: Orbis, 1993.

Horkheimer, Max. "Materialism and Metaphysics." In *Critical Theory: Selected Essays*, translated by Matthew J. O'Connell et al., 10–46. New York: Continuum, 2002.

———. "Traditional and Critical Theory." In *Critical Theory: Selected Essays*, translated by Matthew J. O'Connell et al., 188–243. New York: Continuum, 2002.

Horner, Robyn. *Rethinking God as Gift: Marion, Derrida, and the Limits of Phenomenology*. New York: Fordham University Press, 2001.

Hughes, Kevin. "Remember Bonaventure? (Onto)Theology and Ecstasy." *Modern Theology* 19, no. 4 (Oct. 2003): 529–45.

Ignatius of Loyola. *The Spiritual Exercises of Saint Ignatius*. Translated by George E. Ganss, S.J. Chicago: Loyola Press, 1992.

Irwin, Kevin. "*Lex Orandi, Lex Credendi*—Origins and Meaning: State of the Question." *Liturgical Ministry* 11 (Spring 2002): 57–69.

Janicaud, Dominique. "The Theological Turn of French Phenomenology." Translated by Bernard G. Prusak. In *Phenomenology and the*

"Theological Turn": The French Debate, 1–103. New York: Fordham University Press, 2000.

———. *Le tournant théologique de la phénoménologie français*. Paris: Éditions de l'Éclat, 1991.

Jennings, Willie James. *The Christian Imagination: Theology and the Origins of Race*. New Haven: Yale University Press, 2010.

John of Damascus. *De fide orthodoxa*. St. Bonaventure, NY: Franciscan Institute, 1955.

Jones, Tamsin. *A Genealogy of Marion's Philosophy of Religion: Apparent Darkness*. Bloomington: Indiana University Press, 2011.

Jones, William R. *Is God a White Racist? A Preamble to Black Theology*. Boston: Beacon, 1998.

Kadavil, Mathai. *The World as Sacrament: Sacramentality of Creation from the Perspectives of Leonardo Boff, Alexander Schmemann and Saint Ephrem*. Leuven: Peeters, 2005.

Kant, Immanuel. *Religion within the Limits of Reason Alone*. New York: Harper & Row, 1960.

Keller, Catherine, Michael Nausner, and Mayra Rivera, eds. *Postcolonial Theologies: Divinity and Empire*. St. Louis: Chalice, 2004.

Kerr, Fergus. "Foreword: Assessing This 'Giddy Synthesis.'" In *Balthasar at the End of Modernity*, 1–13. Edinburgh: T&T Clark, 1999.

Kilby, Karen. *Balthasar: A (Very) Critical Introduction*. Grand Rapids, MI: Eerdmans, 2012.

Kim, Son-Tae. *Christliche Denkform: Theozentrik oder Anthropozentrik? Die Frage nach dem Subjekt der Geschichte bei Hans Urs von Balthasar und Johann Baptist Metz*. Freiburg: Universitätsverlag, 1999.

Kittel, Gerhard, and Gerhard Friedrich, eds. *Theological Dictionary of the New Testament*. Translated by Geoffrey W. Bromiley. 10 vols. Grand Rapids, MI: Eerdmans, 1964–76.

Lacoste, Jean-Yves. "L'altération: L'autre histoire." *Communio* 7.4, no. 42 (July–Aug. 1982): 83–95.

———. "De la technique à la liturgie." *Communio* 9.2, no. 52 (Mar.–Apr. 1984): 26–37.

———. *Experience and the Absolute: Disputed Questions on the Humanity of Man*. Translated by Mark Raftery-Skehan. New York: Fordham University Press, 2004.

———. *Note sur le temps: Essai sur les raisons de la mémoire et de l'espérance*. Paris: Presses Universitaires de France, 1990.

————. *La phénoménalité de Dieu: Neuf études*. Paris: Éditions du Cerf, 2008.

————. *Présence et parousie*. Geneva: Ad Solem, 2006.

Lacoue-Labarthe, Philippe. *Poetry as Experience*. Translated by Andrea Tarnowski. Stanford, CA: Stanford University Press, 1999.

LaCugna, Catherine Mowry. *God for Us: The Trinity and Christian Life*. San Francisco: HarperCollins, 1993.

Langthaler, Rudolf. *Gottvermissen—Eine theologische Kritik der reinen Vernunft? Die neue Politische Theologie (J. B. Metz) im Spiegel der kantischen Religionsphilosophie*. Regensburg: Verlag Friedrich Pustet, 2000.

Lassalle-Klein, Robert. "Ignacio Ellacuría's Debt to Xavier Zubiri: Critical Principles for a Latin American Philosophy and Theology of Liberation." In Burke and Lassalle-Klein, *Love That Produces Hope*, 88–127.

————. Introduction to Burke and Lassalle-Klein, *Love That Produces Hope*, xii–xxxv.

Leask, Ian, and Eoin Cassidy, eds. *Givenness and God: Questions of Jean-Luc Marion*. New York: Fordham University Press, 2005.

Lee, Michael E. *Bearing the Weight of Salvation: The Soteriology of Ignacio Ellacuría*. New York: Crossroad, 2009.

Levinas, Emmanuel. *Otherwise Than Being, or Beyond Essence*. Translated by Alphonso Lingis. Pittsburgh: Duquesne University Press, 1998.

————. *Totality and Infinity: An Essay on Exteriority*. Translated by Alphonso Lingis. Pittsburgh: Duquesne University Press, 2007.

Lindbeck, George. *The Nature of Doctrine: Religion and Theology in a Post-Liberal Age*. Louisville, KY: Westminster John Knox, 1984.

Löser, Werner, S.J. "The Ignatian Exercises in the Work of Hans Urs von Balthasar." In *Hans Urs von Balthasar: His Life and Work*, edited by David L. Schindler, 103–20. San Francisco: Ignatius Press, 1991.

Lyon, James K. *Paul Celan and Martin Heidegger: An Unresolved Conversation, 1951–1970*. Baltimore: Johns Hopkins University Press, 2006.

Mackinlay, Shane. *Interpreting Excess: Jean-Luc Marion, Saturated Phenomena, and Hermeneutics*. New York: Fordham University Press, 2010.

Maier, Martin. "Karl Rahner: The Teacher of Ignacio Ellacuría." In Burke and Lassalle-Klein, *Love That Produces Hope*, 128–43.

Maldonado-Torres, Nelson. *Against War: Views from the Underside of Modernity*. Durham, NC: Duke University Press, 2008.

Marion, Jean-Luc. *Au lieu de soi: L'approche de Saint Augustin.* Paris: Presses Universitaires de France, 2008.

———. *Being Given: Toward a Phenomenology of Givenness.* Translated by Jeffrey L. Kosky. Stanford, CA: Stanford University Press, 2002.

———. *The Erotic Phenomenon.* Translated by Stephen E. Lewis. Chicago: University of Chicago Press, 2007.

———. *God without Being.* Translated by Thomas A. Carlson. Chicago: University of Chicago Press, 1991.

———. "Heidegger and Descartes." In *Critical Heidegger,* edited by Christopher Macann, 67–96. New York: Routledge, 1996.

———. *The Idol and Distance: Five Studies.* Translated by Thomas A. Carlson. New York: Fordham University Press, 2001.

———. *In Excess: Studies of Saturated Phenomena.* Translated by Robyn Horner and Vincent Berraud. New York: Fordham University Press, 2002.

———. "Le phénoménalité du sacrement: être et donation." *Communio* 26.5, no. 157 (Sept.–Oct. 2001): 59–76.

———. "Le présent et le don." *Communio* 2.6, no. 14 (Nov.–Dec. 1977): 50–70.

———. *Prolegomena to Charity.* Translated by Stephen Lewis. New York: Fordham University Press, 2002.

———. *Reduction and Givenness: Investigations of Husserl, Heidegger, and Phenomenology.* Translated by Thomas A. Carlson. Evanston, IL: Northwestern University Press, 1998.

———. "Le saint invisible." *Communio* 34.5, no. 205 (Sept.–Oct. 2009): 77–86.

———. "Thomas Aquinas and Onto-theo-logy." In *Mystics: Presence and Aporia,* edited by Michael Kessler and Christian Sheppard, 38–74. Chicago: University of Chicago Press, 2003.

Maritain, Jacques. *Man and the State.* Washington, DC: Catholic University of America Press, 1998.

Martinez, Gaspar. *Confronting the Mystery of God: Political, Liberation, and Public Theologies.* New York: Continuum, 2001.

Massingale, Bryan. *Racial Justice and the Catholic Church.* Maryknoll, NY: Orbis, 2010.

Mbiti, John. "An African Views American Black Theology." In Cone and Wilmore, *Black Theology: A Documentary History,* vol. 1, 379–84.

McAfee Brown, Robert. *Gustavo Gutiérrez.* Atlanta: John Knox, 1980.

———. "Spirituality and Liberation: The Case for Gustavo Gutiérrez." *Worship* 58, no. 5 (1984): 395–404.

McGinn, Bernard. "The Letter and the Spirit: Spirituality as an Academic Discipline." In Dreyer and Burrows, *Minding the Spirit*, 25–41.

McGrath, Sean. *The Early Heidegger and Medieval Philosophy: Phenomenology for the Godforsaken*. Washington, DC: Catholic University of America Press, 2006.

———. "Heidegger's Approach to Aquinas: Opposition, *Destruktion*, Unbelief." In *Belief and Metaphysics*, edited by Connor Cunningham and Peter M. Candler Jr., 260–90. London: SCM, 2007.

McIntosh, Mark A. *Christology from Within: Spirituality and the Incarnation in Hans Urs von Balthasar*. Notre Dame, IN: University of Notre Dame Press, 1996.

———. *Mystical Theology: The Integrity of Spirituality and Theology*. Malden, MA: Blackwell, 1998.

Merton, Thomas. *Zen and the Birds of Appetite*. New York: New Directions, 1968.

Metz, Johann Baptist. *The Advent of God*. Translated by John Drury. New York: Newman Press, 1970.

———. "Christians and Jews after Auschwitz: Being a Meditation Also on the End of Bourgeois Religion." In *Love's Strategy: The Political Theology of Johann Baptist Metz*, edited by John K. Downey, 39–52. Harrisburg, PA: Trinity Press International, 1999.

———. *Christliche Anthropozentrik: Über die Denkform des Thomas von Aquin*. Munich: Kösel-Verlag, 1962.

———. "The Church after Auschwitz." In *A Passion for God*, 121–32.

———. "The Courage to Pray." In *The Courage to Pray*, coauthored with Karl Rahner, translated by Sarah O'Brien Twohig, 1–28. New York: Crossroad, 1981.

———. "Facing the Jews: Christian Theology after Auschwitz." In *Faith and the Future: Essays on Theology, Solidarity, and Modernity*, 38–48. Maryknoll, NY: Orbis, 1995.

———. *Faith in History and Society: Toward a Practical Fundamental Theology*. Translated by J. Matthew Ashley. New York: Crossroad, 2007.

———. *Followers of Christ: The Religious Life and the Church*. Translated by Thomas Linton. New York: Paulist, 1978.

———. "Freiheit als philosophisch-theologisches Grenzproblem." In *Gott in Welt: Festgabe für Karl Rahner*, edited by Johann Baptist Metz et al., 287–311. Freiburg: Herder, 1964.

————. "Heidegger und das Problem der Metaphysik." *Scholastik* 28 (1953): 1–22.

————. *Memoria Passionis: Ein provizierendes Gedächtnis in pluralistischer Gesellschaft.* Freiburg im Breisgau: Verlag Herder, 2006.

————. "Monotheism and Democracy: Religion and Politics on Modernity's Ground." In *A Passion for God*, 138–49.

————. *Mystik der offenen Augen: Wenn Spiritualität aufbricht.* Freiburg im Breisgau: Verlag Herder, 2011.

————. *A Passion for God: The Mystical-Political Dimension of Christianity.* Translated by J. Matthew Ashley. Mahwah, NJ: Paulist, 1998.

————. *Poverty of Spirit.* Translated by John Drury. Inclusive-language version by Carole Farris. Mahwah, NJ: Paulist, 1998.

————. "Theologische und Metaphysische Ordnung." *Zeitschrift für katholische Theologie* 83 (1961): 1–14.

————. "Theology as Theodicy?" In *A Passion for God*, 54–71.

————. *Theology of the World.* Translated by William Glen-Doepel. New York: Herder and Herder, 1969.

————. "Toward a Christianity of Political Compassion." In Burke and Lassalle-Klein, *Love That Produces Hope*, 250–53.

Mignolo, Walter D. *Local Histories/Global Designs: Coloniality, Subaltern Knowledges, and Border Thinking.* Princeton, NJ: Princeton University Press, 2000.

Milbank, John, Catherine Pickstock, and Graham Ward, eds. *Radical Orthodoxy: A New Theology.* New York: Routledge, 1999.

Moltmann, Jürgen. *The Trinity and the Kingdom: The Doctrine of God.* Translated by Margaret Kohl. Minneapolis: Fortress, 1991.

Mongrain, Kevin. "Poetics and Doxology: Von Balthasar on Poetic Resistance to Modernity's Turn to the Subject." *Pro Ecclesia* 16, no. 4 (2007): 381–415.

————. *The Systematic Thought of Hans Urs von Balthasar: An Irenaean Retrieval.* New York: Crossroad, 2002.

Montejo, Carlos Luy. *Armut und Spiritualität: Der Beitrag Gustavo Gutiérrez zur Theologie der Evangelisierung.* Frankfurt am Main: Peter Lang, 2006.

Morrill, Bruce T. *Anamnesis as Dangerous Memory: Political and Liturgical Theology in Dialogue.* Collegeville, MN: Liturgical Press, 2000.

Nava, Alexander. *The Mystical and Prophetic Thought of Simone Weil and Gustavo Gutiérrez: Reflections on the Mystery and Hiddenness of God.* Albany: SUNY Press, 2001.

Nichols, Aidan, O.P. *Scattering the Seed: A Guide through Balthasar's Early Writings on Philosophy and the Arts.* Washington, DC: Catholic University of America Press, 2006.

Nietzsche, Friedrich. *The Gay Science: With a Prelude in Rhymes and an Appendix of Songs.* Translated by Walter Kaufmann. New York: Random House, 1974.

Nilson, Jon. *Hearing Past the Pain: Why White Catholic Theologians Need Black Theology.* Mahwah, NJ: Paulist, 2007.

Nordstokke, Kjell. *Council and Context in Leonardo Boff's Ecclesiology: The Rebirth of the Church among the Poor.* Translated by Brian Mac-Neil. Lewiston, NY: Edwin-Mellen, 1996.

O'Regan, Cyril. "Crossing Hegel." In *Counter-Experiences: Reading Jean-Luc Marion,* edited by Kevin Hart, 95–150. Notre Dame, IN: University of Notre Dame Press, 2007.

———. "Hans Urs von Balthasar and the Unwelcoming of Heidegger." In *The Grandeur of Reason: Reason, Tradition, and Universalism,* edited by Connor Cunningham and Peter M. Candler Jr., 264–98. London: SCM, 2010.

———. *Theology and the Spaces of Apocalyptic.* Milwaukee: Marquette University Press, 2009.

———. "Von Balthasar's Valorization and Critique of Heidegger's Genealogy of Modernity." In *Christian Spirituality and the Culture of Modernity: The Thought of Louis Dupré,* edited by Peter Casarella and George P. Schner, S.J., 123–58. Grand Rapids, MI: Eerdmans, 1998.

Ostovich, Steven. "Carl Schmitt, Political Theology, and Eschatology." *KronoScope* 7 (2007): 49–66.

Paul VI, Pope. *Nostra Aetate: Declaration on the Relation of the Church to Non-Christian Religions.* A declaration of the Second Vatican Council. October 28, 1965. www.vatican.va.

Pears, Angie. *Doing Contextual Theology.* New York: Routledge, 2010.

Péguy, Charles. *The Mystery of the Holy Innocents, and Other Poems.* Translated by Pansy Pakenham. New York: Harper and Brothers, 1956.

Peperzak, Adriaan. "Religion after Onto-theology?" In *Religion after Metaphysics,* edited by Mark A. Wrathall, 104–22. New York: Cambridge University Press, 2003.

Peterson, Erik. *Monotheism as a Political Problem.* In *Theological Tractates.* Edited and translated by Michael J. Hollerich. Stanford, CA: Stanford University Press, 2011.

Petrella, Ivan. *Beyond Liberation Theology: A Polemic.* London: SCM, 2008.

———, ed. *Latin American Liberation Theology: The Next Generation.* Maryknoll, NY: Orbis, 2005.

Pickstock, Catherine. *After Writing: On the Liturgical Consummation of Philosophy.* Malden, MA: Blackwell, 1998.

Pico, J. Hernández. "La oración en los procesos latinoamericanos de liberación." In *Espiritualidad de la liberación,* edited by A. Cussiánovich et al., 159–85. Lima: CEP, 1980.

Przywara, Erich. *Analogia Entis: Metaphysik; Ur-Struktur und All-Rhythmus.* Einsiedeln: Johannes Verlag, 1962.

Quash, Ben. *Theology and the Drama of History.* Cambridge: Cambridge University Press, 2005.

Raboteau, Albert J. *Slave Religion: The "Invisible Institution" in the Antebellum South.* New York: Oxford University Press, 1980.

———. *A Sorrowful Joy.* The Harold M. Wit Lectures at Harvard Divinity School. Mahwah, NJ: Paulist, 2002.

Rahner, Karl. "Current Problems in Christology." In *Theological Investigations,* vol. 1, 149–213. New York: Crossroad, 1982.

———. *Hearer of the Word.* Translated by Joseph Donceel. New York: Continuum, 1994.

———. *Spirit in the World.* Translated by William Dych, S.J. New York: Continuum, 1994.

Ramey, Lauri. *Slave Songs and the Birth of African American Poetry.* New York: Palgrave Macmillan, 2008.

Ricoeur, Paul. *From Text to Action: Essays in Hermeneutics II.* Evanston, IL: Northwestern University Press, 1991.

Rissing, Michaela, and Thilo Rissing. *Politische Theologie: Schmitt – Derrida – Metz; Eine Einführung.* Munich: Wilhelm Fink Verlag, 2009.

Rivera, Mayra. *The Touch of Transcendence: A Postcolonial Theology of God.* Louisville, KY: Westminster John Knox, 2007.

Roberts, J. Deotis. *Liberation and Reconciliation: A Black Theology.* 2nd ed. Louisville, KY: Westminster John Knox, 2005.

Sachs, Nelly. *The Seeker, and Other Poems.* Translated by Ruth and Matthew Mead and Michael Hamburger. New York: Farrar, Straus and Giroux, 1970.

Safranski, Rüdiger. *Martin Heidegger: Between Good and Evil.* Translated by Ewald Osers. Cambridge, MA: Harvard University Press, 1998.

Said, Edward. *Orientalism.* New York: Vintage Books, 1979.

Savage, Robert. *Hölderlin after the Catastrophe: Heidegger – Adorno – Brecht.* Rochester, NY: Camden House, 2008.

Schindler, D.C. *Hans Urs von Balthasar and the Dramatic Structure of Truth.* New York: Fordham University Press, 2004.

Schmemann, Alexander. "Worship in a Secular Age." In *For the Life of the World*, 117–34. New York: St. Vladimir's Seminary Press, 1973.

Schmitt, Carl. *The Leviathan in the State Theory of Thomas Hobbes: Meaning and Failure of a Political Symbol.* Translated by George Schwab and Erna Hilfstein. Westport, CT: Greenwood, 1996.

———. *Political Theology: Four Chapters on the Concept of Sovereignty.* Translated by George Schwab. Foreword by Tracy B. Strong. Chicago: University of Chicago Press, 2005.

———. *Political Theology II: The Myth of the Closure of Any Political Theology.* Translated by Michael Hoelzl and Graham Ward. Malden, MA: Polity, 2008.

Schneiders, Sandra M., I.H.M. "The Discipline of Christian Spirituality and Catholic Theology." In *Exploring Christian Spirituality: Essays in Honor of Sandra M. Schneiders, I.H.M.*, edited by Bruce H. Lescher and Elizabeth Liebert, S.N.J.M., 196–212. Mahwah, NJ: Paulist, 2006.

———. "A Hermeneutical Approach to the Study of Christian Spirituality." In Dreyer and Burrows, *Minding the Spirit*, 49–60.

———. "The Study of Christian Spirituality: Contours and Dynamics of a Discipline." In Dreyer and Burrows, *Minding the Spirit*, 5–24.

Schrijvers, Joeri. "In (the) Place of the Self: A Critical Study of Jean-Luc Marion's 'Au lieu de soi: L'approche de Saint Augustin.'" *Modern Theology* 25, no. 4 (Oct. 2009): 661–86.

Schuster, Ekkehard, and Reinhold Boschert-Kimmig, eds. *Hope against Hope: Johann Baptist Metz and Elie Wiesel Speak Out on the Holocaust.* Translated by J. Matthew Ashley. Mahwah, NJ: Paulist, 1999.

Scott, Mark S.M. "Shades of Grace: Origen and Gregory of Nyssa's Soteriological Exegesis of the 'Black and Beautiful' Bride in Song of Songs 1:5." *Harvard Theological Review* 99, no. 1 (2006): 65–83.

Segundo, Juan Luis. *Berdiaeff: Une réflexion chrétienne sur la personne.* Paris: Éditions Montaigne, 1963.

———. *The Christ of the Ignatian Exercises.* Vol. 4 of *Jesus of Nazareth: Yesterday and Today.* Translated by John Drury. Maryknoll, NY: Orbis, 1987.

———. *Faith and Ideologies.* Vol. 1 of *Jesus of Nazareth: Yesterday and Today.* Translated by John Drury. Maryknoll, NY: Orbis, 1984.

————. *Grace and the Human Condition*. Vol. 2 of *A Theology for Artisans of a New Humanity*. Translated by John Drury. Maryknoll, NY: Orbis, 1973.

————. *The Historical Jesus of the Synoptics*. Vol. 2 of *Jesus of Nazareth: Yesterday and Today*. Translated by John Drury. Maryknoll, NY: Orbis, 1985.

————. *The Humanist Christology of Paul*. Vol. 3 of *Jesus of Nazareth: Yesterday and Today*. Translated by John Drury. Maryknoll, NY: Orbis, 1986.

————. *The Liberation of Theology*. Translated by John Drury. Maryknoll, NY: Orbis, 1985.

————. *Our Idea of God*. Vol. 3 of *A Theology for Artisans of a New Humanity*. Translated by John Drury. Maryknoll, NY: Orbis, 1974.

Sheldrake, Philip. *Spirituality and Theology: Christian Living and the Doctrine of God*. London: Darton, Longman and Todd, 1998.

Sobrino, Jon. "Ignacio Ellacuría, the Human Being, and the Christian: 'Taking the Crucified People Down from the Cross.'" In Burke and Lassalle-Klein, *Love That Produces Hope*, 1–67.

————. *Spirituality of Liberation: Toward Political Holiness*. Maryknoll, NY: Orbis, 1988.

Sobrino, Jon, Ignacio Ellacuría, et al. *Companions of Jesus: The Jesuit Martyrs of El Salvador*. Maryknoll, NY: Orbis, 1990.

Soulen, R. Kendall. *The God of Israel and Christian Theology*. Minneapolis: Fortress, 1996.

Steck, Christopher. *The Ethical Thought of Hans Urs von Balthasar*. New York: Crossroad, 2001.

Swan, Laura, ed. *The Benedictine Tradition*. Collegeville, MN: Liturgical Press, 2007.

Tanner, Kathryn. *Christ the Key*. New York: Cambridge University Press, 2010.

————. *The Politics of God: Christian Theologies and Social Justice*. Minneapolis: Augsburg-Fortress, 1992.

————. "Theology at the Limits of Phenomenology." In *Counter-Experiences: Reading Jean-Luc Marion*, edited by Kevin Hart, 201–31. Notre Dame, IN: University of Notre Dame Press, 2007.

Taubes, Jacob. *The Political Theology of Paul*. Edited by Aleida Assmann and Jan Assmann. Translated by Dana Hollander. Stanford, CA: Stanford University Press, 2004.

Taylor, Charles. *A Catholic Modernity: Charles Taylor's Marianist Award Lecture*. Edited by James L. Heft. New York: Oxford University Press, 1999.

———. *A Secular Age*. Cambridge, MA: Harvard University Press, 2007.

———. *Sources of the Self: The Making of the Modern Identity*. Cambridge, MA: Harvard University Press, 1989.

Teresa of Ávila. *The Interior Castle*. Translated by Kieran Kavanaugh, O.C.D., and Otilio Rodriguez, O.C.D. Mahwah, NJ: Paulist, 1979.

Thatamanil, John. "Tillich and the Postmodern." In *The Cambridge Companion to Paul Tillich*, edited by Russell Re Manning, 288–303. New York: Cambridge University Press, 2009.

Thirion, Benoît. *L'appel dans la pensée de Jean-Louis Chrétien: Contexte et introduction*. Paris: L'Harmattan, 2002.

Torrell, Jean-Pierre, O.P. *Christ and Spirituality in St. Thomas Aquinas*. Translated by Bernhard Blankenhorn, O.P. Washington, DC: Catholic University of America Press, 2011.

———. *St. Thomas Aquinas*. Vol. 2, *Spiritual Master*. Translated by Robert Royal. Washington, DC: The Catholic University of America Press, 2003.

Townes, Emilie M. *In a Blaze of Glory: Womanist Spirituality as Social Witness*. Nashville: Abingdon, 1995.

Tracy, David. "African American Thought: The Discovery of Fragments." In *Black Faith and Public Talk: Critical Essays on James H. Cone's "Black Theology and Black Power,"* edited by Dwight N. Hopkins, 29–38. Maryknoll, NY: Orbis, 1999.

———. *Analogical Imagination: Christian Theology and the Culture of Pluralism*. New York: Crossroad, 1981.

Turner, Denys. *The Darkness of God: Negativity in Christian Mysticism*. New York: Cambridge University Press, 1999.

———. *Faith, Reason, and the Existence of God*. New York: Cambridge University Press, 2004.

———. "Marxism, Liberation Theology, and the Way of Negation." In *The Cambridge Companion to Liberation Theology*, edited by Christopher Rowland, 229–47. 2nd ed. New York: Cambridge University Press, 2007.

Tutu, Desmond M. "Black Theology/African Theology—Soul Mates or Antagonists?" In Cone and Wilmore, *Black Theology: A Documentary History*, vol. 1, 385–92. Maryknoll, NY: Orbis, 1993.

Viller, Marcel, ed. *Dictionnaire de spiritualité: Ascétique et mystique, doctrine et histoire*. Paris: G. Beauchesne and Sons.

Vogel, Dwight W. "Liturgical Theology: A Conceptual Geography." In *Primary Sources of Liturgical Theology: A Reader*, edited by Dwight W. Vogel, 3–14. Collegeville, MN: Liturgical Press, 2000.

Wainwright, Geoffrey. *Doxology: The Praise of God in Worship, Doctrine, and Life*. New York: Oxford University Press, 1980.

Welte, Bernhard. "God in Heidegger's Thought." *Philosophy Today* 26, no. 1 (Spring 1982): 85–100.

Westphal, Merold. *Overcoming Onto-theology: Toward a Postmodern Christian Faith*. New York: Fordham University Press, 2001.

———. *Transcendence and Self-Transcendence: On God and the Soul*. Bloomington: Indiana University Press, 2004.

Wigley, Stephen. *Karl Barth and Hans Urs von Balthasar: A Critical Engagement*. New York: T&T Clark, 2007.

Williams, Delores S. *Sisters in the Wilderness: The Challenge of Womanist God-Talk*. Maryknoll, NY: Orbis, 2003.

Wilmore, Gayraud S. *Black Religion and Black Radicalism: An Interpretation of the Religious History of African Americans*. 3rd ed. Maryknoll, NY: Orbis, 2004.

Wirzba, Norman. "The Witness of Humility." In Benson and Wirzba, *Words of Life*, 233–51.

Wolin, Richard, ed. *The Heidegger Controversy: A Critical Reader*. Cambridge, MA: MIT Press, 1993.

Wüthrich, Matthias D. "Lament for Naught? An Inquiry into the Suppression of Lament in Systematic Theology: The Example of Karl Barth." In *Evoking Lament*, edited by Eva Harasta and Brian Brock, 60–76. New York: T&T Clark, 2009.

Yancy, George, ed. *Christology and Whiteness: What Would Jesus Do?* New York: Routledge, 2012.

Zimmerman, Michael. *Heidegger's Confrontation with Modernity: Technology, Politics, and Art*. Bloomington: Indiana University Press, 1990.

Zubiri, Xavier. *Man and God*. Translated by Joaquín Redondo, Thomas Fowler, and Nelson Orringer. Lanham, MD: University Press of America, 2009.

———. *Nature, History, God*. Translated by Thomas B. Fowler. Washington, DC: University Press of America, 1981.

INDEX

Adorno, Theodor: on Auschwitz, 202, 207, 373n77; *Dialectic of Enlightenment* (coauthored by Horkheimer), 25, 182, 340n26; and Heidegger, 183–84; *Negative Dialectics*, 184, 377n13

aesthetics, 23, 83–95, 109, 138, 144, 160, 166, 191, 216, 220, 222, 258–59, 284, 286, 298–99, 302, 304, 306–7, 330, 352n24, 353n35, 386n2

Agamben, Giorgio, 341n30

agonistic prayer, 2, 152, 199, 206, 240, 279, 311, 320

analogy: and Balthasar, 73, 75–83, 87–89, 92, 99, 104, 106, 109; and Cone, 284, 295–98; and liberation theology, 220, 222, 229, 232, 251, 254, 256, 262; and Metz, 172–73, 177, 193–94, 208; and post-Balthasarian thought, 112, 126, 134, 137. *See also* Przywara, Erich

Anderson, Victor, 295, 305–9

apocalyptic, 103, 118, 134, 225, 236, 314, 353n36; and Metz, 176, 181, 188, 190–91, 194–95, 197, 200, 215, 217, 230–31, 374n90

apophasis, 331–32; and Balthasar, 73, 77, 79, 86–87, 353n35; and Caputo/Derrida, 22, 112, 115–16, 118, 121, 167, 171, 191, 207, 209, 277, 283, 299–302, 341n29; and post-Balthasarian thought, 126–27, 129–30, 132, 138–40, 149–50, 253

apostolic spirituality, 89, 152, 197, 221, 275, 278, 337n9

Aquinas, Thomas: and Balthasar, 79–82; and Caputo, 116–17; and Chrétien, 151, 153; and Heidegger, 52, 79–82, 116, 128, 173, 352n17; and Marion, 125, 128–29, 359n25, 361n39, 361n43; and Metz, 173–76, 367n6; and prayer, 14, 335n3. *See also* analogy; Przywara, Erich

Aristotle, 21, 78–79, 339n19

ANDREW PREVOT

is assistant professor of theology

at Boston College.

(14) God desires first

(15) Really good def. of doxology
- Shared w/ others
- Christ fully incarnates prayer + doxology

(17) Theology as thinking prayer

(13) Semi-def. of prayer

(17) - Prayer has action, living

(18) Spirituality is imitating Christ

(25) Contemplation must be contemplation in action

(26-27) <u>Prayer</u> is Counterviolent in that it prepares followers for resistance, gives glory to God instead of self + leaders.

- Asks humanity to play a part
- Training in hospitality + responsibility
- Believe that definitively lover despite hate of world

(28) Clear priority to prayers of victims of history